TOEPLITZ
THEIR APPLICATIONS

BY

ULF GRENANDER

&

GABOR SZEGÖ

UNIVERSITY OF CALIFORNIA PRESS

BERKELEY AND LOS ANGELES

1958

UNIVERSITY OF CALIFORNIA PRESS
BERKELEY AND LOS ANGELES
CALIFORNIA

CAMBRIDGE UNIVERSITY PRESS
LONDON, ENGLAND

This book was written with the partial support of
the Office of Naval Research, United States Navy,
and the Office of Ordnance Research, United States
Army; reproduction in whole or part is permitted
for any purpose of the United States Government.

Printed in Great Britain at the University Press, Cambridge
(Brooke Crutchley, University Printer)

PREFACE

The principal subject of this monograph is the study of certain Hermitian forms whose matrices depend on the difference of the two indices; matrices of this kind have the form $(c_{\nu-\mu})$. Here $\{c_n\}$ is a certain given sequence of complex constants and we assume that $c_{-n} = \bar{c}_n$. In the case of finite matrices the integers μ and ν range either from 0 to n or from $-n$ to $+n$; in the case of infinite matrices they range from 0 to $+\infty$ or from $-\infty$ to $+\infty$. The corresponding concept for functionals is that of a function (or kernel) of two real variables having the form $K(x-y)$, i.e. depending on the difference of the variables x and y; here $K(u)$ is a complex-valued function of the real variable u and $K(-u) = \overline{K(u)}$.

The following special cases are of particular importance. The quantities c_n are the coefficients of a power series, or the Fourier coefficients of a real function integrable in the sense of Lebesgue, or the Fourier–Stieltjes coefficients of a distribution function; in all these cases we assume that $c_{-n} = \overline{c_n}$. The history of these forms is not without interest; it is closely related to various remarkable problems of the modern theory of functions. In 1910, O. Toeplitz studied forms of the type mentioned (without assuming that they have the Hermitian character) in their relation to Laurent series and called them L-forms. In the investigations of Toeplitz these forms appear as illustrations of the spectral theory of Hilbert. About the same time C. Carathéodory obtained necessary and sufficient conditions for the Fourier coefficients of a harmonic function in order to characterize the regularity and positivity of such a function within a circle. The conditions of Carathéodory have been transformed by Toeplitz and the connection of Carathéodory's problem with the L-forms has been established. For the principal theorem of Carathéodory various proofs have been offered, some of them exhibiting interesting relations of these questions to older ideas due to Kronecker, Stieltjes and others. We mention the following names: E. Fischer, G. Frobenius, G. Herglotz, F. Riesz, I. Schur and G. Szegö. The Bibliography at the end of the present monograph gives the specific references.

In the early twenties, G. Szegö studied in detail the distribution of the eigenvalues of the sections of Toeplitz forms associated with a function defined in $[-\pi, \pi]$ and integrable in the sense of Lebesgue.

In this connection he introduced a new class of polynomials which are orthogonal on the unit circle relative to a given weight function. These polynomials are closely related to the Toeplitz forms. In this investigation the notion of the reproducing kernel appears probably for the first time; this notion has influenced to some extent the ideas dealt with in the paper[6] of the same author† in relation to an arbitrary curve of the complex plane. About the same time S. Bergman[1] and S. Bochner[1] began investigations centering around the similar and more general concept of the reproducing kernel.

The corresponding problems for functions $K(x-y)$ have been investigated by M. Mathias[1] and S. Bochner[2], p. 74.

In recent years, new interest has been paid to this subject in view of its natural occurrence in the theory of stochastic processes. This is true especially for prediction and interpolation problems in stationary processes. Indeed, several of the important results obtained by A. N. Kolmogorov and N. Wiener can be reduced to problems studied in the theory of Toeplitz forms. The probability problem is easily translated to Hilbert space terminology, and it is then isomorphic to a problem concerning Toeplitz forms. An important group of statistical questions related to stationary processes (especially linear estimation and testing linear hypotheses) has also been treated successfully with the aid of Toeplitz forms. The same is true for certain distribution problems for quadratic forms of normally distributed stochastic variables.

This revival of interest had its reaction in this country; we mention especially the names of J. L. Doob, M. Kac, S. Kakutani, M. Rosenblatt and G. Szegö. Various mathematicians of the Russian school, as N. I. Achieser, J. Geronimus and M. G. Krein, obtained new and important results. We mention also the Scandinavian statisticians U. Grenander, K. Karhunen and H. Wold.

The first part of the present exposition is devoted to the theory of Toeplitz forms. The second part deals with applications, in particular to the calculus of probability and mathematical statistics. Neither part claims completeness in any way. Our purpose has been to elucidate the principal ideas of this remarkable chapter of modern analysis and to help the interested student of mathematical statistics to acquire a working knowledge of the subject. The somewhat protracted chapter 1 explains not only the notation employed but

† Numbers in square brackets refer to the Bibliography.

contains also the definition of important auxiliary concepts and the exposition of basic results which will be used later. This arrangement avoids interruptions in the main text. For the same reason, bibliographic explanations and other comments have been placed in an Appendix. We assume that the reader is in possession of the fundamental facts of the theory of functions.

In chapters 2 and 3 certain topics appear which were treated in the book on orthogonal polynomials by G. Szegö. In view of the progress made in this subject since the publication of that book (1939) it was possible to bring some details in an improved setting. The other chapters contain partly old and partly more recent results, some older facts in a new setting, and finally some completely new results. Chapters 1–6 and chapter 9 have been prepared by Szegö, the other chapters by Grenander.

The research from which the present book originated was partly supported by the Office of Naval Research, United States Navy. The idea of preparing a monograph on Toeplitz forms was suggested to the authors by Professor Jerzy Neyman, Director of the Statistical Laboratory at the University of California in Berkeley; we convey our thanks for his friendly interest in our undertaking. We are indebted to the following persons for valuable suggestions of mathematical and formal nature: Professor S. Karlin, California Institute of Technology; Dr A. Novikoff, Johns Hopkins University, Baltimore, Md.; Professor M. Riesz, University of Lund, Sweden; Dr M. Rosenblatt and Professor A. Zygmund, University of Chicago. Finally, our thanks go to Mrs Leonore Veltfort for the careful preparation of the typescript, and to Mrs Ann E. Szegö for her aid in reading the proofs and preparing the index.

September 1955

UNIVERSITY OF STOCKHOLM, SWEDEN
STANFORD UNIVERSITY, CALIF.

CONTENTS

PART I: TOEPLITZ FORMS

PART II: APPLICATIONS OF TOEPLITZ FORMS

PART I

TOEPLITZ FORMS

CHAPTER 1

PRELIMINARIES

1.1. Notation

The text is divided into two parts, each part into chapters, each chapter into sections. The numbering of the formulas starts anew in each section. Theorems are not numbered; they are quoted by the number of the section in which they occur.

The symbol $A \subset B$ indicates that the set A is contained in the set B.

The symbol $x \in A$ indicates that x is an element of the set A.

Let $\{S_\nu\}$ denote a denumerable sequence of sets, $\nu = 1, 2, 3, \ldots$. The set of elements belonging to at least one of the sets S_ν is called the union of the sets S_ν, in symbol $\bigcup_{\nu=1}^{\infty} S_\nu$. The set of elements common to all S_ν is denoted by $\bigcap_{\nu=1}^{\infty} S_\nu$.

The symbol $[a, b]$ is used for a finite interval $a \leq x \leq b$. If it is stated explicitly we permit $a = -\infty$ or $b = +\infty$.

We write $\delta_{nm} = 0$ or 1, according as $n \neq m$ or $n = m$.

A matrix A with elements $a_{\mu\nu}$ is denoted by $A = (a_{\mu\nu})$; if the matrix A is of the square type, its determinant is denoted by $\det A = \det (a_{\mu\nu})$. The unit form is denoted by I. The trace of a matrix (or of a quadratic or Hermitian form) A is denoted by $\operatorname{tr} A$. We denote by A' the transposed matrix, by $\bar{A}$ the matrix with conjugate complex elements; we write $A^* = \bar{A}'$.

A quadratic form F_n of the real variables $x_0, x_1, \ldots, x_n$ is called positive (positive definite) if $F_n > 0$ for all real x_j except if all x_j are zero. It is called nonnegative (nonnegative semidefinite) if $F_n \geq 0$ for all x_j and $F_n = 0$ for some x_j not all zero. The definitions are similar for Hermitian forms.

For arbitrary complex x, $x \neq 0$, we write $\operatorname{sgn} x = |x|^{-1} x$.

Let $\rho(x) = \sum_{\nu=0}^{n} c_\nu x^\nu$ be a polynomial of degree n. We define the 'reciprocal' polynomial by $\rho^*(x) = \sum_{\nu=0}^{n} \bar{c}_{n-\nu} x^\nu = x^n \bar{\rho}(x^{-1})$.

We write $a_n \cong b_n$ if $b_n \neq 0$ and $\lim_{n\to\infty} a_n/b_n = 1$. The symbols $a_n = O(b_n)$, $a_n = o(b_n)$ signify that $b_n > 0$ and a_n/b_n is bounded or tends to zero as

$n \to \infty$, respectively. Similar notation is used if n is replaced by a continuous variable x, $x \to \infty$.

A function $\alpha(x)$ defined in the finite or infinite interval $[a, b]$ is called a distribution function if it is monotonically nondecreasing. It is called of the *finite type* if its range consists of a finite number of values. In the opposite case it is called of the *infinite type*.

Let $f(x)$ be a continuous function in the interval $[a, b]$. The modulus of continuity $\omega(\delta)$ of $f(x)$ is defined as $\max |f(x') - f(x'')|$ for all values of x' and x'' in $[a, b]$ such that $|x' - x''| \leq \delta$.

Let $f(z) = \sum\limits_{n=0}^{\infty} c_n z^n$ be an analytic function of the complex variable z regular in the open unit circle $|z| < 1$. We say that $f(z)$ belongs to the class H_2 if the integral

$$\frac{1}{2\pi} \int_{-\pi}^{\pi} |f(r\,e^{ix})|^2 \, dx$$

is bounded for all $r < 1$. This condition is equivalent to the fact that the series $\sum\limits_{n=0}^{\infty} |c_n|^2$ is convergent.

1.2. Integrals. Classes of functions. Inequalities

(a) We assume the knowledge of the elementary properties of the Riemann and Lebesgue integrals as well as of the Stieltjes–Riemann and Stieltjes–Lebesgue integrals. We note the formula for integration by parts:

$$\int_a^b f(x) \, d\alpha(x) = f(b) \, \alpha(b) - f(a) \, \alpha(a) - \int_a^b f'(x) \, \alpha(x) \, dx. \qquad (1)$$

Here $f(x)$ has a continuous derivative, $\alpha(x)$ is a distribution function, the left-hand integral is of the Stieltjes–Riemann type, $[a, b]$ is a finite interval.

(b) Let $p \geq 1$ and $\alpha(x)$ a distribution function of the infinite type in $[a, b]$. We denote by

$$L_p[d\alpha(x); a, b] \qquad (2)$$

the space of all complex-valued functions $F(x)$ which are measurable with respect to $\alpha(x)$ and for which the Stieltjes–Lebesgue integral

$$\int_a^b |F(x)|^p \, d\alpha(x) \qquad (3)$$

exists. In particular, if $w(x) \geq 0$ is Lebesgue integrable, we denote by

$$L_p[w(x) \, dx; a, b] \qquad (4)$$

the space of all complex-valued functions $F(x)$ which are measurable in the Lebesgue sense and for which

$$\int_a^b |F(x)|^p w(x)\, dx \tag{5}$$

exists. It is assumed that $w(x)$ is not a 'zero-function', i.e. $w(x)$ is not zero almost everywhere. In the special case $w(x)=1$ we denote this space by $L_p(a, b)$; in the special case $a=-\pi$, $b=\pi$ we write simply L_p. For the class L_1 we use the shorter symbol L.

(c) We denote by $C(a, b)$ the class of all complex-valued functions which are continuous in the finite interval $[a, b]$. The class C consists of all complex-valued functions $f(x)$ which are continuous in $[-\pi, \pi]$ and for which $f(-\pi)=f(\pi)$. This is equivalent to the class of all functions which are continuous and periodic with period 2π.

(d) We note two important inequalities.

Hölder's inequality. Let $u(x)$ be of the class L_p, $v(x)$ of the class L_q, where $p>0$, $q>0$ and $1/p+1/q=1$; $a \leq x \leq b$. We have then

$$\left| \int_a^b u(x)\, v(x)\, dx \right| \leq \left\{ \int_a^b |u(x)|^p\, dx \right\}^{1/p} \left\{ \int_a^b |v(x)|^q dx \right\}^{1/q}.$$

The special case $p=q=2$ is Schwarz's inequality.

Minkowski's inequality. Let $p>1$ and $u(x)$, $v(x)$ two functions of the class L_p; $a \leq x \leq b$. Then

$$\left\{ \int_a^b |u(x)+v(x)|^p\, dx \right\}^{1/p} \leq \left\{ \int_a^b |u(x)|^p dx \right\}^{1/p} + \left\{ \int_a^b |v(x)|^p\, dx \right\}^{1/p}.$$

1.3. Structure of monotonic functions. Sequences of monotonic functions

(a) Let $\alpha(x)$ be a distribution function of the infinite type in the interval $[-\pi, \pi]$. Then $\alpha(x)$ has at most a denumerable number of discontinuities which are all of the first kind; that is, the limits $\alpha(x+0)$ and $\alpha(x-0)$ exist everywhere. Moreover, $\alpha(x)$ is differentiable almost everywhere. Finally, the following important decomposition holds:

$$\alpha(x) = \alpha_j(x) + \alpha_s(x) + \alpha_a(x), \tag{1}$$

where

(i) all the three functions on the right are non-decreasing;

(ii) $\alpha_j(x)$ (jump function) has the following form:

$$\alpha_j(x) = \Sigma \lambda_k h(x-t_k)$$

(a finite or infinite sum), where $h(x) = 0$ for $x < 0$, $h(x) = 1$ for $x > 0$ and $\lambda_k > 0$; the discontinuities t_k of $\alpha_j(x)$ are identical with those of $\alpha(x)$;

(iii) $\alpha_s(x)$ (singular function) is continuous, strictly increasing and $\alpha'_s(x) = 0$ almost everywhere;

(iv) $\alpha_a(x)$ is strictly increasing and absolutely continuous so that the derivative $\alpha'_a(x)$ (which exists almost everywhere) is of the class L and for any two values x' and x'' we have

$$\int_{x'}^{x''} \alpha'_a(x)\, dx = \alpha_a(x'') - \alpha_a(x').$$

Of course some of the components in (1) may be missing.

If $w(x)$ belongs to L and $w(x) \geqq 0$ almost everywhere, then the indefinite integral $\int_{-\pi}^{x} w(t)\, dt$ is of the type $\alpha_a(x)$.

(b)   THEOREM. *Let $\{\alpha_n(x)\}$ be a sequence of distribution functions in $[-\pi, \pi]$, and let*

$$\lim_{n \to \infty} \alpha_n(x) = \alpha(x) \tag{2}$$

exist for each x. Then $\alpha(x)$ is a distribution function and for every function $f(x)$ of the class C we have

$$\lim_{n \to \infty} \int_{-\pi}^{\pi} f(x)\, d\alpha_n(x) = \int_{-\pi}^{\pi} f(x)\, d\alpha(x). \tag{3}$$

The limit function $\alpha(x)$ is obviously nondecreasing. Let

$$-\pi = x_0 < x_1 < x_2 < \ldots < x_{m-1} < x_m = \pi$$

be an arbitrary subdivision of $[-\pi, \pi]$. We denote by m_μ and M_μ the minimum and maximum of $f(x)$ in $[x_{\mu-1}, x_\mu]$, respectively. Then

$$\int_{-\pi}^{\pi} f(x)\, d\alpha_n(x) \leqq \sum_{\mu=1}^{m} M_\mu [\alpha_n(x_\mu) - \alpha_n(x_{\mu-1})],$$

$$\limsup_{n \to \infty} \int_{-\pi}^{\pi} f(x)\, d\alpha_n(x) \leqq \sum_{\mu=1}^{m} M_\mu [\alpha(x_\mu) - \alpha(x_{\mu-1})].$$

For an appropriate subdivision the right-hand side comes arbitrarily close to the integral on the right of (3). A similar estimation of the lim inf in the opposite direction is possible. This yields (3).

(c) The following 'selection theorem' is of great importance (see Appendix).

THEOREM. *Let $\{\alpha_n(x)\}$ be a sequence of distribution functions in $[-\pi, \pi]$, and let $\{\alpha_n(x)\}$ be uniformly bounded*

$$|\alpha_n(x)| \leqq A,$$

where A is independent of n and x. [This condition is, of course, equivalent to the boundedness of $\{\alpha_n(\pm\pi)\}$.] *Then a subsequence $\{\alpha_{n_j}(x)\}$ can be selected so that for each x*

$$\lim_{j \to \infty} \alpha_{n_j}(x) = \alpha(x)$$

exists.

The limit $\alpha(x)$ will be, of course, a distribution function.

1.4. Monotonic functions with vanishing derivative

(a) Following the notation of 1.3 (a) we consider the function

$$\beta(x) = \alpha_j(x) + \alpha_s(x); \qquad (1)$$

this is a distribution function whose absolutely continuous component is missing. Using this symbol we prove the following important theorem:

THEOREM. *Let ϵ be an arbitrary positive number. We can decompose the interval $I: [-\pi, \pi]$ in a finite number of intervals such that for a certain class I_1 of these intervals and for the complementary class I_2 the following inequalities hold:*

$$\int_{I_1} dx < \epsilon, \qquad \int_{I_2} d\beta(x) < \epsilon. \qquad (2)$$

(b) As a preparation we deal first with the following lemma:

LEMMA. *Let $-\pi = x_0 < x_1 < \ldots < x_{m-1} < x_m = \pi$ be an arbitrary subdivision of the interval $I: [-\pi, \pi]$. We have then*

$$\inf \sum_{\mu=1}^{m} \min\{x_\mu - x_{\mu-1}, \alpha_s(x_\mu) - \alpha_s(x_{\mu-1})\} = 0,$$

where the symbol inf *refers to all possible subdivisions.*

In other words, δ being an arbitrary positive number, we can find a subdivision of I such that

$$\sum_{\mu=1}^{m} \min\{x_\mu - x_{\mu-1}, \alpha_s(x_\mu) - \alpha_s(x_{\mu-1})\} < \delta. \qquad (3)$$

For the proof of the lemma we generalize the inf in question in the following manner. We denote by $[x', x'']$ an arbitrary interval of I and let $x_0, x_1, ..., x_m$ be now an arbitrary subdivision of the interval $[x', x'']$,

$$x_0 = x' < x_1 < x_2 < ... < x_{m-1} < x_m = x''.$$

We write

$$\inf \sum_{\mu=1}^{m} \min \{x_\mu - x_{\mu-1}, \alpha_s(x_\mu) - \alpha_s(x_{\mu-1})\} = h(x', x'').$$

We wish to prove that $h(-\pi, \pi) = 0$.

Clearly $h(x', x'') + h(x'', x''') = h(x', x''')$ provided $x' \leq x'' \leq x'''$. We write $h(-\pi, x) = h(x)$. This function is nondecreasing. Moreover,

$$h(x', x'') = h(x'') - h(x') < x'' - x',$$

so that $h(x)$ is absolutely continuous. Also

$$h(x'') - h(x') \leq \alpha_s(x'') - \alpha_s(x'),$$

so that $h'(x) = 0$ almost everywhere. Hence $h(x) = \text{const.}$, and since $h(-\pi) = 0$, we have generally $h(x) = 0$, $h(\pi) = 0$.

(c) In possession of this lemma the proof of the theorem in (a) is easy. We determine first a subdivision of I such that (3) holds. We denote by K_1 those intervals for which $x_\mu - x_{\mu-1} < \alpha_s(x_\mu) - \alpha_s(x_{\mu-1})$ and by K_2 the others. Further, we denote [as in 1.3 (a)] by λ_k the jumps of $\alpha_j(x)$ produced at the points t_k, respectively. The sum $\Sigma \lambda_k$ being convergent, we can determine N such that $\lambda_{N+1} + \lambda_{N+2} + ... < \delta$. Then we consider those elements of the finite set $t_1, t_2, ..., t_N$ which lie in K_2; we surround these points by small intervals (belonging to K_2) whose total length is less than δ and denote the remaining part of K_2 by I_2. Thus I_1 consists of the intervals K_1 and, in addition, of the small intervals just constructed which are in K_2.

In view of (3) the total length of I_1 is less than $\delta + \delta = 2\delta$. On the other hand,

$$\int_{I_2} d\alpha_j(x) \leq \lambda_{N+1} + \lambda_{N+2} + ... < \delta,$$

$$\int_{I_2} d\alpha_s(x) \leq \int_{K_2} d\alpha_s(x) = \sum_{K_2} \min \{x_\mu - x_{\mu-1}, \alpha_s(x_\mu) - \alpha_s(x_{\mu-1})\} < \delta.$$

We now choose $2\delta = \epsilon$. This establishes (2).

1.5. Linear functionals

A linear functional $L(f)$ defined for all functions $f(x)$ of the class C [cf. 1.2 (c)], is characterized by the following conditions: (i) For each f of C it has a definite real or complex value. (ii) Let f_1 and f_2 be of C, c_1 and c_2 constants; then

$$L(c_1 f_1 + c_2 f_2) = c_1 L(f_1) + c_2 L(f_2). \tag{1}$$

Such a functional is called bounded if the quantity

$$\sup_{|f| \leqq 1} |L(f)| = \|L\| \tag{2}$$

is finite. This sup is called the *norm* of $L(f)$. A bounded linear functional can be written in the following form:

$$L(f) = \int_{-\pi}^{\pi} f(x) \, d\alpha(x), \tag{3}$$

where $\alpha(x)$ is a function of bounded variation depending only on the functional. The norm of $L(f)$ is $\int_{-\pi}^{\pi} |d\alpha(x)|$, i.e. the total variation of $\alpha(x)$.

A bounded functional is called nonnegative if $f(x) \geqq 0$ implies $L(f) \geqq 0$ for all functions $f(x) \in C$. The necessary and sufficient condition for the nonnegative character of the functional (3) is that $\alpha(x)$ is a nondecreasing function (a distribution function). The norm of (3) is in this case $\alpha(\pi) - \alpha(-\pi)$; this is the value of the functional for $f = 1$.

1.6. Lebesgue integrals

We use the symbols L and C as defined in 1.2. We note the following two important theorems:

(a) THEOREM. *Let $\{f_n(x)\}$ be a sequence of nonnegative functions belonging to L. We assume that* $\lim_{n \to \infty} f_n(x) = f(x)$ *exists almost everywhere and* $\int_{-\pi}^{\pi} f_n(x) \, dx \leqq A$. *Then $f(x)$ is of the class L and*

$$\int_{-\pi}^{\pi} f(x) \, dx \leqq A.$$

(b) THEOREM. *Let $f(x)$ belong to L. The Poisson integral*

$$\frac{1}{2\pi}\int_{-\pi}^{\pi} f(\theta)\,\frac{1-r^2}{1-2r\cos(x-\theta)+r^2}\,d\theta,$$

where $0\leq r<1$, has the limit $f(x)$, as $r\to 1-0$, for almost all values of x.

If $f(x)$ belongs to the class C, Poisson's integral tends uniformly to $f(x)$, $-\pi\leq x\leq\pi$, as $r\to 1-0$.

1.7. Vector space, scalar product, length, completeness

(a) First let us consider the N-dimensional complex Euclidean vector space. A vector $\mathbf{f}$ is defined by its N complex components (projections) f_k; $k=1,2,\ldots,N$. Let $\mathbf{f}=(f_k)$, $\mathbf{g}=(g_k)$ be two given vectors; we define their scalar product by

$$(\mathbf{f},\mathbf{g})=f_1\bar{g}_1+f_2\bar{g}_2+\ldots+f_N\bar{g}_N. \tag{1}$$

The length of $\mathbf{f}$ is defined by $\|\mathbf{f}\|=(\mathbf{f},\mathbf{f})^{\frac{1}{2}}$.

Without entering in the systematic (axiomatic) treatment of these concepts we point out a few generalizations and analogous definitions.

Let $\rho_1,\rho_2,\ldots,\rho_N$ be given positive numbers. We may define the scalar product of $\mathbf{f}$ and $\mathbf{g}$ by

$$\rho_1 f_1\bar{g}_1+\rho_2 f_2\bar{g}_2+\ldots+\rho_N f_N\bar{g}_N. \tag{2}$$

This is a generalization of (1). We obtain in a corresponding way a generalization of the definition of the length.

Other examples of vector spaces and scalar products are the following.

The complex Hilbert space $\mathbf{f}=(f_k)$, where $k=1,2,\ldots$ and the infinite series $\Sigma\,|f_k|^2$ is convergent. The definition of $(\mathbf{f},\mathbf{g})$ corresponding to (1) is obvious.

The space $L_2=L_2(a,b)$, where a and b are real numbers ($a=-\infty$ or $b=+\infty$ are also permitted). We define, if $f(x)$ and $g(x)$ are two functions (vectors) of L_2,

$$(f,g)=\int_a^b f(x)\,\overline{g(x)}\,dx. \tag{3}$$

The length (magnitude) of a function $f(x)$ is

$$\|f\|=(f,f)^{\frac{1}{2}}=\left\{\int_a^b |f(x)|^2\,dx\right\}^{\frac{1}{2}}. \tag{4}$$

An important generalization is the following:

$$(f,g) = \int_a^b f(x)\,\overline{g(x)}\,d\alpha(x), \quad \|f\| = \left\{\int_a^b |f(x)|^2\,d\alpha(x)\right\}^{\frac{1}{2}}, \tag{5}$$

where $\alpha(x)$ is a given distribution function in $[a,b]$; $\alpha(b)-\alpha(a)>0$. In the case when $\alpha(x)$ is absolutely continuous, we have $\alpha'(x)=w(x)$ almost everywhere and

$$(f,g) = \int_a^b f(x)\,\overline{g(x)}\,w(x)\,dx, \quad \|f\| = \left\{\int_a^b |f(x)|^2\,w(x)\,dx\right\}^{\frac{1}{2}}. \tag{6}$$

Here the so-called weight function $w(x)$ is nonnegative and of the class L. The case of a zero-function $w(x)$ is excluded. Obviously (3) is the analog of (1), (5) and (6) are analogs of (2).

(b) The 'length' of a vector can be defined independently of the concept of the scalar product. The definitions in (4), (5) and (6) are the natural concepts of the length in the complex spaces $L_2(a,b)$, $L_2[d\alpha(x);\ a,b]$, $L_2[w(x)\,dx;\ a,b]$, respectively. We point out the following important definition in $L_p[d\alpha(x);\ a,b]$:

$$\|f\| = \|f\|_p = \left\{\int_a^b |f(x)|^p\,d\alpha(x)\right\}^{1/p}, \quad p \geqq 1. \tag{7}$$

We mention also the other important definition:

$$\|f\| = \|f\|_\infty = \max|f(x)|, \quad -\pi \leqq x \leqq \pi,$$

where $f(x) \in C$.

(c) Let us consider the space $L_p[d\alpha(x);\ a,b]$, $p \geqq 1$. We say that the functions

$$f_0(x), f_1(x), \ldots, f_n(x), \ldots \tag{8}$$

of this space are *complete* in this space if any function $f(x)$ of the space can be approximated with arbitrary accuracy by a finite linear combination of the functions (8). The approximation is measured by the integral (7). In other words, if $f(x)$ and ϵ are given, $\epsilon > 0$, we can find a function of the form

$$\phi(x) = c_0 f_0(x) + c_1 f_1(x) + \ldots + c_n f_n(x),$$

where the coefficients c_ν are suitable complex constants such that

$$\int_a^b |f(x)-\phi(x)|^p\,d\alpha(x) < \epsilon. \tag{9}$$

1.8. Orthogonal systems

(a) A system of functions $\{\phi_n(x)\}$, where $\phi_n(x) \in L_2(a,b)$, is called orthonormal in $[a,b]$ if

$$(\phi_n, \phi_m) = \int_a^b \phi_n(x) \overline{\phi_m(x)}\, dx = \delta_{nm}. \tag{1}$$

In general, we let n and m run over all nonnegative integers. In some cases however, it is advisable to let n and m run over all integers from $-\infty$ to $+\infty$. For instance, the functions $\{e^{inx}\}$, where n ranges over the integers from $-\infty$ to $+\infty$, are orthonormal in $[-\pi, \pi]$.

Let $f(x)$ be a function of $L_2(a,b)$. The Fourier coefficients of $f(x)$ with respect to the orthonormal system $\{\phi_n(x)\}$ are defined by

$$c_n = (f, \phi_n) = \int_a^b f(x) \overline{\phi_n(x)}\, dx, \quad n = 0, 1, 2, \ldots. \tag{2}$$

They are the coefficients of the formal Fourier series of $f(x)$:

$$c_0 \phi_0(x) + c_1 \phi_1(x) + c_2 \phi_2(x) + \ldots + c_n \phi_n(x) + \ldots. \tag{3}$$

It is well known that for each n we have

$$\sum_{\nu=0}^{n} |c_\nu|^2 \leq \int_a^b |f(x)|^2\, dx = \|f\|^2, \tag{4}$$

so that $\sum_{n=0}^{\infty} |c_n|^2$ is convergent and

$$\sum_{n=0}^{\infty} |c_n|^2 \leq \|f\|^2. \tag{5}$$

We say that the system $\{\phi_n(x)\}$ is complete if in (5) the $=$ sign holds for every function $f(x)$ of the class $L_2(a,b)$. This property is equivalent to the special case $\alpha(x) = x$, $p = 2$ of the definition formulated in 1.7 (c). It is also equivalent to the fact that the partial sums of the Fourier series (3) converge in the mean [i.e. in the sense of $L_2(a,b)$] towards $f(x)$.

Sometimes we consider systems $\{f_n(x)\}$ which are orthonormal in the following sense:

$$(f_n, f_m) = \int_a^b f_n(x) \overline{f_m(x)}\, d\alpha(x) = \delta_{nm}, \tag{6}$$

where $\alpha(x)$ is a given distribution function defined in $[a, b]$.

(b) *Theorem of F. Riesz and E. Fischer.* Let $\{c_n\}$ be any sequence of complex numbers such that $\sum_{n=0}^{\infty} |c_n|^2$ is convergent. There exists a function $f(x) \in L_2(a, b)$ so that the relations (2) hold. In the case when the system $\{\phi_n(x)\}$ is complete, the function $f(x)$ is uniquely determined, except of course for a set of measure zero. We have

$$\lim_{n \to \infty} \| f(x) - s_n(x) \| = 0,$$

where $s_n(x)$ are the partial sums of the series (3).

(c) *Orthogonalization.* Let

$$f_0(x), \ f_1(x), \ f_2(x), \ ..., \ f_n(x), \ ... \tag{7}$$

be given complex-valued functions in $L_2(a, b)$ such that any finite subset of (7) is linearly independent; this means that a relation $\sum_{\nu=0}^{m} \gamma_\nu f_\nu(x) = 0$, with constant coefficients γ_ν, can hold for all x (except for a set of measure zero) only if all coefficients γ_ν are zero.

There exists a uniquely determined system

$$\phi_0(x), \ \phi_1(x), \ \phi_2(x), \ ..., \ \phi_n(x), \ ..., \tag{8}$$

so that the following two conditions are satisfied:

(i) $\qquad \phi_n(x) = l_{n0} f_0(x) + l_{n1} f_1(x) + ... + l_{nn} f_n(x),$

where the coefficients l_{nm} are properly chosen constants and $l_{nn} > 0$;

(ii) We have
$$(\phi_n, \phi_m) = \delta_{nm}.$$

The relations (ii) mean that the functions $\{\phi_n(x)\}$ are orthonormal in $[a, b]$. The transition from the given system $\{f_n(x)\}$ to the orthonormal system $\{\phi_n(x)\}$ is called *orthogonalization.*

A proof of existence and a direct representation of the functions $\phi_n(x)$ is not difficult. The Hermitian form

$$\| u_0 f_0(x) + u_1 f_1(x) + ... + u_n f_n(x) \|^2,$$

where the length is defined by 1.7 (4), is positive definite so that the determinants
$$D_n = \det((f_\mu, f_\nu)), \quad \mu, \nu = 0, 1, ..., n, \tag{9}$$

are all positive. Now we can verify that the functions

$$\phi_n(x) = (D_{n-1} D_n)^{-\frac{1}{2}} \begin{vmatrix} (f_0, f_0) & (f_1, f_0) & \cdots & (f_n, f_0) \\ (f_0, f_1) & (f_1, f_1) & \cdots & (f_n, f_1) \\ \cdots & \cdots & \cdots & \cdots \\ (f_0, f_{n-1}) & (f_1, f_{n-1}) & \cdots & (f_n, f_{n-1}) \\ f_0(x) & f_1(x) & \cdots & f_n(x) \end{vmatrix}, \tag{10}$$

$$n = 1, 2, 3, ...,$$

satisfy indeed conditions (i) and (ii). The coefficient of $f_n(x)$ in $\phi_n(x)$ is $(D_{n-1}/D_n)^{\frac{1}{2}}$. For $n=0$ we have $\phi_0(x) = D_0^{-\frac{1}{2}} f_0(x)$.

The uniqueness of the system $\{\phi_n(x)\}$ can be shown as follows. First, we express each $f_k(x)$ as a linear combination of the functions $\phi_l(x)$, $l \leqq k$; hence $(\phi_n, f_k) = 0$ for all $k \leqq n-1$. If another linear combination $\tilde{\phi}_n(x)$ of the form (i) existed satisfying again the conditions $(\tilde{\phi}_n, f_k) = 0$, $k \leqq n-1$, we would be able to form $\lambda \phi_n(x) + \mu \tilde{\phi}_n(x)$ with $\lambda \neq 0$, $\mu \neq 0$ involving only $f_0, f_1, \ldots, f_{n-1}$. Hence

$$\| \lambda \phi_n(x) + \mu \tilde{\phi}_n(x) \| = 0$$

would follow, that is,

$$\lambda \phi_n(x) + \mu \tilde{\phi}_n(x) = 0,$$

except for a set of measure zero. In view of (ii) there must be $|\lambda| = |\mu|$, and since the coefficient of $f_n(x)$ in (i) is positive, we conclude that $\phi_n(x) = \tilde{\phi}_n(x)$. On account of the linear independence of the functions f the coefficients l_{nm} are uniquely determined.

(d) The process of orthogonalization remains essentially unchanged if the scalar product (ϕ_n, ϕ_m) is defined by (6), where $\alpha(x)$ is a given distribution function in $[a, b]$. A representation like (10) is valid again. The case $d\alpha(x) = w(x) \, dx$ is of particular interest. We mention the following two examples.

(i) Let $f_n(x) = x^n$ so that $\phi_n(x)$ is a polynomial of degree n in which the coefficient of x^n is positive. We have

$$\int_a^b \phi_n(x) \, \phi_m(x) \, d\alpha(x) = \delta_{nm}, \quad n, m = 0, 1, 2, \ldots. \tag{11}$$

(ii) Let $f_n(x) = e^{inx}$ so that $\phi_n(x)$ is a polynomial of degree n in e^{ix} in which the coefficient of e^{inx} is positive. We have

$$\int_{-\pi}^{\pi} \phi_n(x) \, \overline{\phi_m(x)} \, d\alpha(x) = \delta_{nm}, \quad n, m = 0, 1, 2, \ldots. \tag{12}$$

1.9. Approximations

(a) We shall use frequently the following important theorem:

THEOREM OF WEIERSTRASS. *Let $f(x)$ be of the class C (1.2). To an arbitrary $\epsilon > 0$ a trigonometric polynomial $t(x)$ can be found such that we have, uniformly for all real x,*

$$| f(x) - t(x) | < \epsilon.$$

(b) A more refined formulation of the theorem of Weierstrass is furnished by the following theorem:

THEOREM. *Let $\omega(\delta)$ be the modulus of continuity of a function $f(x)$ of the class C (1.1). For each n a trigonometric polynomial $t(x)$ of degree n can be found such that*

$$|f(x) - t(x)| < A\omega(2\pi/n).$$

Here A is an absolute constant.

As an example we mention the case of a function $f(x)$ satisfying the Lipschitz condition

$$|f(x') - f(x'')| < K\,|x' - x''\,|^\alpha, \quad 0 < \alpha < 1.$$

We have $\omega(\delta) = O(\delta^\alpha)$. Then $f(x)$ can be approximated by a trigonometric polynomial of degree n with an accuracy of order $n^{-\alpha}$. Another interesting condition is that of Lipschitz–Dini:

$$\omega(\delta) = O[|\log\delta|^{-1-\lambda}], \quad \lambda > 0.$$

The order of approximation is then $(\log n)^{-1-\lambda}$.

'If the function $f(x)$ belongs to a certain subclass Γ of C, the approximating trigonometric polynomials $t(x)$ can be chosen from the same subclass Γ.' This assertion holds for the following subclasses:

(i) $f(x)$ is an even function, $f(-x) = f(x)$.
(ii) $f(x)$ is an odd function, $f(-x) = -f(x)$.
(iii) $f(x)$ is of the 'power series type', i.e.

$$\int_{-\pi}^{\pi} f(x)\,e^{inx}\,dx = 0, \quad n = 1, 2, 3, \dots.$$

In the first case $t(x)$ will be a cosine polynomial, in the second a sine polynomial, in the third a polynomial in e^{ix}.

(c) THEOREM. *Let $f(x)$ be a function of the class L. To any $\epsilon > 0$ a trigonometric polynomial $t(x)$ can be found such that*

$$\int_{-\pi}^{\pi} |f(x) - t(x)|\,dx < \epsilon.$$

In the case when $f(x) \geq m$, we can choose $t(x)$ in such a way that $t(x) \geq m$.
A similar theorem holds for the approximations by polynomials. The inequality expresses the completeness of the system $\{e^{inx}\}$, $n = 0$, $\pm 1, \pm 2, \dots$, in the space $L[dx; -\pi, \pi]$.

For the proof let us assume first that $f(x)$ is bounded from below, $f(x) \geq m$. Let ω be a positive number, $\omega \geq m$. We define the function $f_\omega(x)$ as follows:

$$f_\omega(x) = \begin{cases} f(x) & \text{if } f(x) \leq \omega, \\ \omega & \text{if } f(x) \geq \omega. \end{cases}$$

Since $f_\omega(x) \leq f(x)$ we have

$$\int_{-\pi}^{\pi} |f(x) - f_\omega(x)| \, dx \leq \int_{f(x) \geq \omega} f(x) \, dx, \qquad (1)$$

and the last integral is less than $\tfrac{1}{2}\epsilon$ provided ω is sufficiently large. Now $f_\omega(x)$ is bounded, $m \leq f_\omega(x) \leq \omega$, hence $f_\omega(x) \in L_2$, so that it can be approximated in the L_2 sense by the partial sums of its Fourier series [1.8 (a)], consequently also by the Fejér means of this series. Thus we can find a trigonometric polynomial $t(x)$ satisfying the condition $t(x) \geq m$ and the inequality

$$\int_{-\pi}^{\pi} |f_\omega(x) - t(x)| \, dx < (2\pi)^{\frac{1}{2}} \left\{ \int_{-\pi}^{\pi} |f_\omega(x) - t(x)|^2 \, dx \right\}^{\frac{1}{2}} < \tfrac{1}{2}\epsilon. \qquad (2)$$

Combining the inequalities (1) and (2) we obtain the theorem.

This argument requires only a slight modification if $f(x)$ is unbounded from below.

(d) A similar argument yields the completeness of the system $\{e^{inx}\}$, $n = 0, \pm 1, \pm 2, \ldots$, in the space $L_p[dx; -\pi, \pi]$, where $p > 1$. For $p \leq 2$ we use Hölder's inequality [1.2 (d)] as in (2); for $p > 2$ we take into account that $\max |t(x)| \leq \max |f_\omega(x)|$, so that

$$\int_{-\pi}^{\pi} |f_\omega(x) - t(x)|^p \, dx \leq (2 \max |f_\omega(x)|)^{p-2} \int_{-\pi}^{\pi} |f_\omega(x) - t(x)|^2 \, dx.$$

Finally, Minkowski's inequality [1.2 (d)] must be used.

Let $\alpha(x)$ be an arbitrary distribution function in the interval $[-\pi, \pi]$, and let $p \geq 1$. The functions $\{e^{inx}\}$, $n = 0, \pm 1, \pm 2, \ldots$, are complete in the space $L_p[d\alpha(x); -\pi, \pi]$.

1.10. Toeplitz forms

We consider three classes of functions. In each case we associate with every function of the class a form of Hermitian character which we call a Toeplitz form.

(a) Let

$$a_0 + 2 \sum_{n=1}^{\infty} r^n (a_n \cos nx + b_n \sin nx) \qquad (1)$$

be the expansion of a harmonic function in the polar coordinates r, x where the coefficients $a_0, a_1, b_1, a_2, b_2, ..., a_n, b_n, ...$ are real. We introduce the complex numbers

$$c_n = a_n - ib_n, c_{-n} = \bar{c}_n = a_n + ib_n, \quad n = 0, 1, 2, ...; \; b_0 = 0, \qquad (2)$$

so that $(c_{\nu-\mu})$ will be a Hermitian matrix, $\mu, \nu = 0, 1, 2, ..., n$. We consider the Hermitian forms

$$T_n = \Sigma c_{\nu-\mu} u_\mu \bar{u}_\nu, \quad \mu, \nu = 0, 1, ..., n, \qquad (3)$$

and call them the *Toeplitz forms* associated with the harmonic function (1).

Let $f(x)$ be a real-valued function of the class L, and

$$f(x) \sim \sum_{n=-\infty}^{\infty} c_n e^{inx} \qquad (4)$$

its Fourier series, where

$$c_n = \frac{1}{2\pi} \int_{-\pi}^{\pi} e^{-inx} f(x) \, dx; \quad c_{-n} = \bar{c}_n. \qquad (5)$$

We call the Hermitian forms (3) in this case the *Toeplitz forms* associated with the function $f(x)$. We have

$$T_n = \frac{1}{2\pi} \int_{-\pi}^{\pi} | u_0 + u_1 e^{ix} + u_2 e^{2ix} + ... + u_n e^{nix} |^2 f(x) \, dx. \qquad (6)$$

Finally, we consider a distribution function $\alpha(x)$ defined in $[-\pi, \pi]$ and form its Fourier–Stieltjes coefficients:

$$c_n = \frac{1}{2\pi} \int_{-\pi}^{\pi} e^{-inx} \, d\alpha(x); \quad c_{-n} = \bar{c}_n. \qquad (7)$$

The corresponding Hermitian forms (3) are called again the *Toeplitz forms* associated with the distribution function $\alpha(x)$. We have in this case

$$T_n = \frac{1}{2\pi} \int_{-\pi}^{\pi} | u_0 + u_1 e^{ix} + u_2 e^{2ix} + ... + u_n e^{nix} |^2 \, d\alpha(x). \qquad (8)$$

In the special case of a constant, $a_0 = 1$ in (1), or $f(x) = 1$ in (4), or $\alpha(x) = x$ in (7), we have $c_0 = 1$, $c_n = 0$, $n \neq 0$, and T_n reduces to the unit form
$$T_n = | u_0 |^2 + | u_1 |^2 + ... + | u_n |^2.$$

It is also interesting to observe that for the special system

$$u_0 = u_1 = ... = u_n = (n+1)^{-\frac{1}{2}}$$

(for which $T_n = 1$) the expression (6) will reduce to the nth Fejér mean of $f(x)$.

(b) The following theorem and the theorem of (c) express a basic property of the Toeplitz forms:

THEOREM (concerning harmonic functions). *The series* (1) *is convergent in the unit circle* $r < 1$ *and represents there a positive harmonic function if and only if the Toeplitz forms* (3) *are nonnegative for all values of* n. *The only exception is when* (1) *is identically zero.*

The expression

$$T_n(r, \theta) = \Sigma c_{\nu-\mu} r^{|\mu-\nu|} e^{i(\mu-\nu)\theta} u_\mu \bar{u}_\nu, \quad \mu, \nu = 0, 1, \ldots, n,$$

defines a harmonic function of the polar coordinates r, θ so that its nonnegativity for $r = 1$ involves the same property for $r < 1$. Let (1) represent a regular and positive harmonic function $f(r, x)$ for $r < 1$; since

$$T_n(r, \theta) = \frac{1}{2\pi} \int_{-\pi}^{\pi} |u_0 + u_1 e^{ix} + u_2 e^{2ix} + \ldots + u_n e^{nix}|^2 f(r, x - \theta) \, dx,$$

$$(9)$$

we have $T_n(r, \theta) \geqq 0$ and also $T_n(1, 0) = T_n \geqq 0$.

Conversely, we assume that $T_n \geqq 0$, thus $T_n(1, \theta) \geqq 0$, hence $T_n(r, \theta) \geqq 0$, $r < 1$, θ arbitrary real. In particular, we have $T_n(r, 0) \geqq 0$. From $T_n \geqq 0$ we conclude that $c_0^2 - |c_n|^2 \geqq 0$, $|c_n| \leqq c_0$, so that (1) is convergent for $r < 1$ and represents a regular harmonic function $f(r, x)$. Now let $0 < \rho < 1$ and x_0 an arbitrary fixed real value. We choose in (9)

$$u_0 + u_1 e^{ix} + u_2 e^{2ix} + \ldots + u_n e^{nix} = (1 - \rho^2)^{\frac{1}{2}} \sum_{\nu=0}^{n} \rho^\nu e^{i\nu(x - x_0)},$$

so that for $n \to \infty$

$$\frac{1}{2\pi} \int_{-\pi}^{\pi} \left| \frac{(1-\rho^2)^{\frac{1}{2}}}{1 - \rho\, e^{i(x - x_0)}} \right|^2 f(r, x) \, dx$$

$$= \frac{1}{2\pi} \int_{-\pi}^{\pi} \frac{1 - \rho^2}{1 - 2\rho \cos(x - x_0) + \rho^2} f(r, x) \, dx \geqq 0.$$

If $\rho \to 1 - 0$, this expression [Poisson's integral, 1.6 (b)] approaches $f(r, x_0)$ so that $f(r, x)$ is nonnegative in the unit circle $r < 1$. According to the extremum principle on harmonic functions it must be positive unless it is identically zero.

This establishes the theorem.

(c) THEOREM (concerning functions of the class L). *The function $f(x)$ in* (4) *is nonnegative (except for a set of measure zero) if and only if the Toeplitz forms* (6) *are nonnegative for all values of n.*

The proof follows very much the same line as in (b). If we have $f(x) \geq 0$ almost everywhere, the forms (6) are clearly nonnegative. Conversely, if $T_n \geq 0$ for all n, we conclude as before that

$$\frac{1}{2\pi} \int_{-\pi}^{\pi} \frac{1-\rho^2}{1-2\rho \cos(x-x_0)+\rho^2} f(x)\, dx \geq 0.$$

In view of 1.6 (b) this expression approaches $f(x_0)$ when $\rho \to 1-0$ for almost all x_0 and this establishes the assertion.

1.11. Trigonometric moment problem

(a) Let $\alpha(x)$ be a distribution function in $[-\pi, \pi]$ and

$$c_n = \frac{1}{2\pi} \int_{-\pi}^{\pi} e^{-inx}\, d\alpha(x), \quad n=0, \pm 1, \pm 2, \ldots, \tag{1}$$

its Fourier–Stieltjes coefficients. The representation 1.10 (8) holds for the associated Toeplitz forms. These forms are nonnegative semidefinite and even positive definite unless $\alpha(x)$ is of the finite type. In the latter case we denote the jumps of $\alpha(x)$ by $\lambda_1, \lambda_2, \ldots, \lambda_m$ produced at the points $t_1, t_2, \ldots, t_m$ ($-\pi \leq t_1 < t_2 < \ldots < t_{m-1} < t_m < \pi$); we have then

$$T_n = \frac{1}{2\pi} \sum_{j=1}^{m} \lambda_j \, | u_0 + u_1 e^{it_j} + u_2 e^{2it_j} + \ldots + u_n e^{nit_j} |^2. \tag{2}$$

Hence T_n is positive definite if $n \leq m$ and nonnegative semidefinite for $n > m$.

In general, the Toeplitz determinants D_n (the determinants of the form T_n) are all positive. The special case (2) is the only exception; we have in this case $D_n > 0$ for $n \leq m$ and $D_n = 0$ for $n > m$.

The *trigonometric moment problem* can be formulated as follows: *Let c_n be a sequence of complex constants, $c_{-n} = \bar{c}_n$. What are the necessary and sufficient conditions in order that a distribution function $\alpha(x)$ exists for which the equations* (1) *hold?*

(b) The nonnegativity of the Toeplitz forms 1.10 (3) is certainly a necessary condition. Now this condition is also sufficient, as it can be shown by the following argument. First we show by the argument used in the proof of 1.10 (b) that 1.10 (1) converges for $r < 1$ and represents a regular harmonic function $f(r, x)$ in the unit circle $r < 1$. Moreover, $f(r, x) \geqq 0$ and, in view of the extremum principle on harmonic functions, we have $f(r, x) > 0$ unless $f(r, x)$ is identically zero.

Further we form

$$F(r, x) = \tfrac{1}{2} a_0 x^2 - \sum_{n=1}^{\infty} \frac{a_n \cos nx + b_n \sin nx}{n^2} r^n. \tag{3}$$

The latter sum represents a harmonic function which is regular for $r < 1$ and continuous for $r \leqq 1$. Moreover, for a fixed r, the expression $F(r, x)$ is a convex function of x since

$$\frac{d^2}{dx^2} F(r, x) = f(r, x) > 0.$$

Hence for any values of x_1 and x_2 from $[-\pi, \pi]$ we have

$$F(r, x_1) + F(r, x_2) - 2F(r, \tfrac{1}{2}(x_1 + x_2)) \geqq 0,$$

and the same inequality holds for the boundary values $F(x)$:

$$F(x_1) + F(x_2) - 2F(\tfrac{1}{2}(x_1 + x_2)) \geqq 0.$$

Such a function $F(x)$ is absolutely continuous and its derivative $F'(x) = \alpha(x)$ exists almost everywhere and is nondecreasing. We have

$$\frac{1}{2\pi} \int_{-\pi}^{\pi} (F(x) - \tfrac{1}{2} a_0 x^2) e^{-inx} dx = -\frac{c_n}{n^2},$$

$$\frac{1}{2\pi} \int_{-\pi}^{\pi} (F'(x) - a_0 x) e^{-inx} dx = -i \frac{c_n}{n}, \quad n = 1, 2, 3, \ldots.$$

From the last relation, integrating by parts, (1) will follow.

1.12. Representation of L. Fejér and F. Riesz for nonnegative trigonometric polynomials

(a) THEOREM. *Any nonnegative trigonometric polynomial in x can be written as the square of the modulus of a polynomial in z of equal degree where z is on the unit circle, $z = e^{ix}$.*

That is, if

$$f(x) = a_0 + 2 \sum_{k=1}^{n} (a_k \cos kx + b_k \sin kx) \tag{1}$$

is nonnegative for all real values of x, a polynomial $g(z) = \sum_{j=0}^{n} d_j z^j$ exists such that $f(x) = |g(z)|^2$, $z = e^{ix}$.

This representation can be obtained by inserting first

$$\cos kx = \tfrac{1}{2}(z^k + z^{-k}), \quad \sin kx = \frac{1}{2i}(z^k - z^{-k}).$$

Then $f(x)$ will be of the form $z^{-n}G(z)$, where $G(z)$ is a polynomial of degree $2n$ satisfying the relation $G(z) = G^*(z)$. Hence the zeros of $G(z)$ must be symmetrical with respect to the unit circle, i.e. with every zero z_0, where $0 < |z_0| < 1$, also $(\bar{z}_0)^{-1}$ will be a zero; we can ascertain by differentiation that the zeros z_0 and $(\bar{z}_0)^{-1}$ are of the same multiplicity. Moreover, the zeros of $G(z)$ on the unit circle, if they exist, are of even multiplicity. Finally, if 0 is a zero of order m of $G(z)$, the same polynomial $G(z)$ must have ∞ as a zero of the same order.† Taking all these facts into account, we see that $G(z)$ must have the form

$$G(z) = A z^m \prod_{\mu=1}^{p} (z - \alpha_\mu)(z - (\bar{\alpha}_\mu)^{-1}) \prod_{\nu=1}^{q} (z - \beta_\nu)^2.$$

Here A is a constant,

$$0 < |\alpha_\mu| < 1, \quad |\beta_\nu| = 1, \quad m + 2p + 2q = 2n - m.$$

Now $f(x)$ being nonnegative we have

$$f(x) = |G(z)| = |A| \prod_{\mu=1}^{p} |z - \alpha_\mu| |z - (\bar{\alpha}_\mu)^{-1}| \prod_{\nu=1}^{q} |z - \beta_\nu|^2$$

$$= \left| A^{\frac{1}{2}} \prod_{\mu=1}^{p} \alpha_\mu^{-\frac{1}{2}}(z - \alpha_\mu) \prod_{\nu=1}^{q} (z - \beta_\nu) \right|^2, \quad z = e^{ix}. \qquad (2)$$

This yields the desired polynomial $g(z)$.

(b) Let z_0 be any zero of $g(z)$, $|z_0| \neq 1$; we obtain another representation of $f(x)$ by replacing $g(z)$ by

$$\frac{1 - \bar{z}_0 z}{z - z_0} g(z).$$

Repeating this procedure we can gradually remove all the zeros from the interior of the unit circle resulting in a representation

$$f(x) = |g(z)|^2, \quad z = e^{ix},$$

---

† A polynomial has 0 as a zero of order m if its *first* m coefficients (those of $1, z, z^2, \ldots, z^{m-1}$) vanish. A polynomial has ∞ as a zero of order m if its *last* m coefficients vanish.

in which $g(z) \neq 0$ for $|z| < 1$; if we impose the additional condition that $g(0)$ be real and positive, the representation will be *uniquely* determined.

In a similar fashion we can remove all zeros from the exterior of the unit circle.

The representation in question can be expressed also in terms of the coefficients of $f(x)$ and $g(z)$ as follows:

$$\frac{1}{2\pi}\int_{-\pi}^{\pi} e^{-ikx}f(x)\,dx = a_k - ib_k$$

$$= \bar{d}_0 d_k + \bar{d}_1 d_{k+1} + \ldots + \bar{d}_{n-k}d_n;$$

$$k = 0, 1, 2, \ldots, n;\ b_0 = 0. \quad (3)$$

1.13. The class H_2

(a) We consider an analytic function $g(z) = \sum\limits_{n=0}^{\infty} d_n z^n$ of the class H_2 (1.1).

By the theorem of F. Riesz and E. Fischer [1.8 (b)] there exists a complex-valued function $h(\theta)$ of the class L_2 such that

$$\frac{1}{2\pi}\int_{-\pi}^{\pi} h(\theta)\,e^{-in\theta}\,d\theta = \begin{cases} d_n, & n = 0, 1, 2, \ldots, \\ 0, & n = -1, -2, \ldots. \end{cases} \quad (1)$$

Hence for $r < 1$ by Parseval's relation

$$\frac{1}{2\pi}\int_{-\pi}^{\pi} h(\theta)\,\frac{1-r^2}{1-2r\cos(x-\theta)+r^2}\,d\theta = \sum_{n=0}^{\infty} d_n r^n e^{inx} = g(re^{ix}), \quad (2)$$

so that in view of 1.6 (b) the limit

$$\lim_{r \to 1-0} g(re^{ix}) = h(x) \quad (3)$$

exists for almost all x. We use the natural notation $h(x) = g(e^{ix})$ and we have again by Parseval's formula

$$\frac{1}{2\pi}\int_{-\pi}^{\pi} |g(e^{ix})|^2 e^{-ikx}\,dx = \bar{d}_0 d_k + \bar{d}_1 d_{k+1} + \bar{d}_2 d_{k+2} + \ldots, \quad k = 0, 1, 2, \ldots. \quad (4)$$

A simple consequence of (4) is the following relation:

$$\lim_{r \to 1-0}\frac{1}{2\pi}\int_{-\pi}^{\pi} |g(re^{ix})|^2 F(x)\,dx = \frac{1}{2\pi}\int_{-\pi}^{\pi} |g(e^{ix})|^2 F(x)\,dx, \quad (5)$$

valid for an arbitrary trigonometric polynomial $F(x)$. We have furthermore

$$\lim_{r \to 1-0} \frac{1}{2\pi} \int_{-\pi}^{\pi} |g(re^{ix})|^2 |G(re^{ix})|^2 dx = \frac{1}{2\pi} \int_{-\pi}^{\pi} |g(e^{ix})|^2 |G(e^{ix})|^2 dx,$$

$$(6)$$

where $G(z)$ is a polynomial in z.

(b) The function $g(e^{ix})$ just defined has the important property that $\log |g(e^{ix})|$ *is integrable in the sense of Lebesgue.* Here we assume, of course, that $g(z)$ is not identically zero.

For the proof let $g(0) \neq 0$ [otherwise we would consider $z^{-m}g(z)$, where m denotes the order of the zero $z = 0$]; we assume that $g(0) = 1$. By the formula of Jacobi–Jensen we have

$$\frac{1}{2\pi} \int_{-\pi}^{\pi} \log |g(re^{ix})| dx = \log \prod_{k=1}^{p} \frac{r}{|\alpha_k|} \geq 0,$$

where $\alpha_1, \alpha_2, \ldots, \alpha_p$ denote the zeros of $g(z)$ within the circle of radius r. Hence if I_1 is the set of x-values for which $\log |g(re^{ix})| \geq 0$ and I_2 the complementary set, we have

$$\int_{-\pi}^{\pi} |\log|g(re^{ix})|| dx = \int_{I_1} \log |g(re^{ix})| dx - \int_{I_2} \log |g(re^{ix})| dx$$

$$= 2 \int_{I_1} \log |g(re^{ix})| dx - \int_{-\pi}^{\pi} \log |g(re^{ix})| dx$$

$$\leq 2 \int_{I_1} \log |g(re^{ix})| dx = \int_{I_1} \log |g(re^{ix})|^2 dx$$

$$< \int_{I_1} |g(re^{ix})|^2 dx \leq \int_{-\pi}^{\pi} |g(re^{ix})|^2 dx < 2\pi \sum_{n=0}^{\infty} |d_n|^2.$$

In view of 1.6 (a) we find that $\log |g(e^{ix})|$ is integrable and

$$\int_{-\pi}^{\pi} |\log|g(e^{ix})|| dx \leq 2\pi \sum_{n=0}^{\infty} |d_n|^2.$$

1.14. Positive representation

(a) Our purpose is to extend the representation of nonnegative trigonometric polynomials discussed in 1.12 to more general functions. The relation 1.12 (3) will serve as a guide.

Let $f(x)$ be a real-valued function of the class L but not a zero function. *What is the necessary and sufficient condition in order that an analytic function* $g(z) = \sum\limits_{n=0}^{\infty} d_n z^n$ *of the class* H_2 *exists such that*

$$\frac{1}{2\pi}\int_{-\pi}^{\pi} e^{-ikx} f(x)\, dx = \bar{d}_0 d_k + \bar{d}_1 d_{k+1} + \bar{d}_2 d_{k+2} + \ldots, \quad k = 0, 1, 2, \ldots. \tag{1}$$

The answer is as follows: $f(x)$ *must be nonnegative for almost all values of* x *and* $\log f(x)$ *must be in* L.

As an illustration, we mention the function $f(x) = |g(e^{ix})|^2$, where $g(z)$ is in H_2 and $g(e^{ix})$ is defined as in 1.13 (a). The essential content of the theorem is that the functions $|g(e^{ix})|^2$ yield all functions $f(x)$, $f(x) \geq 0$, for which $\log f(x) \in L$.

(b) We prove first that the condition is sufficient. The integral

$$\frac{1}{2\pi}\int_{-\pi}^{\pi} \log f(\theta)\, \frac{1-r^2}{1-2r\cos(x-\theta)+r^2}\, d\theta \tag{2}$$

represents a harmonic function of the polar coordinates r, x which is regular in the circle $r < 1$. We form the analytic function $h(z)$ whose real part (2) is, and we assume that $h(0)$ is real. Writing

$$g(z) = e^{\frac{1}{2}h(z)} = \sum_{n=0}^{\infty} d_n z^n$$

we have

$$|g(re^{ix})|^2 = \exp\{\Re h(re^{ix})\}$$

$$= \exp\left\{\frac{1}{2\pi}\int_{-\pi}^{\pi} \log f(\theta)\, \frac{1-r^2}{1-r\cos(x-\theta)+r^2}\, d\theta\right\}$$

$$\leqq \frac{1}{2\pi}\int_{-\pi}^{\pi} f(\theta)\, \frac{1-r^2}{1-2r\cos(x-\theta)+r^2}\, d\theta. \tag{3}$$

Here we used Jensen's inequality (see Appendix). Thus integrating we have

$$\frac{1}{2\pi}\int_{-\pi}^{\pi} |g(re^{ix})|^2\, dx \leqq \frac{1}{2\pi}\int_{-\pi}^{\pi} f(\theta)\, d\theta, \tag{4}$$

so that $g(z)$ belongs to H_2. Also we find

$$\sum_{n=0}^{\infty} |d_n|^2 \leqq \frac{1}{2\pi}\int_{-\pi}^{\pi} f(\theta)\, d\theta. \tag{5}$$

By 1.6 (b) we find for almost all x

$$\lim_{r \to 1-0} |g(r e^{ix})|^2 = \exp\{\log f(x)\} = f(x), \tag{6}$$

so that by 1.6 (a)

$$\frac{1}{2\pi} \int_{-\pi}^{\pi} f(x) \, dx \leqq \lim_{r \to 1-0} \frac{1}{2\pi} \int_{-\pi}^{\pi} |g(r e^{ix})|^2 \, dx = \sum_{n=0}^{\infty} |d_n|^2. \tag{7}$$

Comparing (5) and (7) we obtain

$$\frac{1}{2\pi} \int_{-\pi}^{\pi} f(x) \, dx = \sum_{n=0}^{\infty} |d_n|^2, \tag{8}$$

which is the special case $k=0$ of (1).

We apply now the last result to the function $f(x) \, | \, 1 + \eta \, e^{ikx}|^2$, where η is a complex constant and k a positive integer. We obtain

$$\frac{1}{2\pi} \int_{-\pi}^{\pi} f(x) \, | \, 1 + \eta \, e^{ikx}|^2 \, dx = \lim_{r \to 1-0} \frac{1}{2\pi} \int_{-\pi}^{\pi} |g(r e^{ix}) \, (1 + \eta r^k \, e^{ikx})|^2 \, dx,$$

so that

$$\frac{1}{2\pi} \int_{-\pi}^{\pi} f(x) \, e^{-ikx} \, dx = \lim_{r \to 1-0} \frac{1}{2\pi} \int_{-\pi}^{\pi} |g(r e^{ix})|^2 \, e^{-ikx} \, dx,$$

from which the general case (1) follows without difficulty.

(c) In order to prove that the condition is necessary, we assume the existence of a function $g(z)$ of the class H_2 such that (1) holds. In addition, 1.13 (4) holds so that all Fourier coefficients of $f(x) - |g(e^{ix})|^2$ are zero, hence $f(x) = |g(e^{ix})|^2 \geqq 0$, except for a set of measure zero.

In view of 1.13 (b) we conclude now that $\log f(x)$ is L-integrable.

(d) We note the following inequality which will be useful in 3.2:

$$\exp\left\{\frac{1}{2\pi} \int_{-\pi}^{\pi} \log f(\theta) \, \frac{1 - r^2}{1 - 2r \cos(x - \theta) + r^2} \, d\theta\right\} \leqq \frac{1}{1 - r^2} \frac{1}{2\pi} \int_{-\pi}^{\pi} f(\theta) \, d\theta. \tag{9}$$

Indeed, by Cauchy's inequality,

$$|g(r e^{ix})|^2 = \left|\sum_{n=0}^{\infty} d_n r^n e^{inx}\right|^2 \leqq \sum_{n=0}^{\infty} |d_n|^2 \sum_{n=0}^{\infty} r^{2n}.$$

Now we combine (3) and (8).

(e) Let $f(x)$ be nonnegative for almost all values of x and $\log f(x)$ of the class L. The function $g(z)$ defined in (b) is uniquely determined. For the sake of clarity we write sometimes $g(z) = g(f; z)$. We note that

$$[g(0)]^2 = [g(f; 0)]^2 = \exp\left\{\frac{1}{2\pi}\int_{-\pi}^{\pi}\log f(\theta)\,d\theta\right\} \tag{10}$$

is the *geometric mean of* $f(\theta)$.

1.15. Functions of the class C

(a) Let $f(x)$ be a function of the class C which is positive for all real values of x. Then the condition of 1.14 (a) is satisfied and the Poisson integral 1.14 (2) has a limit for *all* values of x. Hence the equation 1.14 (6) holds for all x, or $|g(f; e^{ix})|^2 = f(x)$ for all x. However, the existence of the limit of $\operatorname{sgn} g(f; re^{ix})$, $r \to 1-0$, can be stated in general only for almost all x.

(b) We introduce now a further restriction on the function $f(x)$.

THEOREM. *Let* $f(x)$ *be a positive function of the class C with the modulus of continuity* $\omega(\delta)$. *We assume that the integral*

$$\int_0^{\delta_0}\delta^{-1}\omega(\delta)\,d\delta, \quad \delta_0 > 0, \tag{1}$$

is convergent. Then $g(f; z) = g(z)$ *is continuous in the closed unit circle* $|z| \leqq 1$.

The condition concerning (1) is satisfied if $\omega(\delta) = K\delta^\alpha$, $0 < \alpha < 1$ (Lipschitz condition), or $\omega(\delta) = K\,|\log\delta\,|^{-1-\lambda}, \lambda > 0$ (Lipschitz–Dini condition). If the integral (1) is convergent, the integral

$$\int_{-\pi}^{\pi}(\log f(\theta) - \log f(x))\,\operatorname{ctg}\frac{x-\theta}{2}\,d\theta$$

is absolutely convergent and hence the integral

$$\int_{-\pi}^{\pi}\log f(\theta)\,\operatorname{ctg}\frac{x-\theta}{2}\,d\theta$$

exists in the sense of Cauchy's principal value. Now we have for $r < 1$

$$\operatorname{sgn} g(f; re^{ix}) = \exp\left\{\frac{i}{4\pi}\int_{-\pi}^{\pi}\log f(\theta)\,\frac{2r\sin(x-\theta)}{1 - 2r\cos(x-\theta) + r^2}\,d\theta\right\}$$

$$= \exp\left\{\frac{i}{4\pi}\int_{-\pi}^{\pi}(\log f(\theta) - \log f(x))\frac{2r\sin(x-\theta)}{1 - 2r\cos(x-\theta) + r^2}\,d\theta\right\},$$

and we have to show that the last integral has a limit as $r \to 1-0$.

Let ϵ be an arbitrary positive number. We have

$$\lim_{r \to 1-0} \int_{|x-\theta| > \epsilon} (\log f(\theta) - \log f(x)) \frac{2r \sin(x-\theta)}{1 - 2r \cos(x-\theta) + r^2} d\theta$$

$$= \int_{|x-\theta| > \epsilon} (\log f(\theta) - \log f(x)) \operatorname{ctg} \frac{x-\theta}{2} d\theta.$$

On the other hand, $1 - 2r \cos(x-\theta) + r^2 \geqq 2r(1 - \cos(x-\theta))$; so

$$\left| \int_{|x-\theta| \leqq \epsilon} (\log f(\theta) - \log f(x)) \frac{2r \sin(x-\theta)}{1 - 2r \cos(x-\theta) + r^2} d\theta \right|$$

$$\leqq \int_{|x-\theta| \leqq \epsilon} |\log f(\theta) - \log f(x)| \frac{|\sin(x-\theta)|}{1 - \cos(x-\theta)} d\theta,$$

and the last integral is arbitrarily small with ϵ [in view of the condition regarding $\omega(\delta)$].

Thus we have

$$\lim_{r \to 1-0} \operatorname{sgn} g(f; re^{ix}) = \exp\left\{ \frac{i}{4\pi} \int_{-\pi}^{\pi} \log f(\theta) \operatorname{ctg} \frac{x-\theta}{2} d\theta \right\},$$

where the last integral is taken in the sense of Cauchy's principal value.

(c) Finally, we prove the following theorem which will be of importance in the asymptotic evaluation of the orthogonal polynomials to be discussed in chapter 3.

THEOREM. *Let $f(x)$ be a positive function of the class C with the modulus of continuity*

$$\omega(\delta) \leqq K\delta^\alpha, \quad 0 < \alpha \leqq 1 \quad \text{(Lipschitz condition)}, \tag{2}$$

or

$$\omega(\delta) \leqq K |\log \delta|^{-1-\lambda}, \quad \lambda > 0 \quad \text{(Lipschitz–Dini condition)}. \tag{3}$$

(In both cases $K > 0$ is a fixed constant.) According to 1.9 (b) for any integer m we can find a positive trigonometric polynomial $t(x)$ of degree m satisfying the condition

$$|f(x) - t(x)| < A\omega(2\pi/m).$$

For the associated analytic functions $g(f; z)$ and $g(t; z)$ the following inequality holds:

$$|g(f; z) - g(t; z)| < B\omega(2\pi/m) \log m, \quad |z| \leqq 1.$$

Here A is an absolute constant, while B depends on K, α (or λ) and on the minimum and maximum of $f(x)$.

Since the difference of $|g(f; e^{ix})|^2$ and $|g(t; e^{ix})|^2$ is of the order $\omega(2\pi/m)$, it suffices to prove that the difference of $\operatorname{sgn} g(f; e^{ix})$ and $\operatorname{sgn} g(t; e^{ix})$ is of the order $\omega(2\pi/m) \log m$. According to (b) we have to show that

$$\int_{-\pi}^{\pi} (\log f(\theta) - \log t(\theta)) \operatorname{ctg} \frac{x-\theta}{2} d\theta = \omega(2\pi/m) \log m . O(1).$$

The last integral can also be written in the following form:

$$\int_{-\pi}^{\pi} (\log f(\theta) - \log t(\theta) - \log f(x) + \log t(x)) \operatorname{ctg} \frac{x-\theta}{2} d\theta. \qquad (4)$$

Since $\log f(\theta) - \log f(x) = \omega(|\theta - x|) O(1)$ and $t(\theta)$ is a differentiable function, the integral (4) is absolutely convergent.

Let η be a fixed positive number. We denote by $E = E(x, \eta)$ the set of all θ-values defined by the condition $|\theta - x| \leq \eta$ and by E' the complementary set with respect to the interval $[-\pi, \pi]$. We take

$$\int_{E} |\log f(\theta) - \log f(x)| \left| \operatorname{ctg} \frac{x-\theta}{2} \right| d\theta$$

$$= O(1) \int_{E} \omega(|\theta - x|) |\theta - x|^{-1} d\theta = O(1) \int_{0}^{\eta} \delta^{-1} \omega(\delta) d\delta,$$

$$\int_{E} |\log t(\theta) - \log t(x)| \left| \operatorname{ctg} \frac{x-\theta}{2} \right| d\theta$$

$$= O(m) \int_{E} |\theta - x| |\theta - x|^{-1} d\theta = O(m\eta).$$

In the second case we have used S. Bernstein's inequality [1.16 (a)]:

$$|t(\theta) - t(x)| \leq |\theta - x| \max |t'(\theta)|$$

$$\leq m |\theta - x| \max |t(\theta)|.$$

Now the integral (4) extended over E' will be

$$\omega(2\pi/m) O(1) \int_{E'} |\theta - x|^{-1} d\theta = \omega(2\pi/m) \log \frac{1}{\eta} O(1).$$

In the case (2) we choose $\eta = m^{-\alpha-1}$. We have

$$\int_{0}^{\eta} \delta^{-1} \omega(\delta) d\delta = O(\eta^{\alpha}) = O(m^{-\alpha}), \quad m\eta = O(m^{-\alpha}).$$

In the case (3) we choose $\eta = m^{-1} (\log m)^{-\lambda}$ and we have

$$\int_0^\eta \delta^{-1} \omega(\delta)\, d\delta = O\left(\left(\log\frac{1}{\eta}\right)^{-\lambda}\right) = O((\log m)^{-\lambda}), \quad m\eta = O((\log m)^{-\lambda}).$$

1.16. Theorem of S. Bernstein

(a) THEOREM. *Let $f(x)$ be a trigonometric polynomial of degree n and* $\max |f(x)| = M$. *Then*
$$\max |f'(x)| \leqq nM. \tag{1}$$

Both maxima are taken for all real values of x (or for $-\pi \leqq x \leqq \pi$).

The inequality (1) is the best possible as the example

$$f(x) = M \cos n\,(x - x_0)$$

shows, x_0 arbitrary real.

(b) The following special case of S. Bernstein's inequality is particularly simple:

THEOREM. *Let $F(z)$ be a polynomial of degree n and $\max | F(z) | = M$ when z ranges over the unit circle $|z| \leqq 1$. Then*

$$\max | F'(z) | \leqq nM, \quad |z| \leqq 1. \tag{2}$$

The equality sign holds if $F(z) = \epsilon M z^n$, where $|\epsilon| = 1$. This inequality (2) follows by applying (1) to the trigonometric polynomial $F(e^{ix})$ of x.

A simple direct proof for (2) can be deduced from the fact that the Fejér means of a power series about $z = 0$ do not exceed in the absolute value the maximum modulus of the function, $|z| \leqq 1$. Indeed, it suffices to prove (2) for $z = 1$. Now if we write

$$F(z) = c_0 + c_1 z + c_2 z^2 + \ldots + c_n z^n,$$

we have for $|z| = 1$

$$| c_n + c_{n-1} z + c_{n-2} z^2 + \ldots + c_0 z^n | \leqq M,$$

so that

$$| c_n + (c_n + c_{n-1}) + (c_n + c_{n-1} + c_{n-2}) + \ldots + (c_n + c_{n-1} + \ldots + c_1)| \leqq nM,$$

which is the assertion.

1.17. Faber polynomials

(a) In order to save space, we deal at present only with the following case. Let l be an analytic Jordan curve in the complex x-plane. We denote by $x=h(z)$, $z=H(x)$ the one-to-one and conformal mapping of the exterior of l onto the exterior of the unit circle in the z-plane, $|z|>1$, normalized by the condition that $x=\infty$ corresponds to $z=\infty$ and dx/dz is real and positive for $x=z=\infty$. We then have

$$
\left.
\begin{aligned}
h(z) &= cz+c_0+c_1z^{-1}+c_2z^{-2}+..., \quad c>0, \\
H(x) &= dx+d_0+d_1x^{-1}+d_2x^{-2}+..., \quad d>0,
\end{aligned}
\right\} \tag{1}
$$

for $|z|>1$ and in a neighbourhood of $x=\infty$, respectively. The quantity $c=d^{-1}$ is called the *transfinite diameter* of the curve l. Since l is analytic, the mapping will be one-to-one and conformal even for $|z|\geqq r$, where $0<r<1$ and r is sufficiently near to 1. In particular, it will define a one-to-one correspondence of the curve l and the unit circle $|z|=1$. The linear magnification $|dx/dz|=|h'(z)|$ is bounded away from zero and infinity uniformly for $|z|\geqq 1$ (even for $|z|\geqq r$).

Further, we consider a weight function $w(x)$ on the curve l defined in the following manner. Let $\Delta(x)$ be an analytic function different from zero in the closed exterior of l (including at $x=\infty$) and let $\Delta(\infty)>0$; we set $w(x)=|\Delta(x)|^2$, where x is on l. The weight function $w(x)$ being given, the analytic function $\Delta(x)$ can be computed by the procedure of 1.14 (b) interpreting $w(x)$ as a function of z defined on the unit circle $|z|=1$; here $x=h(z)$, $z=H(x)$.

Faber polynomials $f_n(x)$ associated with the curve l and the weight function $w(x)$ are defined now as follows. The function

$$
g_n(x) = [\Delta(x)]^{-1}[H'(x)]^{\frac{1}{2}}[H(x)]^n \tag{2}
$$

is regular at the finite points of the closed exterior of l and has a pole of order n at $x=\infty$. Hence the Laurent expansion of $g_n(x)$ about $x=\infty$ begins with $[\Delta(\infty)]^{-1}c^{-n-\frac{1}{2}}x^n$ and proceeds in terms of decreasing powers of x. The polynomial part of this expansion is the nth Faber polynomial $f_n(x)$.

(b) We mention the following examples.

(i) l is the unit circle $|x|=1$, $h(z)=z$, $H(x)=x$. The function $\Delta(x)$ can be derived from the weight function $w(x)$ as in 1.14 (b). Denoting the expansion of $[\Delta(x)]^{-1}$ about $x=\infty$ by $\sum\limits_{m=0}^{\infty}u_mx^{-m}$, we have

$$
f_n(x) = u_0x^n+u_1x^{n-1}+...+u_{n-1}x+u_n. \tag{3}
$$

(ii) l is the interval $-1\leqq x\leqq 1$ and $w(x)=(1-x^2)^{-\frac{1}{2}}$. This is in fact a degenerated case, since this curve l is not analytic (it can be inter-

preted as the limiting case of an ellipse with foci at -1 and $+1$).
Likewise the weight function is not analytic on l. Nevertheless, there
is no difficulty in extending the definition of the Faber polynomials
given above to this case. We have

$$H(x) = x + (x^2 - 1)^{\frac{1}{2}},$$

$$\Delta(x) = \left(1 + \frac{x}{(x^2 - 1)^{\frac{1}{2}}}\right)^{\frac{1}{2}} = [H'(x)]^{\frac{1}{2}},$$

so that $g_n(x) = [x + (x^2 - 1)^{\frac{1}{2}}]^n$. The function

$$f_n(x) = [x + (x^2 - 1)^{\frac{1}{2}}]^n + [x - (x^2 - 1)^{\frac{1}{2}}]^n \tag{4}$$

has the same polynomial part as $g_n(x)$ and it is in fact equal to $2T_n(x)$
where $T_n(x)$ is the nth Tchebychev polynomial, $n > 1$.

(c) We prove the following

THEOREM. *Let the curve l and the weight function $w(x)$ satisfy the
conditions formulated in* (a) *and also let $g_n(x)$ and $f_n(x)$ have the same
meaning as in* (a). *There are two constants M and r, $M > 0$, $0 < r < 1$,
such that the following inequality holds uniformly on l:*

$$|f_n(x) - g_n(x)| < Mr^n. \tag{5}$$

We interpret the functions $H'(x)$ and $\Delta(x)$ [hence also $g_n(x)$] as
functions of z by using the correspondence $x = h(z)$, $z = H(x)$. If r is
less than 1 but sufficiently near to 1, this correspondence will remain
conformal and one-to-one for $|z| \geq r$; also $\Delta(x)$ will be regular and
different from zero for $|z| \geq r$. We denote by l_r the Jordan curve
corresponding to $|z| = r$ in the x-plane. On applying Cauchy's
theorem in the ring-shaped domain bounded by l_r and by a large
circle, we obtain, if x is on l,

$$g_n(x) - f_n(x) = \frac{1}{2\pi i} \int_{l_r} \frac{g_n(\xi) - f_n(\xi)}{\xi - x} \, d\xi = \frac{1}{2\pi i} \int_{l_r} \frac{g_n(\xi)}{\xi - x} \, d\xi.$$

The integration is extended in the *negative* sense. The first integrand
is of order $O(|\xi|^{-2})$ as $\xi \to \infty$ so that the contribution of the large circle
vanishes. On l_r we have $|H(\xi)| = |z| = r$, so that $g_n(\xi) = O(r^n)$. This
yields the inequality (5).

The functions $g_n(x)$, hence also the polynomials $f_n(x)$, are uniformly
bounded on the curve l.

1.18. Eigenvalues of Hermitian forms

In this section the indices μ and ν assume the integer values
$0, 1, 2, \ldots, n$.

(a) Let $A = \Sigma a_{\mu\nu} u_\mu \bar{u}_\nu$ be a Hermitian form, i.e. $a_{\nu\mu} = \bar{a}_{\mu\nu}$; we denote
by $I = \Sigma \, |\, u_\mu \,|^2$ the unit form. The values of the parameter λ for which
the Hermitian form $A - \lambda I$ is singular, i.e. $\det (A - \lambda I) = 0$, are called
the eigenvalues of A. They are all real.

Let B be a positive definite Hermitian form of the same variables
u_μ as above. The values of λ for which the form $A - \lambda B$ is singular,
$\det (A - \lambda B) = 0$, are called the eigenvalues of A with respect to B.
They are again real. Moreover, the smallest (largest) eigenvalue
represents the minimum (maximum) of the form A under the side
condition $B = 1$.

(b) We prove the following frequently useful theorem:

THEOREM. *Let $A = \Sigma a_{\mu\nu} u_\mu \bar{u}_\nu$ be a Hermitian form for which the sum
of the moduli of the elements in each row is under a common bound:*

$$|a_{\mu 0}| + |a_{\mu 1}| + \ldots + |a_{\mu n}| \leqq M, \quad \mu = 0, 1, 2, \ldots, n. \tag{1}$$

Then we have for the eigenvalues λ_ν of A:

$$|\lambda_\nu| \leqq M, \quad \nu = 0, 1, 2, \ldots, n. \tag{2}$$

It suffices to show that the form A is in the absolute value not
greater than M provided the variables u_μ are subjected to the condition $I = 1$. Now for each eigenvalue λ we have with proper u_μ, not
all zero,
$$\lambda u_\mu = a_{\mu 0} u_0 + a_{\mu 1} u_1 + \ldots + a_{\mu n} u_n, \quad \mu = 0, 1, \ldots, n.$$

Let $\max |\, u_\mu \,| = |\, u_k \,| > 0$; then

$$|\lambda| \, |\, u_k \,| \leqq (|\, a_{k0}\,| + |\, a_{k1}\,| + \ldots + |\, a_{kn}\,|) |\, u_k \,| \leqq M \,|\, u_k \,|,$$

and this yields the assertion.

(c) Another important fact which plays a role in the investigations
of H. Weyl and R. Courant on the eigenvalues of a membrane (see
Appendix), is the following:

THEOREM. *Let A and B be two Hermitian forms, the second positive
definite. We denote the eigenvalues of A with respect to B by $\lambda_0, \lambda_1, \ldots, \lambda_n$,
ordered in nondecreasing order. Then λ_ν, $\nu \geqq 1$, can be characterized by
the following extremum property. We denote the vector $(u_0, u_1, \ldots, u_n)$ by*

u *and let* $\mathbf{a}_1, \mathbf{a}_2, \ldots, \mathbf{a}_\nu$ *be arbitrary vectors in the* $(n+1)$-*dimensional complex space. We denote by* ρ *the minimum of* A/B *for all* **u** *which are not zero and satisfy the side conditions*

$$(\mathbf{a}_1, \mathbf{u}) = (\mathbf{a}_2, \mathbf{u}) = \ldots = (\mathbf{a}_\nu, \mathbf{u}) = 0. \tag{3}$$

Then $\lambda_\nu = \max \rho$ *for all possible choices of the vectors* $\mathbf{a}_1, \mathbf{a}_2, \ldots, \mathbf{a}_\nu$.

For $\nu = 0$ we have no auxiliary conditions and λ_0 is simply the minimum of A/B for all **u**.

The proof can be based on the following standard representation:

$$\frac{A}{B} = \frac{\Sigma \lambda_\nu |\xi_\nu|^2}{\Sigma |\xi_\nu|^2},$$

where the ξ_ν are linearly independent linear forms of the variables u_μ. By definition $\rho \leq A/B$, where we may choose any vector **u** satisfying the linear conditions (3). We add to these the conditions $\xi_{\nu+1} = \ldots = \xi_n = 0$ imposing altogether n linear conditions on **u**. There is always a non-zero vector **u** satisfying these conditions; the corresponding ξ cannot be all zero, so that $\xi_0, \xi_1, \ldots, \xi_\nu$ are not all zero. Hence

$$\rho \leq \frac{\lambda_0 |\xi_0|^2 + \lambda_1 |\xi_1|^2 + \ldots + \lambda_\nu |\xi_\nu|^2}{|\xi_0|^2 + |\xi_1|^2 + \ldots + |\xi_\nu|^2} \leq \lambda_\nu.$$

On the other hand, let us take for $\mathbf{a}_1, \ldots, \mathbf{a}_\nu$ the vectors whose projections are the conjugates of the coefficients of $\xi_0, \ldots, \xi_{\nu-1}$ (as linear forms of $u_0, \ldots, u_n$). Then $\xi_0 = \ldots = \xi_{\nu-1} = 0$, and

$$\rho = \min \frac{\lambda_\nu |\xi_\nu|^2 + \lambda_{\nu+1} |\xi_{\nu+1}|^2 + \ldots + \lambda_n |\xi_n|^2}{|\xi_\nu|^2 + |\xi_{\nu+1}|^2 + \ldots + |\xi_n|^2}$$

for all possible $\xi_\nu, \ldots, \xi_n$ which is exactly λ_ν.

This proves the assertion.

We note the following simple consequence. Let A, B; A', B' be two pairs of Hermitian forms, B and B' positive definite, and let $A/B \leq A'/B'$ for all **u**. Denoting the eigenvalues of these pairs by λ_ν and λ'_ν (ordered in nondecreasing order), we have

$$\lambda_\nu \leq \lambda'_\nu, \quad \nu = 0, 1, 2, \ldots, n. \tag{4}$$

From these inequalities we further conclude the following. Let $D(A), D(B), D(A'), D(B')$ denote the determinants of the given forms which we assume now to be all positive definite. Then

$$\frac{D(A)}{D(B)} \leq \frac{D(A')}{D(B')}. \tag{5}$$

1.19. Measure space

Let X be an abstract space of elements x. In X we define a family $\mathfrak{X}$ of subsets S, $S \subset X$; $\mathfrak{X}$ is supposed to be a *Borel field*, i.e. the following three conditions are satisfied:

(i) The total space belongs to $\mathfrak{X}$, $X \in \mathfrak{X}$.

(ii) The complement of any set in the family belongs also to it, $S^* \in \mathfrak{X}$ if $S \in \mathfrak{X}$.

(iii) The union of any denumerable sequence of sets

$$S_\nu \in \mathfrak{X}, \quad \nu = 1, 2, \ldots,$$

belongs to the family, $\bigcup\limits_{\nu=1}^{\infty} S_\nu \in \mathfrak{X}$.

With each set $S \in \mathfrak{X}$ we associate a nonnegative number $\mu(S)$ in such a way that the set-function $\mu(S)$ is *completely additive*:

$$\mu\left(\bigcup_{\nu=1}^{\infty} S_\nu\right) = \sum_{\nu=1}^{\infty} \mu(S_\nu) \text{ if } S_\nu \in \mathfrak{X}, \quad \nu = 1, 2, \ldots,$$

for disjoint sets S_ν.

Then μ is said to be a *measure* and we can proceed in defining $(\mathfrak{X})$-measurable functions and the integral

$$\int_X f(x) \, d\mu(x),$$

in the same way as in the case when μ is the ordinary Lebesgue measure on the real line. When there is no danger of confusion we shall write dx instead of $d\mu(x)$.

We shall suppose that μ is *σ-finite*, i.e. there exists a decomposition of the whole space X into a denumerable number of measurable subsets each of which has a finite μ-measure.

The space X together with the Borel field and the measure forms a *measure space* and is denoted by the symbol $(X, \mathfrak{X}, \mu)$.

1.20. Linear operators

(a) Without going into detail we remind the reader of some basic concepts belonging to the theory of Hilbert spaces. A collection $\mathfrak{H}$ of elements h is said to form a *Hilbert space* if:

1. $\mathfrak{H}$ is a linear space, i.e. if f, $g \in \mathfrak{H}$, then $af + bg$ is defined and belongs to $\mathfrak{H}$. Here a and b are arbitrary complex constants and the

usual rules for addition of vectors and multiplication with scalars are supposed to be valid in $\mathfrak{H}$.

2. An inner product (f, g) with the usual properties is defined for each pair of elements f and g in $\mathfrak{H}$. The number $\|f\| = (f, f)^{\frac{1}{2}}$ is called the *norm* of the element f.

3. $\mathfrak{H}$ is complete, i.e. if we have a Cauchy sequence $h_\nu \in \mathfrak{H}$, $\|h_\nu - h_\mu\| \to 0$ as $\nu, \mu \to \infty$, there is an element $h \in \mathfrak{H}$ so that $\|h - h_\nu\| \to 0$ as $\nu \to \infty$.

We already met some examples of Hilbert spaces in 1.7. The following case is of importance. We consider the set $L_2(X)$ of all complex-valued and $(\mathfrak{X})$-measurable functions $f(x)$ defined on X which are quadratically integrable:

$$\int_X |f(x)|^2 d\mu(x) < \infty.$$

Defining addition and scalar multiplication in the obvious way and the scalar product by

$$(f, g) = \int_X f(x) \overline{g(x)}\, d\mu(x),$$

it can be shown that $L_2(X)$ is a Hilbert space.

(b) If with each element $f \in \mathfrak{H}$ an element $L(f) \in \mathfrak{H}$ is associated such that $L(af + bg) = aL(f) + bL(g)$, L is called a *linear operator*. Sometimes we let L take values of another Hilbert space. If for every pair $f, g \in \mathfrak{H}$ we have $(Lf, g) = (f, Lg)$ we say that L is *Hermitian*.

An especially important case is when

$$\|L\| = \sup_{\|f\|=1} \|L(f)\| < \infty. \tag{1}$$

Then L is said to be *bounded* and the number $\|L\|$ in (1) is called the norm of L.

Such a case is the projection operator. Let M be a closed linear manifold in $\mathfrak{H}$. It can be shown (see Appendix) that to each $f \in \mathfrak{H}$ there is an element h such that

$$f = g + h, \quad g \perp M, \quad h \in \mathfrak{H}.$$

By $g \perp M$ we mean that each $x \in M$ is orthogonal to g, i.e. $(g, x) = 0$. Clearly the transformation $Pf = h$ is linear and bounded, $\|P\| \leq 1$. P is said to be a projection on M and one can easily show that the projections are completely characterized by the following conditions:

(i) $PPx = Px$, or $P^2 = P$.

(ii) P is Hermitian.

Another important type of bounded operators are the *unitary* operators (transformations). A linear operator U is said to be unitary if

(i) $(Uf, Ug) = (f, g)$ for all $f, g \in \mathfrak{H}$.

(ii) Uf maps $\mathfrak{H}$ onto the whole space $\mathfrak{H}$.

It is clear that such a transformation has an inverse U^{-1} which is also linear and bounded, $\| U^{-1} \| = \| U \| = 1$.

(c) One of the main problems in the theory of Hilbert spaces is the representation of wide classes of linear transformations using simpler ones as building stones. An important result is the following:

THEOREM OF HILBERT. *Any Hermitian bounded linear transformation L can be represented in the following form:*

$$L = \int_{-M}^{M} \lambda \, dE_\lambda. \tag{2}$$

Here E_λ is a resolution of the identity, i.e. a one-parameter family of projections E_λ such that

$$E_{\lambda_1} E_{\lambda_2} = E_\lambda, \quad \lambda = \min(\lambda_1, \lambda_2), \quad E_{-M} = O, \quad E_M = I,$$

where $M = \| L \|$.

If we require that E_λ should be continuous to the right, the family E_λ is uniquely determined.

The set of points of increase of E_λ on the interval $[-M, M]$ is called the *spectrum* of L. For instance, when L is a Hermitian matrix interpreted as a transformation in n-space, (2) is the usual representation of the matrix in diagonal form after a rotation of the coordinate axes; the spectrum consists then of the eigenvalues of the matrix.

CHAPTER 2

ORTHOGONAL POLYNOMIALS.
ALGEBRAIC PROPERTIES

2.1. Definition

(a) Let $\alpha(x)$ be a distribution function of the infinite type, $-\pi \leqq x \leqq \pi$, and

$$c_n = \frac{1}{2\pi} \int_{-\pi}^{\pi} e^{-inx} \, d\alpha(x) \tag{1}$$

its Fourier–Stieltjes coefficients. We form a system of polynomials

$$\phi_0(z), \phi_1(z), \phi_2(z), \dots, \phi_n(z), \dots \tag{2}$$

of the complex variable z which are orthonormal on the unit circle $|z| = 1, z = e^{ix}$, with the weight $(2\pi)^{-1} \, d\alpha(x)$. More precisely, they satisfy the following conditions:

(i) $\phi_n(z)$ is a polynomial of degree n in which the coefficient of z^n is real and positive;

(ii) $\dfrac{1}{2\pi} \displaystyle\int_{-\pi}^{\pi} \phi_n(z) \, \overline{\phi_m(z)} \, d\alpha(x) = \delta_{nm}, \quad z = e^{ix}; \; n, m = 0, 1, 2, \dots. \tag{3}$

The system $\{\phi_n(z)\}$ is uniquely determined by the conditions (i) and (ii). We mention the particularly important case of an absolutely continuous distribution function $\alpha(x)$; then $d\alpha(x) = f(x) \, dx$, where $f(x)$ is nonnegative and L-integrable (not a zero function).

(b) From the general formula 1.8 (10) we conclude the following explicit representation of these polynomials:

$$\phi_n(z) = (D_{n-1} D_n)^{-\frac{1}{2}} \begin{vmatrix} c_0 & c_{-1} & c_{-2} & \cdots & c_{-n} \\ c_1 & c_0 & c_{-1} & \cdots & c_{-n+1} \\ \cdots & \cdots & \cdots & \cdots & \cdots \\ c_{n-1} & c_{n-2} & c_{n-3} & \cdots & c_{-1} \\ 1 & z & z^2 & \cdots & z^n \end{vmatrix} \tag{4}$$

$$= (D_{n-1} D_n)^{-\frac{1}{2}} \begin{vmatrix} c_0 z - c_{-1} & c_{-1} z - c_{-2} & \cdots & c_{-n+1} z - c_{-n} \\ c_1 z - c_0 & c_0 z - c_{-1} & \cdots & c_{-n+2} z - c_{-n+1} \\ \cdots & \cdots & \cdots & \cdots \\ c_{n-1} z - c_{n-2} & c_{n-2} z - c_{n-3} & \cdots & c_0 z - c_{-1} \end{vmatrix},$$

$$n = 1, 2, 3, \dots, \tag{5}$$

where $D_n = \det(c_{\nu-\mu})_0^n$ is the determinant of the Toeplitz form

$$\sum_{\mu,\nu=0,1,\ldots,n} c_{\nu-\mu} u_\mu \bar{u}_\nu = \frac{1}{2\pi} \int_{-\pi}^{\pi} |u_0 + u_1 e^{ix} + u_2 e^{2ix} + \ldots + u_n e^{nix}|^2 \, d\alpha(x).$$
(6)

Since (6) is positive definite we have $D_n > 0$ for all n. We call these determinants D_n the *Toeplitz determinants* associated with the distribution $d\alpha(x)$. We note that

$$\phi_0(z) = D_0^{-\frac{1}{2}} = c_0^{-\frac{1}{2}}.$$
(7)

The second representation (5) arises from the first one, namely, (4), by an easy transformation of the determinant.

For later purposes it is useful to introduce a special notation for the coefficient k_n of z^n and for the constant term l_n in the polynomial $\phi_n(z)$. We have

$$k_n = (D_{n-1}/D_n)^{\frac{1}{2}},$$
(8)

$$l_n = (-1)^n (D_{n-1} D_n)^{-\frac{1}{2}} \begin{vmatrix} c_{-1} & c_{-2} & \cdots & c_{-n} \\ c_0 & c_{-1} & \cdots & c_{-n+1} \\ \cdots & \cdots & \cdots & \cdots \\ c_{n-2} & c_{n-3} & \cdots & c_{-1} \end{vmatrix}.$$
(9)

2.2. Extremum properties

(a) THEOREM. *The polynomial $k_n^{-1} \phi_n(z)$ minimizes the integral*

$$\frac{1}{2\pi} \int_{-\pi}^{\pi} |g(z)|^2 \, d\alpha(x), \quad z = e^{ix},$$
(1)

where $g(z) = z^n + a_1 z^{n-1} + \ldots + a_n$ is an arbitrary polynomial of degree n in which the coefficient of z^n is 1. The minimum itself is $k_n^{-2} = D_n/D_{n-1}$.

This follows by representing $g(z)$ in the form

$$g(z) = v_0 \phi_0(z) + v_1 \phi_1(z) + \ldots + v_n \phi_n(z),$$
(2)

where $v_0, v_1, \ldots, v_n$ are complex variables and v_n is subjected to the condition $v_n k_n = 1$. Now, $z = e^{ix}$,

$$\frac{1}{2\pi} \int_{-\pi}^{\pi} |g(z)|^2 \, d\alpha(x) = |v_0|^2 + |v_1|^2 + \ldots + |v_n|^2 \geq |v_n|^2 = k_n^{-2}.$$

(b) THEOREM. *Let $g(z)$ be an arbitrary polynomial of degree n satisfying the side condition*

$$\frac{1}{2\pi} \int_{-\pi}^{\pi} |g(z)|^2 \, d\alpha(x) = 1, \quad z = e^{ix}. \tag{3}$$

Let a be a fixed complex constant. The maximum of $|g(a)|^2$ for all polynomials satisfying the above conditions, is attained for

$$g(z) = \epsilon[s_n(a,a)]^{-\frac{1}{2}} s_n(a,z), \tag{4}$$

where

$$s_n(a,z) = \sum_{\nu=0}^{n} \overline{\phi_\nu(a)} \, \phi_\nu(z). \tag{5}$$

The maximum itself will be $s_n(a,a)$.

The polynomials $s_n(a,z)$ are called the *kernel polynomials* of the distribution $d\alpha(x)$.

Indeed, assuming (2), the side condition (3) will be $\sum_{\nu=0}^{n} |v_\nu|^2 = 1$. Then by Cauchy's inequality

$$|g(a)|^2 \leq \sum_{\nu=0}^{n} |v_\nu|^2 \sum_{\nu=0}^{n} |\phi_\nu(a)|^2 = \sum_{\nu=0}^{n} |\phi_\nu(a)|^2 = s_n(a,a).$$

The equation sign can easily be discussed.

(c) The kernel polynomial can be characterized by a similar orthogonality property as the polynomial $\phi_n(z)$.

THEOREM. *Let $g(z)$ be any polynomial of degree n. Then*

$$\frac{1}{2\pi} \int_{-\pi}^{\pi} s_n(a,z) \overline{g(z)} \, d\alpha(x) = \overline{g(a)}, \quad z = e^{ix}. \tag{6}$$

Indeed, representing $g(z)$ in the form (2) the integral in (6) will be

$$\sum_{\nu=0}^{n} \overline{\phi_\nu(a)} \, \overline{v_\nu} = \overline{g(a)}.$$

It is obvious that $s_n(a,z)$ is the only polynomial of degree n in z satisfying condition (6).

Using this characterization (with $g(z) = z^\nu$, $\nu = 0, 1, 2, ..., n$) we verify easily the representation

$$
s_n(a, z) = -D_n^{-1}
\begin{vmatrix}
c_0 & c_{-1} & \cdots & c_{-n+1} & c_{-n} & 1 \\
c_1 & c_0 & \cdots & c_{-n+2} & c_{-n+1} & \bar{a} \\
\cdots & \cdots & \cdots & \cdots & \cdots & \cdots \\
c_n & c_{n-1} & \cdots & c_1 & c_0 & \bar{a}^n \\
1 & z & \cdots & z^{n-1} & z^n & 0
\end{vmatrix}. \tag{7}
$$

(d) From the representation (7) we conclude the identity

$$
s_n(a, z) = (\bar{a}z)^n \, s_n(\bar{z}^{-1}, \bar{a}^{-1}). \tag{8}
$$

In particular,

$$
s_n(0, z) = \sum_{\nu=0}^{n} \overline{\phi_\nu(0)} \, \phi_\nu(z) = \sum_{\nu=0}^{n} l_\nu \phi_\nu(z)
$$
$$
= k_n z^n \overline{\phi}_n(z^{-1}) = k_n \phi_n^*(z), \tag{9}
$$

and

$$
s_n(0, 0) = \sum_{\nu=0}^{n} |\phi_\nu(0)|^2 = \sum_{\nu=0}^{n} |l_\nu|^2 = k_n^2 = D_{n-1}/D_n. \tag{10}
$$

In (9) we used the notation $\phi_n^*(z) = z^n \overline{\phi}_n(z^{-1})$ (see 1.1).

A proof of (8) can be based also on the extremum property given in (b).

2.3. Zeros. Identities

(a) We prove the following:

THEOREM. *For $|a| < 1$ all zeros of the kernel polynomial $s_n(a, z)$ lie in $|z| > 1$. For $|a| > 1$ all zeros of $s_n(a, z)$ lie in $|z| < 1$. For $|a| = 1$ all zeros of $s_n(a, z)$ lie on $|z| = 1$. The zeros of the orthogonal polynomials $\phi_n(z)$ are all in $|z| < 1$.*

Let z_0 be a zero of $s_n(a, z)$. We define a new distribution $d\alpha_1(x)$ by

$$
d\alpha_1(x) = \left| \frac{s_n(a, z)}{z - z_0} \right|^2 d\alpha(x), \quad z = e^{ix}.
$$

Then we consider the following extremum problem:

$$
|g(a)|^2 = \max; \quad \frac{1}{2\pi} \int_{-\pi}^{\pi} |g(z)|^2 \, d\alpha_1(x) = 1, \quad z = e^{ix},
$$

where $g(z)$ is an arbitrary *linear* function. Obviously this maximum is attained for $g(z) = \text{const.} (z - z_0)$. Thus it is sufficient to prove the theorem for $n = 1$. We have from 2.2 (7)

$$s_1(a, z) = - D_1^{-1} \begin{vmatrix} c_0 & c_{-1} & 1 \\ c_1 & c_0 & \bar{a} \\ 1 & z & 0 \end{vmatrix},$$

so that

$$z_0 = \frac{c_0 - \bar{c}_1 \bar{a}}{c_1 - c_0 \bar{a}}.$$

This yields the assertion since $|c_1| < c_0$. The statement concerning $\phi_n(z)$ follows from 2.2 (9).

(b) We have the following identities:

$$s_n(a, z) = \sum_{\nu=0}^{n} \overline{\phi_\nu(a)} \, \phi_\nu(z) = \frac{\overline{\phi_{n+1}^*(a)} \, \phi_{n+1}^*(z) - \overline{\phi_{n+1}(a)} \, \phi_{n+1}(z)}{1 - \bar{a}z}, \qquad (1)$$

$$k_n z \phi_n(z) = k_{n+1} \phi_{n+1}(z) - l_{n+1} \phi_{n+1}^*(z), \qquad (2)$$

$$k_n \phi_{n+1}(z) = k_{n+1} z \phi_n(z) + l_{n+1} \phi_n^*(z). \qquad (3)$$

The proof of the first identity follows from 2.2 (6). Indeed, we have $[g(z)$ is a polynomial of degree $n]$,

$$\frac{1}{2\pi} \int_{-\pi}^{\pi} \frac{\overline{\phi_{n+1}^*(a)} \, \phi_{n+1}^*(z) - \overline{\phi_{n+1}(a)} \, \phi_{n+1}(z)}{1 - \bar{a}z} \, \overline{g(z)} \, d\alpha(x)$$

$$= \overline{g(a)} \frac{1}{2\pi} \int_{-\pi}^{\pi} \frac{\overline{\phi_{n+1}^*(a)} \, \phi_{n+1}^*(z) - \overline{\phi_{n+1}(a)} \, \phi_{n+1}(z)}{1 - \bar{a}z} \, d\alpha(x)$$

$$+ \frac{1}{2\pi} \int_{-\pi}^{\pi} \{ \overline{\phi_{n+1}^*(a)} \, \phi_{n+1}^*(z) - \overline{\phi_{n+1}(a)} \, \phi_{n+1}(z) \} \frac{\overline{g(z)} - \overline{g(a)}}{1 - \bar{a}z} \, d\alpha(x), \quad z = e^{ix}.$$

The last integral vanishes since we may write

$$g(z) - g(a) = (z - a) \, r(z),$$

where $r(z)$ is of degree $n - 1$ and

$$\int_{-\pi}^{\pi} \phi_{n+1}^*(z) \, \overline{zr(z)} \, d\alpha(x) = \int_{-\pi}^{\pi} \phi_{n+1}(z) \, \overline{zr(z)} \, d\alpha(x) = 0, \quad z = e^{ix}.$$

Hence

$$\frac{\overline{\phi_{n+1}^*(a)} \, \phi_{n+1}^*(z) - \overline{\phi_{n+1}(a)} \, \phi_{n+1}(z)}{1 - \bar{a}z} = c s_n(a, z),$$

where c is independent of z. Interchanging a and z and taking the conjugate-complex values of both sides, we see that c is also independent of a. Writing $z=a=0$, we obtain

$$k_{n+1}^2 - |\, l_{n+1}\,|^2 = c \sum_{\nu=0}^n |\, l_\nu\,|^2,$$

so that $c=1$ by 2.2 (10).

Comparison of the coefficients of $\bar{a}^n$ in the first identity leads to the second one. By taking the reciprocal polynomial of both sides of (2) and eliminating $\phi_{n+1}^*(z)$ we obtain the third identity.

2.4. Examples

(a) The previous results remain valid in the following more general situation. Let

$$c_0, c_1, c_2, \ldots, c_N \tag{1}$$

denote given complex constants, c_0 real and $c_{-n}=\bar{c}_n$; $n=1,2,\ldots,N$. We assume, moreover, that the Hermitian form

$$\Sigma c_{\nu-\mu} u_\mu \bar{u}_\nu, \quad \mu,\nu=0,1,2,\ldots,N, \tag{2}$$

is *positive definite*. Another way of formulating this condition is as follows. We introduce a 'linear functional' $L(f)$ defined for an arbitrary trigonometric polynomial $f(x)$ of a degree not exceeding N. Moreover, we assume that $L(f)$ is 'positive', i.e. that $L(f) \geqq 0$ whenever $f(x)$ is a nonnegative trigonometric polynomial, with the equation sign only if $f(x)$ is identically zero (cf. 1.5). Writing

$$L(e^{-inx})=c_n, \quad L(e^{inx})=c_{-n}, \quad n=0,1,2,\ldots,N, \tag{3}$$

we have

$$L\{|\, u_0 + u_1 e^{ix} + u_2 e^{2ix} + \ldots + u_N e^{Nix}\,|^2\} = \sum_{\mu,\nu=0,1,\ldots,N} c_{\nu-\mu} u_\mu \bar{u}_\nu. \tag{4}$$

In view of the theorem of L. Fejér and F. Riesz (1.12) it is clear that the positivity of the functional $L(f)$ is equivalent to the positive-definite character of the Hermitian form (2).

Under these conditions there is no difficulty in defining the system $\{\phi_n(z)\}$, $0 \leqq n \leqq N$, satisfying conditions corresponding to (i) and (ii) in 2.1; condition (i) remains unchanged, condition (ii) becomes in this case:

$$L\{\phi_n(z)\,\overline{\phi_m(z)}\} = \delta_{nm}, \quad z=e^{ix}; \ n,m=0,1,2,\ldots,N. \tag{5}$$

All results of the previous sections hold provided $n \leq N$ except the identities 2.3 (1), (2), (3) for which $n \leq N-1$ must be assumed.

(b) We consider a distribution function $\alpha(x)$ of the *finite* type, assuming that $\alpha(x)$ has jump points x_k with the positive jumps $2\pi\rho_k$, respectively, $k=0, 1, 2, ..., N$. The points x_k are distinct and situated in the interval $-\pi \leq x < \pi$. We define

$$c_n = \sum_{k=0}^{N} \rho_k e^{-inx_k}, \quad n=0, \pm1, \pm2, ..., \pm N, \tag{6}$$

so that

$$\sum_{\mu,\nu=0,1,...,N} c_{\nu-\mu} u_\mu \overline{u}_\nu = \sum_{k=0}^{N} \rho_k \mid u_0 + u_1 e^{ix_k} + u_2 e^{2ix_k} + ... + u_N e^{Nix_k} \mid^2 \tag{7}$$

is a positive-definite Hermitian form. Hence the results of (a) are applicable.

(c) Finally, we consider another important, completely different class of distributions. We assume that $d\alpha(x) = w(x)\,dx$, where $[w(x)]^{-1}$ is a positive trigonometric polynomial of the precise degree p. According to 1.12 (b) this trigonometric polynomial can be written in the normalized form $\mid g(z) \mid^2$, $z = e^{ix}$, where $g(z)$ is a polynomial of the precise degree p in z whose zeros are all in the interior of the unit circle. Assuming that the highest coefficients of $g(z)$ (that is, the coefficient of z^p) is positive, we have

$$\phi_n(z) = z^{n-p} g(z), \quad n=p, p+1, p+2, ... \tag{8}$$

Indeed, if $\gamma(z)$ is of degree $n-1$ we have $(z=e^{ix})$

$$\int_{-\pi}^{\pi} z^{n-p} g(z) \overline{\gamma(z)} \mid g(z) \mid^{-2} dx = \frac{1}{i} \int_{\mid z \mid =1} \frac{z^{n-1}\overline{\gamma}(z^{-1})}{z^p \overline{g}(z^{-1})} dz.$$

In the last integral the denominator is a polynomial in z whose zeros are all outside of the unit circle $\mid z \mid > 1$. The numerator is a polynomial of degree $n-1$ in z; thus the integrand is regular for $\mid z \mid \leq 1$ so that the integral is $=0$.

CHAPTER 3

ORTHOGONAL POLYNOMIALS.
LIMIT PROPERTIES

3.1. A limit theorem

(a) THEOREM. *Let $\alpha(x)$ be a distribution function of the infinite type. We consider the Toeplitz forms*

$$T_n = \frac{1}{2\pi} \int_{-\pi}^{\pi} |u_0 + u_1 z + u_2 z^2 + \ldots + u_n z^n|^2 \, d\alpha(x),$$

$$z = e^{ix}; \; n = 0, 1, 2, \ldots, \quad (1)$$

and denote by μ_n the minimum of T_n under the side condition $u_0 = 1$. Then

$$\lim_{n \to \infty} \mu_n = \mu = G(w) = \exp\left\{ \frac{1}{2\pi} \int_{-\pi}^{\pi} \log w(x) \, dx \right\}, \quad (2)$$

where $w(x)$ is the almost everywhere existing derivative of $\alpha(x)$. In the case where $\log w(x)$ is not L-integrable, $G(w)$ has to be replaced by zero.

Of course, $w(x)$ is the derivative of the absolutely continuous part of $\alpha(x)$ (1.3 and 1.4).

We observe that the minimum μ_n remains unchanged if the side condition $u_0 = 1$ is replaced by the other side condition $u_n = 1$. According to 2.2 (a) the solution of this second minimum problem is given by $k_n^{-1}\phi_n(z)$, where k_n and $\phi_n(z)$ have the same meaning as in chapter 2. Thus in the original minimum problem (min $T_n, u_0 = 1$) the minimum is attained for the reciprocal polynomial $k_n^{-1}\phi_n^*(z)$. We note that in view of 2.3 the zeros of this polynomial are in $|z| > 1$.

The minima μ_n are nonincreasing as n increases. Hence $\lim_{n \to \infty} \mu_n = \mu$ exists. The evaluation of μ will be done in several steps.

(b) The minimum μ_n remains unchanged if we impose on the polynomial $\sum_{j=0}^{n} u_j z^j, u_0 = 1$, the condition to be different from zero in the unit circle $|z| < 1$. In this case we have

$$\exp\left\{ \frac{1}{2\pi} \int_{-\pi}^{\pi} \log \left| \sum_{j=0}^{n} u_j z^j \right|^2 dx \right\} = 1, \quad z = e^{ix}.$$

Using the refined formulation of the theorem of L. Fejér-F. Riesz

[1.12 (b)], we see that μ_n can be considered as the minimum of the expression

$$\frac{1}{2\pi} \int_{-\pi}^{\pi} k(x) \, d\alpha(x)$$

for all nonnegative trigonometric polynomials $k(x)$ of degree n for which $G(k)=1$. Or

$$\mu_n = \min \, [G(k)]^{-1} \frac{1}{2\pi} \int_{-\pi}^{\pi} k(x) \, d\alpha(x) \tag{3}$$

for all nonnegative trigonometric polynomials $k(x)$ of degree n for which $G(k) > 0$.

(c) Now by the inequality for the arithmetic and geometric means:

$$\frac{1}{2\pi} \int_{-\pi}^{\pi} k(x) \, d\alpha(x) \geqq \frac{1}{2\pi} \int_{-\pi}^{\pi} k(x) \, w(x) \, dx \geqq G(kw) = G(k) \, G(w), \tag{4}$$

so that $\mu_n \geqq G(w)$ and also $\mu \geqq G(w)$. On the other hand,

$$\mu \leqq [G(k)]^{-1} \frac{1}{2\pi} \int_{-\pi}^{\pi} k(x) \, d\alpha(x), \tag{5}$$

where $k(x)$ is *any* nonnegative trigonometric polynomial which is not identically zero. By the theorem of Weierstrass the same inequality will hold for any positive continuous function $k(x)$.

(d) We prove first $\mu = G(w)$ in the special case when $\alpha(x)$ is absolutely continuous, $\alpha'(x) = w(x)$ almost everywhere, assuming also that $w(x) \geqq m > 0$. Hence $G(w) > 0$. Let ϵ be an arbitrary positive number; by the approximation theorem of 1.9 (c) we can find a trigonometric polynomial $t(x)$ such that

$$\frac{1}{2\pi} \int_{-\pi}^{\pi} |\, w(x) - t(x)\,|\, dx < \epsilon, \quad t(x) \geqq m. \tag{6}$$

We choose in (5), $k(x) = [t(x)]^{-1}$, so that

$$\mu \leqq G(t) \frac{1}{2\pi} \int_{-\pi}^{\pi} \frac{w(x)}{t(x)} \, dx$$

$$< G(w) \, G\left(\frac{t}{w}\right) \left\{1 + \frac{1}{2\pi m} \int_{-\pi}^{\pi} |\, w(x) - t(x)\,|\, dx\right\}$$

$$< G(w) \, G\left(\frac{t}{w}\right) (1 + m^{-1}\epsilon).$$

Also

$$\log G\left(\frac{t}{w}\right) = \frac{1}{2\pi} \int_{-\pi}^{\pi} [\log t(x) - \log w(x)]\, dx$$

$$< \frac{1}{2\pi m} \int_{-\pi}^{\pi} |\, t(x) - w(x)\, |\, dx < m^{-1}\epsilon.$$

Consequently for $\epsilon \to 0$ we have $\mu \leq G(w)$, so that indeed $\mu = G(w)$.

(e) Next we remove the restriction $w(x) \geq m > 0$. Let $w(x)$ be an arbitrary nonnegative function of the class L. [We allow also $G(w) = 0$.] If ϵ is an arbitrary positive number, we have

$$\mu = \mu(w) \leq \mu(w + \epsilon) = G(w + \epsilon).$$

Now let $\eta > 0$ be fixed. We have

$$\int_{w(x) > \eta} \log [w(x) + \epsilon]\, dx - \int_{w(x) > \eta} \log w(x)\, dx < \frac{\epsilon}{\eta} 2\pi,$$

so that

$$\int_{-\pi}^{\pi} \log [w(x) + \epsilon]\, dx$$

$$= \int_{w(x) \leq \eta} \log [w(x) + \epsilon]\, dx + \int_{w(x) > \eta} \log [w(x) + \epsilon]\, dx$$

$$\leq \int_{w(x) > \eta} \log [w(x) + \epsilon]\, dx < \int_{w(x) > \eta} \log w(x)\, dx + \frac{\epsilon}{\eta} 2\pi,$$

provided $\eta + \epsilon < 1$. Thus

$$\limsup_{\epsilon \to 0} \int_{-\pi}^{\pi} \log [w(x) + \epsilon]\, dx \leq \int_{w(x) > \eta} \log w(x)\, dx,$$

and so for $\eta \to 0$

$$\limsup_{\epsilon \to 0} \int_{-\pi}^{\pi} \log [w(x) + \epsilon]\, dx \leq \int_{-\pi}^{\pi} \log w(x)\, dx,$$

provided that the last integral exists. Otherwise the right-hand side (hence also the left-hand side) is $-\infty$. Hence in every case

$$G(w + \epsilon) \to G(w)$$

as $\epsilon \to 0$.

This establishes the proof of the theorem in the absolutely continuous case.

(f) Finally, we consider the general case of an arbitrary distribution function $\alpha(x)$. Since $\mu \geqq \mu(w)$ it suffices to prove the opposite inequality $\mu \leqq \mu(w)$. In view of (5) we must prove the following assertion:

We denote by $\beta(x) = \alpha_j(x) + \alpha_s(x)$ the component of the distribution function $\alpha(x)$ which is not absolutely continuous (1.3). *Let δ be an arbitrary positive number and $h(x)$ an arbitrary positive continuous function. We can construct another positive and continuous function $k(x)$ such that the following inequality holds:*

$$[G(k)]^{-1} \left\{ \frac{1}{2\pi} \int_{-\pi}^{\pi} k(x)\, w(x)\, dx + \frac{1}{2\pi} \int_{-\pi}^{\pi} k(x)\, d\beta(x) \right\}$$

$$< [G(h)]^{-1} \frac{1}{2\pi} \int_{-\pi}^{\pi} h(x)\, w(x)\, dx + \delta. \quad (7)$$

The left-hand side is an upper bound for μ.

For the proof we employ the theorem in 1.4 (a). We define $k(x) = \epsilon$ in the intervals I_1. Now let $\eta > 0$ be given; denoting one typical interval I_2 by $[a, b]$ we denote by I_2' the intervals arising from I_2 by excluding $[a, a+l]$ and $[b-l, b]$ from each $[a, b]$, where l is chosen so small that the total length of $I_2 - I_2'$ is $< \eta$. We define $k(x) = h(x)$ in I_2', and in the remaining intervals $I_2 - I_2'$ the function $k(x)$ should be linear and in the whole continuous.† If ϵ is sufficiently small, we have $\min k(x) = \epsilon$, $\max k(x) = \max h(x)$. Now

$$\left| \int_{-\pi}^{\pi} \log k(x)\, dx - \int_{-\pi}^{\pi} \log h(x)\, dx \right| \leqq \left| \int_{I_1} \log k(x)\, dx \right|$$

$$+ \left| \int_{I_2 - I_2'} \log k(x)\, dx \right| + \left| \int_{I_1} \log h(x)\, dx \right| + \left| \int_{I_2 - I_2'} \log h(x)\, dx \right|$$

$$< \epsilon \log \frac{1}{\epsilon} + \eta \log \frac{1}{\epsilon} + \epsilon O(1) + \eta O(1).$$

Now we choose $\eta = (\log 1/\epsilon)^{-2}$ so that $G(k) > (1 - \delta')\, G(h)$, where $\delta' \to 0$ as ϵ tends to zero.

---

† Suppose the interval to the right of an I_2 interval (denoted by $[a, b]$) is an I_1 interval; then $k(x)$ will be linear in $[b-l, b]$, varying between an ordinate of $h(x)$ and ϵ. Suppose the interval to the right is another I_2, then $k(x)$ will be linear in $[b-l, b+l]$, varying between two ordinates of $h(x)$.

On the other hand,

$$\frac{1}{2\pi}\int_{-\pi}^{\pi}[k(x)-h(x)]\,w(x)\,dx < 2\max h(x)\int_{I_1+(I_2-I_2')}w(x)\,dx=\delta''.$$

The total length of I_1 is less than ϵ, the total length of I_2-I_2' is less than η; hence $\delta''\to 0$ as ϵ tends to zero. Finally,

$$\int_{-\pi}^{\pi}k(x)\,d\beta(x)=\int_{I_1+I_2}k(x)\,d\beta(x).$$

The integral over I_1 is less than $\epsilon\int_{-\pi}^{\pi}d\beta(x)$. The integral over I_2 is less than $\max h(x)\int_{I_2}d\beta(x) < \epsilon\max h(x)$.

This establishes (7) provided ϵ is sufficiently small. Thus the proof of the theorem is complete.

3.2. Generalization

(a) THEOREM. *Let $\alpha(x)$ be a distribution function of the infinite type. We consider the Toeplitz form*

$$T_n=\frac{1}{2\pi}\int_{-\pi}^{\pi}|\,u_0+u_1z+u_2z^2+\ldots+u_nz^n\,|^2\,d\alpha(x),\quad z=e^{ix}.\quad(1)$$

Let $\zeta=re^{i\phi}$ be a fixed complex number, $|\,\zeta\,|<1$. We denote by $\mu_n(\zeta)$ the minimum of T_n under the side condition

$$u_0+u_1\zeta+u_2\zeta^2+\ldots+u_n\zeta^n=1.\quad(2)$$

Then

$$\lim_{n\to\infty}\mu_n(\zeta)=\mu(\zeta)$$
$$=(1-|\,\zeta\,|^2)\exp\left\{\frac{1}{2\pi}\int_{-\pi}^{\pi}\frac{1-r^2}{1-2r\cos(\phi-x)+r^2}\log w(x)\,dx\right\},\quad(3)$$

where $w(x)$ is the almost everywhere existing derivative of $\alpha(x)$. In the case when $\log w(x)$ is not L-integrable, the limit (3) must be replaced by zero.

We denote the expression on the right of (3) by $(1-|\,\zeta\,|^2)\,G(w;\zeta)$. The quantity $G(w;\zeta)$ is a mean value of $w(x)$ depending on ζ and represents a generalization of the geometric mean $G(w)$ to which it reduces if $\zeta=0$.

The mean value $G(w; \zeta)$ admits of an important interpretation. Let $\log w(x)$ be of the class L. Substituting in 1.14: $f(x) = w(x)$, we find that $G(w; \zeta) = |g(\zeta)|^2$, where $g(z) = g(w; z)$ is the analytic function defined in 1.14 (e).

Using 1.14 (9) we obtain the following inequality valid for an arbitrary L-integrable function $w(x)$, $w(x) \geqq 0$,

$$(1 - |\zeta|^2) G(w; \zeta) \leqq \frac{1}{2\pi} \int_{-\pi}^{\pi} w(x) \, dx. \tag{4}$$

(b) The sequence $\{\mu_n(\zeta)\}$ is nonincreasing, so that the limit $\lim_{n \to \infty} \mu_n(\zeta) = \mu(\zeta)$ exists. In order to prove that $\mu(\zeta) = (1 - |\zeta|^2) G(w; \zeta)$ we point out first that the polynomial $\Sigma u_j z^j$ for which the minimum $\mu_n(\zeta)$ is attained must be again different from zero in the unit circle $|z| < 1$. Indeed, if it should have a zero z_0 with $|z_0| < 1$, we consider

$$\frac{1 - \bar{z}_0 z}{z - z_0} \frac{\zeta - z_0}{1 - \bar{z}_0 \zeta} \Sigma u_j z^j,$$

satisfying the side condition (2). We see easily that on the unit circle $|z| = 1$ this polynomial has a smaller modulus than the original one which is a contradiction. We denote the square modulus of the minimum polynomial, $z = e^{ix}$, by $k(x)$, so that in view of the side condition we have $G(k; \zeta) = 1$.

Using now the inequality (4) we find

$$\mu_n(\zeta) \geqq (1 - |\zeta|^2) G(w; \zeta) G(k; \zeta) = (1 - |\zeta|^2) G(w; \zeta), \tag{5}$$

and the same inequality holds for $\mu(\zeta)$. On the other hand, if $k(x)$ is an arbitrary nonnegative trigonometric polynomial with $G(k; \zeta) > 0$, we have

$$\mu(\zeta) \leqq [G(k; \zeta)]^{-1} \frac{1}{2\pi} \int_{-\pi}^{\pi} k(x) \, d\alpha(x). \tag{6}$$

From here on the proof follows a line similar to that in the special case $\zeta = 0$ discussed in 3.1.

3.3. Completeness

(a) The following application of the theorem in 3.1 is of importance:

THEOREM. *Let $\alpha(x)$ be a distribution function of the infinite type. The functions $1, e^{ix}, e^{2ix}, \ldots, e^{nix}, \ldots$, are closed in the space*

$$L_2[d\alpha(x); -\pi, \pi], \tag{1}$$

if and only if

$$\int_{-\pi}^{\pi} \log w(x)\, dx = -\infty, \qquad (2)$$

where $w(x)$ denotes the almost everywhere existing derivative of the distribution function $\alpha(x)$.

We note that the functions $\{e^{\pm nix}\}$, $n = 0, 1, 2, \ldots$, are always closed in the space (1). The meaning of the condition (2) is that the integral

$$\int_{-\pi}^{\pi} \overset{+}{\log} \frac{1}{w(x)}\, dx$$

is divergent.

(b) We use the theorem proved in 3.1. We first show that condition (2) is *necessary*. Indeed, if $\log w(x)$ is L-integrable we have, by 3.1, $\mu_n \geqq \mu$, where μ is a fixed positive number. Now by the definition of μ_n we have

$$\frac{1}{2\pi} \int_{-\pi}^{\pi} |\, e^{-ix} - (A_0 + A_1 e^{ix} + \ldots + A_{n-1} e^{i(n-1)x})\, |^2\, d\alpha(x) \geqq \mu_n \geqq \mu \quad (3)$$

for all possible choice of the complex constants $A_0, A_1, \ldots, A_{n-1}$. Thus e^{-ix} cannot be approximated in (1) with an accuracy $< \mu$.

On the other hand, we prove that the condition $\mu = 0$ is *sufficient*. Indeed, in this case μ_n will be arbitrarily small with increasing n. This means that the integral in (3) can be made arbitrarily small; thus e^{-ix} can be approximated in the space (1) with arbitrary accuracy. For the same reason e^{-2ix} can be approximated by an expression of the form $B_0 e^{-ix} + B_1 + B_2 e^{ix} + \ldots + B_{n-1} e^{i(n-2)x}$. Replacing here $B_0 e^{-ix}$ by a suitable approximation of the form $C_0 + C_1 e^{ix} + C_2 e^{2ix} + \ldots + C_m e^{mix}$, we obtain the desired approximation for e^{-2ix}. Continuing this process we can show that any e^{-kix}, k positive integer, can be approximated by a linear combination of a finite number of the functions 1, e^{ix}, e^{2ix}, ...

3.4. Kernel function. Asymptotic formula of $\varphi_n(z)$ for $|z| > 1$

We introduce in this section the important concept of the kernel function associated with a given distribution function $\alpha(x)$. It arises from the kernel polynomials $s_n(a, z)$ defined in 2.2 (b) by the limiting process $n \to \infty$.

(a) THEOREM. *Let $\alpha(x)$ be a distribution function of the infinite type, $w(x)$ the almost everywhere existing derivative of $\alpha(x)$. We assume that $\log w(x)$ is L-integrable. We denote by $g(z) = g(w, z)$ the analytic function defined in 1.14 (e) $[f(x) = w(x)]$. Finally, let $\{\phi_n(z)\}$ be the orthonormal system of polynomials associated with the distribution function $\alpha(x)$ (2.1).*

We have the following formulas:

$$\lim_{n \to \infty} s_n(\zeta, \zeta) = s(\zeta, \zeta) = \sum_{n=0}^{\infty} |\phi_n(\zeta)|^2 = \frac{1}{1 - |\zeta|^2} \frac{1}{|g(\zeta)|^2}, \quad |\zeta| < 1, \ (1)$$

$$\lim_{n \to \infty} s_n(\zeta, z) = s(\zeta, z) \doteq \sum_{n=0}^{\infty} \overline{\phi_n(\zeta)} \phi_n(z) = \frac{1}{1 - \bar{\zeta} z} \frac{1}{\overline{g(\zeta)}} \frac{1}{g(z)},$$

$$|\zeta| < 1, |z| < 1, \quad (2)$$

$$\lim_{n \to \infty} k_n = [G(w)]^{-\frac{1}{2}} = [g(0)]^{-1}, \tag{3}$$

$$\lim_{n \to \infty} z^{-n} \phi_n(z) = [\bar{g}(z^{-1})]^{-1}, \quad |z| > 1, \tag{4}$$

$$\lim_{n \to \infty} \phi_n(z) = 0, \quad |z| < 1. \tag{5}$$

We recall briefly the definition of the function $g(z) = g(w; z)$. We have $g(z) = e^{\frac{1}{2}h(z)}$, where $h(z)$ is regular in the unit circle $|z| < 1$ and $\Re h(z)$ is defined by the Poisson integral associated with $\log w(x)$ [1.14 (2)]. The function $g(z)$ is regular and different from zero in $|z| < 1$ and $g(0)$ is real and positive.

The symbol k_n has the same meaning as in 2.1 (8), i.e.

$$\phi_n(z) = k_n z^n + \ldots.$$

(b) In the minimum problem of 3.2 we introduce the variables v_j defined by the rearrangement

$$\sum_{j=0}^{n} u_j z^j = \sum_{j=0}^{n} v_j \phi_j(z).$$

We have then

$$T_n = \sum_{j=0}^{n} |v_j|^2$$

and the side condition 3.2 (2) becomes

$$\sum_{j=0}^{n} v_j \phi_j(\zeta) = 1.$$

Thus by Cauchy's inequality,

$$1 = \left| \sum_{j=0}^{n} v_j \phi_j(\zeta) \right|^2 \leqq \sum_{j=0}^{n} |v_j|^2 \sum_{j=0}^{n} |\phi_j(\zeta)|^2 = s_n(\zeta, \zeta) \sum_{j=0}^{n} |v_j|^2,$$

so that

$$\mu_n(\zeta) = \min \sum_{j=0}^{n} |v_j|^2 = \frac{1}{s_n(\zeta, \zeta)}. \tag{6}$$

Hence (1) follows by using 3.2 (3). This result yields also the convergence of (2) for $|\zeta| < 1$, $|z| < 1$, and of course (5). The function $s(\zeta, z)$ is called the *kernel function* associated with $\alpha(x)$.

Formula (3) follows from 2.2 (10).

(c) We proceed now to the proof of (4). We consider the function

$$1 - z^n \overline{\phi}_n(z^{-1}) g(z) = d_{n0} + d_{n1} z + d_{n2} z^2 + \dots,$$

which is regular and of the class H_2 in the unit circle $|z| < 1$. Using the notation $z = r e^{ix}$, $r < 1$, we have

$$\sum_{\nu=0}^{\infty} |d_{n\nu}|^2 r^{2\nu} = \frac{1}{2\pi} \int_{-\pi}^{\pi} |1 - z^n \overline{\phi}_n(z^{-1}) g(z)|^2 dx$$

$$= 1 - 2\Re \frac{1}{2\pi} \int_{-\pi}^{\pi} z^n \overline{\phi}_n(z^{-1}) g(z) \, dx$$

$$+ \frac{1}{2\pi} \int_{-\pi}^{\pi} |z^n \overline{\phi}_n(z^{-1})|^2 |g(z)|^2 dx.$$

But

$$\frac{1}{2\pi} \int_{-\pi}^{\pi} z^n \overline{\phi}_n(z^{-1}) g(z) \, dx = k_n g(0), \quad z = r e^{ix},$$

and [1.13 (6), 1.14 (6)]

$$\lim_{r \to 1} \frac{1}{2\pi} \int_{-\pi}^{\pi} |z^n \overline{\phi}_n(z^{-1})|^2 |g(z)|^2 dx = \frac{1}{2\pi} \int_{-\pi}^{\pi} |\phi_n(e^{ix})|^2 |g(e^{ix})|^2 dx$$

$$= \frac{1}{2\pi} \int_{-\pi}^{\pi} |\phi_n(e^{ix})|^2 w(x) \, dx$$

$$\leqq \frac{1}{2\pi} \int_{-\pi}^{\pi} |\phi_n(e^{ix})|^2 d\alpha(x) = 1.$$

Consequently,

$$\sum_{\nu=0}^{\infty} |d_{n\nu}|^2 \leqq 2 - 2 k_n g(0).$$

Thus for $|z| < 1$,

$$|1 - z^n \overline{\phi}_n(z^{-1}) g(z)|^2 \leq \sum_{\nu=0}^{\infty} |d_{n\nu}|^2 \sum_{\nu=0}^{\infty} |z|^{2\nu} = (1 - |z|^2)^{-1} [2 - 2k_n g(0)],$$

and the last expression tends to zero when $n \to \infty$ [cf. (3)]. This completes the proof of (4).

The representation (2) of the kernel function follows from the identity 2.3 (1) taking (4) and (5) into account.

3.5. Asymptotic formula of $\varphi_n(z)$ for $|z| = 1$

(a) The purpose of this section is to prove the following theorem:

THEOREM. *Let $w(x)$ be a positive function of the class C satisfying the conditions of the theorem in* 1.15 (c) *[$f(x) = w(x)$]. We denote the orthonormal polynomials associated with the distribution $w(x)\,dx$, $-\pi \leq x < \pi$, by $\phi_n(z)$, assuming that the coefficient of z^n in $\phi_n(z)$ is real and positive* (cf. 2.1). *We denote by $g(w; z)$ the analytic function defined in* 1.14 (e) *[$f(x) = w(x)$]. Then the following asymptotic formula holds:*

$$\phi_n(z) \doteq z^n / \overline{g(w;\ z)} + \omega(2\pi/n) \log n . O(1), \quad z = e^{ix}, \ -\pi \leq x \leq \pi. \quad (1)$$

For the O-term a bound can be obtained in which only the constants K, α (or λ) [cf. 1.15 (c)] *and the minimum and maximum of the function $w(x)$ occur.*

The main term in (1) is identical with the main term appearing in 3.4 (4); the latter formula is valid for $|z| > 1$, the present formula for $|z| = 1$. According to 1.15 (b) we have $|g(w; e^{ix})|^2 = w(x)$. The modulus of continuity $\omega(\delta)$ is of the special form defined in 1.15 (c).

(b) The function $[w(x)]^{-1}$ satisfies a condition of the same form as $w(x)$ [with the same α or λ as $w(x)$ but K must be replaced by another constant depending on K and on the minimum of $w(x)$]. Using the theorem in 1.15 (c) we can find a trigonometric polynomial $t(x)$ of degree m such that

$$|[w(x)]^{-1} - t(x)| < B\omega(2\pi/m), \quad (2)$$

where B depends on K and on the minimum of $w(x)$. Of course $t(x)$ is positive provided m is sufficiently large. The function $g(t; z)$ is analytic in the closed unit circle $|z| \leq 1$, and we have $|g(t; e^{ix})|^2 = t(x)$.

In view of the theorem in 1.15 (b) the function $g(w; z)$ is regular for $|z| < 1$ and continuous for $|z| \leq 1$; moreover,

$$|g(w; e^{ix}) g(t; e^{ix})|^2 = w(x) t(x) = 1 + \omega(2\pi/m) . O(1). \tag{3}$$

Consequently,

$$|g(w; 0) g(t; 0)|^2 = 1 + \omega(2\pi/m) . O(1). \tag{4}$$

Let $\{\psi_n(z)\}$ be the orthonormal set of polynomials associated with the distribution $[t(x)]^{-1} dx$, $-\pi \leq x \leq \pi$. Writing for the sake of brevity $g(t; z) = \gamma(z)$, we have, by 2.4 (c),

$$\psi_n(z) = z^n \overline{\gamma}(1/z), \quad n \geq m. \tag{5}$$

(c) Now we rearrange the polynomial $\phi_m(z)$ corresponding to the weight function $w(x)$ as a linear combination of the polynomials $\psi_\nu(z)$ corresponding to the weight function $[t(x)]^{-1}$:

$$\phi_m(z) = \sum_{\nu=0}^{m} \alpha_\nu \psi_\nu(z) = \alpha_m \psi_m(z) + \frac{1}{2\pi} \int_{-\pi}^{\pi} [t(x)]^{-1} \phi_m(\zeta) \sum_{\nu=0}^{m-1} \overline{\psi_\nu(\zeta)} \psi_\nu(z) \, dx$$

$$= \alpha_m \psi_m(z) + \frac{1}{2\pi} \int_{-\pi}^{\pi} \{[t(x)]^{-1} - w(x)\} \phi_m(\zeta) \sum_{\nu=0}^{m-1} \overline{\psi_\nu(\zeta)} \psi_\nu(z) \, dx$$

$$+ \frac{1}{2\pi} \int_{-\pi}^{\pi} w(x) \phi_m(\zeta) \sum_{\nu=0}^{m-1} \overline{\psi_\nu(\zeta)} \psi_\nu(z) \, dx, \quad \zeta = e^{ix}. \tag{6}$$

The last term vanishes because of the orthogonality property of the $\phi_m(z)$.

We denote by k_m and $k'_m = \gamma(0)$ the highest coefficients of $\phi_m(z)$ and $\psi_m(z)$, respectively; then $\alpha_m = k_m/k'_m = k_m[\gamma(0)]^{-1}$. Furthermore, by 3.1 (a), we have

$$[g(w; 0)]^2 = G(w) \leq \mu_m(w) = k_m^{-2} \leq \frac{1}{2\pi} \int_{-\pi}^{\pi} w(x) \, |\gamma(z)/\gamma(0)|^2 \, dx$$

$$= [\gamma(0)]^{-2} \frac{1}{2\pi} \int_{-\pi}^{\pi} w(x) t(x) \, dx, \quad z = e^{ix}.$$

Multiplying these inequalities by $[g(w; 0)]^{-2}$ we obtain, in view of (4) and (2),

$$\left. \begin{array}{l} 1 \leq k_m^{-2} [g(w; 0)]^{-2} \leq 1 + \omega(2\pi/m) . O(1), \\[2mm] k_m = [g(w; 0)]^{-1} + \omega(2\pi/m) . O(1), \\[2mm] \alpha_m = 1 + \omega(2\pi/m) . O(1). \end{array} \right\} \tag{7}$$

(d) Our next purpose is to find a bound for

$$\max |\phi_m(z)| = H = H(m), \quad |z| = 1.$$

Using (7), (5) and (2) we find from (6)

$$H \leqq O(1) + \omega(2\pi/m) . O(1) H \max_{|z|=1} \int_{-\pi}^{\pi} \left| \sum_{\nu=0}^{m-1} \overline{\psi_\nu(\zeta)} \, \psi_\nu(z) \right| dx, \quad \zeta = e^{ix}.$$

(8)

Now by 2.3 (1)

$$\sum_{\nu=0}^{m-1} \overline{\psi_\nu(\zeta)} \, \psi_\nu(z) = \frac{\overline{\gamma(\zeta)} \, \gamma(z) - \overline{\gamma^*(\zeta)} \, \gamma^*(z)}{1 - \bar{\zeta}z}.$$

(9)

We show that

$$\int_{-\pi}^{\pi} \left| \sum_{\nu=0}^{m-1} \overline{\psi_\nu(\zeta)} \, \psi_\nu(z) \right| dx = O(\log m), \quad \zeta = e^{ix}, \quad |z| = 1.$$

(10)

Indeed, the numerator of the fraction on the right of (9) is a polynomial of degree m in z vanishing for $z = \zeta$. Hence, by S. Bernstein's inequality [cf. in particular 1.16 (b)], the kernel polynomial (9) is uniformly $O(m)$. Thus the arc $|\zeta - z| \leqq m^{-1}$ contributes to (10) a quantity which is $O(m).O(m^{-1}) = O(1)$, while the contribution of the complementary arc $|\zeta - z| > m^{-1}$ will be

$$O(1) \int_{|\zeta-z|>m^{-1}} \frac{dx}{|1 - \bar{\zeta}z|} = O(\log m).$$

Using (10) we find from (8)

$$H \leqq O(1) + H\omega(2\pi/m) \log m . O(1),$$

so that $H = O(1)$. Now we conclude from (6), in view of (7), (5), (2) and $H = O(1)$, that for $|z| = 1$

$$\phi_m(z) = [1 + \omega(2\pi/m) \, O(1)] \, z^m \overline{\gamma(z)} + \omega(2\pi/m) \log m . O(1).$$

Finally we have, by the theorem in 1.15 (c),

$$g(w^{-1}; z) - g(t; z) = [g(w; z)]^{-1} - \gamma(z) = \omega(2\pi/m) \log m . O(1),$$

and this yields the assertion.

CHAPTER 4

THE TRIGONOMETRIC MOMENT PROBLEM

We refer to the formulation of this problem in 1.11. First we deal in 4.1 with the 'finite' moment problem, which is essentially a problem of algebraic character.

4.1. A theorem of C. Carathéodory

(a) THEOREM. Let $c_1, c_2, ..., c_n$ be given complex constants not all zero, $n > 1$. There exists an integer m, $1 \leqq m \leqq n$, and certain constants ρ_k, ϵ_k; $k = 1, 2, ..., m$, such that $\rho_k > 0$, $|\epsilon_k| = 1$, $\epsilon_k \neq \epsilon_l$ if $k \neq l$, and

$$c_\nu = \sum_{k=1}^{m} \rho_k \epsilon_k^\nu, \quad \nu = 1, 2, ..., n. \tag{1}$$

The integer m and the constants ρ_k, ϵ_k are uniquely determined. This basic theorem can be formulated also as follows:

$$c_\nu = \int_{-\pi}^{\pi} e^{-i\nu x} d\alpha(x), \quad \nu = 1, 2, ..., n, \tag{2}$$

where $\alpha(x)$ is a distribution function of the finite type defined in the following way. It has jumps at those points x for which e^{-ix} coincides with one of the numbers ϵ_k and the corresponding jump is ρ_k.

(b) We write $c_{-\nu} = \bar{c}_\nu, \nu = 1, 2, ..., n$, and define c_0 by the condition that the Hermitian form

$$\Sigma c_{\mu-\nu} u_\mu \bar{u}_\nu, \quad \mu, \nu = 0, 1, 2, ..., n, \tag{3}$$

shall have the minimum zero when $\Sigma |u_\nu|^2 = 1$. Thus the eigenvalues of (3) are nonnegative. They cannot be all zero (otherwise all c_ν must be zero), and since their sum [the trace of (3)] is $(n+1) c_0$, we conclude that c_0 must be positive. We shall prove (1) for $\nu = 0, 1, 2, ..., n$, so that $c_0 = \Sigma \rho_k$ and (1) will hold for $\nu = 0, \pm 1, ..., \pm n$.

Let us define the linear operation L by the conditions

$$L(z^\nu) = L(e^{i\nu x}) = c_\nu, \quad \nu = 0, \pm 1, ..., \pm n, \tag{4}$$

so that L is defined for an arbitrary trigonometric polynomial of degree n. The form (3) can be written as follows:

$$L\{|u_0 + u_1 z + u_2 z^2 + ... + u_n z^n|^2\}, \quad z = e^{ix}. \tag{5}$$

(c) We denote by μ_h the smallest eigenvalue of the hth section of (3), that is,

$$\mu_h = \min L\{|\, u_0 + u_1 z + \ldots + u_h z^h\,|^2\}, \quad z = e^{ix}, \qquad (6)$$

where $|\,u_0\,|^2 + \ldots + |\,u_h\,|^2 = 1$. Obviously,

$$\mu_0 \geqq \mu_1 \geqq \ldots \geqq \mu_n = 0. \qquad (7)$$

Since $\mu_0 = c_0 > 0$, there exists an integer $m, 1 \leqq m \leqq n$, such that $\mu_{m-1} > 0, \mu_m = 0$. We have then

$$\left.\begin{array}{l} L\{|\, g_{m-1}(z)\,|^2\} > 0; \\[4pt] L\{|\, g_m(z)\,|^2\} \geqq 0, \quad L\{|\, G(z)\,|^2\} = 0, \quad z = e^{ix}, \end{array}\right\} \qquad (8)$$

where $g_{m-1}(z)$ is an *arbitrary* polynomial of degree $m-1$, not identically zero, $g_m(z)$ is an *arbitrary* polynomial of degree m, and $G(z)$ is a *special* polynomial of the precise degree m. The determinant D_h of the Hermitian form in (6) is positive for $h \leqq m-1$ and 0 for $h \geqq m$.

Let p be an integer, $-(n-m) \leqq p \leqq n$. Since for any complex ϵ

$$L\{|\, G(z) + \epsilon z^p\,|^2\} \geqq 0, \quad z = e^{ix},$$

we have

$$L\{G(z)\,\bar{z}^p\} = 0, \quad z = e^{ix}, \; -(n-m) \leqq p \leqq n. \qquad (9)$$

Let us consider these equations first for $0 \leqq p < m$. They determine the polynomial $G(z)$ (except for a constant factor) uniquely. Indeed, if $G_1(z)$ should be another polynomial of precise degree m satisfying the same equations $(0 \leqq p < m)$, we could determine the constants a and b so that $aG(z) + bG_1(z)$ is of degree $m-1$; now

$$L\{|\, aG(z) + bG_1(z)\,|^2\} = |\,a\,|^2 L\{|\, G(z)\,|^2\} + 2\Re a\bar{b}L\{G(z)\,\overline{G_1(z)}\}$$

$$+ |\,b\,|^2 L\{|\, G_1(z)\,|^2\} = 0, \quad z = e^{ix},$$

which contradicts the first equation (8) unless $aG(z) + bG_1(z) = 0$. From this characterization of $G(z)$ and in view of $D_m = 0$ we conclude the representation

$$G(z) = D_{m-1}^{-1} \begin{vmatrix} c_0 & c_1 & \cdots & c_m \\ c_{-1} & c_0 & \cdots & c_{m-1} \\ \cdots & \cdots & \cdots & \cdots \\ c_{-(m-1)} & c_{-(m-2)} & \cdots & c_1 \\ 1 & z & \cdots & z^m \end{vmatrix}. \qquad (10)$$

The polynomial $G(z)$ has been normalized by the condition that its highest coefficient is equal to 1.

(d) We denote by $\epsilon_1, \epsilon_2, \ldots, \epsilon_m$ the zeros of $G(z)$. We shall prove that

$$|\epsilon_k| = 1 \quad \text{and} \quad \epsilon_k \neq \epsilon_l \quad \text{if} \quad k \neq l. \tag{11}$$

Moreover, we shall prove that (1) holds with

$$\rho_k = L\{G_k(z)\} = L\{|\,G_k(z)\,|^2\}, \quad z = e^{ix},$$

$$G_k(z) = \frac{1}{G'(\epsilon_k)} \frac{G(z)}{z - \epsilon_k}. \tag{12}$$

In view of the first part of (8) this implies that $\rho_k > 0$.

(e) In order to prove the first part of (11) we note that for arbitrary complex v_0, v_1,

$$L\left\{ \left| \frac{G(z)}{z - \epsilon_k} \right|^2 |\,v_0 + v_1 z\,|^2 \right\} = \Sigma \gamma_{\mu - \nu} v_\mu \bar{v}_\nu > 0, \quad z = e^{ix}; \ \mu, \nu = 0, 1,$$

with the sign of equality if $v_0 + v_1 z = z - \epsilon_k$. This corresponds to the special case $m = 1$ of (8). More precisely we have, instead of (4),

$$L\left\{ \left| \frac{G(z)}{z - \epsilon_k} \right|^2 z^\nu \right\} = \gamma_\nu, \quad z = e^{ix}; \ \nu = 0, \pm 1,$$

so that $\gamma_0 > 0$ and $\gamma_0 = |\gamma_1|$. Also $z - \epsilon_k$ plays here the role of $G(z)$. Thus ϵ_k is the root of $\begin{vmatrix} \gamma_0 & \gamma_1 \\ 1 & z \end{vmatrix} = 0$, hence $\epsilon_k = \gamma_1/\gamma_0$, $|\epsilon_k| = 1$.

(f) For the proof of the second part of (11) we assume that $m \geq 2$. Then

$$L\left\{ \left| \frac{G(z)}{(z - \epsilon_k)(z - \epsilon_l)} \right|^2 |\,v_0 + v_1 z + v_2 z^2\,|^2 \right\} = \Sigma \delta_{\mu - \nu} v_\mu \bar{v}_\nu, \quad z = e^{ix}; \ \mu, \nu = 0, 1, 2,$$

with the sign of equality if $v_0 + v_1 z + v_2 z^2 = (z - \epsilon_k)(z - \epsilon_l)$. This corresponds to the special case $m = 2$ of (8) so that $\delta_0 > 0, \delta_0 > |\,\delta_1\,|$ and

$$\begin{vmatrix} \delta_0 & \delta_1 & \delta_2 \\ \delta_{-1} & \delta_0 & \delta_1 \\ \delta_{-2} & \delta_{-1} & \delta_0 \end{vmatrix} = 0. \tag{13}$$

Also ϵ_k and ϵ_l are the roots of the equation

$$\begin{vmatrix} \delta_0 & \delta_1 & \delta_2 \\ \delta_{-1} & \delta_0 & \delta_1 \\ 1 & z & z^2 \end{vmatrix} = 0. \tag{14}$$

Thus we have to show that

$$(\delta_0\delta_1 - \delta_{-1}\delta_2)^2 - 4(\delta_0^2 - |\delta_1|^2)(\delta_1^2 - \delta_0\delta_2) \neq 0. \tag{15}$$

Now (13) can be written as follows: $(\delta_0^2 - |\delta_1|^2)^2 = |\delta_1^2 - \delta_0\delta_2|^2$, so that $\delta_0\delta_2 = \delta_1^2 + (\delta_0^2 - |\delta_1|^2)e^{it}$, t real. In view of

$$\delta_0\delta_1 - \delta_{-1}\delta_2 = (\delta_0^2 - |\delta_1|^2)(\delta_1/\delta_0 - \bar{\delta}_1 e^{it}/\delta_0),$$

the left-hand side of (15) will be

$$(\delta_0^2 - |\delta_1|^2)^2 \{(\delta_1/\delta_0 - \bar{\delta}_1 e^{it}/\delta_0)^2 + 4e^{it}\}$$
$$= 4e^{it}(\delta_0^2 - |\delta_1|^2)^2(-r^2\sin^2 u + 1) \neq 0,$$

where $\delta_1 e^{-it/2}/\delta_0 = re^{iu}$, $0 < r < 1$, has been written.

(g) Now we prove that $\rho_k = L\{G_k(z)\} = L\{|G_k(z)|^2\}$, $z = e^{ix}$ (so that ρ_k is real and positive). Indeed,

$$L\{G_k(z)\overline{(G_k(z) - 1)}\} = \frac{1}{G'(\epsilon_k)} L\{G(z)\overline{h(z)}\}, \quad z = e^{ix}, \tag{16}$$

where

$$h(z) = \frac{G_k(z) - 1}{z^{-1} - \epsilon_k^{-1}} = -\epsilon_k z \frac{G_k(z) - G_k(\epsilon_k)}{z - \epsilon_k}$$

is a polynomial of degree $m - 1$ so that (16) vanishes in view of (9).

(h) Finally, we prove that for all polynomials $f(z)$ of degree n we have

$$L\{f(z)\} = \sum_{k=1}^{m} \rho_k f(\epsilon_k), \quad z = e^{ix}. \tag{17}$$

Writing $f(z) = z^\nu$, (1) will follow.

Given $f(z)$, there exist polynomials $q(z)$ (degree $n - m$) and $r(z)$ (degree $m - 1$) such that

$$f(z) = G(z)q(z) + r(z), \quad f(\epsilon_k) = r(\epsilon_k),$$

$$r(z) = \sum_{k=1}^{m} r(\epsilon_k)G_k(z) = \sum_{k=1}^{m} f(\epsilon_k)G_k(z).$$

Now, in view of (9), $L\{G(z)q(z)\} = 0$, $z = e^{ix}$, so that

$$L\{f(z)\} = L\{r(z)\} = \sum_{k=1}^{m} f(\epsilon_k)L\{G_k(z)\},$$

which is the assertion.

(k) One more remark is necessary concerning the uniqueness of the quantities m, ϵ_k, ρ_k. Let (1) hold for $-n \leqq \nu \leqq n$. The form (3) can be written then as follows:

$$\sum_{k=1}^{m} \rho_k \mid u_0 + u_1 \epsilon_k + u_2 \epsilon_k^2 + \ldots + u_n \epsilon_k^n \mid^2,$$

so that m is the rank of (3). Next we show that the ϵ_k are the zeros of the polynomial (10). Indeed, if $G(z) = u_0 + u_1 z + \ldots + u_m z^m$ is the polynomial of degree m with zeros $\epsilon_1, \epsilon_2, \ldots, \epsilon_m$, we have

$$u_0 c_{-\alpha} + u_1 c_{-\alpha+1} + \ldots + u_m c_{-\alpha+m} = \sum_{k=1}^{m} \rho_k \epsilon_k^{-\alpha} G(\epsilon_k) = 0,$$

$$u_0 + u_1 \epsilon_k + \ldots + u_m \epsilon_k^m = 0, \quad \alpha = 0, 1, \ldots, m-1,$$

so that the determinant of this system must be zero. Finally, (17) holds and writing $f(z) = G_k(z)$, formula (12) for ρ_k follows.

4.2. The trigonometric moment problem

The theorem of C. Carathéodory proved in the foregoing section serves as the basis of another approach to the trigonometic moment problem formulated in 1.11 (a). This approach is essentially different from that dealt with in 1.11 (b).

(a) Let $\{c_n\}$ be the given sequence of moments, $c_{-n} = \bar{c}_n$. We assume that the Toeplitz forms T_n defined by 1.10 (3) are nonnegative. We denote the minimum of T_n under the side condition $\Sigma \mid u_\nu \mid^2 = 1$ by $\rho_0^{(n)}$ so that $\rho_0^{(n)}$ is a nonincreasing sequence of nonnegative numbers. According to 4.1 we can find for each n a representation of the form

$$\left. \begin{aligned} c_0 - \rho_0^{(n)} &= \sum_{k=1}^{m} \rho_k, \\ c_\nu &= \sum_{k=1}^{m} \rho_k \epsilon_k^\nu, \quad \nu = \pm 1, \pm 2, \ldots, \pm n, \end{aligned} \right\} \tag{1}$$

where m, ρ_k, ϵ_k depend on n, $1 \leqq m \leqq n$, $\rho_k > 0$, $\mid \epsilon_k \mid = 1$.

We define the distribution function $\alpha_n(x)$ in $[-\pi, \pi]$ in the following way: $\alpha_n(x) - \rho_0^{(n)} x$ is a distribution function of the finite type having jumps at the points x for which e^{-ix} coincides with one of the numbers ϵ_k and the corresponding jump is $2\pi \rho_k$. Since for $\nu \neq 0$

$$\int_{-\pi}^{\pi} e^{-i\nu x} dx = 0,$$

we have, in view of (1),

$$\begin{cases} \dfrac{1}{2\pi}\int_{-\pi}^{\pi} d\alpha_n(x)=\dfrac{1}{2\pi}\int_{-\pi}^{\pi} d[\alpha_n(x)-\rho_0^{(n)}x]+\rho_0^{(n)}=c_0, \\[2mm] \dfrac{1}{2\pi}\int_{-\pi}^{\pi} e^{-i\nu x}\,d\alpha_n(x)=\dfrac{1}{2\pi}\int_{-\pi}^{\pi} e^{-i\nu x}\,d[\alpha_n(x)-\rho_0^{(n)}x]=c_\nu, \\[2mm] \hspace{4cm}\nu=\pm 1,\,\pm 2,\,...,\,\pm n. \end{cases} \tag{2}$$

We assume that $\alpha_n(-\pi)=0$ and also that $\alpha_n(x)$ is continuous from the right.

(b) Since

$$0<\sum_{k=1}^{m}\rho_k=c_0-\rho_0^{(n)}\leqq c_0,$$

the distribution functions $\{\alpha_n(x)\}$ are uniformly bounded. By the theorem in 1.3 (c) we can select a subsequence $\alpha_{n_j}(x)$ for which

$$\lim_{j\to\infty}\alpha_{n_j}(x)=\alpha(x)$$

exists and $\alpha(x)$ is a distribution function. Moreover [1.3 (3)] for each integer ν

$$\lim_{j\to\infty}\int_{-\pi}^{\pi}e^{-i\nu x}\,d\alpha_{n_j}(x)=\int_{-\pi}^{\pi}e^{-i\nu x}\,d\alpha(x).$$

If j is sufficiently large, the left-hand integral is $=2\pi c_\nu$. Thus $\alpha(x)$ is a solution of the trigonometric moment problem.

CHAPTER 5

EIGENVALUES OF TOEPLITZ FORMS

In his papers [1, 2, 3] O. Toeplitz has studied the distribution of the 'eigenvalues' of an infinite matrix $T = (c_{\nu-\mu})$, where the indices μ and ν range from $-\infty$ to $+\infty$. A value λ is called an eigenvalue of the matrix T if the matrix $T - \lambda I$ has no bounded inverse; here I denotes the unit matrix. Assuming that the Laurent series $\sum\limits_{n=-\infty}^{\infty} c_n z^n$ is convergent in the ring $r' < |z| < r''$, where $0 < r' < 1 < r''$, Toeplitz proved [[3], pp. 360–1], that these eigenvalues coincide with the set of the complex values this Laurent series assumes *on* the unit circle $|z| = 1$. If $c_{-n} = \bar{c}_n$ the matrix T is Hermitian and the eigenvalues are, of course, all real.

In the present chapter we shall consider *finite* Toeplitz forms which are sections of an infinite one defined as in 1.10. In this case the result mentioned reappears in a modified (asymptotic) form.

5.1. Equal distribution

(a) The asymptotic distribution of the eigenvalues of Toeplitz forms as well as of other related forms to be studied in chapter 6 can be expressed in the terminology of the theory of 'equal distributions' due to H. Weyl (see Appendix).

DEFINITION. *For each n we consider a set of $n+1$ real numbers $a_1^{(n)}, a_2^{(n)}, \ldots, a_{n+1}^{(n)}$ and another set of the same kind $b_1^{(n)}, b_2^{(n)}, \ldots, b_{n+1}^{(n)}$. We assume that for each ν and n*

$$|a_\nu^{(n)}| < K, \quad |b_\nu^{(n)}| < K, \tag{1}$$

where K is independent of ν and n.

We say that the sets $\{a_\nu^{(n)}\}$ and $\{b_\nu^{(n)}\}$, $n \to \infty$, are equally distributed in the interval $[-K, K]$ if the following holds. Let $F(t)$ be an arbitrary continuous function in the interval $[-K, K]$; we have then

$$\lim_{n \to \infty} \frac{\sum\limits_{\nu=1}^{n+1} [F(a_\nu^{(n)}) - F(b_\nu^{(n)})]}{n+1} = 0. \tag{2}$$

(b) It is well known that the limit relation (2) will be proved for all continuous functions $F(t)$ if it holds for certain special sets of continuous functions. We mention two such special sets.

(i) $F(t) = t^s, s = 0, 1, 2, \ldots$. We have then

$$\lim_{n \to \infty} \frac{\sum_{\nu=1}^{n+1} [(a_\nu^{(n)})^s - (b_\nu^{(n)})^s]}{n+1} = 0. \tag{3}$$

(ii) $F(t) = \log(1 + zt)$ where z is real and $|z| < K^{-1}$. We have then

$$\lim_{n \to \infty} \left\{ \frac{(1 + za_1^{(n)})(1 + za_2^{(n)}) \ldots (1 + za_{n+1}^{(n)})}{(1 + zb_1^{(n)})(1 + zb_2^{(n)}) \ldots (1 + zb_{n+1}^{(n)})} \right\}^{1/(n+1)} = 1. \tag{4}$$

(c) From (i) or (ii) we derive the general theorem (2) by a familiar argument of the theory of equal distributions. We show, in particular, how (i) [i.e. (3)] can be concluded from (ii) [i.e. from (4)]. Assuming (4) we have

$$\lim_{n \to \infty} \frac{\sum_{\nu=1}^{n+1} [\log(1 + za_\nu^{(n)}) - \log(1 + zb_\nu^{(n)})]}{n+1} = 0.$$

The quotient following the limit sign is a single-valued and analytic function of the complex variable z provided $|z| < K^{-1}$. It is uniformly bounded in z and n provided $|z| < (2K)^{-1}$. (It is understood that all these functions are equal to zero if $z = 0$.) According to the assumption the limit relation holds for real z within the circle mentioned; owing to Vitali's theorem it will hold for all complex values from the same circle, and uniformly within a sufficiently small circle about $z = 0$. Hence the corresponding limit relation will hold for the coefficients of z^s. But these relations are identical with (3).

5.2. Asymptotic distribution of eigenvalues

(a) Let $f(x)$ be a real-valued function of the class L,

$$c_n = \frac{1}{2\pi} \int_{-\pi}^{\pi} e^{-inx} f(x) \, dx, \quad n = 0, \pm 1, \pm 2, \ldots, \tag{1}$$

its Fourier coefficients. We consider the finite Toeplitz forms

$$\begin{aligned} T_n(f) &= \sum_{\mu, \nu = 0, 1, 2 \ldots, n} c_{\nu-\mu} u_\mu \bar{u}_\nu \\ &= \frac{1}{2\pi} \int_{-\pi}^{\pi} |u_0 + u_1 e^{ix} + u_2 e^{2ix} + \ldots + u_n e^{nix}|^2 f(x) \, dx, \\ &\qquad\qquad\qquad\qquad\qquad\qquad n = 0, 1, 2, \ldots. \tag{2} \end{aligned}$$

The eigenvalues of the Hermitian form $T_n(f)$ are defined as the roots of the characteristic equation $\det T_n(f-\lambda)=0$; we denote them by

$$\lambda_1^{(n)}, \lambda_2^{(n)}, ..., \lambda_{n+1}^{(n)}. \tag{3}$$

As well known, these values are all real.

We observe that if a and b are arbitrary real numbers, the eigenvalues associated with the function $a+bf(x)$ will be $a+b\lambda_\nu^{(n)}$. Also the eigenvalues of $f(x+x_0)$, x_0 real constant, are the same as those of $f(x)$. Finally, let $f_1(x)$ and $f_2(x)$ be two real-valued functions of the class L and $\lambda_\nu^{(n)}$, $\mu_\nu^{(n)}$ the corresponding eigenvalues, each set ordered in a nondecreasing way. If $f_1(x)\leqq f_2(x)$ for all x, then $\lambda_\nu^{(n)}\leqq\mu_\nu^{(n)}$ for all ν. This follows from 1.18 (4).

Assume, for the sake of simplicity, that the eigenvalues of $f(x)$ are simple; then to each eigenvalue $\lambda_\nu^{(n)}$ a nonvanishing eigenvector $(u_{\nu 0}, u_{\nu 1}, ..., u_{\nu n})$ belongs, determined except a scalar factor, such that $T_n(f)-\lambda_\nu^{(n)}I=0$ for these values of u_p. Here I is the unit form $\Sigma\,|\,u_p\,|^2$.

Our purpose is to study the asymptotic distribution of the eigenvalues (3) as $n\to\infty$. Under suitable regularity conditions the Laurent series

$$\sum_{n=-\infty}^{\infty} c_n e^{inx} \tag{4}$$

represents the function $f(x)$; thus (see the introduction to this chapter) it can be expected that the eigenvalues (3) will be related to the values the function $f(x)$ assumes.

In some cases we are also interested in the asymptotic characterization of the eigenvectors associated with the function $f(x)$ as $n\to\infty$ [cf. 7.4 (c).]

(b) We assume that $m\leqq f(x)\leqq M$ for all real x. Then from (2)

$$m\leqq T_n(f)\leqq M \tag{5}$$

follows provided that the variables u_p are subjected to the condition

$$I=\sum_{p=0}^{n}|\,u_p\,|^2=\frac{1}{2\pi}\int_{-\pi}^{\pi}|\,u_0+u_1 e^{ix}+u_2 e^{2ix}+...+u_n e^{nix}\,|^2 dx=1.$$

Hence we have

$$m\leqq\lambda_\nu^{(n)}\leqq M, \quad \nu=1,2,...,n+1. \tag{6}$$

Our main theorem can be formulated as follows:

THEOREM. *Let $f(x)$ be a real-valued function of the class L. We denote by m and M the 'essential' lower and upper bound of $f(x)$, respectively,* *and assume that m and M are finite. If $F(\lambda)$ is any continuous function defined in the finite interval $m \leq \lambda \leq M$, we have*

$$\lim_{n \to \infty} \frac{F(\lambda_1^{(n)}) + F(\lambda_2^{(n)}) + \ldots + F(\lambda_{n+1}^{(n)})}{n+1} = \frac{1}{2\pi} \int_{-\pi}^{\pi} F[f(x)] \, dx. \qquad (7)$$

The essential lower bound of $f(x)$ is defined as the largest number m for which the inequality $f(x) \geq m$ holds with the exception of a set of measure 0. The definition of the essential upper bound is quite similar. Of course we may have in general $m = -\infty$ or $M = +\infty$.

We order the eigenvalues (3) in a nondecreasing way:

$$\lambda_1^{(n)} \leq \lambda_2^{(n)} \leq \ldots \leq \lambda_{n+1}^{(n)}. \qquad (8)$$

Then

$$\lambda_1^{(n)} \geq m, \quad \lambda_{n+1}^{(n)} \leq M. \qquad (9)$$

A consequence of the theorem is that

$$\lim_{n \to \infty} \lambda_1^{(n)} = m, \quad \lim_{n \to \infty} \lambda_{n+1}^{(n)} = M, \qquad (10)$$

and these equations will hold [see (f)] also in case $m = -\infty$ or $M = +\infty$. Similar limit relations hold for $\lambda_\nu^{(n)}$ and $\lambda_{n+2-\nu}^{(n)}$, where ν is fixed and $n \to \infty$.

(c) Using the definition of 5.1 (a) the limit relation (7) can be expressed as follows. The sets

$$\{\lambda_\nu^{(n)}\} \quad \text{and} \quad \left\{ f\left(-\pi + \frac{2\nu\pi}{n+2} \right) \right\}, \quad n \to \infty,$$

are equally distributed. Corresponding to the two special cases (i) and (ii) pointed out in 5.1 (b), we have the following special consequences of (7):

(i) $F(\lambda) = \lambda^s$, $s = 0, 1, 2, \ldots$, so that

$$\lim_{n \to \infty} \frac{(\lambda_1^{(n)})^s + (\lambda_2^{(n)})^s + \ldots + (\lambda_{n+1}^{(n)})^s}{n+1} = \frac{1}{2\pi} \int_{-\pi}^{\pi} [f(x)]^s \, dx. \qquad (11)$$

(ii) Let $m > 0$ so that $\lambda_\nu^{(n)} \geq m > 0$ holds. Denoting the determinant of the Toeplitz form (2) by $D_n(f)$ (Toeplitz determinant) we have $D_n(f) > 0$ and

$$\lim_{n \to \infty} [D_n(f)]^{1/(n+1)} = \exp\left\{ \frac{1}{2\pi} \int_{-\pi}^{\pi} \log f(x) \, dx \right\}. \qquad (12)$$

Since

$$D_n(f) = \lambda_1^{(n)} \lambda_2^{(n)} \ldots \lambda_{n+1}^{(n)},$$

5

we have

$$\log D_n(f) = \log \lambda_1^{(n)} + \log \lambda_2^{(n)} + \ldots + \log \lambda_{n+1}^{(n)},$$

so that (12) is indeed equivalent to the special case $F(\lambda) = \log \lambda$, $\lambda > 0$.

(d) We indicate now a proof of (ii), that is, of the limit relation (12). This will yield a proof of (7), and of course also the assertion (i).

The limit formula (12) is a simple consequence of the theorem proved in 3.1. Indeed, the minimum μ_n of the Toeplitz form $T_n(f)$ under the side condition $u_0 = 1$ (or $u_n = 1$) is $D_n(f)/D_{n-1}(f)$, where $D_n(f)$ is the determinant of $T_n(f)$ [cf. 2.2 (a)]. Hence by using the theorem quoted,

$$\lim_{n \to \infty} \frac{D_n(f)}{D_{n-1}(f)} = \exp \left\{ \frac{1}{2\pi} \int_{-\pi}^{\pi} \log f(x)\, dx \right\}. \tag{13}$$

This implies of course (12).

(e) More than the limit relations (10) hold: if ϵ is an arbitrarily small positive quantity, the number of those eigenvalues (3) for which $m \leqq \lambda_\nu^{(n)} < m + \epsilon$ [or $M - \epsilon < \lambda_\nu^{(n)} \leqq M$] holds, tends to $+\infty$ with n.

(f) Let $m = -\infty$. In order to prove the first relation (10) we define for any positive ω the function $f_\omega(x)$ as follows:

$$f_\omega(x) = \begin{cases} f(x) & \text{if } f(x) \geqq -\omega, \\ -\omega & \text{if } f(x) \leqq -\omega. \end{cases}$$

We must have then $\quad \lim_{\omega \to \infty} [\inf f_\omega(x)] = -\infty.$

Denoting by $\lambda_\nu^{(n)}(\omega)$ the eigenvalues of $f_\omega(x)$ ordered as the $\lambda_\nu^{(n)}$ are, we have $\lambda_1^{(n)} \leqq \lambda_1^{(n)}(\omega)$ since $f(x) \leqq f_\omega(x)$. Thus

$$\limsup_{n \to \infty} \lambda_1^{(n)} \leqq \limsup_{n \to \infty} \lambda_1^{(n)}(\omega) = \inf f_\omega(x).$$

This establishes the assertion.

We deal in a similar fashion with the case $M = +\infty$, and more generally with the eigenvalues $\lambda_\nu^{(n)}$, $\lambda_{n+2-\nu}^{(n)}$ where ν is fixed, $n \to \infty$.

5.3. Examples

(a) Let $f(x)$ be a trigonometric polynomial of the first order:

$$f(x) = a_0 + 2(a_1 \cos x + b_1 \sin x) = a_0 - 2(a_1^2 + b_1^2)^{\frac{1}{2}} \cos(x - \xi). \tag{1}$$

We exclude the case $f(x) = a_0$ so that a_1 and b_1 are not both zero. The meaning of ξ is clear: $f(\xi)$ is the minimum of $f(x)$. We prove that in this case the eigenvalues $\lambda_\nu^{(n)}$ are (except for the order) the following ordinates:

$$f\left(\xi + \frac{\nu\pi}{n+2}\right), \quad \nu = 1, 2, \ldots, n+1. \tag{2}$$

In view of the remark on the eigenvalues of $a + bf(x)$ and $f(x + x_0)$ [cf. 5.2 (a)] it suffices to discuss the case $f(x) = -2\cos x$. We have then

$$T_n(f) = \sum_{p=0}^{n} |u_p|^2 - \sum_{p=0}^{n-1} (u_p \bar{u}_{p+1} + \bar{u}_p u_{p+1}). \tag{3}$$

The eigenvalues satisfy the well-known characteristic equation

$$\Delta_n(\lambda) = \begin{vmatrix} -\lambda & -1 & 0 & \ldots & 0 \\ -1 & -\lambda & -1 & \ldots & 0 \\ 0 & -1 & -\lambda & \ldots & 0 \\ \ldots & \ldots & \ldots & \ldots & \ldots \\ 0 & 0 & 0 & -1 & -\lambda \end{vmatrix} = 0. \tag{4}$$

Expanding this determinant we obtain the recurrence relation

$$\Delta_n(\lambda) = -\lambda \Delta_{n-1}(\lambda) - \Delta_{n-2}(\lambda), \quad n = 2, 3, 4, \ldots, \tag{5}$$

to which the 'initial conditions' $\Delta_0(\lambda) = -\lambda$, $\Delta_1(\lambda) = \lambda^2 - 1$ have to be added. Equation (5) holds also for $n = 1$ provided we define $\Delta_{-1}(\lambda) = 1$. Introducing the notation $\lambda = -2\cos x$, (5) will be

$$\Delta_n(-2\cos x) = 2\cos x \cdot \Delta_{n-1}(-2\cos x) - \Delta_{n-2}(-2\cos x). \tag{6}$$

The equation $\rho^2 = 2\cos x \cdot \rho - 1$ has the roots $e^{\pm ix}$ so that

$$\Delta_n(-2\cos x) = A e^{inx} + B e^{-inx},$$

where the constants A, B can be determined from the cases $n = -1$ and $n = 0$. Thus

$$\Delta_n(-2\cos x) = \frac{\sin(n+2)x}{\sin x}. \tag{7}$$

This yields the eigenvalues

$$\lambda_\nu^{(n)} = -2\cos\frac{\nu\pi}{n+2}, \quad \nu = 1, 2, \ldots, n+1. \tag{8}$$

5-2

(b) The same case (1) can be dealt with by another method which is not without interest. It makes use of a pair of identities which can be formulated as follows. Let

$$x_\nu = \frac{\nu\pi}{n+2}, \quad l_{\nu\mu} = \left(\frac{2}{n+2}\right)^{\frac{1}{2}} \sin(\mu+1)x_\nu,$$

$$\nu = 1, 2, ..., n+1; \ \mu = 0, 1, ..., n. \quad (9)$$

We have then identically in the complex variables u_p, $z = e^{ix}$:

$$\left.\begin{array}{l}
\dfrac{1}{2\pi}\displaystyle\int_{-\pi}^{\pi} |\, u_0 + u_1 z + ... + u_n z^n\,|^2\, dx \\[2mm]
\qquad\qquad = \displaystyle\sum_{\nu=1}^{n+1} |\, l_{\nu 0} u_0 + l_{\nu 1} u_1 + ... + l_{\nu n} u_n\,|^2, \\[4mm]
\dfrac{1}{2\pi}\displaystyle\int_{-\pi}^{\pi} \cos x\, |\, u_0 + u_1 z + ... + u_n z^n\,|^2\, dx \\[2mm]
\qquad\qquad = \displaystyle\sum_{\nu=1}^{n+1} \cos x_\nu\, |\, l_{\nu 0} u_0 + l_{\nu 1} u_1 + ... + l_{\nu n} u_n\,|^2.
\end{array}\right\} \quad (10)$$

From (10) we obtain the eigenvalues $-2\cos x_\nu$ and also the eigenvectors $(l_{\nu 0}, l_{\nu 1}, ..., l_{\nu n})$.

Equations (10) follow from the well-known formula of 'mechanical quadrature'

$$\frac{1}{2\pi}\int_{-\pi}^{\pi} \phi(x)\, dx = \frac{1}{2N}\sum_{\nu=-N+1}^{N} \phi\left(\frac{\nu\pi}{N}\right), \quad (11)$$

holding for any trigonometric polynomial $\phi(x)$ whose degree does not exceed $2N-1$. We choose with real u_μ

$$\phi(x) = \tfrac{1}{2}(a + b\cos x)\left|\sum_{\mu=0}^{n} u_\mu e^{i(\mu+1)x} - \sum_{\mu=0}^{n} u_\mu e^{-i(\mu+1)x}\right|^2,$$

where a and b are parameters. This trigonometric polynomial is of degree $2n+3$ so that (11) will be applicable with $N = n+2$. Since

$$\int_{-\pi}^{\pi} (a + b\cos x)\sum_{\mu=0}^{n} u_\mu e^{i(\mu+1)x}\sum_{\mu=0}^{n} u_\mu e^{i(\mu+1)x}\, dx = 0,$$

we have

$$\frac{1}{2\pi}\int_{-\pi}^{\pi} \phi(x)\, dx = \frac{1}{2\pi}\int_{-\pi}^{\pi} (a + b\cos x)\left|\sum_{\mu=0}^{n} u_\mu e^{i(\mu+1)x}\right|^2 dx.$$

On the other hand,

$$\frac{1}{2(n+2)}\sum_{\nu=-n-1}^{n+2}\phi\left(\frac{\nu\pi}{n+2}\right)=\frac{1}{2(n+2)}\sum_{\nu=-n-1}^{n+2}\phi(x_\nu)$$

$$=\frac{1}{n+2}\sum_{\nu=-n-1}^{n+2}(a+b\cos x_\nu)$$

$$\times\left|\sum_{\mu=0}^{n}u_\mu\sin(\mu+1)x_\nu\right|^2.$$

We used here the symbol x_ν in an extended sense, namely, for all ν with $-n-1\leq\nu\leq n+2$. The quantity in the latter sum does not change if x_ν is replaced by $-x_\nu$ and it vanishes for $x_\nu=0$ or π. This results in the following expression:

$$\frac{2}{n+2}\sum_{\nu=1}^{n+1}(a+b\cos x_\nu)\left|\sum_{\mu=0}^{n}u_\mu\sin(\mu+1)x_\nu\right|^2,$$

which yields the formulas (10).

(c) Let $f(x)$ be the reciprocal of a positive trigonometric polynomial of the first order. For the sake of simplicity we consider

$$f(x)=\frac{1-r^2}{1-2r\cos x+r^2}=\sum_{n=-\infty}^{\infty}r^{|n|}e^{inx},\quad 0<r<1,\tag{12}$$

this specialization being without importance. The characteristic equation is in this case:

$$\Delta_n(\lambda)=\begin{vmatrix}1-\lambda & r & r^2 & \dots & r^n\\ r & 1-\lambda & r & \dots & r^{n-1}\\ r^2 & r & 1-\lambda & \dots & r^{n-2}\\ \dots & \dots & \dots & \dots & \dots\\ r^n & r^{n-1} & r^{n-2} & \dots & 1-\lambda\end{vmatrix}=0.\tag{13}$$

Multiplying the second row of this determinant by r, subtracting it from the first and performing a similar operation with the columns, we find

$$\Delta_n(\lambda)=\begin{vmatrix}1-\lambda-r^2(1+\lambda) & r\lambda & 0 & \dots & 0\\ r\lambda & 1-\lambda & r & \dots & r^{n-1}\\ 0 & r & 1-\lambda & \dots & r^{n-2}\\ \dots & \dots & \dots & \dots & \dots\\ 0 & r^{n-1} & r^{n-2} & \dots & 1-\lambda\end{vmatrix}$$

$$=[1-\lambda-r^2(1+\lambda)]\Delta_{n-1}(\lambda)-r^2\lambda^2\Delta_{n-2}(\lambda),\quad n=2,3,4,\dots.\tag{14}$$

This recurrence relation holds also for $n=1$ provided we put $\Delta_{-1}(\lambda)=1$.

In order to find an explicit representation of $\Delta_n(\lambda)$, we write conveniently

$$\lambda = \frac{1-r^2}{1-2r\cos x + r^2} = f(x) \tag{15}$$

and form the equation

$$\begin{aligned}\rho^2 &= [1-\lambda-r^2(1+\lambda)]\rho - r^2\lambda^2 \\ &= -2\lambda r\rho \cos x - r^2\lambda^2\end{aligned} \tag{16}$$

with the roots $-\lambda r e^{\pm ix}$. Following a similar procedure as in (a) it is easy to verify the formula

$$\begin{aligned}\Delta_n(\lambda) &= \frac{(-\lambda r)^{n+1}}{1-r^2}\left(\frac{\sin(n+2)x}{\sin x} - 2r\frac{\sin(n+1)x}{\sin x} + r^2\frac{\sin nx}{\sin x}\right) \\ &= \frac{(-\lambda r)^{n+1}}{1-r^2}p_n(\cos x).\end{aligned} \tag{17}$$

The expression $p_n(t)$ defined by (17) is a polynomial of degree $n+1$ in $t=\cos x$. It has $n+1$ real and distinct zeros $\cos t_\nu^{(n)}$, where

$$0 < t_1^{(n)} < t_2^{(n)} < \ldots < t_{n+1}^{(n)} < \pi,$$

and the eigenvalues (ordered in increasing order) will be

$$\lambda_\nu^{(n)} = f(t_{n+2-\nu}^{(n)}), \quad \nu = 1, 2, \ldots, n+1. \tag{18}$$

The evaluation of the zeros $t_\nu^{(n)}$ in explicit terms does not seem to be feasible. However, it is easy to show that they are separated by the quantities x_ν used in (b). Indeed, $1 \leq \nu \leq n+1$,

$$p_n(\cos x_\nu) = (-1)^\nu \cdot 2r(1 - r\cos x_\nu),$$

so that

$$\operatorname{sgn} p_n(\cos x_\nu) = (-1)^\nu.$$

Also we see by direct substitution that the latter equation holds for $\nu = 0$, so that

$$0 < t_1^{(n)} < x_1 < t_2^{(n)} < x_2 < \ldots < t_{n+1}^{(n)} < x_{n+1} < \pi. \tag{19}$$

It is easy to obtain an asymptotic expression for the 'extreme' eigenvalues $\lambda_\nu^{(n)}$, $\lambda_{n+2-\nu}^{(n)}$, where ν is fixed and $n \to \infty$. We have

$$\begin{aligned}\lim_{n\to\infty} n^{-1}p_n\left(\cos\frac{z}{n}\right) &= (1-r)^2\frac{\sin z}{z}, \\ \lim_{n\to\infty}(-1)^{n+1}n^{-1}p_n\left(-\cos\frac{z}{n}\right) &= (1+r)^2\frac{\sin z}{z}.\end{aligned} \tag{20}$$

Here z is an arbitrary complex number and the relations (20) hold uniformly for $|z| \leq R$. Consequently for fixed ν

$$t_\nu^{(n)} \cong \pi - t_{n+2-\nu}^{(n)} \cong \frac{\nu\pi}{n+2},$$

so that

$$\lambda_\nu^{(n)} = f\left(\pi + \frac{\nu\pi + \epsilon}{n+2}\right), \quad \lambda_{n+2-\nu}^{(n)} = f\left(\frac{\nu\pi + \epsilon}{n+2}\right), \tag{21}$$

where $\epsilon = \epsilon_\nu^{(n)} \to 0$ as $n \to \infty$. Compare (21) with (2).

(d) A generalization of the case dealt with in (c) is the following: $f(x) = [\phi(x)]^{-1}$, where $\phi(x)$ is a positive trigonometric polynomial. If $\phi(x)$ is of the precise degree p we can represent it in the form $|\delta(z)|^2$, $z = e^{ix}$, where $\delta(z)$ is a polynomial of the precise degree p not vanishing in the unit circle $|z| \leq 1$; also we may assume that $\delta(0) > 0$ [cf. 1.12 (b)]. By using the notation introduced in 1.14 (e) we have $g(f; z) = [\delta(z)]^{-1}$.

In this case the Toeplitz determinants $D_n(f)$ can be computed in explicit terms, at least for $n \geq p$. (A discussion of the eigenvalues seems to be difficult.) Indeed, we have for the geometric mean of $f(x)$:

$$G(f) = \exp\left\{\frac{1}{2\pi}\int_{-\pi}^{\pi} \log f(x)\,dx\right\} = \exp\left\{-\frac{1}{\pi}\int_{-\pi}^{\pi} \Re \log \delta(z)\,dx\right\}$$

$$= \exp\{-2\Re \log \delta(0)\} = [\delta(0)]^{-2}, \quad z = e^{ix}, \tag{22}$$

since $\Re \log \delta(z)$ is a regular harmonic function throughout the unit circle $|z| \leq 1$. Now by the theorem of 3.1:

$$G(f) \leq \mu_n = \frac{D_n(f)}{D_{n-1}(f)} \leq \frac{1}{2\pi}\int_{-\pi}^{\pi} \left|\frac{u_0 + u_1 z + \ldots + u_n z^n}{\delta(z)}\right|^2 dx,$$

where $z = e^{ix}$ and $u_0 = 1$; $u_1, u_2, \ldots, u_n$ are arbitrary complex. Let $n \geq p$; we choose

$$u_0 + u_1 z + \ldots + u_n z^n = \frac{\delta(z)}{\delta(0)},$$

so that

$$G(f) \leq \frac{D_n(f)}{D_{n-1}(f)} \leq [\delta(0)]^{-2} = G(f), \quad \frac{D_n(f)}{D_{n-1}(f)} = G(f)$$

follows. Hence for $n \geq p$

$$D_n(f) = D_{p-1}(f)\,[G(f)]^{n-p+1}. \tag{23}$$

In this special case it is easy to confirm 5.2 (12) and 5.2 (13).

A representation of $D_{p-1}(f)$ will be found in 5.5.

5.4. Extreme eigenvalues

Let $f(x)$ be a function of the class L, $-\pi \leq x \leq \pi$. We denote by m and M the essential lower bound and the essential upper bound of $f(x)$, respectively. We order the eigenvalues $\lambda_\nu^{(n)}$ of $f(x)$ again in a non-decreasing way so that the inequalities 5.2 (8) are satisfied. According to 5.2 (b) the relations

$$\lim_{n \to \infty} \lambda_\nu^{(n)} = m, \quad \lim_{n \to \infty} \lambda_{n+2-\nu}^{(n)} = M, \tag{1}$$

hold for any *fixed* value of ν. Our purpose is now to investigate the mode of this convergence, in particular the order of magnitude of the differences $\lambda_\nu^{(n)} - m$ and $M - \lambda_{n+2-\nu}^{(n)}$ as n becomes large. It will be necessary to introduce certain restrictions on the function $f(x)$.

(a) We consider a class of functions satisfying the following condition:

CONDITION A. *Let $f(x)$ be of the class C. Let $\min f(x) = f(x_0) = m$ and let $x = x_0$ be the only value of x (mod 2π) for which this minimum is attained. Moreover, we assume that $f(x)$ has a continuous second derivative in a certain neighborhood of x_0. Finally, let $f''(x_0) \neq 0$.*

Obviously $f''(x_0) > 0$, and we have

$$\lim_{x \to x_0} \frac{f(x)}{1 - \cos(x - x_0)} = f''(x_0). \tag{2}$$

We prove then the following theorem:

THEOREM. *Let $f(x)$ satisfy condition A. We have for a fixed ν and $n \to \infty$*

$$\left.\begin{array}{l} \lambda_\nu^{(n)} - m \cong f(x_0 + \nu\pi/n) - f(x_0) \cong c\nu^2\pi^2/n^2, \\ c = \tfrac{1}{2}f''(x_0), \quad \nu = 1, 2, 3, \ldots. \end{array}\right\} \tag{3}$$

A similar result holds for $\lambda_{n+2-\nu}^{(n)}$. As an example we mention

$$f(x) = b_0 - \sum_{n=1}^{\infty} b_n \cos nx,$$

where $b_n > 0$ and $\Sigma n^2 b_n$ is convergent. Then $x_0 = 0$,

$$m = b_0 - \sum_{n=1}^{\infty} b_n, \quad c = \tfrac{1}{2} \sum_{n=1}^{\infty} n^2 b_n.$$

(b) We prove the theorem by making use of the following simple lemma:

LEMMA. *Let $f(x)$ satisfy condition A and let $x_0 = 0$, $f(0) = m = 0$. To a given $\epsilon > 0$ we can find two functions $\underline{f}(x)$ and $\bar{f}(x)$ satisfying the following conditions:*

(i)
$$\underline{f}(x) = (1 - \cos x)\,[a + b(1 - \cos x)]^{-1},$$

$$\bar{f}(x) = (1 - \cos x)\,[c + d(1 - \cos x)],$$

where a, b, c, d are positive constants;

(ii) *for all x we have* $\quad \underline{f}(x) \leqq f(x) \leqq \bar{f}(x);$

(iii) *we have*
$$|f''(0) - \underline{f}''(0)| < \epsilon, \quad |f''(0) - \bar{f}''(0)| < \epsilon.$$

For the proof we form the function $F(x) = (1 - \cos x)^{-1} f(x)$ which is positive and continuous; $F(0) = f''(0)$. First we determine a neighborhood $[-x', x']$ of $x = 0$ in which $F(x) < F(0) + \frac{1}{2}\epsilon = c$ holds; then we choose d so large that $d(1 - \cos x') > \max F(x)$. As a result the second inequalities in (ii) and (iii) will hold. By applying a similar reasoning to $[F(x)]^{-1}$ the function $\underline{f}(x)$ can be obtained.

(c) In view of the remark made in 5.2 (a) concerning the eigenvalues of two functions $f_1(x), f_2(x)$ satisfying the inequality $f_1(x) \leqq f_2(x)$, it suffices to prove the above theorem for the special functions $\underline{f}(x)$, $\bar{f}(x)$ defined in the lemma.

The case of $\underline{f}(x)$ can be reduced to that treated in 5.3 (c) since

$$\frac{1 - \cos x}{a + b(1 - \cos x)} = \alpha - \beta \frac{1 - r^2}{1 - 2r \cos x + r^2}$$

$$= \alpha - \frac{\beta(1 - r^2)}{(1 - r)^2 + 2r(1 - \cos x)}.$$

Here a, b are given positive numbers and α, β, r can be determined in such a manner that $\alpha, \beta > 0$, $0 < r < 1$. Indeed,

$$\alpha = \frac{1}{b}, \quad \beta = \frac{1 - r}{1 + r}\frac{1}{b}, \quad \frac{(1 - r)^2}{2r} = \frac{a}{b}.$$

Thus for a function of the type $\underline{f}(x)$ the assertion follows from 5.3 (21).

(d) As to the function $\bar{f}(x)$ we can assume that it has the form

$$\bar{f}(x) = 1 - \cos x + d(1 - \cos x)^2, \quad d > 0. \tag{4}$$

We compare the eigenvalues $\lambda_\nu^{(n)}$ of $f(x)$ with the eigenvalues

$$\lambda_\nu = 1 - \cos x_\nu \quad \text{of} \quad 1 - \cos x,$$

where x_ν has the same meaning as in 5.3 (9). We shall use the vectors

$$\mathbf{l}_\nu: \quad l_{\nu 0}, l_{\nu 1}, \ldots, l_{\nu n},$$

$$\mathbf{u}: \quad u_0, u_1, \ldots, u_n,$$

where $l_{\nu \mu}$ is defined by 5.3 (9). By the inequality 1.18 (4) we have

$$\lambda_\nu < \lambda_\nu^{(n)} < T_n(\bar f)/\Sigma\,|\,u_p\,|^2 = T_n(\bar f)/|\,\mathbf{u}\,|^2,$$

where

$$T_n(\bar f) = \frac{1}{2\pi} \int_{-\pi}^{\pi} (1 - \cos x)\,|\,u_0 + u_1 z + \ldots + u_n z^n\,|^2\,dx$$

$$+ \frac{d}{2\pi} \int_{-\pi}^{\pi} (1 - \cos x)^2\,|\,u_0 + u_1 z + \ldots + u_n z^n\,|^2\,dx, \quad z = e^{ix}, \quad (5)$$

is the nth Toeplitz form associated with the function $\bar f(x)$; the inequality holds for any nonzero vector $\mathbf{u}$ satisfying certain suitable $\nu - 1$ side conditions.

We choose the real constants $A_1, A_2, \ldots, A_\nu$ not all zero so that the vector

$$\mathbf{u} = A_1 \mathbf{l}_1 + A_2 \mathbf{l}_2 + \ldots + A_\nu \mathbf{l}_\nu \qquad (6)$$

satisfies these side conditions. We adopt the normalization

$$\mathbf{u}^2 = A_1^2 + A_2^2 + \ldots + A_\nu^2 = 1. \qquad (7)$$

Now the first part of (5) is, in view of 5.3 (10),

$$\sum_{h=1}^{n+1} (1 - \cos x_h)\,(\mathbf{l}_h, \mathbf{u})^2 = \sum_{h=1}^{n+1} \lambda_h (\mathbf{l}_h, \mathbf{u})^2 = \sum_{h=1}^{\nu} \lambda_h A_h^2 \leq \lambda_\nu \sum_{h=1}^{\nu} A_h^2 = \lambda_\nu \cong f(\nu \pi/n)$$

provided ν is fixed and $n \to \infty$. We show that the second part of (5) is $O(n^{-3})$. Indeed, $(1 - \cos x)^2 = \frac{1}{4}\,|\,1 - z\,|^4$, and

$$\frac{1}{2\pi} \int_{-\pi}^{\pi} |\,(1-z)^2\,(u_0 + u_1 z + \ldots + u_n z^n)\,|^2\,dx$$

$$= \frac{1}{2\pi} \int_{-\pi}^{\pi} \left|\,\sum_{h=0}^{n+2} (u_h + u_{h-2} - 2u_{h-1})\,z^h\,\right|^2\,dx$$

$$= \sum_{h=0}^{n+2} |\,u_h + u_{h-2} - 2u_{h-1}\,|^2, \quad u_{-2} = u_{-1} = u_{n+1} = u_{n+2} = 0.$$

But for fixed, ν, h and k,

$$u_h = A_1 l_{1h} + A_2 l_{2h} + \ldots + A_\nu l_{\nu h},$$

$$u_h^2 < l_{1h}^2 + l_{2h}^2 + \ldots + l_{\nu h}^2 = O(n^{-3})$$

since $l_{kh}=O(n^{-\frac{1}{2}}x_k)=O(n^{-\frac{3}{2}})$. Similar bounds hold for u_{n-h}. Further we have for *any* h

$$(u_h+u_{h-2}-2u_{h-1})^2 \le \sum_{k=1}^{\nu}(l_{kh}+l_{k,h-2}-2l_{k,h-1})^2,$$

$$l_{kh}+l_{k,h-2}-2l_{k,h-1}=\left(\frac{2}{n+2}\right)^{\frac{1}{2}}[\sin(h+1)x_k+\sin(h-1)x_k-2\sin hx_k]$$

$$=\left(\frac{2}{n+2}\right)^{\frac{1}{2}}2\sin hx_k(\cos x_k-1)=O(n^{-\frac{1}{2}}x_k^2)$$

$$=O(n^{-\frac{1}{2}}n^{-2})=O(n^{-\frac{5}{2}})$$

and

$$\sum_{h=0}^{n+2}n^{-5}=O(n^{-4}).$$

This establishes the assertion.

5.5. Refinement of the distribution theorem

In certain cases the theorem proved in 5.2 can be refined in the sense that for appropriate functions $f(x)$ and $F(\lambda)$ the limit of the expression

$$(n+1)\left\{\frac{F(\lambda_1^{(n)})+F(\lambda_2^{(n)})+\ldots+F(\lambda_{n+1}^{(n)})}{n+1}-\frac{1}{2\pi}\int_{-\pi}^{\pi}F[f(x)]\,dx\right\}$$

$$=F(\lambda_1^{(n)})+F(\lambda_2^{(n)})+\ldots+F(\lambda_{n+1}^{(n)})-(n+1)\frac{1}{2\pi}\int_{-\pi}^{\pi}F[f(x)]\,dx$$

as $n\to\infty$, can be asserted and even evaluated. Such a case is

$$F(\lambda)=\log\lambda,\quad \lambda>0,$$

provided that $f(x)$ satisfies certain restrictive conditions. This leads to a refinement of the limit theorem 5.2 (12) on Toeplitz determinants, without involving of course the corresponding refinements of the limit theorem 5.2 (11).

(a) We consider a class of functions satisfying the following condition.

CONDITION B. *Let $f(x)$ be a positive function of the class C. Moreover, we assume that $f'(x)$ exists and satisfies the Lipschitz condition*

$$|f'(x_1)-f'(x_2)|<K|x_1-x_2|^\alpha,\quad K>0,0<\alpha<1. \tag{1}$$

We denote by $g(z) = g(f; z)$ the analytic function associated with the function $f(x)$ in the sense of 1.14 (e). This function is regular and different from zero in the open unit circle $|z| < 1$. We show that in the present case (that is, under condition B) it is continuous in the closed unit circle $|z| \leq 1$. Indeed, let us form the function

$$\log g(z) = h(z) = \frac{1}{4\pi} \int_{-\pi}^{\pi} \log f(x) \frac{1 + z e^{-ix}}{1 - z e^{-ix}} dx = \sum_{n=0}^{\infty} h_n z^n, \quad |z| < 1; \quad (2)$$

the coefficients h_n of this power series are closely related to the Fourier coefficients of the function $\log f(x)$. This function satisfies also condition B, consequently we have $h_n = O(n^{-1-\alpha})$. (See Appendix.) Hence $h(z)$ and $g(z)$ are continuous for $|z| \leq 1$, $f(x) = |g(e^{ix})|^2$ and

$$\frac{1}{\pi} \iint \left| \frac{g'(z)}{g(z)} \right|^2 d\sigma = \frac{1}{\pi} \iint |h'(z)|^2 d\sigma = \sum_{n=0}^{\infty} n |h_n|^2 \qquad (3)$$

is finite, the latter series being convergent; here $d\sigma$ denotes the area element of the unit circle.

Now we have the following theorem:

THEOREM. *Let $f(x)$ satisfy condition B; we denote by $G(f)$ the geometric mean of $f(x)$ and by $g(z) = g(f; z)$ the analytic function defined in 1.14 (e). If $D_n(f)$ is the determinant of the n-th Toeplitz form associated with the function $f(x)$, we have*

$$\lim_{n \to \infty} \frac{D_n(f)}{[G(f)]^{n+1}} = \exp \left\{ \frac{1}{\pi} \iint \left| \frac{g'(z)}{g(z)} \right|^2 d\sigma \right\}. \qquad (4)$$

The integration on the right is extended over the unit circle $|z| \leq 1$.

The existence of this limit (not necessarily its finiteness) is easy to establish, even for arbitrary nonnegative functions $f(x)$ for which $f(x)$ and $\log f(x)$ belong to the class L. Indeed, according to 3.1 the quantity $D_n(f)/D_{n-1}(f)$ is never less than $G(f)$ (which is its limit as $n \to \infty$), so that

$$\frac{D_n(f)}{[G(f)]^{n+1}} \geq \frac{D_{n-1}(f)}{[G(f)]^n}. \qquad (5)$$

Thus the ratio in question is nondecreasing.

(b) For the proof of the theorem we consider first the special case $f(x) = [\phi(x)]^{-1}$, where $\phi(x)$ is a positive trigonometric polynomial of the precise degree p. This is the special case dealt with in 5.3 (d); following the notation introduced there we have

$$g(z) = g(f; z) = [\delta(z)]^{-1}, \quad G(f) = [g(f; 0)]^2 = [\delta(0)]^{-2}.$$

Also, in view of 5.3 (23)

$$\frac{D_n(f)}{[G(f)]^{n+1}}=\frac{D_{p-1}(f)}{[G(f)]^p}, \quad n\geqq p. \tag{6}$$

In order to verify (4) we evaluate first the determinant $D_{p-1}(f)$ of the Toeplitz form

$$T_{p-1}(f)=\frac{1}{2\pi}\int_{-\pi}^{\pi}\left|\sum_{\mu=0}^{p-1}u_\mu e^{-i\mu x}\right|^2 f(x)\,dx$$

$$=\frac{1}{2\pi}\int_{-\pi}^{\pi}\left|\frac{u(z)}{\delta(z)}\right|^2 dx, \quad z=e^{ix}, \tag{7}$$

where

$$u(z)=\sum_{\mu=0}^{p-1}u_\mu z^{p-1-\mu}. \tag{8}$$

We denote the (distinct) zeros of $\delta(z)$ by $z_0,z_1,\ldots,z_{p-1}$ so that

$$\delta(z)=\gamma(z_0-z)(z_1-z)\ldots(z_{p-1}-z), \tag{9}$$

where $|z_\mu|>1$ and the product $\gamma z_0 z_1\ldots z_{p-1}$ is real and positive. Now, by Lagrange's formula,

$$\frac{u(z)}{\delta(z)}=\sum_{\nu=0}^{p-1}\frac{u(z_\nu)}{\delta'(z_\nu)}\frac{1}{z-z_\nu}=\sum_{\nu=0}^{p-1}\frac{v_\nu}{z-z_\nu}, \tag{10}$$

where

$$v_\nu=\frac{u(z_\nu)}{\delta'(z_\nu)}=\frac{1}{\delta'(z_\nu)}\sum_{\mu=0}^{p-1}u_\mu z_\nu^{p-1-\mu}, \quad \nu=0,1,\ldots,p-1. \tag{11}$$

This system (11) represents a linear transformation of $\{u_\mu\}$ into $\{v_\nu\}$ with the Jacobian

$$J=\frac{\partial(v_0,v_1,\ldots,v_{p-1})}{\partial(u_0,u_1,\ldots,u_{p-1})}=\frac{\Pi(z_\kappa-z_\lambda)}{\delta'(z_0)\,\delta'(z_1)\ldots\delta'(z_{p-1})},$$
$$\kappa<\lambda;\ \kappa,\lambda=0,1,\ldots,p-1. \tag{12}$$

Inserting for $\delta'(z_\nu)$ the expression obtained from (9) by differentiation and by the substitution $z=z_\nu$, we find the following other form of the Jacobian:

$$J=(-1)^{\frac{1}{2}p(p+1)}\gamma^{-p}\Pi(z_\kappa-z_\lambda)^{-1}. \tag{13}$$

(c) Employing (7) and (10) we find the following transformation of $T_{p-1}(f)$:

$$T_{p-1}(f)=\sum_{\nu,\mu=0,1,\ldots,p-1}v_\nu\bar{v}_\mu\frac{1}{2\pi}\int_{-\pi}^{\pi}\frac{dx}{(z-z_\nu)(\bar{z}-\bar{z}_\mu)}, \quad z=e^{ix}. \tag{14}$$

The coefficient of $v_\nu \bar{v}_\mu$ can be written as a line integral extended over the unit circle $|z| = 1$:

$$\frac{1}{2\pi i} \int \frac{dz/z}{(z-z_\nu)(z^{-1}-\bar{z}_\mu)} = \frac{1}{2\pi i} \int \frac{dz}{(z-z_\nu)(1-\bar{z}_\mu z)} = \frac{1}{z_\nu \bar{z}_\mu - 1}. \quad (15)$$

The determinant of (14) is

$$\det\left(\frac{1}{z_\nu \bar{z}_\mu - 1}\right) = \frac{1}{z_0 z_1 \cdots z_{p-1}} \det\left(\frac{1}{\bar{z}_\mu - z_\nu^{-1}}\right)$$

$$= \frac{1}{z_0 z_1 \cdots z_{p-1}} \frac{\Pi(\bar{z}_\kappa - \bar{z}_\lambda)(z_\lambda^{-1} - z_\kappa^{-1})}{\Pi(\bar{z}_\mu - z_\nu^{-1})} = \frac{\Pi |z_\kappa - z_\lambda|^2}{\Pi |\bar{z}_\mu z_\nu - 1|}. \quad (16)$$

Consequently,

$$D_{p-1}(f) = |J|^2 \det\left(\frac{1}{z_\nu \bar{z}_\mu - 1}\right) = \frac{|\gamma|^{-2p}}{\Pi |\bar{z}_\mu z_\nu - 1|}, \quad (17)$$

and, in view of (6), $G(f) = (\gamma z_0 z_1 \cdots z_{p-1})^{-2}$,

$$\frac{D_n(f)}{[G(f)]^{n+1}} = \frac{|z_0 z_1 \cdots z_{p-1}|^{2p}}{\Pi |\bar{z}_\mu z_\nu - 1|}, \quad \mu, \nu = 0, 1, \ldots, p-1; \ n \geq p. \quad (18)$$

(d) We evaluate now the right-hand expression in (4) in the present case $f(x) = [\phi(x)]^{-1}$. We have

$$\frac{g'(z)}{g(z)} = -\frac{\delta'(z)}{\delta(z)} = \frac{1}{z_0 - z} + \frac{1}{z_1 - z} + \ldots + \frac{1}{z_{p-1} - z}, \quad (19)$$

so that integrating over the unit circle $|z| \leq 1$,

$$\frac{1}{\pi} \iint \left|\frac{g'(z)}{g(z)}\right|^2 d\sigma = \sum_{\nu, \mu = 0, 1, \ldots, p-1} \frac{1}{\pi} \iint \frac{d\sigma}{(z-z_\nu)(\bar{z}-\bar{z}_\mu)}. \quad (20)$$

The integral in the general term of this sum can be written as follows:

$$\int_0^1 \int_{-\pi}^{\pi} \frac{r\,dr\,dx}{(r e^{ix} - z_\nu)(r e^{-ix} - \bar{z}_\mu)} = \int_0^1 r\,dr \int_{|\zeta|=1} \frac{d\zeta/i\zeta}{(r\zeta - z_\nu)(r\zeta^{-1} - \bar{z}_\mu)}. \quad (21)$$

The integration with respect to ζ leads to

$$\frac{2\pi}{\bar{z}_\mu z_\nu - r^2},$$

so that we obtain for (21)

$$2\pi \int_0^1 \frac{r\,dr}{\bar{z}_\mu z_\nu - r^2} = [-\pi \log(\bar{z}_\mu z_\nu - r^2)]_0^1 = \pi \log \frac{\bar{z}_\mu z_\nu}{\bar{z}_\mu z_\nu - 1}.$$

Hence $\quad \exp\left\{\dfrac{1}{\pi}\displaystyle\int\int\left|\dfrac{g'(z)}{g(z)}\right|^2 d\sigma\right\}=\Pi\,\dfrac{\bar{z}_\mu z_\nu}{\bar{z}_\mu z_\nu-1}=\dfrac{|z_0 z_1 \cdots z_{p-1}|^{2p}}{\Pi\,|\bar{z}_\mu\,z_\nu-1|}.$ (22)

Comparison of this with (18) establishes the theorem in the special case $f(x)=[\phi(x)]^{-1}$.

Both sides of (17) being continuous functions of the zeros

$$z_0, z_1, \ldots, z_{p-1},$$

the restriction concerning the distinctness of these zeros can easily be removed.

(e) In order to prove (4) generally, we approximate the function $f(x)$ by a function $f_1(x)=[\phi(x)]^{-1}$ of the special form dealt with in (b)–(d). Let $0<\epsilon<1$ and

$$1-\epsilon<\dfrac{f(x)}{f_1(x)}<1+\epsilon. \tag{23}$$

From the minimum property of $D_n(f)/D_{n-1}(f)$ proved in 2.2 (a) [cf. 5.2 (d)] we conclude that

$$(1-\epsilon)\dfrac{D_n(f_1)}{D_{n-1}(f_1)}<\dfrac{D_n(f)}{D_{n-1}(f)}<(1+\epsilon)\dfrac{D_n(f_1)}{D_{n-1}(f_1)}. \tag{24}$$

Hence for all n

$$(1-\epsilon)^{n+1}D_n(f_1)<D_n(f)<(1+\epsilon)^{n+1}D_n(f_1). \tag{25}$$

Also

$$(1-\epsilon)\,G(f_1)<G(f)<(1+\epsilon)\,G(f_1), \tag{26}$$

so that

$$\left(\dfrac{1-\epsilon}{1+\epsilon}\right)^{n+1}\dfrac{D_n(f_1)}{[G(f_1)]^{n+1}}<\dfrac{D_n(f)}{[G(f)]^{n+1}}<\left(\dfrac{1+\epsilon}{1-\epsilon}\right)^{n+1}\dfrac{D_n(f_1)}{[G(f_1)]^{n+1}}. \tag{27}$$

(f) Introducing the notation $z=re^{it}$ we rewrite (2) as follows:

$$h(re^{it})=\dfrac{1}{4\pi}\int_{-\pi}^{\pi}\log f(x+t)\dfrac{1+re^{-ix}}{1-re^{-ix}}dx, \quad r<1, \tag{28}$$

so that by differentiating with respect to t

$$izh'(z)=\dfrac{1}{4\pi}\int_{-\pi}^{\pi}\dfrac{f'(x+t)}{f(x+t)}\dfrac{1+re^{-ix}}{1-re^{-ix}}dx \tag{29}$$

follows. In view of 1.6 we find that $\Re[izh'(z)]$ has the limit $f'(t)/f(t)$ as $r\to 1$, and this limit satisfies a Lipschitz condition [cf. (1)]. By Privalov's theorem (see Appendix) the same will be true for $\Im[izh'(z)]$, and so for the function $h'(z)$ itself, and naturally also for $\{[g(z)]^{-1}\}'$.

We expand now $[g(z)]^{-1}$ in a power series $\sum\limits_{n=0}^{\infty} g_n z^n$, where $g_n = O(n^{-1-\alpha})$, and denote its pth partial sum by $s_p(z)$. In view of general theorems on approximations (see Appendix), $s_p(z)$ yields an approximation of order $O(p^{-1-\alpha} \log p)$ in the closed unit circle $|z| \leq 1$ as $p \to \infty$. [Hence $s_p(z)$ will be different from zero in this circle provided p is large enough.] Thus $|s_p(e^{ix})|^{-2} = f_p(x)$ approximates $f(x)$ with the same degree of accuracy so that from (27)

$$\left(\frac{1-\epsilon_p}{1+\epsilon_p}\right)^p \frac{D_{p-1}(f_p)}{[G(f_p)]^p} \leq \frac{D_{p-1}(f)}{[G(f)]^p} \leq \left(\frac{1+\epsilon_p}{1-\epsilon_p}\right)^p \frac{D_{p-1}(f_p)}{[G(f_p)]^p} \qquad (30)$$

follows, where $\epsilon_p = O(p^{-1-\alpha} \log p)$. But $(1+\epsilon_p)^p \to 1$ as $p \to \infty$ and by (d)

$$\frac{D_{p-1}(f_p)}{[G(f_p)]^p} = \exp\left\{ \frac{1}{\pi} \int\int \left|\frac{s_p'(z)}{s_p(z)}\right|^2 d\sigma \right\}. \qquad (31)$$

Hence it suffices to show that the right-hand expression in (31) tends to that in (4) as $p \to \infty$. This fact is equivalent to

$$\lim_{p \to \infty} \int\int |s_p(z)|^2 \left|\frac{s_p'(z)}{s_p(z)}\right|^2 d\sigma = \int\int \frac{1}{|g(z)|^2} \left|\frac{g'(z)}{g(z)}\right|^2 d\sigma,$$

which is obvious since these integrals are equal to

$$\pi \sum_{n=1}^{p} n |g_n|^2 \quad \text{and} \quad \pi \sum_{n=1}^{\infty} n |g_n|^2,$$

respectively.

This completes the proof of the theorem.

CHAPTER 6

GENERALIZATIONS AND ANALOGS OF TOEPLITZ FORMS

In this chapter we deal with various instances of Hermitian and quadratic forms which are either generalizations or analogs of Toeplitz forms. We are interested primarily in the asymptotic distribution of the eigenvalues of these forms. As to the definition of equal distribution, cf. 5.1 (a).

6.1. Special cases

In this introductory paragraph we enumerate the types of Hermitian and quadratic forms to be dealt with in the rest of the chapter.

(a) Let $\{f_n(x)\}$, $n = 0, 1, 2, \ldots$, be given complex-valued functions of the class $C(a, b)$ which are linearly independent. We denote by $\{\phi_n(x)\}$, $n = 0, 1, 2, \ldots$, the orthonormal system of functions arising from the given system by the process of orthogonalization. This process has been described in 1.8 (c).

Let $f(x)$ be a function of the class $L(a, b)$. We consider the Hermitian form

$$H_n(f) = \int_a^b | u_0 f_0(x) + u_1 f_1(x) + \ldots + u_n f_n(x) |^2 f(x)\, dx \qquad (1)$$

under the side condition $H_n(1) = 1$. The eigenvalues λ are defined as the roots of the algebraic equation

$$\det\{H_n(f) - \lambda H_n(1)\} = \det\{H_n(f - \lambda)\} = 0.$$

By a suitable linear transformation of the variables this problem can be replaced by the following equivalent one. We consider the Hermitian form

$$K_n(f) = \int_a^b | v_0 \phi_0(x) + v_1 \phi_1(x) + \ldots + v_n \phi_n(x) |^2 f(x)\, dx \qquad (2)$$

under the side condition

$$K_n(1) = \int_a^b | v_0 \phi_0(x) + v_1 \phi_1(x) + \ldots + v_n \phi_n(x) |^2 dx = \sum_{p=0}^{n} | v_p |^2 = I = 1.$$

$$(3)$$

6

The eigenvalues λ defined above are the same for which

$$\det\{K_n(f) - \lambda I\} = \det\{K_n(f-\lambda)\} = 0$$

(I is the unit form).

The Hermitian forms $H_n(f)$ and $K_n(f)$ are, of course, finite sections of certain Hermitian forms of infinitely many variables.

The following special cases are of particular interest:

(i) $a = -\pi$, $b = \pi$, $f_n(x) = \phi_n(x) = (2\pi)^{-\frac{1}{2}} e^{inx}$. The forms $H_n(f) = K_n(f)$ are now identical with the Toeplitz forms defined in 1.10.

(ii) $a = -1$, $b = 1$, $f_n(x) = x^n$, $\phi_n(x) = (n+\frac{1}{2})^{\frac{1}{2}} P_n(x)$, where $P_n(x)$ is the nth Legendre polynomial. The forms $H_n(f)$ are in this case of the Hankel type to be considered in 6.3.

(iii) Let $w(x) \geqq 0$ be a weight function defined in the interval $[a, b]$ excluding the case of a zero function; let $f_n(x) = [w(x)]^{\frac{1}{2}} x^n$ and $\phi_n(x) = [w(x)]^{\frac{1}{2}} p_n(x)$, where $\{p_n(x)\}$ is the system of the orthonormal polynomials associated with $w(x)$ (cf. 6.4). Instead of $w(x)\, dx$ more generally $d\alpha(x)$ can be considered, where $\alpha(x)$ is a given distribution function.

(b) Let l be an analytic Jordan curve in the complex x-plane. Orthogonalizing the system $\{x^n\}$ on this curve, we obtain a system $\{p_n(x)\}$ of polynomials characterized by the following conditions:

(α) $p_n(x)$ is a polynomial of degree n in which the coefficient of x^n is positive:

(β) $$\int_l p_n(x) \overline{p_m(x)} \,|dx| = \delta_{nm}, \quad n, m = 0, 1, 2, \ldots; \tag{4}$$

here $|dx|$ is the arc element of the curve l.

This system $\{p_n(x)\}$ is closely related to the conformal mapping $x = h(z)$, $z = H(x)$ defined in 1.17 (a), establishing a one-to-one correspondence of the exterior of the curve l (in the x-plane) with the exterior of the unit circle (in the z-plane). This mapping carries $x = \infty$ into $z = \infty$. It defines also a one-to-one correspondence of the curve l itself with the unit circle $|z| = 1$, $z = e^{i\theta}$. Thus any function $f(x)$ defined on the curve l can be interpreted as a function of z on the unit circle $z = e^{i\theta}$, or simply as a function of the real variable θ, $-\pi \leqq \theta \leqq \pi$.

Let $f(x)$ be a real-valued function defined on the curve l and belonging to the class L. (This means that $f(x)$ as a function of θ is of the class L.) We consider the eigenvalues of the form

$$H_n(f) = \int_l |u_0 + u_1 x + u_2 x^2 + \ldots + u_n x^n|^2 f(x) \,|dx|;$$

$$\text{side condition } H_n(1) = 1; \tag{5}$$

or, what is the same, the eigenvalues of

$$K_n(f) = \int_l |v_0 p_0(x) + v_1 p_1(x) + \ldots + v_n p_n(x)|^2 f(x) |dx|;$$

$$\text{side condition } K_n(1) = I = 1. \quad (6)$$

The eigenvalue problem for the form (5) will be dealt with in 6.2. These eigenvalues are asymptotically $(n \to \infty)$ so distributed as the values of $f(x)$ taken at $n+1$ points of the curve l corresponding to equidistant points on the unit circle $z = e^{i\theta}$. These values can be represented as follows:

$$f(x_{\nu n}), \quad x_{\nu n} = h\left\{\exp\frac{2\nu\pi i}{n+2}\right\}, \quad \nu = 1, 2, \ldots, n+1, \quad (7)$$

where $h(z)$ has the same meaning as in 1.17 (a).

In the case when l is the unit circle, the forms $H_n(f)$ coincide with the Toeplitz forms defined in 1.10. In the degenerated case when l is the interval $-1 \leqq x \leqq 1$, the forms $H_n(f)$ are of the Hankel type to be considered in 6.3.

More generally we may introduce a weight function $w(x) \geqq 0$ on the curve l [$w(x)$ is not a zero function], and form the system $\{p_n(x)\}$ of polynomials satisfying (α) and, instead of (β), the following condition:

$$\int_l p_n(x) \overline{p_m(x)} w(x) |dx| = \delta_{nm}, \quad n, m = 0, 1, 2, \ldots. \quad (8)$$

Instead of $w(x)|dx|$, more generally, $d\alpha(x)$ can be considered, where $\alpha(x)$ is a given distribution function on l.

(c) Further, we define three classes of Hermitian forms, each being generalizations of the Toeplitz forms.† For this purpose we consider the class of real-valued functions $f(r, x)$, $0 \leqq r \leqq 1$, periodic in x with period 2π, satisfying the following condition:

CONDITION C. *The coefficients $\psi_n(r)$ of the Fourier series*

$$f(r, x) \sim \sum_{n=-\infty}^{\infty} \psi_n(r) e^{inx} \quad (9)$$

are continuous and there exists a constant M such that

$$\sum_{n=-\infty}^{\infty} \max|\psi_n(r)| \leqq M. \quad (10)$$

The maxima are taken in the interval $0 \leqq r \leqq 1$.

---

† Strictly they generalize only such Toeplitz forms as correspond to functions $f(x)$ with an absolutely convergent Fourier series.

Obviously, $\psi_{-n}(r) = \overline{\psi_n(r)}$; the Fourier series of $f(r,x)$ is absolutely convergent and the function $f(r,x)$ of the two variables r and x is continuous.

We shall consider the following three Hermitian forms:

$$\Sigma\psi_{\nu-\mu}\left(\frac{\mu+\nu}{2n+2}\right)u_\mu\overline{u}_\nu, \quad \Sigma\psi_{\nu-\mu}\left(\frac{\min(\mu,\nu)}{n+1}\right)u_\mu\overline{u}_\nu, \left.\begin{array}{}\\\\\\\end{array}\right\}$$
$$\Sigma\psi_{\nu-\mu}\left(\frac{\max(\mu,\nu)}{n+1}\right)u_\mu\overline{u}_\nu \quad \mu,\nu = 0,1,2,\dots,n. \tag{11}$$

In all these cases we adopt the side condition $I = 1$. In 6.5 we shall discuss the asymptotic distribution of the eigenvalues of these forms as $n \to \infty$. It will be shown that they are asymptotically so distributed as the values of $f(r,x)$ taken at 'regularly distributed' points of the rectangle $0 \leqq r \leqq 1$, $-\pi \leqq x \leqq \pi$; for instance, we may choose for these points

$$r = p/P, \quad x = -\pi + 2q\pi/Q; \quad p = 1,2,\dots,P; \quad q = 1,2,\dots,Q,$$

where $P = P(n)$, $Q = Q(n)$ and $P(n)\,Q(n) \cong n$ as $n \to \infty$.

6.2. Hermitian forms associated with a curve of the complex plane

In this section we deal with the eigenvalues $\lambda_\nu^{(n)}$ of the form $H_n(f)$ defined by 6.1 (5) under the side condition $H_n(1) = 1$; they are the roots of the equation $\det\{H_n(f-\lambda)\} = 0$. We assume that the curve l is *analytic*. In this discussion the concepts and results of 1.17 will be instrumental.

We prove the following theorem:

THEOREM. *Let $f(x)$ be a real-valued bounded function defined on the analytic curve l and belonging there to the class L; let $m \leqq f(x) \leqq M$. The eigenvalues $\lambda_1^{(n)}, \lambda_2^{(n)}, \dots, \lambda_{n+1}^{(n)}$ of the Hermitian form $H_n(f)$ under the side condition $H_n(1) = 1$ satisfy the inequalities $m \leqq \lambda_\nu^{(n)} \leqq M$. Moreover, if $F(\lambda)$ is a continuous function defined in the interval $m \leqq \lambda \leqq M$, we have*

$$\lim_{n\to\infty}\frac{F(\lambda_1^{(n)}) + F(\lambda_2^{(n)}) + \dots + F(\lambda_{n+1}^{(n)})}{n+1}$$
$$= \frac{1}{2\pi}\int_{|z|=1}F[f(x)]\,|\,dz\,| = \frac{1}{2\pi}\int_{-\pi}^{\pi}F[f(x)]\,d\theta. \tag{1}$$

Here $f(x)$ must be interpreted as a function of z (or θ) in the conformal mapping $x = h(z)$, $z = H(x)$, $|\,z\,| = 1$, $z = e^{i\theta}$.

The expression on the right of (1) can be written also in the form

$$\frac{1}{2\pi} \int_l F[f(x)] \, |H'(x)| \, |dx|.$$

This generalizes, of course, theorem 5.2 (b).

The result (1) holds also in the degenerated case when l is the interval $-1 \leq x \leq 1$ (cf. 6.3).

(a) Denoting the determinant of the form $H_n(f)$ by $D_n(f)$ we have

$$\frac{D_n(f)}{D_n(1)} = \lambda_1^{(n)} \lambda_2^{(n)} \dots \lambda_{n+1}^{(n)}. \tag{2}$$

As in the case of the Toeplitz forms (associated with the unit circle) dealt with in 5.2 it suffices to show that for $m > 0$ we have

$$\lim_{n \to \infty} \frac{1}{n+1} \log \frac{D_n(f)}{D_n(1)} = \frac{1}{2\pi} \int_{-\pi}^{\pi} \log f(x) \, d\theta. \tag{3}$$

We shall prove the sharper statement

$$\lim_{n \to \infty} \left\{ \frac{D_n(f)}{D_n(1)} : \frac{D_{n-1}(f)}{D_{n-1}(1)} \right\} = \exp \left\{ \frac{1}{2\pi} \int_{-\pi}^{\pi} \log f(x) \, d\theta \right\}, \tag{4}$$

and the still sharper equation

$$\lim_{n \to \infty} c^{-2n-1} \frac{D_n(f)}{D_{n-1}(f)} = 2\pi \exp \left\{ \frac{1}{2\pi} \int_{-\pi}^{\pi} \log f(x) \, d\theta \right\}. \tag{5}$$

Here c is the transfinite diameter of the curve l (1.17).

Writing in the last relation $f(x) = 1$ we find

$$\lim_{n \to \infty} c^{-2n-1} \frac{D_n(1)}{D_{n-1}(1)} = 2\pi. \tag{6}$$

From (5) and (6) we conclude indeed (4), and from this, of course, (3) follows.

(b) Equation (5) is a consequence of the following theorem:

THEOREM. Let $f(x)$ be nonnegative and of the class L on the analytic curve l. We denote by μ_n the minimum of the form $H_n(f)$ [6.1 (5)] under the side condition $u_n = 1$. Then

$$\lim_{n \to \infty} (c^{-2n-1} \mu_n) = 2\pi \exp \left\{ \frac{1}{2\pi} \int_{-\pi}^{\pi} \log f(x) \, d\theta \right\}. \tag{7}$$

If $\log f(x)$ is not integrable, the right-hand expression must be replaced by zero.

This is obviously a generalization of the absolutely continuous case of theorem 3.1 (a); the unit circle is replaced by an arbitrary analytic curve. [It would be an easy matter to extend further this theorem by considering a distribution $d\alpha(x)$ instead of $f(x)\,dx$.] Since

$$\mu_n = D_n(f)/D_{n-1}(f),$$

from (7) we obtain (5).

The argument follows the pattern set in 3.1 so that we can be brief.

(c) By the inequality for the arithmetic and geometric means:

$$H_n(f) \geq 2\pi \exp\left\{ \frac{1}{2\pi} \int_{-\pi}^{\pi} \log |u_0 + u_1 x + \dots + u_n x^n|^2 \, d\theta \right\}$$

$$\times \exp\left\{ \frac{1}{2\pi} \int_{-\pi}^{\pi} \log f(x)\,d\theta \right\} \exp\left\{ \frac{1}{2\pi} \int_{-\pi}^{\pi} \log |h'(z)|\,d\theta \right\}, \quad (8)$$

where $x = h(z)$, $|z| = 1$, $z = e^{i\theta}$.

Now for an arbitrary complex value of α:

$$\frac{1}{2\pi} \int_{-\pi}^{\pi} \log |x - \alpha|\,d\theta = \frac{1}{2\pi} \int_{-\pi}^{\pi} \log |h(z) - \alpha|\,d\theta \geq \log c. \quad (9)$$

Indeed, if α is in the exterior of l, $\alpha = h(z_0)$, $|z_0| > 1$, the function

$$\log \left| \frac{h(z) - h(z_0)}{z - z_0} \right|$$

is regular-harmonic for $|z| \geq 1$ so that its mean value on the unit circle is $= \log c$. On the other hand,

$$\frac{1}{2\pi} \int_{-\pi}^{\pi} \log |z - z_0|\,d\theta = \log |z_0| > 0.$$

If α is in the interior of l, the function

$$\log \left| \frac{h(z) - \alpha}{z} \right|$$

will be regular-harmonic for $|z| \geq 1$ so that (9) holds with the sign $=$. Taking

$$\frac{1}{2\pi} \int_{-\pi}^{\pi} \log |h'(z)|\,d\theta = \log c$$

into account we find from (8)

$$H_n(f) \geq 2\pi \, |\, u_n \,|^2 c^{2n+1} \exp\left\{\frac{1}{2\pi}\int_{-\pi}^{\pi} \log f(x)\, d\theta\right\},$$

hence

$$c^{-2n-1}\mu_n \geq 2\pi \exp\left\{\frac{1}{2\pi}\int_{-\pi}^{\pi} \log f(x)\, d\theta\right\}. \tag{10}$$

(d) We assume (temporarily) that $f(x) \geq m > 0$. If $\epsilon > 0$ is given, we can find, owing to the approximation theorem 1.9 (c), a trigonometric polynomial $t(\theta)$ of θ such that

$$\int_{-\pi}^{\pi} |f(x) - t(\theta)|\, d\theta < \epsilon, \quad t(\theta) \geq m.$$

In view of 1.12 the function $t(\theta)$ can be written in the form $|\, D(z)\,|^2$, $z = e^{i\theta}$, where $D(z)$ is regular and different from zero for $|\,z\,| \geq 1$ [including $z = \infty$, $D(\infty) > 0$]. Thus $t(\theta) = |\,\Delta(x)\,|^2$, x on l, where $\Delta(x)$ satisfies the conditions of 1.17 (a).

We form now the Faber polynomials $f_n(x)$ defined in 1.17 (a). The leading term of $f_n(x)$ is $[\Delta(\infty)]^{-1} c^{-n-\frac{1}{2}} x^n$, so that

$$\mu_n \leq [\Delta(\infty)]^2 c^{2n+1} \int_l |f_n(x)|^2 f(x)\,|\, dx\,|.$$

Using theorem 1.17 (c) we find

$$c^{-2n-1}\mu_n \leq [\Delta(\infty)]^2 \int_l |\, g_n(x)\,|^2 f(x)\, dx + O(r^n)$$

$$\leq [\Delta(\infty)]^2 \int_l |[\Delta(x)]^{-1}[H'(x)]^{\frac{1}{2}}[H(x)]^n|^2 f(x)\,|\, dx\,| + O(r^n),$$

Hence
$$0 < r < 1.$$

$$\limsup_{n \to \infty} c^{-2n-1}\mu_n \leq [\Delta(\infty)]^2 \int_{-\pi}^{\pi} [t(\theta)]^{-1} f(x)\, d\theta. \tag{11}$$

The last integral is equal to

$$2\pi + \int_{-\pi}^{\pi} \frac{f(x) - t(\theta)}{t(\theta)}\, d\theta < 2\pi + m^{-1}\int_{-\pi}^{\pi} |f(x) - t(\theta)|\, d\theta < 2\pi + m^{-1}\epsilon,$$

also

$$[\Delta(\infty)]^2 = \exp\left\{\frac{1}{2\pi}\int_{-\pi}^{\pi} \log t(\theta)\, d\theta\right\}$$

$$= \exp\left\{\frac{1}{2\pi}\int_{-\pi}^{\pi} \log f(x)\, d\theta\right\}\exp\left\{\frac{1}{2\pi}\int_{-\pi}^{\pi}[\log t(\theta) - \log f(x)]\, d\theta\right\}$$

and

$$\int_{-\pi}^{\pi} [\log t(\theta) - \log f(x)] \, d\theta < m^{-1} \int_{-\pi}^{\pi} |t(\theta) - f(x)| \, d\theta < m^{-1} \epsilon.$$

Thus the result (7) is established for $f(x) \geqq m > 0$. This restriction can be removed in the same fashion as it was done in 3.1 (e).

6.3. Hankel forms

We shall deal with the degenerated case of the form $H_n(f)$ [6.1 (5)] when the curve l is a finite interval. The proof of 6.2 requires only slight modifications in this case and it does not seem necessary to discuss them in detail.

(a) Let $a \leqq x \leqq b$ be a finite interval, $f(x)$ a real-valued function of the class $L(a, b)$. The quadratic form

$$H_n(f) = \int_a^b (u_0 + u_1 x + u_2 x^2 + \ldots + u_n x^n)^2 f(x) \, dx = \sum_{\mu, \nu = 0, 1, \ldots, n} c_{\mu+\nu} u_\mu u_\nu \tag{1}$$

is called a form of the Hankel type, the corresponding matrix $(c_{\mu+\nu})$ a matrix of the Hankel type. In a similar fashion as Toeplitz matrices of the form $(c_{\nu-\mu})$ are connected with the trigonometric moment problem, the Hankel matrices of the form $(c_{\mu+\nu})$ are associated with the ordinary (power) moment problem. This is true not only in the case of a finite interval (which we consider in the present section) but in that of the half-infinite interval $0 \leqq x < +\infty$ and also in that of the whole infinite interval $-\infty < x < +\infty$.

(b) For the sake of simplicity we assume that $a = -1$, $b = +1$. By a suitable linear transformation $H_n(f)$ is transformed into

$$K_n(f) = \int_{-1}^{1} [v_0 p_0(x) + v_1 p_1(x) + \ldots + v_n p_n(x)]^2 f(x) \, dx, \tag{2}$$

where $p_n(x) = (n + \tfrac{1}{2})^{\frac{1}{2}} P_n(x)$ and $P_n(x)$ is the nth Legendre polynomial. The eigenvalue problems $\det\{H_n(f) - \lambda H_n(1)\} = \det\{H_n(f-\lambda)\} = 0$ and $\det\{K_n(f) - \lambda I\} = \det\{K_n(f-\lambda)\} = 0$ are identical. If $\lambda_\nu^{(n)}$ denote the eigenvalues defined as the roots of these equations, we have the limit relation 6.2 (1). In this case the conformal mapping $x = h(z)$, $z = H(x)$ will carry the complex x-plane cut along the interval $[-1, +1]$

into the exterior of the unit circle of the z-plane, $|z| > 1$. It can be represented by the elementary relations:

$$x = \tfrac{1}{2}(z + z^{-1}), \quad z = x + (x^2 - 1)^{\frac{1}{2}}. \tag{3}$$

The unit circle $z = e^{i\theta}$ is transformed into $x = \cos\theta$, that is, into the interval $[-1, +1]$ described twice. The transfinite diameter of this interval is $c = \tfrac{1}{2}$.

The limit relation can be written as follows:

$$\lim_{n \to \infty} \frac{F(\lambda_1^{(n)}) + F(\lambda_2^{(n)}) + \cdots + F(\lambda_{n+1}^{(n)})}{n+1} = \frac{1}{\pi} \int_{-1}^{+1} F[f(x)] (1 - x^2)^{-\frac{1}{2}} \, dx$$

$$= \frac{1}{\pi} \int_0^{\pi} F[f(\cos\theta)] \, d\theta, \tag{4}$$

where $F(\lambda)$ is defined as in 6.2 (1). Thus the eigenvalues are asymptotically distributed as the equidistant ordinates of the function $f(\cos\theta), 0 \leq \theta \leq \pi$.

Let $f(x) \in L$, $f(x) \geq 0$. Denoting by $D_n(f)$ the determinant of the form $H_n(f)$, $a = -1$, $b = +1$, we have [cf. 6.2 (5)]

$$\lim_{n \to \infty} 2^{2n+1} \frac{D_n(f)}{D_{n-1}(f)} = 2\pi \exp\left\{ \frac{1}{\pi} \int_{-1}^{+1} \log f(x) (1 - x^2)^{-\frac{1}{2}} dx \right\}$$

$$= 2\pi \exp\left\{ \frac{1}{\pi} \int_0^{\pi} \log f(\cos\theta) \, d\theta \right\}. \tag{5}$$

[If $\log f(\cos\theta)$ is not integrable, the right-hand side of (5) must be replaced by zero.] From this we can derive the relation (4) as in 6.2.

Similar results hold for arbitrary finite values of a and b. In the general case the transfinite diameter is $c = \tfrac{1}{4}(b - a)$.

6.4. Orthogonal polynomials

(a) Let $f(x)$ be a function of the class $L(-1, +1)$; we assume that $f(x) \geq 0$, excluding the case of a zero function. We can form a system $\{p_n(x)\}$ of polynomials satisfying the following conditions:

(α) $p_n(x)$ is of degree n and the coefficient k_n' of x^n in $p_n(x)$ is positive:

$$(\beta) \qquad \int_{-1}^1 p_n(x) p_m(x) f(x) \, dx = \delta_{nm}, \quad n, m = 0, 1, 2, \ldots. \tag{1}$$

They are called the *orthonormal polynomials* associated with the weight function $f(x)$. These polynomials are related to the Hankel forms in a similar manner as the polynomials $\phi_n(z)$ discussed in chapters 2 and 3 are to the Toeplitz forms. Instead of the distribution $f(x)\,dx$ more general distributions of the form $d\alpha(x)$ can be considered.

(b) Between the two classes of orthogonal polynomials just mentioned an important relationship exists. This can be formulated in the following theorem:

THEOREM. *Let* $\{p_n(x) = k'_n x^n + ...\}$ *and* $\{\phi_n(z) = k_n z^n + ...\}$ *be the two systems of orthonormal polynomials associated with the weight functions*

$$\left.\begin{array}{ll} f(x), & -1 \leq x \leq +1, \\ f(\cos\theta)\,|\sin\theta|\,, & z = e^{i\theta}, \quad -\pi \leq \theta \leq \pi, \end{array}\right\} \tag{2}$$

respectively. We have then the following identities:

$$\left.\begin{array}{ll} p_n(x) = (2\pi)^{-\frac{1}{2}}(1 + l_{2n}/k_{2n})^{-\frac{1}{2}}\{z^{-n}\phi_{2n}(z) + z^n\phi_{2n}(z^{-1})\} \\ \qquad = (2\pi)^{-\frac{1}{2}}(1 - l_{2n}/k_{2n})^{-\frac{1}{2}}\{z^{-n+1}\phi_{2n-1}(z) + z^{n-1}\phi_{2n-1}(z^{-1})\}, \\ \qquad\qquad\qquad\qquad\qquad\qquad\qquad\qquad\qquad x = \tfrac{1}{2}(z + z^{-1}). \end{array}\right\} \tag{3}$$

The second weight function (2) is even, so that the coefficients of $\phi_n(z)$ are all real [cf. 2.1 (4) or (5)]. We have $l_n = \phi_n(0)$.

For the proof we note first that the two right-hand expressions occurring in (3) are identical; this follows from the relation 2.3 (3) taking the identity 2.2 (10) into account. Thus it suffices to discuss the first equation. The right-hand expression is a polynomial of degree n in $\tfrac{1}{2}(z + z^{-1}) = x$ and the coefficient of x^n is positive. We show that

$$\int_{-1}^{1}\{z^{-n}\phi_{2n}(z) + z^n\phi_{2n}(z^{-1})\}(z^\nu + z^{-\nu})f(x)\,dx = 0, \quad 0 \leq \nu \leq n-1, \quad z = e^{ix}.$$

(Linear combinations of $z^\nu + z^{-\nu} = 2\cos\nu\theta$ represent the most general polynomial of degree $n-1$ in $x = \cos\theta$.) Indeed,

$$\int_{-\pi}^{\pi}\phi_{2n}(z)\,\bar{z}^{n-\nu}f(\cos\theta)\,|\sin\theta|\,d\theta = \int_{-\pi}^{\pi}\phi_{2n}(z)\,\bar{z}^{n+\nu}f(\cos\theta)\,|\sin\theta|\,d\theta = 0,$$

and these relations remain valid if we replace θ by $-\theta$ (or z by $z^{-1} = \bar{z}$). Hence (3) holds except perhaps a positive constant factor.

Now in view of the orthonormal property of $\phi_m(z)$:

$$\frac{1}{2\pi}\int_{-\pi}^{\pi}\mid z^{-n}\phi_{2n}(z)+z^n\phi_{2n}(z^{-1})\mid^2 f(\cos\theta)\mid\sin\theta\mid d\theta$$

$$=\frac{1}{2\pi}\int_{-\pi}^{\pi}\{\mid\phi_{2n}(z)\mid^2+\mid\phi_{2n}(z^{-1})\mid^2+2\Re\phi_{2n}(z)\,\overline{z^{2n}\phi_{2n}(z^{-1})}\}$$
$$\times f(\cos\theta)\mid\sin\theta\mid d\theta$$

$$=2+2l_{2n}/k_{2n},$$

and this proves the assertion.

(c) By means of (3) many problems concerning Hankel forms can be reduced to the corresponding problems involving Toeplitz forms.

Let us denote the determinant of the Hankel form $H_n(f)$ by $D_n(f)=D_n$ and that of the nth Toeplitz form corresponding to the weight function $f(\cos\theta)\mid\sin\theta\mid$ by Δ_n. Then the highest coefficients of the orthonormal polynomials can be written as follows:

$$k'_n=(D_{n-1}/D_n)^{\frac{1}{2}},\quad k_n=(\Delta_{n-1}/\Delta_n)^{\frac{1}{2}}.\qquad(4)$$

Concerning the second equation, cf. 2.1 (8); the first equation follows in a similar way. From the first identity (3) we conclude

$$\left.\begin{array}{l}k'_n=(2\pi)^{-\frac{1}{2}}(1+l_{2n}/k_{2n})^{-\frac{1}{2}}k_{2n}.2^n,\\[2mm]\dfrac{D_n}{D_{n-1}}=2\pi(1+l_{2n}/k_{2n})\dfrac{\Delta_n}{\Delta_{n-1}}2^{-2n}.\end{array}\right\}\qquad(5)$$

In view of 3.4 (3) and (5) we find

$$\lim_{n\to\infty}2^{2n}\frac{D_n}{D_{n-1}}=2\pi\exp\left\{\frac{1}{\pi}\int_0^{\pi}\log\left[f(\cos\theta)\mid\sin\theta\mid\right]d\theta\right\}.$$

Since

$$\exp\left\{\frac{1}{\pi}\int_0^{\pi}\log\sin\theta\,d\theta\right\}=\frac{1}{2},$$

this yields again 6.3 (5).

(d) Using theorem 3.4 (a) [in particular the limit relations (3), (4) and (5)] we obtain the following theorem:

THEOREM. *Let $f(x)$ be a nonnegative weight function in $[-1,1]$ such that $f(\cos\theta)$ and $\log f(\cos\theta)$ are of the class L. If $\{p_n(x)\}$ denotes the associated orthonormal system of polynomials, we have for all x not on the segment $[-1,+1]$*

$$\lim_{n\to\infty}z^{-n}p_n(x)=(2\pi)^{-\frac{1}{2}}[g(z^{-1})]^{-1}.\qquad(6)$$

Here $x = \frac{1}{2}(z + z^{-1})$, $|z| > 1$, *and* $g(z)$ *is the analytic function, regular and different from zero in the unit circle* $|z| < 1$, *which corresponds to the function* $f(\cos \theta) |\sin \theta|$ *in the sense of* 1.14 (e). *We have for almost all* θ

$$\lim_{r \to 1-0} |g(re^{i\theta})|^2 = f(\cos \theta)|\sin \theta|.$$

6.5. Hermitian forms associated with a function of two variables

We deal here with the eigenvalues $\lambda_\nu^{(n)}$ of the forms 6.1 (11). The procedure is similar in any of the three cases; thus we shall consider throughout this paragraph the first case. We shall prove the following theorem:

THEOREM. *Let the function* $f(r, x)$ *satisfy condition* C [6.1 (c)]. *We denote the eigenvalues of the first Hermitian form* 6.1 (11) *by* $\lambda_\nu^{(n)}$. *We have then* $|\lambda_\nu^{(n)}| \leq M$. *Moreover, if* $F(\lambda)$ *is any continuous function defined for* $-M \leq \lambda \leq M$, *we have*

$$\lim_{n \to \infty} \frac{F(\lambda_1^{(n)}) + F(\lambda_2^{(n)}) + \ldots + F(\lambda_{n+1}^{(n)})}{n+1} = \frac{1}{2\pi} \int_{-\pi}^{\pi} \int_0^1 F[f(r, x)]\, dr\, dx. \quad (1)$$

In the special case when $f(r, x)$ is independent of r, this is an assertion on Toeplitz forms. The limit relation (1) is equivalent to the distribution property formulated at the end of 6.1 (c).

The inequality $|\lambda_\nu^{(n)}| \leq M$ follows from theorem 1.18 (b).

The distribution theorem is equivalent [cf. 5.1 (b)] to any of the following two special cases.

(i) Let s be any positive integer; then

$$\lim_{n \to \infty} \frac{(\lambda_1^{(n)})^s + (\lambda_2^{(n)})^s + \ldots + (\lambda_{n+1}^{(n)})^s}{n+1} = \frac{1}{2\pi} \int_{-\pi}^{\pi} \int_0^1 [f(r, x)]^s\, dr\, dx. \quad (2)$$

(ii) Let $\lambda_\nu^{(n)} \geq m > 0$ for all ν and n. Denoting by D_n the determinant of the first form 6.1 (11), we have

$$\lim_{n \to \infty} D_n^{1/(n+1)} = \exp\left\{\frac{1}{2\pi} \int_{-\pi}^{\pi} \int_0^1 \log f(r, x)\, dr\, dx\right\}. \quad (3)$$

(a) Before starting with the proof we make a few preliminary remarks. A sufficient condition for $\lambda_\nu^{(n)} \geq m > 0$ is the following:

$$\min \psi_0(r) \geq m + \sum_{\substack{-\infty < n < \infty; \\ n \neq 0}} \max |\psi_n(r)|. \quad (4)$$

This condition implies among others that $\psi_0(r) \geq m > 0$.

Indeed, if A_n is the matrix of the first form 6.1 (11),

$$A_n - mI = \rho(I+K), \quad \rho = \prod_{p=0}^{n} \left[\psi_0 \left(\frac{p}{n+1} \right) - m \right],$$

where I is the unit matrix. The elements of the matrix K in the principal diagonal are zero, and outside of the principal diagonal they are of the form

$$\psi_{\nu-\mu}(r) \, [\psi_0(r') - m]^{-\frac{1}{2}} [\psi_0(r'') - m]^{-\frac{1}{2}}, \quad \mu \neq \nu,$$

where r, r', r'' are certain values in $0, 1$. In view of the theorem in 1.18 (b) the eigenvalues of K are in the absolute value not greater than

$$\sum \max | \psi_n(r) | \, [\min \psi_0(r) - m]^{-1} \leq 1,$$

so that the form corresponding to $A_n - mI$ is nonnegative.

(b) We observe that $\lambda_\nu^{(n)} \geq m$ (holding for each ν and n) has the consequence that $f(r, x) \geq m$. It is sufficient to show this for $m = 0$.

From $\lambda_\nu^{(n)} \geq 0$ it follows that

$$\sum_{\mu, \nu = 0, 1, \ldots, n} \psi_{\nu-\mu} \left(\frac{\mu+\nu}{2n+2} \right) u_\mu \bar{u}_\nu \geq 0.$$

Let $0 < r - \epsilon < r + \epsilon < 1$. We choose $u_p = e^{-ipx}$, x real, provided that p satisfies the condition

$$r - \epsilon \leq \frac{p}{n+1} \leq r + \epsilon; \tag{5}$$

otherwise let $u_p = 0$. Hence, if μ and ν satisfy the inequalities (5),

$$\sum \psi_{\nu-\mu} \left(\frac{\mu+\nu}{2n+2} \right) e^{i(\nu-\mu)x} \geq 0. \tag{6}$$

Let N be a fixed positive integer. We form the Nth Fejér mean of the trigonometric polynomial (6). According to the fundamental property of these means we have

$$\sum_{|\mu-\nu| \leq N} \left(1 - \frac{|\mu-\nu|}{N} \right) \psi_{\nu-\mu} \left(\frac{\mu+\nu}{2n+2} \right) e^{i(\nu-\mu)x} \geq 0. \tag{7}$$

Let $R = R(r, \epsilon, n)$ be the number of the terms $\mu = \nu$ in (6) or (7), so that $R(r, \epsilon, n) \to \infty$ as $n \to \infty$ (r, ϵ fixed). If k is fixed, $| k | \leq N$, the number of the terms $\nu - \mu = k$ is $R(r, \epsilon, n) + O(1)$ as $n \to \infty$. Dividing (7) by $R(r, \epsilon, n)$ and passing to the limit $n \to \infty$ and then to $\epsilon \to 0$, we find

$$\sum_{|k| \leq N} \left(1 - \frac{|k|}{N} \right) \psi_k(r) e^{ikx} \geq 0. \tag{8}$$

This being true for each N, we have $f(r, x) \geq 0$.

(c) For the proof of the theorem we intend to prove (2). Let ϵ be arbitrary and let l be chosen so that

$$\sum_{|n| > l} \max |\psi_n(r)| < \epsilon. \tag{9}$$

We consider the trigonometric polynomial of the lth degree

$$f_l(r, x) = \sum_{n=-l}^{l} \psi_n(r) e^{inx}. \tag{10}$$

We denote the matrix of the first form 6.1 (11) associated with the function $f_l(r, x)$ by $A_n^{(l)}$ and write

$$A_n = A_n^{(l)} + D. \tag{11}$$

The sum of the moduli of the elements in any row of D is less than ϵ so that the same holds for the eigenvalues of D, hence also for the values of $A_n - A_n^{(l)}$ as $I = \Sigma |u_p|^2 = 1$. By theorem 1.18 (c) we have for the eigenvalues $\lambda_\nu^{(n)}$ and $\lambda_\nu^{(n, l)}$ of A_n and $A_n^{(l)}$ (each set ordered in non-decreasing order)

$$|\lambda_\nu^{(n)} - \lambda_\nu^{(n, l)}| < \epsilon. \tag{12}$$

If s is a positive integer, we have, since $|\lambda_\nu^{(n)}| \leq M$, $|\lambda_\nu^{(n, l)}| \leq M$,

$$|(\lambda_\nu^{(n)})^s - (\lambda_\nu^{(n, l)})^s| < s M^{s-1} \epsilon.$$

A similar inequality holds for $[f(r, x)]^s - [f_l(r, x)]^s$. Consequently it will be sufficient to prove the theorem for a trigonometric polynomial $f_l(r, x)$.

(d) To simplify the notation we assume that the original function $f(r, x)$ itself is a trigonometric polynomial of degree l. Hence the matrix A_n will have elements different from zero only in $2l + 1$ 'lines' parallel to the principal diagonal. Replacing all these elements except those in the 'line h' by 0 ($-l \leq h \leq l$), a matrix B_{nh} will result. Clearly,

$$A_n = \sum_{h=-l}^{l} B_{nh}. \tag{13}$$

We denote by $\operatorname{tr} A$ the *trace* of an arbitrary matrix A (1.1). Hence the sum $(\lambda_1^{(n)})^s + (\lambda_2^{(n)})^s + \ldots + (\lambda_{n+1}^{(n)})^s$ occurring in (2) is $\operatorname{tr} A_n^s$, where A_n^s is the sth power of the matrix A_n. Now

$$A_n^s = \sum B_{nh_1} B_{nh_2} \ldots B_{nh_s}, \tag{14}$$

where $h_1, h_2, \ldots, h_s$ run independently from $-l$ to l. Thus it suffices to show that

$$\lim_{n \to \infty} \frac{\operatorname{tr}(B_{nh_1} B_{nh_2} \ldots B_{nh_s})}{n+1}$$

$$= \frac{1}{2\pi} \int_{-\pi}^{\pi} e^{i(h_1 + h_2 + \ldots + h_s)x} dx \int_0^1 \psi_{h_1}(r)\, \psi_{h_2}(r) \ldots \psi_{h_s}(r)\, dr. \tag{15}$$

The right-hand side is, of course, zero unless $\Sigma h_i = 0$, in which case it reduces to the second integral (integral in r).

For the sake of convenience we use for the matrices

$$B_{nh_1}, B_{nh_2}, \ldots, B_{nh_s}$$

the following alternate notation:

$$(g_{\mu\nu}^{(1)}), (g_{\mu\nu}^{(2)}), \ldots, (g_{\mu\nu}^{(s)}), \tag{16}$$

where $\mu, \nu = 0, 1, \ldots, n$. In these matrices all terms are zero except those for which $\nu - \mu = h_1, h_2, \ldots, h_s$, respectively. The general element $g_{\mu\nu}$ of their product is

$$g_{\mu\nu_1}^{(1)} g_{\nu_1\nu_2}^{(2)} \ldots g_{\nu_{s-2}\nu_{s-1}}^{(s-1)} g_{\nu_{s-1}\nu}^{(s)}, \tag{17}$$

where $\nu_1, \nu_2, \ldots, \nu_{s-1}$ vary independently from 0 to n. Now all terms of $g_{\mu\nu}$ will vanish except if

$$\nu_1 - \mu = h_1, \nu_2 - \nu_1 = h_2, \ldots, \nu - \nu_{s-1} = h_s. \tag{18}$$

A consequence of these conditions is that $\nu - \mu = \Sigma h_i$. But the elements $g_{\mu\nu}$ contribute to the trace only if $\mu = \nu$, so that (15) will be trivial if $\Sigma h_i \neq 0$.

Let $\Sigma h_i = 0$, $\mu = \nu$; we have then

$$\left.\begin{array}{l} \nu_1 = \mu + h_1, \quad \nu_2 = \mu + h_1 + h_2, \ldots, \\ \nu_s = \nu = \mu + h_1 + h_2 + \ldots + h_s = \mu, \end{array}\right\} \tag{19}$$

and the trace in question will be

$$\sum_{\mu=0}^{n} g_{\mu\mu} = \sum_{\mu=0}^{n}{}' \psi_{h_1}\left(\frac{2\mu + h_1}{2n+2}\right) \psi_{h_2}\left(\frac{2\mu + 2h_1 + h_2}{2n+2}\right) \psi_{h_3}\left(\frac{2\mu + 2h_1 + 2h_2 + h_3}{2n+2}\right)$$

$$\ldots \psi_{h_s}\left(\frac{2\mu + 2h_1 + \ldots + 2h_{s-1} + h_s}{2n+2}\right). \tag{20}$$

In the sum Σ' we have to suppress all terms in which at least one of the quantities $\mu + h_1, \mu + h_1 + h_2, \ldots, \mu + h_1 + \ldots + h_s$ fails to be in the range $0, n$. This can not happen if we assume that $sl \leqq \mu \leqq n - sl$.

Multiplying (20) by $(n+1)^{-1}$ and passing to the limit $n \to \infty$ we find

$$\int_0^1 \psi_{h_1}(r)\, \psi_{h_2}(r) \ldots \psi_{h_s}(r)\, dr,$$

and this proves (15).

Thus the proof of the theorem is complete.

CHAPTER 7

FURTHER GENERALIZATIONS

7.1. Eigenvalues of Hilbert–Schmidt kernels

We refer to sections 1.19 and 1.20. The definitions and notations introduced in those sections are used in the following.

(a) There is an important class of bounded linear Hermitian operators L which are similar to the example mentioned at the end of 1.20 in so far as their spectrum forms a discrete point set. They are defined by the condition that for any bounded sequence $f_1, f_2, \ldots \epsilon \mathfrak{H}$, $\|f_\nu\| \leq C$, there is a subsequence $f_{\nu_1}, f_{\nu_2}, \ldots$ such that $L(f_{\nu_j}), j = 1, 2, \ldots$ converges (in the sense of the topology corresponding to the norm). Such operators are said to be *completely continuous*, and they have been shown (see Appendix) to have a discrete spectrum with zero as its only limit point (if any).

We consider a measure space $(S, \mathfrak{S}, m)$ and a function $K(s, t)$ defined on the product space $S \times S$ and measurable with respect to the product measure. If the kernel $K(s, t)$ is Hermitian, i.e. $K(s, t) = \overline{K(t, s)}$, and quadratically integrable over $S \times S$:

$$\iint_{S \times S} |K(s, t)|^2 \, dm(s) \, dm(t) < \infty,$$

then the operator

$$Lf = \int_S K(s, t) f(t) \, dm(t)$$

is defined for $f \epsilon L_2(S)$ and assumes as values elements in the same Hilbert space. L is immediately seen to be linear, Hermitian and bounded. It is said to be an operator of the *Hilbert–Schmidt* type, and it is not difficult to show (see Appendix) that it is completely continuous.

Let us denote the points of the spectrum of L by $\lambda_\nu, \nu = 1, 2, \ldots$. In order to describe the distribution of these 'eigenvalues' we introduce the *distribution function*

$$N(x) = \begin{cases} -\text{number of } \lambda_\nu \geq x & \text{if } x > 0, \\ \text{number of } \lambda_\nu \leq x & \text{if } x < 0. \end{cases}$$

In general, our purpose will be to study the distribution of the eigenvalues when the measure space is changed in a certain way to be described in the next section. We shall obtain then various distributions distinguished by an index α which takes values of a directed set A. We will consider the behavior of the normalized distribution functions $D_\alpha(x) = K_\alpha^{-1} N(x)$, where the K_α are some appropriately chosen constants.

(b) We shall say that the distribution D_α of the eigenvalues $\lambda_\nu^{(\alpha)}, \nu = 1, 2, \ldots, |\lambda_\nu^{(\alpha)}| \leqq M$, converges to a distribution D characterized by the nondecreasing function $D(x)$ if for every interval $[a, b]$ not containing zero and whose endpoints are continuity points of $D(x)$ we have

$$\lim_\alpha [D_\alpha(b) - D_\alpha(a)] = D(b) - D(a). \tag{1}$$

The limit corresponds to the partial ordering of the directed set A; $D(x)$ will in general be bounded at $\pm M$, but it can be infinite at $x = 0$.

It will usually be convenient to prove this by using the moments

$$\mu_s^{(\alpha)} = K_\alpha^{-1} \sum_{\nu=1}^\infty (\lambda_\nu^{(\alpha)})^s.$$

Suppose that the operators are bounded, $\| L^{(\alpha)} \| \leqq M$, and that the moments converge to the finite values

$$\mu_s = \int_{-M}^M x^s dD(x) \quad \text{for } s \geqq 2.$$

If $0 \notin [a, b]$ and $\epsilon > 0$ is given, we can approximate the characteristic function $c(x)$ of the interval $[a, b]$ by polynomials $p_1(x)$, $p_2(x)$, so that

$$\left. \begin{aligned} p_1(x) &\leqq c(x) \leqq p_2(x), \\ p_2(x) - p_1(x) &\leqq \epsilon, \end{aligned} \right\} \quad x \in [-M, M];$$

the second inequality holds except for very small neighborhoods of a and b. In addition,

$$p_2(x) - p_1(x) \leqq \epsilon x^2;$$

finally, the polynomials do not contain terms of degree zero and one. This follows from Weierstrass's approximation theorem and from the fact that $x^{-2} c(x)$ is continuous for $x \neq a, b$. But then

$$K_\alpha^{-1} \sum_{\nu=1}^\infty p_1(\lambda_\nu^{(\alpha)}) \leqq K_\alpha^{-1} [D_\alpha(b) - D_\alpha(a)] = K_\alpha^{-1} \sum_{\nu=1}^\infty c(\lambda_\nu^{(\alpha)}) \leqq K_\alpha^{-1} \sum_{\nu=1}^\infty p_2(\lambda_\nu^{(\alpha)})$$

and passing to the limits

$$\int_{-M}^M p_1(x) dD(x) \leqq \underline{\lim_\alpha}, \quad \overline{\lim_\alpha} K_\alpha^{-1} [D_\alpha(b) - D_\alpha(a)] \leqq \int_{-M}^M p_2(x) dD(x).$$

Now we only have to observe that

$$\int_{-M}^{M} x^2 dD(x) < \infty \tag{2}$$

and (1) follows easily.

For the case when L is a matrix of the type $n \times n$, the eigenvalues are n in number and we do not have the difficulty arising from a possible limit point at $x = 0$. Then we can define the distribution functions by

$$N(x) = \text{number of } \lambda_\nu \leq x,$$

and the normalizing constant K_α is chosen as n. The condition (2) is no longer necessary.

7.2. General Toeplitz forms

(a) We consider two measure spaces $(X, \mathfrak{X}, \mu)$ and $(S, \mathfrak{S}, \nu)$ and a function $\phi(x, s)$ measurable with respect to the product measure $d\mu d\nu$. This function will be used as a kernel to define an integral operator. Before doing this however, we have to introduce another concept.

Let S_α be $(\mathfrak{S})$-measurable sets of finite measure in S for each α belonging to a directed set A. We assume that $\alpha_1 < \alpha_2$ implies $S_{\alpha_1} \subset S_{\alpha_2}$ and that $\lim S_\alpha = S$. We denote the set of $(\mathfrak{S})$-measurable functions bounded on S_α and vanishing outside by $\mathfrak{F}_\alpha$.

Assuming that the kernel is bounded in S_α,

$$| \phi(x, s) | \leq c_\alpha < \infty$$

for $x \in X$, $s \in S_\alpha$, the integral

$$\int_S \phi(x, s) u(s) ds = Tu$$

exists if $u \in \mathfrak{F}_\alpha$ and defines a linear transformation T. In the cases we are going to study, the following three conditions will be satisfied.

(i) The set of elements $u(s)$ belonging to some $\mathfrak{F}_\alpha$, belongs to $L_2(S)$ and is dense in $L_2(S)$.

(ii) The set of elements Tu, where u runs through all the sets $\mathfrak{F}_\alpha$, is dense in $L_2(X)$.

(iii) $\| Tu \| = \| u \|$ for all u for which T is defined. Then, using a standard argument (see Appendix), T can be extended continuously to a linear, unitary transformation from $L_2(S)$ to $L_2(X)$.

Under these conditions we will call $\phi(x, s)$ an *orthogonal kernel*.

(b) Starting from T and a bounded $(\mathfrak{X})$-integrable function $f(x)$ we will define a transformation K in the following way. Consider the set

$$e_\lambda = \{x \,|\, f(x) \leqq \phi\} \in \mathfrak{X}.$$

For any $u \in L_2(S)$ we can write $Tu = \phi_1(x) + \phi_2(x)$, where

$$\phi_1(x) = 0, x \in e_\lambda^*, \quad \phi_2(x) = 0, x \in e_\lambda.$$

Since T is unitary it has an inverse T^{-1} and we can define the family of linear operators $\quad E_\lambda u = T^{-1}c_\lambda(x)\,Tu = T^{-1}\phi_1,$

where $c_\lambda(x)$ stands for the linear transformation defined by the multiplication with the characteristic function of the set e_λ. We have $\|E_\lambda u\| \leqq \|u\|$ and $E_\lambda^2 = T^{-1}c_\lambda^2(x)\,T = E_\lambda$. Now E_λ is Hermitian, since

$$(E_\lambda u, v) = (T^{-1}c_\lambda(x)\,Tu, v) = (c_\lambda(x)\,Tu, Tv) = (Tu, c_\lambda(x)\,Tv) = (u, E_\lambda v);$$

E_λ must be a projection operator (see 1.20). If $\lambda \leqq \mu$ we find

$$E_\lambda E_\mu = T^{-1}c_\lambda(x)\,c_\mu(x)\,T = T^{-1}c_\lambda(x)\,T = E_\lambda.$$

Introducing $\sup_x |f(x)| = M$ it follows

$$E_\lambda = O \text{ if } \lambda < -M, \quad E_\lambda = I \text{ if } \lambda > M,$$

so that E_λ is a resolution of the identity.

We define the new operator K by the relation

$$K = \int_{-M}^{M} \lambda\, dE_\lambda.$$

We have for the bilinear form

$$(u, Kv) = \int_{-M}^{M} \lambda\, d(u, E_\lambda v) = \int_{-M}^{M} \lambda\, d\int_{e_\lambda} Tu\overline{Tv}\, dx = \int_{X} f(x)\, Tu\overline{Tv}\, dx.$$

If $u, v \in \mathfrak{F}_\alpha$ we can write this as

$$(u, Kv) = \int_S \int_S K(s, t)\, u(s)\, \overline{u(t)}\, ds\, dt,$$

where the kernel $K(s, t)$ is given by

$$K(s, t) = \int_X f(x)\, \phi(x, s)\, \overline{\phi(x, t)}\, dx,$$

so that K can be considered as an integral operator (or rather the extension of one).

The kernel K [or $K(f)$ as we sometimes write in order to point out the dependence upon f] is called a *Toeplitz operator*. Its spectrum is easily obtained in the following way. We shall say that a point λ belongs to the set of values ('Wertevorrat') of $f(x)$ if for any $\epsilon > 0$

$$\mu\{x \mid \lambda - \epsilon \leq f(x) \leq \lambda + \epsilon\} > 0.$$

If λ is such a number it is clear that

$$E_{\lambda + \epsilon} - E_{\lambda - \epsilon} = T^{-1}[c_{\lambda + \epsilon}(x) - c_{\lambda - \epsilon}(x)] T \neq O$$

and the converse is obvious. Hence the spectrum of K coincides with the set of values of $f(x)$. In particular we have $\| K \| = \operatorname*{ess\,sup}_{x} | f(x) |$.

Let us note the very simple rules of composition. Of course $K(af + bg) = aK(f) + bK(g)$, and we conclude also $K(fg) = K(f) K(g)$ immediately from the relation $K = T^{-1} f(x) T$, where $f(x)$ stands for the operator defined by multiplying with the function $f(x)$.

Now let us consider an operator K_α transforming $L_2(S_\alpha)$ into itself, such that if $u \in L_2(S_\alpha)$

$$K_\alpha u = \int_{S_\alpha} K(s, t) \,\overline{u(t)}\, dt.$$

Since

$$\int_S \int_S | K_\alpha(s, t) |^2 \, ds \, dt \leq c_\alpha^2 [\nu(S_\alpha)]^2 < \infty,$$

K_α is a Hilbert–Schmidt kernel (see 7.1). It is called a *finite Toeplitz operator* in contrast to K which is the infinite Toeplitz operator. Denoting the eigenvalues of K_α by $\lambda_\nu^{(\alpha)}$, $\nu = 1, 2, \dots$, our main problem will be the study of their distribution $\mathfrak{D}_\alpha$ for 'large' values of α.

(c) Let us consider some examples. We choose S as the set of integers and ν as counting measure. Let

$$\phi(x, s) = \phi_s(x), \quad s = \dots -1, 0, 1, \dots$$

be a complete orthonormal system in $L_2(X)$. Then T is a unitary transformation from the Hilbert space $L_2(S)$ of sequences with a convergent sum of squares to $L_2(X)$. K can be represented by the infinite *Toeplitz matrix*

$$M(f) = \left\{ \int_X f(x)\, \phi_s(x)\, \overline{\phi_t(x)}\, dx;\ s, t = \dots, -1, 0, 1, \dots \right\}.$$

For S_α we choose the set of integers between $-\alpha$ and α so that K_α is represented by a finite section of $M(f)$ which we write as follows:

$$M_\alpha(f) = \left\{ \int_X f(x)\, \phi_s(x)\, \overline{\phi_t(x)}\, dx;\ -\alpha \leqq s, t \leqq \alpha \right\} = [M(f)]_\alpha.$$

Specializing X as the interval $[-\pi, \pi]$ and μ as the Lebesgue measure we may choose the ϕ's as follows:

$$\phi_s(x) = (2\pi)^{-\frac{1}{2}} e^{isx},$$

and obtain the *classical Toeplitz matrices*

$$M_\alpha(f) = \left\{ \frac{1}{2\pi} \int_{-\pi}^{\pi} e^{i(s-t)x} f(x)\, dx;\ -\alpha \leqq s, t \leqq \alpha \right\},$$

studied in considerable detail in the previous chapters. Another possibility is to choose X as $[-1, 1]$ and μ as the measure with density $(1-x)^\alpha (1+x)^\beta$ with respect to the Lebesgue measure. Then it is natural to choose the ϕ's as the Jacobi polynomials.

If we let both X and S be the whole real line and μ and ν be the Lebesgue measure, we might define again $\phi(x, s) = (2\pi)^{-\frac{1}{2}} e^{isx}$; for T we choose the Fourier–Plancherel transform. The operator K will be represented by the integral kernel

$$K(s, t) = \frac{1}{2\pi} \int_{-\infty}^{\infty} e^{i(s-t)x} f(x)\, dx,$$

which is a *Toeplitz kernel*.

Many more examples could be mentioned, and we shall deal with several cases in this and the next chapter. In particular, we will be interested in the eigenvalue distribution of Toeplitz forms associated with the classical systems of orthogonal functions. As a preparation we will investigate first (in 7.3 and 7.4) how Toeplitz operators can be approximated in a certain sense by operators with eigenvalue distributions which are known or at least can be treated easier than the given ones.

7.3. A metric for Toeplitz operators

(a) In section 1.20 we introduced the norm $\|K\|$ which is a metric for operators K. This norm is somewhat too 'strong' for our purpose and we will find it convenient to introduce another one. It can be written as follows:

$$| K_\alpha | = \left\{ [\nu(S_\alpha)]^{-1} \int_S \int_S | K(s,t) |^2 ds\,dt \right\}^{\frac{1}{2}}.$$

One may note that the two norms can easily be expressed in terms of the eigenvalues:

$$\| K \| = \max_j | \lambda_j^{(\alpha)} |, \quad | K_\alpha |^2 = [\nu(S_\alpha)]^{-1} \sum_{\nu=1}^{\infty} (\lambda_\nu^{(\alpha)})^2.$$

For later purposes we shall need a bound for $| GH |$ (for the norm of the product of two operators); we find easily, all the integrations taken over S_α,

$$| GH |^2 = [\nu(S_\alpha)]^{-1} \int\int \left| \int G(s,u)\, H(u,t)\, du \right|^2 ds\,dt$$

$$= [\nu(S_\alpha)]^{-1} \int\int\int\int G(s,u)\, G(s,v)\, H(u,t)\, \overline{H(v,t)}\, du\,dv\,ds\,dt$$

$$= [\nu(S_\alpha)]^{-1} \int\int\int F(u,v)\, H(u,t)\, \overline{H(v,t)}\, du\,dv\,dt,$$

where we employed the notation

$$F(u,v) = \int G(s,u)\, \overline{G(s,v)}\, ds.$$

Hence

$$| GH |^2 \leq [\nu(S_\alpha)]^{-1} \| F \| \int\int | H(u,t) |^2 du\,dt = \| F \| \cdot | H |^2 \leq \| G \|^2 | H |^2,$$

which proves the relation

$$| GH | \leq \| G \| \cdot | H |. \tag{1}$$

(b) It is easy to find some simple but useful bounds for the norm of $K_\alpha(f)$ where f is given. As easily seen

$$\int_S K(s,t)\, \overline{K(t,\tau)}\, dt = \int_X [f(x)]^2\, \phi(x,s)\, \overline{\phi(x,\tau)}\, dx,$$

so that

$$\int_{s\in S_\alpha, t\in S} | K(s,t) |^2 ds\,dt = \int_{S_\alpha} \int_X [f(x)]^2 | \phi(x,s) |^2 dx\,ds.$$

If the orthogonal kernel is uniformly bounded

$$| \phi(x, s) | \leq c_\alpha \leq c < \infty, \quad x \in X, s \in S,$$

we have

$$| K_\alpha |^2 \leq c \int_X [f(x)]^2 \, dx,$$

so that

$$| K_\alpha | \leq c^{\frac{1}{2}} \| f \|.$$

On the other hand if

$$\int_X | \phi(x, s) |^2 \, dx \leq K, \quad s \in S, \tag{2}$$

we find

$$| K_\alpha | \leq K^{\frac{1}{2}} \operatorname*{ess\,sup}_x | f(x) |.$$

Note that when S is the set of integers and $\phi(x, s) = \phi_s(x)$ forms an orthonormal system, (2) is automatically satisfied with $K = 1$.

Recapitulating, we have

(i) $\| K \|, \| K_\alpha \| \leq \operatorname*{ess\,sup}_x | f(x) |.$

(ii) If $| \phi(x, s) | \leq c < \infty$, then $| K_\alpha | \leq c^{\frac{1}{2}} \| f \|.$

(iii) If $\int_S | \phi(x, s) |^2 \, dx \leq K < \infty$, then $| K_\alpha | \leq K^{\frac{1}{2}} \operatorname*{ess\,sup}_x | f(x) |.$

7.4. Approximations of Toeplitz operators

(a) Given a Toeplitz operator K_α we want to study its eigenvalue distribution $\mathfrak{D}_\alpha$ in the asymptotic sense. It will usually be convenient to consider a slightly different operator L_α, not necessarily a Toeplitz operator, but of the Hilbert–Schmidt type. L_α should approximate K_α in the following sense:

(i) It should be uniformly bounded in both norms,

$$\| L_\alpha \| \leq k < \infty, \quad | L_\alpha | \leq l < \infty.$$

(ii) $\lim_\alpha | L_\alpha - K_\alpha | = 0.$

Suppose that we can find an operator L_α satisfying these conditions such that its eigenvalue moments tend (in the way described in 7.1) to those of $\mathfrak{D}$; we shall prove then that the same holds for K_α.

Writing

$$K_\alpha = L_\alpha + \Delta_\alpha,$$

we find by taking the sth iterate (s is an arbitrary positive integer)

$$K_\alpha^s = L_\alpha^s + R_\alpha, \tag{1}$$

where R_α is a finite sum (the number of terms does not depend on α), a typical term of which can be written as follows: $A_1 A_2 \ldots A_q$, $q \leqq s$. Here the factors A_j are either L_α or Δ_α, but at least one of them is Δ_α. Using 7.3 (1) the sum R_α can be written as $A_\alpha B_\alpha = E_\alpha$ with $|A_\alpha|$ bounded and $\lim_\alpha |B_\alpha| = 0$. But

$$| [\nu(S_\alpha)]^{-1} \operatorname{tr} E_\alpha |^2$$

$$= \left| [\nu(S_\alpha)]^{-1} \int_{S_\alpha} E_\alpha(s,s)\, ds \right|^2$$

$$\leqq [\nu(S_\alpha)]^{-1} \int_{S_\alpha} \int_{S_\alpha} |A_\alpha(s,t)|^2\, ds\, dt \, [\nu(S_\alpha)]^{-1} \int_{S_\alpha} \int_{S_\alpha} |B_\alpha(s,t)|^2\, ds\, dt,$$

which tends to zero for increasing α. Denoting the eigenvalues of K_α and L_α by λ_j and l_j, respectively, we find by taking the trace of both sides of (1)

$$[\nu(S_\alpha)]^{-1} \sum_{j=1}^{\infty} \lambda_j^s = [\nu(S_\alpha)]^{-1} \sum_{j=1}^{\infty} l_j^s + o(1).$$

Choosing the constants K_α in 7.1 as $\nu(S_\alpha)$ we see, in view of the convergence of the moments of l_j, that the moments of λ_j also converge. This is true for each s (according to a remark made in 7.1 it is sufficient to consider $s \geqq 2$), and we have proved that $\mathfrak{D}_\alpha$ tends to $\mathfrak{D}$. Thus we have the following theorem:

THEOREM. *Let the Toeplitz form K_α be approximated by the Hilbert–Schmidt operator L_α so that* (i) *and* (ii) *are satisfied and* (iii), *the eigenvalue moments $\mu_s^{(\alpha)}$ of L_α, $s \geqq 2$, tend to the moments of a distribution $\mathfrak{D}$ with $\mu_2(\mathfrak{D}) < \infty$. Then the eigenvalue distribution of K_α tends also to $\mathfrak{D}$.*

(b) Dealing with Toeplitz matrices we will consider all $s \geqq 0$. In the rest of this section we discuss only this case, although the results can be extended to arbitrary Toeplitz operators.

Given certain $\alpha \times \alpha$ matrices of the Toeplitz type $K_\alpha^{(1)}, K_\alpha^{(2)}, \ldots, K_\alpha^{(q)}$, and *commutative* Hermitian matrices, $L_\alpha^{(1)}, L_\alpha^{(2)}, \ldots, L_\alpha^{(q)}$, so that $L_\alpha^{(j)}$ approximates $K_\alpha^{(j)}$ as described above. Consider the matrices

$$M_\alpha = K_\alpha^{(1)} K_\alpha^{(2)} \ldots K_\alpha^{(q)}, \quad N_\alpha = L_\alpha^{(1)} L_\alpha^{(2)} \ldots L_\alpha^{(q)}.$$

Suppose that the eigenvalue distribution of N_α tends to $\mathfrak{D}$. Although the matrices M_α are, in general, no longer Hermitian (or even normal), we can still talk about their eigenvalues $\lambda_j, j = 1, 2, \ldots, n$; they are the roots of the equation $\det(M_\alpha - \lambda I) = 0$. These λ_j are not necessarily real; we separate them into real and imaginary parts, $\lambda_j = m_j + in_j$. We shall consider two-dimensional distributions in the complex plane inside a certain fixed circle. On the other hand, N_α is Hermitian and hence its eigenvalues ν_j are real.

As before we can prove for each integer s the convergence of the eigenvalue moments

$$\lim_{\alpha \to \infty} \alpha^{-1} \operatorname{tr} M_\alpha^s = \lim_{\alpha \to \infty} \alpha^{-1} \operatorname{tr} N_\alpha^s = \mu_s, \tag{2}$$

where μ_s is the sth moment corresponding to $\mathfrak{D}$. Now any matrix $A = \{a_{jk};\ j, k = 1, 2, \ldots, \alpha\}$ can be brought, by a unitary transformation U, to a 'superdiagonal' form

$$U^* A U = B = \{b_{jk};\ j, k = 1, 2, \ldots, \alpha\},$$

where $b_{jk} = 0$ for $k > j$. Clearly the eigenvalues ρ_j of A will be given by $b_{jj}, j = 1, 2, \ldots, \alpha$. Forming the trace of the matrix AA^* (which is invariant with respect to unitary transformations) we obtain

$$\operatorname{tr} AA^* = \sum_{j,k=1}^{\alpha} |a_{jk}|^2 = \operatorname{tr} BB^* = \sum_{j,k=1}^{\alpha} |b_{jk}|^2 \geqq \sum_{j=1}^{\alpha} |\rho_j|^2.$$

Applying this inequality to the matrix M_α we find

$$\alpha^{-1} \sum_{j=1}^{\alpha} |\lambda_j|^2 = \alpha^{-1} \sum_{j=1}^{\alpha} (m_j^2 + n_j^2) \leqq |M_\alpha|^2,$$

and since the right member tends to $\lim_{\alpha} |L_\alpha|^2 = \mu_2$ we obtain, by subtracting equation (2) for $s = 0$, that

$$\lim_{\alpha \to \infty} \alpha^{-1} \sum_{j=1}^{\alpha} n_j^2 \leqq 0.$$

Hence the distribution of the imaginary parts of λ_j tends to the distribution concentrated at zero. Thus it follows that the sth moment of the m_j tends to μ_s, and we have proved that, as $\alpha \to \infty$, the distribution of the eigenvalues of M_α becomes more and more concentrated around the real axis; moreover, the real parts will be asymptotically distributed as the eigenvalues of N_α. Nothing is changed in the more general situation

$$M_\alpha = P[K_\alpha^{(1)}, K_\alpha^{(2)}, \ldots, K_\alpha^{(q)}], \quad N_\alpha = P[L_\alpha^{(1)}, L_\alpha^{(2)}, \ldots, L_\alpha^{(q)}],$$

where P is an arbitrary polynomial in q variables with real coefficients.

(c) Is it possible to make asymptotic statements about the *eigenvectors* of a Toeplitz matrix K_α if we know those of an approximating Hermitian matrix L_α? This is indeed possible, but only in the sense of an *average distribution*, as it was the case in the corresponding study of the eigenvalues.

Let K_α have the eigenvalues λ_j corresponding to the eigenvectors ξ_j; similarly, let L_α have the eigenvalues and eigenvectors ν_j and ζ_j, respectively. If we denote the projection operators corresponding to ξ_j and ζ_j by e_j and f_j, respectively, we can write

$$K_\alpha = \sum_{j=1}^{\alpha} \lambda_j e_j, \quad L_\alpha = \sum_{j=1}^{\alpha} \nu_j f_j.$$

Let $[a, b]$ be an interval whose endpoints are continuity points of the limiting distribution $\mathfrak{D}$ of the eigenvalues. If $c(x)$ is the characteristic function of $[a, b]$ and $p(x)$ is a polynomial with real coefficients, we write

$$e = \sum_{a \leq \lambda_j \leq b} e_j, \quad f = \sum_{a \leq \nu_j \leq b} f_j,$$

and we have

$$|p(K_\alpha) - e|^2 = \alpha^{-1} \sum_{j=1}^{\infty} [p(\lambda_j) - c(\lambda_j)]^2.$$

But the limit of this is

$$\int [p(x) - c(x)]^2 \, dD(x),$$

and we can choose a polynomial p so that this integral is as small as desired; a similar conclusion holds for $|p(L_\alpha) - f|$. We obtain then

$$|e - f| \leq |e - p(K_\alpha)| + |p(K_\alpha) - p(L_\alpha)| + |p(L_\alpha) - f|,$$

and since all three terms can be made arbitrarily small we have proved the following theorem:

THEOREM. *Let the Toeplitz matrix K_α be approximated by a Hermitian matrix L_α as described above. Let $[a, b]$ be any continuity interval of the limiting eigenvalue distribution of L_α. The projections e and f upon the two linear manifolds spanned by the eigenvectors belonging to eigenvalues in $[a, b]$ are asymptotically equivalent:*

$$\lim_{\alpha \to \infty} |e - f| = 0. \tag{3}$$

We can interpret (3) in the following slightly more intuitive way. Let us project the eigenvectors ξ_j on the manifold spanned by the ζ_j, $a \leq \nu_j \leq b$, and let us consider the difference

$$\delta_j = \xi_j - f\xi_j.$$

We have, summing over the corresponding values of $j \in J$,

$$\alpha^{-1} \sum_{j \in J} \| \xi_j - f\xi_j \|^2 = \alpha^{-1} \sum_{j \in J} \| (e-f) \xi_j \|^2$$

$$\leq \alpha^{-1} \sum_{j=1}^{\alpha} \| (e-f) \xi_j \|^2,$$

which is easily verified to be just $|e-f|$. The number of $j \in J$ is asymptotically equal to $n\,[D(b) - D(a)]$, so that unless $D(x)$ is constant in $[a, b]$, for any $\epsilon > 0$ *the relative number of the j's for which $\| \delta_j \| > \epsilon$ tends to zero as α increases.*

7.5. Toeplitz forms on product sets

(a) This section deals with some simple but useful remarks. First, let us assume that the Toeplitz operator defined by the kernel

$$K_\alpha(f) = K_\alpha(s, t) = \int_X f(x)\, \phi(x, s)\, \overline{\phi(x, t)}\, dx$$

has a limiting eigenvalue distribution $\mathfrak{D}(f)$ for each bounded and $(\mathfrak{X})$-integrable function $f(x)$ in the sense defined in 7.1; we want to study the Toeplitz form

$$K_{2,\alpha}(f) = K_\alpha(\bar{s}, \bar{t}) = \int_X \int_X f(\bar{x})\, \phi(x_1, s_1)\, \phi(x_2, s_2)\, \overline{\phi(x_1, t_1)}\, \overline{\phi(x_2, t_2)}\, dx_1 dx_2,$$

where $\bar{s} = (s_1, s_2)$, $\bar{t} = (t_1, t_2)$ and $\bar{x} = (x_1, x_2)$. This kernel is defined on the product set $S \times S$. Under the usual condition on $f(\bar{x})$ (boundedness and integrability on $X \times X$) it is also quadratically integrable, and for any $\epsilon > 0$ we can find (see Appendix) certain bounded functions $g_j(x)$ and $h_j(x)$ integrable over X such that

$$f(\bar{x}) = \sum_{j=1}^{r} g_j(x_1)\, h_j(x_2) + d(\bar{x}),$$

where

$$\int_X \int_X [d(\bar{x})]^2\, dx_1 dx_2 < \epsilon.$$

We have

$$K_{2,\alpha}(f) = \sum_{j=1}^{r} K_\alpha(g_j)\, K_\alpha(h_j) + K_{2,\alpha}(d) = H_\alpha + K_{2,\alpha}(d).$$

If we assume that $\phi(x,s)$ is uniformly bounded, $|\phi(x,s)| \leq c$, we find from 7.3 that $|K_{2,\alpha}(d)| \leq (c\varepsilon)^{\frac{1}{2}}$ so that the eigenvalue distributions of $K_{2,\alpha}(f)$ and H_α differ arbitrarily little (see 7.4). Now H_α is an operator which can be treated in a similar way as the polynomials

$$P[K_\alpha^{(1)}, K_\alpha^{(2)}, \ldots, K_\alpha^{(q)}]$$

of the last section.

(b) Let us consider a special situation which is still rather general and occurs frequently. Let f be bounded and $(\mathfrak{X})$-integrable; moreover, let us assume that $K_\alpha(f)$ is (tr)-complete (see the definition of this concept in 8.1) and that the class of Toeplitz forms has a *canonical distribution*. This last property means that there is a measure over (X), not depending upon f, defined by a density $p(x)$ with respect to μ such that for $u > 0$

$$-D(u; f) = \lim_\alpha [\nu(S_\alpha)]^{-1}[\text{number of } \lambda_\nu^{(\alpha)} \geq u]$$

$$= \int_{f(x) \geq u} p(x)\, d\mu(x);$$

we assume also the analogous relation for $u < 0$. A special instance of canonical distributions is that of the classical Toeplitz matrices with $p(x) \equiv 1$ (see chapter 5). We remark that this definition can be extended in a natural way to include canonical distributions that are not absolutely continuous with respect to μ.

Under these assumptions we have for the trace of the sth iterate of $H_\alpha(f)$:

$$[\nu(S_\alpha)]^{-2}\,\mathrm{tr}\,[H_\alpha^s(f)]$$

$$= [\nu(S_\alpha)]^{-2} \sum_{j_1, \ldots, j_s = 1}^{r} \mathrm{tr}\,[K_\alpha(g_{j_1}) \ldots K_\alpha(g_{j_s})]\,\mathrm{tr}\,[K_\alpha(h_{j_1}) \ldots K_\alpha(h_{j_s})]$$

$$= [\nu(S_\alpha)]^{-2} \sum_{j_1, \ldots, j_s = 1}^{r} \mathrm{tr}\,K_\alpha(g_{j_1} \ldots g_{j_s})\,\mathrm{tr}\,K_\alpha(h_{j_1} \ldots h_{j_s}) + o(1).$$

In the second step the (tr)-completeness has been used. But this tends to

$$\sum_{j_1, \ldots, j_s = 1}^{r} \int_X \int_X g_{j_1}(x_1)\, h_{j_1}(x_2) \ldots g_{j_s}(x_1)\, h_{j_s}(x_2)\, p(x_1)\, p(x_2)\, dx_1\, dx_2$$

$$= \int_X \int_X \left[\sum_{j=1}^{r} g_j(x_1)\, h_j(x_2)\right]^s p(x_1)\, p(x_2)\, dx_1\, dx_2.$$

Hence the asymptotic moments of the eigenvalues of $K_{2,\alpha}(f)$ are given by

$$\mu_s(f) = \int_X \int_X [f(\bar{x})]^s \, p(x_1) \, p(x_2) \, dx_1 \, dx_2,$$

i.e. $K_{2,\alpha}(f)$ has a canonical distribution with the density $p(x_1) \, p(x_2)$.

The same proof holds if we assume

$$\int_X |\phi(x,s)|^2 \, dx \leqq k < \infty;$$

we approximate then $f(\bar{x})$ uniformly so that $|d(\bar{x})| \leqq \epsilon, x \in X$. In this case no restriction on $p(x)$ is needed.

(c) Now let us discuss the change of a Toeplitz operator

$$K(s,t) = \int_X f(x) \, \phi(x,s) \, \overline{\phi(x,t)} \, dx$$

under a change of the variables. Let $y = y(x)$ map X in a one-to-one manner onto the space Y. The Borel field $\mathfrak{X}$ is carried over into a Borel field of subsets of Y, say $\mathfrak{Y}$. On $\mathfrak{Y}$ a measure dy is defined such that dx is absolutely continuous with respect to dy. The Radon–Nikodym derivative (see Appendix) will be denoted by dx/dy.

We define $\psi(y,s) = (dx/dy)^{\frac{1}{2}} \, \phi(x,s)$, and this is an orthogonal kernel. For any $u \in L_2(S)$ we have

$$\int_S \psi(y,s) \, u(s) \, ds = (dx/dy)^{\frac{1}{2}} Tu = Vu, \quad \text{say,}$$

and Vu is an element in $L_2(Y)$ with

$$\| Vu \|^2 = \int_Y (dx/dy) \, | Tu |^2 \, dy = \| Tu \|^2.$$

So the metric properties of the operator V from $L_2(S)$ to $L_2(Y)$ are identical with those of T carrying $L_2(S)$ into $L_2(X)$. Hence

$$L(g) = L(s,t) = \int_Y g(y) \, \psi(y,s) \, \overline{\psi(y,t)} \, dy$$

is a Toeplitz operator. $L(g)$ is identical with $L(f)$ if $f(x) = g[y(x)]$. In particular, if $K(f)$ has a canonical distribution with density $p(x)$, $L(g)$ has also a canonical distribution with the density $p[x(y)] \, . \, dy/dx$.

(d) Suppose that the Toeplitz matrices

$$M_n(f) = \left\{ \int_X \phi_\nu(x) \, \overline{\phi_\mu(x)} f(x) \, dx; \; \nu, \mu = 1, 2, \dots, n \right\}$$

have a canonical distribution with density $p(x)$ for bounded and ($\mathfrak{X}$)-measurable functions $f(x)$. Let us consider a function $g(x)$ which is integrable over X but not necessarily bounded. The matrix $M_n(g)$ is still defined since the ϕ's are bounded (see 7.2). Suppose first that $g(x)$ is bounded from below, $m \leq g(x)$. Introducing the bounded and ($\mathfrak{X}$)-measurable function

$$g_M(x) = \begin{cases} g(x) & \text{if } g(x) \leq M, \\ M & \text{otherwise,} \end{cases}$$

it is clear that we have the following relation between the quadratic forms:

$$\int_X \left| \sum_{\nu=1}^{n} z_\nu \phi_\nu(x) \right|^2 g_M(x)\, dx = z^* M_n(g_M)\, z \leq z^* M_n(g)\, z$$

$$= \int_X \left| \sum_{\nu=1}^{n} z_\nu \phi_\nu(x) \right|^2 g(x)\, dx,$$

for any vector $z = (z_1, z_2, \ldots, z_n)$. Denoting the eigenvalues of $M_n(g_M)$ and $M_n(g)$ by $\lambda_\nu(M)$ and λ_ν, respectively, it follows from 1.18 (4) that

$$\lambda_\nu(M) \leq \lambda_\nu, \quad \nu = 1, 2, \ldots, n.$$

Assume that the function

$$\Phi_n(x) = n^{-1} \sum_{\nu=1}^{n} |\phi_\nu(x)|^2$$

is uniformly bounded, $\Phi_n(x) \leq c$ for all n and x. We have then

$$n^{-1} \sum_{\nu=1}^{n} |\lambda_\nu(M) - \lambda_\nu| = n^{-1} \sum_{\nu=1}^{n} [\lambda_\nu - \lambda_\nu(M)]$$

$$= \int_X \Phi_n(x)\, [g(x) - g_M(x)]\, dx \leq c \int_X |g(x) - g_M(x)|\, dx.$$

This quantity can be made arbitrarily small by choosing M large, which implies that the distributions $\mathfrak{D}_n(M)$ and $\mathfrak{D}_n$ of $\lambda_\nu(M)$ and λ_ν, respectively, differ as little as we please. We have for the corresponding limiting distribution functions:

$$D(u; M) = \int_{g_M(x) \geq u} p(x)\, dx.$$

Introducing the sets

$$\{g(x) \geq u\} = E, \quad \{g_M(x) \geq u\} = E_M,$$

we have $E_M \subset E$ and $\mu(E - E_M) \to 0$ as $M \to \infty$ (since g is integrable). Then $D(u; M) \to D(u)$ as $M \to \infty$, since the measure $\int_E p(x)\,dx$ is absolutely continuous with respect to the μ-measure.

This proves that the Toeplitz matrices $M_n(g)$ have a canonical distribution in the more general case when $g(x)$ is only integrable and bounded from below, and $\Phi_n(x)$ is uniformly bounded. By analogous reasoning this result can be extended to integrable functions which are unbounded in both directions.

7.6. The classical Toeplitz forms

In the remaining part of this chapter we shall investigate various types of Toeplitz matrices regarding their eigenvalue distributions beginning with the classical Toeplitz forms. We have already studied this problem in chapter 5, but it will be instructive to compare the method used there with the ideas of the present chapter.

As has been pointed out by various authors, these matrices are closely related to the *circulant (cyclic) matrices*,

$$C = \{c_{\nu\mu};\ \mu, \nu = 1, 2, \ldots, n\},$$

defined by the relation $c_{\nu\mu} = c_{\alpha\beta}$ if $\nu - \mu \equiv \alpha - \beta \pmod{n}$. It is clear that the set of the circulant $n \times n$ matrices is algebraically closed.

We consider the matrix

$$U_n = \{n^{-\frac{1}{2}} e^{2\pi i \nu \mu n};\ \mu, \nu = 1, 2, \ldots, n\} = \begin{pmatrix} \eta_1 \\ \eta_2 \\ \cdots \\ \eta_n \end{pmatrix},$$

where the row vectors η_j are given by

$$\eta_j = (n^{-\frac{1}{2}} e^{2\pi i j/n}, n^{-\frac{1}{2}} e^{2\pi i \cdot 2j/n}, \ldots, n^{-\frac{1}{2}}).$$

U_n is clearly circulant and it is also unitary since

$$\{U_n U_n^*\}_{rs} = n^{-1} \sum_{\nu=1}^{n} e^{2\pi i (r-s)\nu/n} = \delta_{rs}.$$

To a real, bounded and measurable function $f(x)$ a certain $n \times n$ matrix $M_n(f)$ of the Toeplitz type corresponds (see 7.2):

$$M_n(f) = \left\{ \frac{1}{2\pi} \int_{-\pi}^{\pi} e^{i(\nu-\mu)x} f(x)\,dx;\ \mu, \nu = 1, 2, \ldots, n \right\}.$$

Introducing the Cesàro sums

$$f_p(x) = \sum_{\nu=-p}^{p} (1 - |\nu|/p) c_\nu e^{-i\nu x} = \sum_{\nu=-\infty}^{\infty} c'_\nu e^{-i\nu x},$$

where

$$c_\nu = \frac{1}{2\pi} \int_{-\pi}^{\pi} e^{i\nu x} f(x)\, dx,$$

we know that $|f_p(x)| \leq \sup_x |f(x)| = M < \infty$. We define a diagonal matrix D_n by

$$\{D_n\}_{\nu\nu} = f_p(2\pi\nu/n), \quad \nu = 1, 2, \ldots, n,$$

and approximate the Toeplitz matrix $M_n(f)$ by $L_n = U_n^* D_n U_n$. We have

$$\{L_n\}_{\nu\mu} = n^{-1} \sum_{m=1}^{n} e^{2\pi i \nu m/n} f_p(2\pi m/n) e^{-2\pi i m\mu/n} = \sum_{l=-\infty}^{\infty} c'_{\nu-\mu+ln}.$$

Writing $K_n = \{c'_{\nu-\mu}; \ \mu, \nu = 1, 2, \ldots, n\}$ we find easily for large values of n

$$|L_n - K_n|^2 = 2n^{-1} \sum_{\nu=1}^{p} \nu |c'_\nu|^2 \leq 2pn^{-1} \sum_{\nu=1}^{\infty} |c_\nu|^2 = O(n^{-1}),$$

and

$$|K_n - M_n(f)|^2 \leq 2n^{-1} \sum_{\nu=1}^{p} (\nu^2/p^2)(p-\nu)|c_\nu|^2 + 2n^{-1} \sum_{\nu=p+1}^{n} (n-\nu)|c_\nu|^2.$$

For a given $\epsilon > 0$ we can choose p so large that $\sum_{\nu=p+1}^{\infty} |c_\nu|^2 < \epsilon$. Then

$$|M_n(f) - L_n| \leq O(n^{-\frac{1}{2}}) + [O(n^{-1}) + 2\epsilon]^{\frac{1}{2}},$$

so that by choosing first p and then n sufficiently large the distance $|M_n(f) - L_n|$ can be made arbitrarily small.

Now L_n is Hermitian and bounded, $|L_n|$ and $\|L_n\| \leq M$, and has the eigenvalues $f_p(2\pi\nu/n), \nu = 1, 2, \ldots, n$. In view of the continuity of $f_p(x)$ we have for any positive integer s

$$\lim_{n \to \infty} n^{-1} \sum_{\nu=1}^{n} [f_p(2\pi\nu/n)]^s = \frac{1}{2\pi} \int_{-\pi}^{\pi} [f_p(x)]^s\, dx. \tag{1}$$

Also

$$\left| \int_{-\pi}^{\pi} ([f_p(x)]^s - [f(x)]^s)\, dx \right| \leq sM^{s-1} \int_{-\pi}^{\pi} |f_p(x) - f(x)|\, dx$$

$$\leq (2\pi)^{\frac{1}{2}} s M^{s-1} \|f_p - f\| \to 0 \quad \text{as} \quad p \to \infty.$$

8

It is now easily seen, by letting p and n tend to infinity in an appropriate manner, that the left member of (1) tends to

$$\frac{1}{2\pi}\int_{-\pi}^{\pi}[f(x)]^s\,dx,$$

i.e. to the sth moment of $f(x)$ when x is distributed with density $(2\pi)^{-1}$ over the interval $[-\pi,\pi]$ which is the canonical distribution for the classical Toeplitz matrices. This completes the new proof of theorem 5.2.

It also follows immediately that the eigenvectors of $M_n(f)$ are in the sense of 7.4 (c) asymptotically equal to $\eta_j,\ j=1,2,...,n$.

Using a remark made in the last section and noting that in the present case $\Phi_n(x)\equiv 1$, it follows that for any Lebesgue integrable $f(x)$, the matrix $M_n(f)$ has its eigenvalues distributed asymptotically as $f(x)$ with the same canonical distribution.

7.7. Toeplitz forms associated with orthogonal polynomials

(a) Let $w(x)$ be a nonnegative L-integrable weight function in the interval $[-1,1]$ which is not a zero function. We denote the corresponding orthonormal polynomials by $p_\nu(x),\nu=0,1,...$, so that

$$\int_{-1}^{1}p_\mu(x)\,p_\nu(x)\,w(x)\,dx=\delta_{\mu\nu}.$$

If $f(x)$ is a real-valued and continuous function defined for $x\in[-1,1]$, we consider the Toeplitz matrix

$$M_n(f)=\left\{\int_{-1}^{1}p_\mu(x)\,p_\nu(x)f(x)\,w(x)\,dx;\ \mu,\nu=0,1,...,n-1\right\}.$$

In order to study its eigenvalues we first assume that $f(x)$ is a polynomial $h(x)$ of degree ρ. It is well known that the zeros $x_{j\nu},j=1,2,...,\nu$, of $p_\nu(x)$ are real, distinct and situated in $[-1,1]$. If $\mu+\nu+\rho\leq 2n-1$ we obtain by the *Gauss–Jacobi* formula for mechanical quadrature (see Appendix)

$$\int_{-1}^{1}p_\mu(x)\,p_\nu(x)\,h(x)\,w(x)\,dx=\sum_{j=1}^{n}c_j^{(n)}p_\mu(x_{jn})\,p_\nu(x_{jn})\,h(x_{jn}),$$

where the *Christoffel numbers* $c_j^{(n)}$ are positive; they are independent of h. For $h \equiv 1$, $\rho = 0$, this reduces to

$$\delta_{\mu\nu} = \sum_{j=1}^{n} c_j^{(n)} p_\mu(x_{jn}) p_\nu(x_{jn}),$$

so that the matrix O_n with elements

$$[c_j^{(n)}]^{\frac{1}{2}} p_\nu(x_{jn}), \quad j = 1, 2, \ldots, n; \nu = 0, 1, \ldots, n-1,$$

is orthogonal. But $M_n(h) = O_n^* D_n O_n$, where D_n is a diagonal matrix with elements $h(x_{1n}), h(x_{2n}), \ldots, h(x_{nn})$; this means that the eigenvalues of $M_n(h)$ are the values of $h(x)$ at the zeros of $p_n(x)$.

Assume now that the zeros x_{jn} have a limiting distribution Δ over $[-1, 1]$; then $f(x)$ being a given continuous function we approximate $f(x)$ by a polynomial $h(x)$ so that $|f(x) - h(x)| < \epsilon$. If ϵ is sufficiently small the eigenvalue distributions of $M_n(f)$ and $M_n(h)$ differ arbitrarily little. From this and what has just been said about $M_n(h)$, it follows easily that the eigenvalue distributions $\mathfrak{D}_n$ of $M_n(f)$ tend to the distribution of $f(x)$ when x is distributed over $[-1, 1]$ according to Δ. In other words, there exists a canonical distribution and it is identical with Δ.

(b) Now assuming instead that $M_n(f)$ has a canonical distribution Δ [$f(x)$ is still supposed to be continuous] we will show that this implies the convergence of the distribution of the zeros x_{jn} of the orthogonal polynomials towards Δ. We introduce the function

$$\phi(x) = \begin{cases} 1, & x \leq \alpha, \\ 0, & x > \alpha, \end{cases}$$

and $\epsilon > 0$ being given, the functions $\phi_k(x)$, $k = 1, 2$, which are $= 1$ for $x \leq \alpha - \epsilon$ and $x \leq \alpha$, respectively, and $= 0$ for $x \geq \alpha$ and $x \geq \alpha + \epsilon$, respectively; in the remaining intervals $\phi_k(x)$ should be linear. Then $\phi_1(x)$ and $\phi_2(x)$ are continuous and

$$\phi_1(x) \leq \phi(x) \leq \phi_2(x). \tag{1}$$

It is easy to conclude from our assumptions that

$$\lim_{n \to \infty} n^{-1} \sum_{j=1}^{n} \phi_k(x_{jn}) = \int_{-1}^{1} \phi_k(x) \, d\Delta(x),$$

where $\Delta(x)$ is the distribution function corresponding to Δ. From (1) we see, letting ϵ tend to zero, that

$$\lim_{n \to \infty} n^{-1} \sum_{j=1}^{n} \phi(x_{jn}) = \Delta(\alpha)$$

for any continuity point α of Δ, so that the distribution of the zeros tends to Δ. Hence we have proved the following theorem:

THEOREM. *Let $\{p_\nu(x)\}$ be the orthonormal polynomials corresponding to an L-integrable weight function $w(x)$ on $[-1, 1]$. We consider the Toeplitz matrices*

$$M_n(f) = \left\{ \int_{-1}^{1} p_\mu(x)\, p_\nu(x) f(x)\, w(x)\, dx;\ \mu, \nu = 0, 1, \ldots, n-1 \right\},$$

where $f(x)$ is an arbitrary real-valued continuous function. The following two statements are equivalent:

(i) *The Toeplitz matrices $M_n(f)$ have a canonical distribution Δ.*

(ii) *The zeros x_{jn}, $j = 1, 2, \ldots, n$, of the orthogonal polynomial $p_n(x)$ have a distribution tending to Δ when n tends to infinity.*

(c) For a large class of weight functions $w(x)$ it is known (see Appendix) that the second statement above holds. We have indeed the following theorem:

THEOREM. *If the L-integrable weight function $w(x)$ satisfies the condition*

$$\int_{-1}^{1} (1-x^2)^{-\frac{1}{2}} \log w(x)\, dx < \infty, \tag{2}$$

the zeros of the associated orthogonal polynomials converge distribution-wise to $\cos \theta$, where θ is uniformly distributed on $[0, \pi]$.

Applying this theorem to the present problem we see that the Toeplitz matrices associated with the orthogonal polynomials, have a canonical distribution, namely, the one with the density $\pi^{-1}(1-x^2)^{-\frac{1}{2}}$ provided the weight function satisfies the condition (2). We observe that this distribution is independent of the weight function as long as (2) is fulfilled. The deeper reason for this fact will be seen more clearly in 8.1.

As an example we might refer to the Toeplitz forms associated with $w(x) = 1$ and the Legendre polynomials. Another simple case is $w(x) = (1-x^2)^{-\frac{1}{2}}$ and $p_\nu(x) = T_\nu(x)$, the Tchebychev polynomials of the first kind. Substituting $x = \cos\theta$ we have $T_n(x) = \cos n\theta$ so that, changing variables, we see by a simple modification of the argument in 7.5 that these Toeplitz matrices have a canonical distribution $(2\pi)^{-1} . 2 \,|\, d\theta/dx \,| = \pi^{-1}(1 - x^2)^{-\frac{1}{2}}$, as we have just obtained by another method.

7.8. Toeplitz forms and differential equations

It is easy to show that results similar to those obtained hold for Toeplitz matrices associated with the Sturm–Liouville eigenvalue problem. We consider the self-adjoint second-order differential operator $Lv = (pv')' - qv$ and the eigenvalue problem

$$\left.\begin{array}{l} Lv + \lambda\rho v = 0, \\ v(0) = v(\pi) = 0, \end{array}\right\} \quad 0 < x < \pi.$$

Here $p(x), q(x), \rho(x)$ are given functions, $p(x)$ and $\rho(x)$ positive. Under appropriate regularity conditions (see Appendix) we can apply a transformation

$$u = (p\rho)^{\frac{1}{4}} v, \quad t = H(x) = \int_0^x (\rho/p)^{\frac{1}{2}} dx,$$

carrying the problem into

$$\frac{d^2u}{dt^2} - ru + \lambda u = 0, \quad 0 < t < l,$$

$$u(0) = u(l) = 0,$$

where $r(t)$ depends on $p(x)$, $q(x)$, and $\rho(x)$ and the notation $l = H(\pi)$ has been introduced. The normalized eigensolutions of this problem have the following asymptotic behavior (see Appendix):

$$u_n(t) = (2/l)^{\frac{1}{2}} \sin(n\pi t/l) + \epsilon_n(t), \quad \epsilon_n(t) = O(n^{-1}), \quad n = 1, 2, \ldots.$$

Let the normalized eigensolutions of the original problem be

$$v_n(x) = (p\rho)^{-\frac{1}{4}} u_n(t),$$

so that

$$\int_0^l u_m(t)\, u_n(t)\, dt = \int_0^\pi v_m(x)\, v_n(x)\, \rho(x)\, dx = \delta_{mn}, \quad m, n = 1, 2, \ldots.$$

We introduce the Toeplitz matrix

$$M_n(f) = \left\{ m_{\mu\nu} = \int_0^\pi v_\mu(x)\, v_\nu(x) f(x)\, \rho(x)\, dx;\, \mu, \nu = 1, 2, \ldots, n \right\},$$

where $f(x)$ is a continuous real-valued function. We have, of course, for $f(x) \equiv 1$,
$$M_n(1) = I.$$

Now we find by changing variables
$$m_{\mu\nu} = (2/l) \int_0^l \sin(\mu\pi t/l) \sin(\nu\pi t/l) f(x) \, dt + \gamma_{\mu\nu},$$

with a 'remainder' $\gamma_{\mu\nu}$. Introducing the matrix
$$N_n(f) = \left\{ (2/l) \int_0^l \sin(\mu\pi t/l) \sin(\nu\pi t/l) f(x) \, dt;\ \mu,\ \nu = 1, 2, \ldots, n \right\},$$

we have
$$|\, M_n(f) - N_n(f)\,|^2 = n^{-1} \sum_{\mu,\,\nu=1}^{n} \gamma_{\mu\nu}^2.$$

The $\gamma_{\mu\nu}$ are composed of terms of three types of which we treat here only one, namely,
$$\eta_{\mu\nu} = \int_0^1 \sin(\mu\pi t/l) \, a_\nu(t) \, dt,$$

where $a_\nu(t) = O(\nu^{-1})$ uniformly. Hence from Bessel's inequality
$$\sum_{\mu=1}^{n} \eta_{\mu\nu}^2 = O(1) \int_0^1 [a_\nu(t)]^2 \, dt = O(\nu^{-2}),$$

so that $\lim_{n \to \infty} |\, \eta_{\mu\nu}\,| = 0$ and the same holds for the other terms. Since $\|\gamma_{\mu\nu}\|$ is bounded, it follows from theorem 7.4 that the eigenvalue distribution of $N_n(f)$ and $M_n(f)$ are asymptotically the same.

But the general elements of $N_n(f)$ can be written as follows:
$$\frac{2}{\pi} \int_0^\pi \sin \mu s \sin \nu s \, f[H^{-1}(ls/\pi)] \, ds,$$

and we know [cf. Appendix 8.5 (c)] that the eigenvalues of $N_n(f)$ converge distributionwise to $f[H^{-1}(ls/\pi)]$ with s uniformly distributed on $[0, \pi]$. Recapitulating, we conclude that the Toeplitz matrices under consideration have a canonical distribution, namely, that of $H^{-1}(ls/\pi)$, where s is uniform on $[0, \pi]$ with the density $1/\pi$. This distribution has the density $l^{-1}(\rho/p)^{\frac{1}{2}}$ with respect to Lebesgue measure on the interval $[0, \pi]$ of the x-axis.

7.9. The Haar system

All Toeplitz forms we have investigated so far correspond to a system of analytic orthogonal functions. In this section we study the matrices generated by the orthonormal functions of A. Haar (see Appendix); they are not of the previous category. Because of its flexibility and simplicity this example is useful for various purposes.

(a) Haar's system is defined as the following set of functions on $0 \leq x \leq 1$:

$$\chi_0^{(0)}(x) = \quad 1, \quad 0 \leq x \leq 1;$$

$$\chi_0^{(1)}(x) = \begin{cases} 1, & 0 \leq x < \tfrac{1}{2}, \\ -1, & \tfrac{1}{2} < x \leq 1; \end{cases}$$

$$\chi_1^{(1)}(x) = \begin{cases} 2^{\tfrac{1}{2}}, & 0 \leq x < \tfrac{1}{4}, \\ -2^{\tfrac{1}{2}}, & \tfrac{1}{4} < x < \tfrac{1}{2}, \\ 0, & \tfrac{1}{2} < x \leq 1; \end{cases}$$

$$\chi_1^{(2)}(x) = \begin{cases} 0, & 0 \leq x < \tfrac{1}{2}, \\ 2^{\tfrac{1}{2}}, & \tfrac{1}{2} < x < \tfrac{3}{4}, \\ -2^{\tfrac{1}{2}}, & \tfrac{3}{4} < x \leq 1; \end{cases}$$

$$\cdots\cdots\cdots\cdots\cdots$$

$$\chi_m^{(k)}(x) = \begin{cases} 2^{\tfrac{1}{2}m}, & (2k-2)\,2^{-m-1} < x < (2k-1)\,2^{-m-1}, \\ -2^{\tfrac{1}{2}m}, & (2k-1)\,2^{-m-1} < x < (2k)\,2^{-m-1}, \\ 0, & \text{otherwise,} \quad k = 1, 2, 3, \ldots, 2^m. \end{cases}$$

We enumerate these functions by the symbol $\phi_\nu(x)$ using a simple index ν, $\nu = 1, 2, \ldots, n$, so that $n = 2 + 2 + 2^2 + \ldots + 2^m = 2^{m+1}$. They are defined as continuous at $x = 0$ and $x = 1$; we also set

$$\phi_\nu(x) = \tfrac{1}{2}[\phi_\nu(x+0) + \phi_\nu(x-0)].$$

It is well known that the functions $\{\phi_\nu(x); \nu = 1, 2, \ldots\}$ form a complete orthonormal system on $0 \leq x \leq 1$ with the weight function $w(x) \equiv 1$. If $f(x)$ is a real-valued continuous function and ϵ a positive number, we can determine p and c_ν so that

$$|f(x) - f_p(x)| < \epsilon, \quad 0 < x < 1,$$

where

$$f_p(x) = \sum_{\nu=1}^{p} c_\nu \phi_\nu(x).$$

Introducing the midpoints $x_s = (s + \tfrac{1}{2})\, 2^{-m-1}$ of the interval

$$[s \cdot 2^{-m-1}, (s+1) \cdot 2^{-m-1}],$$

and using the fact that the functions $\phi_1(x), \ldots, \phi_n(x)$ are constant on these intervals we obtain immediately

$$\delta_{\mu\nu} = \int_0^1 \phi_\mu(x)\, \phi_\nu(x)\, dx = n^{-1} \sum_{s=0}^{n-1} \phi_\mu(x_s)\, \phi_\nu(x_s).$$

This is equivalent to the fact that the $n \times n$ matrix

$$O_n = \{ n^{-\frac{1}{2}} \phi_\mu(x_\nu);\ \mu = 1, 2, \ldots, n;\ \nu = 0, 1, \ldots, n-1 \}$$

is orthogonal. Also for $n \geqq p$

$$\{ M_n(f_p) \}_{\mu\nu} = \int_0^1 \phi_\mu(x)\, \phi_\nu(x) f_p(x)\, dx = n^{-1} \sum_{s=0}^{n-1} \phi_\mu(x_s)\, \phi_\nu(x_s) f_p(x_s),$$

so that

$$M_n(f_p) = O_n^* D_n O_n,$$

where D_n is a diagonal matrix of the type $n \times n$ with elements $f_p(x_0)$, $f_p(x_1)$, ..., $f_p(x_{n-1})$ in the main diagonal. Now as n tends to infinity the points x_s, $s = 0, 1, \ldots, n-1$, will become uniformly distributed over $[0, 1]$. Hence, since $M_n(f_p)$ has the eigenvalues $f_p(x_s)$, $s = 0, 1, \ldots, n-1$, these are asymptotically distributed as $f_p(x)$ with x uniform on $[0, 1]$. Applying the approximation method of 7.4, the analogous fact is seen to hold for $M_n(f)$. Thus we have proved the following theorem:

THEOREM. *The Toeplitz matrices corresponding to the Haar system have a canonical distribution, namely that one which is uniform over* $[0, 1]$.

(b) In all cases we have considered so far there exists a canonical distribution. By a suitable change of the variable (see 7.5) we may construct cases with any prescribed canonical distribution. One may ask, however, whether there exists always a canonical distribution. The following example answers this question in the negative, as one might expect.

Let $\phi_\nu(x)$ be defined as above. We define an infinite subset E of positive integers by the condition that $\nu \in E$ provided $\phi_\nu(x) \not\equiv 0$ in

$[0, \frac{1}{2}]$; let E^* stand for the complement of E. Let $f(x) = a$ in $[0, \frac{1}{2}]$ and $b(\neq a)$ in $[\frac{1}{2}, 1]$. [We might choose for $f(x)$ a continuous function, by a slight modification of the definition in the neighborhood of $x = \frac{1}{2}$.]

Let ν_k define a one-to-one mapping of the positive integers on themselves, $k = 1, 2, \ldots$. We choose it so that the ratio

$$r_n = n^{-1}\{\text{number of } \nu_k \in E; \ k = 1, 2, \ldots, n\}$$

oscillates as n tends to infinity. This is clearly possible since E is infinite. Now

$$n^{-1}\operatorname{tr} M_n(f) = an^{-1}\sum_{\nu=1}^{n}\int_0^{\frac{1}{2}}[\phi_\nu(x)]^2\,dx + bn^{-1}\sum_{\nu=1}^{n}\int_{\frac{1}{2}}^{1}[\phi_\nu(x)]^2\,dx$$

$$= ar_n + b(1 - r_n) = b + (a - b)r_n,$$

which does not converge. If the eigenvalue distribution of $M_n(f)$ would converge its first moment had to converge (the distribution is bounded); this is, however, apparently not the case. Thus it follows *a fortiori* that no canonical distribution exists.

CHAPTER 8

CERTAIN MATRICES AND INTEGRAL
EQUATIONS OF THE TOEPLITZ TYPE

8.1. Trace complete Toeplitz matrices

(a) With a system $\{\phi_\nu(x); \nu = 0, 1, 2, \ldots\}$ which is orthonormal and complete on the abstract set X, and with a function $f(x)$ we associate certain Toeplitz matrices $M(f)$ in the way discussed in chapter 7; here $f(x)$ is a bounded and real-valued $(\mathfrak{X})$-measurable function. If $g(x)$ is another function of this kind, we have

$$M(f)\,M(g) = M(fg). \tag{1}$$

Indeed this means, more explicitly, that

$$\sum_{k=0}^{\infty} \int_X \phi_\nu(x)\,\overline{\phi_k(x)}f(x)\,dx \int_X \phi_k(x)\,\overline{\phi_\mu(x)}\,g(x)\,dx = \int_X \phi_\nu(x)\,\overline{\phi_\mu(x)}f(x)\,g(x)\,dx,$$

which is identical with *Parseval's* relation or with the *completeness* of the system $\{\phi_\nu(x)\}$.

In the study of *finite* Toeplitz forms there exists an important analog of (1) which is rather essential in dealing with various problems. It is a property of *finite* Toeplitz matrices corresponding in a way to the property (1) of infinite Toeplitz matrices.

Let A be an infinite matrix, $A = \{a_{\nu\mu}; \nu, \mu = 0, 1, \ldots\}$; for the nth section we use the symbol

$$[A]_n = \{a_{\nu\mu}; \nu, \mu = 0, 1, \ldots, n-1\} \text{ (cf. 1.1)}.$$

DEFINITION. *Let K be a class of real-valued functions $f(x)$; we consider the associated class of Toeplitz matrices $M(f)$ and $M_n(f)$. If for every $f_1, f_2, \ldots, f_p \in K$ we have*

$$\lim_{n \to \infty} n^{-1} \operatorname{tr} \{M_n(f_1)\,M_n(f_2) \ldots M_n(f_p) - [M(f_1 f_2 \ldots f_p)]_n\} = 0,$$

we say that the class of Toeplitz matrices is trace complete [(tr)-complete].

(b) The following theorem is useful in establishing the (tr)-completenessfor certain classes of matrices, although the condition is probably far from being necessary:

THEOREM. *Let L be a linear algebra* (see Appendix). *If for every $f \in L$ the elements $m_{\nu\mu}$ of the Toeplitz matrix $M(f)$ satisfy the condition*

$$m_{\nu\mu} = [1 + (\nu-\mu)^2]^{-1} . O(1), \tag{2}$$

the class of matrices considered is (tr)-*complete.*

The bound of $O(1)$ is independent of ν and μ, but it may depend on f. If L is a linear algebra, the conditions $f \in L$, $g \in L$ imply $af(x) + bg(x) \in L$ and $f(x) g(x) \in L$ where a and b are real numbers.

For the proof we consider two sums of the form

$$\Sigma m_{\nu_1\nu_2}(f_1) m_{\nu_2\nu_3}(f_2) \dots m_{\nu_p\nu_1}(f_p), \tag{3}$$

where $m_{\nu\mu}(f_i)$ is the general element of $M(f_i)$. In the first sum, called S_n, the summation is extended over the range

$$0 \le \nu_j \le n-1, \quad j = 1, 2, \dots, p.$$

This corresponds to the first term in the relation defining the (tr)-completeness. In the second sum, called T_n, we sum over

$$0 \le \nu_1 \le n-1,$$
$$0 \le \nu_j < \infty, \quad j = 2, 3, \dots, p.$$

We can assume that $p > 1$; indeed, for $p = 1$ we have $M_n(f_1) = [M(f_1)]_n$ for each n.

The difference $T_n - S_n$ will consist of a finite number (independent of n) of terms of the form (3) where $0 \le \nu_1 \le n-1$; at least one subscript runs from n to infinity and the rest of them (except ν_1) from 0 to infinity. Subscripts belonging to the last category are easily dealt with. Indeed, if μ is one of them, we find

$$\sum_{\mu=0}^{\infty} m_{k\mu}(f) m_{\mu l}(g) = m_{kl}(fg),$$

as we have just seen, and since $fg \in L$ we reduce the situation to the case with $p-1$ factors. In this way we can eliminate all the summations over subscripts of this type.

Hence it is sufficient to consider sums of the form

$$\Sigma m_{\nu_1\nu_2}(f_1) m_{\nu_2\nu_3}(f_2) \dots m_{\nu_q\nu_1}(f_q),$$

with the summation extended over

$$0 \le \nu_1 \le n-1,$$
$$n \le \nu_j < \infty, \quad j = 2, 3, \dots, q.$$

Let k and l be arbitrary integers. If μ is an integer, either $|\mu-k|$ or $|\mu-l|$ is not less than $\frac{1}{2}|k-l|$ so that

$$\sum_{\mu=n}^{\infty} m_{k\mu}(g)\, m_{\mu l}(h)$$

$$= O(1) \sum_{\mu=n}^{\infty} [1+(\mu-k)^2]^{-1} [1+(\mu-l)^2]^{-1}$$

$$= O(1) [1+\tfrac{1}{4}(k-l)^2]^{-1} \sum_{\mu=n}^{\infty} \{[1+(\mu-k)^2]^{-1}+[1+(\mu-l)^2]^{-1}\},$$

and $\sum_{\nu=-\infty}^{\infty}(1+\nu^2)^{-1}$ being convergent, the last expression is

$$= O(1) [1+(k-l)^2]^{-1}.$$

By repeated use of this remark we arrive finally at an expression of the form

$$\Sigma[1+(\nu_2-\nu_1)^2]^{-2},$$

where ν_1 runs from 0 to $n-1$ and ν_2 from n to ∞. This can be written in the form

$$\sum_{k=1}^{\infty} \{[1+k^2]^{-2}+[1+(k+1)^2]^{-2}+\ldots+[1+(k+n-1)^2]^{-2}\}$$

$$< \sum_{k=1}^{\infty} k(1+k^2)^{-2}=O(1).$$

Hence we obtain $T_n-S_n=O(1)$ which proves the assertion.

(c) Before we proceed with the application of this new concept to the study of the eigenvalue distributions of Toeplitz forms, we will consider two simple lemmas:

LEMMA 1. *Let $\{a_\nu(x); \nu=0,1,\ldots\}$ be a complete set of linearly independent functions quadratically integrable over X. We consider the matrix*

$$A_n(f)=\left\{\int_X a_\nu(x)\, a_\mu(x) f(x)\, dx;\ \nu,\mu=0,1,\ldots,n-1\right\},$$

where $f(x)$ is real-valued, bounded and $(\mathfrak{X})$-measurable. The complete orthonormal system obtained from $\{a_\nu(x)\}$ by the Gram–Schmidt orthogonalization [1.8(c)] *is denoted by $\{\phi_\nu(x)\}$, and the associated Toeplitz matrices by $M_n(f)$. Then $M_n(f)$ has the same eigenvalues as $A_n(f)$ has with respect to the positive-definite matrix $A_n(1)$.*

Indeed the latter eigenvalues are defined by

$$\det(A_n(f)-\lambda A_n(1))=0.$$

But we can write

$$\phi_\nu(x) = b_{\nu 0} a_0(x) + b_{\nu 1} a_1(x) + \ldots + b_{\nu\nu} a_\nu(x),$$

where the matrix $B = \{b_{\nu\mu}; \nu, \mu = 0, 1, \ldots, n-1\}$ is nonsingular [since the $a_\nu(x)$ are linearly independent]. We have $M_n(f) = B^* A_n(f) B$, so that, since $M_n(1) = I$,

$$M_n(f) - \lambda I = B^*(A_n(f) - \lambda A_n(1)) B,$$

from which the result follows immediately.

As an application we may consider the case when $X = [-1, 1]$, $dx = $ Lebesgue measure and $a_\nu(x) = x^\nu$. Then $A_n(f)$ is the so-called *Hankel form*

$$H_n(f) = \left\{ \int_{-1}^{1} x^{\nu+\mu} f(x)\, dx;\ \nu, \mu = 0, 1, \ldots, n-1 \right\}.$$

On the other hand, $M_n(f)$ is the Toeplitz form associated with Legendre polynomials. We have seen in 7.7 that the eigenvalues of $M_n(f)$ are distributed asymptotically as $f(\cos\theta)$, where θ is uniform on $[0, \pi]$. Hence the same holds for the eigenvalues defined by

$$\det(H_n(f) - \lambda H_n(1)) = 0.$$

This result was obtained by another method in 6.3.

(d) In order to avoid a minor complication, for the rest of this section we assume that the $a_\nu(x)$ are real-valued. We have the following lemma:

LEMMA 2. *On X we define two measures μ and m, and we consider the corresponding L_2-spaces. Assuming that the measures are absolutely continuous with respect to each other and that the Radon–Nikodym derivative $p = d\mu/dm$ (see Appendix) is bounded away from zero and infinity,*

$$0 < c_1 \leqq d\mu/dm \leqq c_2 < \infty,$$

the two L_2-spaces consist of the same functions, however with different metrics. Let $\{\phi_\nu(x);\ \nu = 0, 1, \ldots\}$ and $\{\psi_\nu(x);\ \nu = 0, 1, \ldots\}$ be the orthonormal systems obtained in the usual way from $\{a_\nu(x);\ \nu = 0, 1, \ldots\}$ using the two metrics corresponding to $d\mu$ and dm. Let us denote the associated Toeplitz forms by $M_n(f)$ and $N_n(f)$.

We assume that $M_n(f)$ has a canonical distribution W and forms a (tr)-complete class. Then $N_n(f)$ has the same canonical distribution W.

Proof. The vectors

$$\phi = (\phi_0, \phi_1, \ldots, \phi_{n-1}), \quad \psi = (\psi_0, \psi_1, \ldots, \psi_{n-1})$$

satisfy $\psi = A\phi$, where A is a nonsingular $n \times n$ matrix. Hence

$$N_n(f) = A^* M_n(fp) A, \qquad (4)$$

so that $M_n(f)$ is similar to $A N_n(f) A^{-1} = A A^* M_n(fp)$. But substituting $f(x) = 1$ in (4) we obtain $I = A^* M_n(p) A$ and $(AA^*)^{-1} = M_n(p)$. Thus $N_n(f)$ has exactly the same eigenvalues as $M_n^{-1}(p) M_n(fp)$. But this matrix behaves for large values of n like $M_n(f)$. To show this we note that

$$M_n^{-1}(p) M_n(fp) - M_n(f) = M_n^{-1}(p) [M_n(pf) - M_n(p) M_n(f)]$$
$$= M_n^{-1}(p) \Delta_n.$$

We know [see (e)] that $\| M_n^{-1}(p) \| \le c_1^{-1}$ and

$$| \Delta_n |^2 = n^{-1} \operatorname{tr} \Delta_n^2$$
$$= n^{-1} \operatorname{tr} \{ M_n^2(pf) - M_n(pf) M_n(p) M_n(f) - M_n(p) M_n(f) M_n(pf)$$
$$+ M_n(p) M_n(f) M_n(p) M_n(f) \}.$$

Using the (tr)-completeness we see that this is equal to

$$o(1) + \int_X \{ [p(x)]^2 [f(x)]^2 - [p(x)]^2 [f(x)]^2 - [p(x)]^2 [f(x)]^2$$
$$+ [p(x)]^2 [f(x)]^2 \} \, dW(x) = o(1),$$

so that from 7.3 (1) we conclude

$$\lim_{n \to \infty} | M_n^{-1}(p) M_n(fp) - M_n(f) | = 0;$$

the rest of the argument goes along the lines of 7.4.

(e) It might be useful to insert a brief motivation of the inequality $\| M_n^{-1}(p) \| \le c_1^{-1}$. We know that $M_n \ge c_1 I_n$, where I_n is the $n \times n$ identity matrix. Or, in terms of quadratic forms, $z^* M_n z \ge c_1 z^* z$. Since M_n is a positive matrix, it has a 'square root', say A, so that $M_n = A^2$. Now writing $z = A^{-1} y$ (A is nonsingular) we obtain

$$z^* M_n z = z^* A A z = y^* y \ge c_1 y^* A^{-1} A^{-1} y = c_1 y^* M_n^{-1} y,$$

which is equivalent to the assertion.

(f) As an example we mention the Toeplitz matrices associated with the polynomials orthonormal with respect to various weight functions, $-1 \leq x \leq 1$. Indeed, we have seen in 7.7 that for a wide class of weight functions we arrive at the same canonical distribution $dW = \pi^{-1}(1-x^2)^{-\frac{1}{2}}\,dx$.

The condition of the boundedness of $d\mu/dx$ may be unnecessary, but it is certainly necessary to impose some condition ensuring absolute continuity. Consider the following simple example: $X = [0, \pi]$, $d\mu = $ Lebesgue measure and $a_0(x) = \pi^{-\frac{1}{2}}$, $a_\nu(x) = (2/\pi)^{\frac{1}{2}} \cos \nu x$, $\nu > 0$. Choosing dm as the Lebesgue measure plus the measure one at the point $x = 0$, we obtain $\phi_\nu(x) = a_\nu(x)$ and

$$\psi_0(x) = (1+\pi)^{-\frac{1}{2}},$$

$$\psi_\nu(x) = \left(\frac{2(1+\pi)}{\pi(3+\pi)}\right)^{\frac{1}{2}} \left(\cos \nu x - \frac{1}{1+\pi}\right), \quad \nu = 1, 2, 3, \ldots.$$

We know (see Appendix, 8.5 (c)) that in this case the $M_n(f)$ are (tr)-complete and have the canonical distribution $dW(x) = \pi^{-1}d\mu$. To study the asymptotic eigenvalue distribution of $N_n(f)$ it is sufficient to consider $\operatorname{tr} N_n(f)$. In view of

$$\int_0^\pi [\psi_\nu(x)]^2 f(x)\,dm(x) = \frac{2(1+\pi)}{\pi(3+\pi)} \int_0^\pi \left[\cos \nu x - \frac{1}{1+\pi}\right]^2 f(x)\,dx$$

$$+ \left[1 - \frac{1}{1+\pi}\right]^2 f(0), \quad \nu > 0,$$

we obtain, using the Riemann–Lebesgue lemma,

$$n^{-1} \operatorname{tr} N_n(f) = n^{-1} \sum_{\nu=0}^n \int_0^\pi [\psi_\nu(x)]^2 f(x)\,dm(x)$$

$$\rightarrow \frac{3 + 2\pi + \pi^2}{\pi(3+\pi)(1+\pi)} \int_0^\pi f(x)\,dx + \frac{2\pi}{(3+\pi)(1+\pi)} f(0)$$

as n tends to infinity. But this is different from the value

$$\int_0^\pi f(x)\,dW(x) = \pi^{-1} \int_0^\pi f(x)\,dx,$$

at which one would arrive if the conclusions of lemma 2 should hold in the present case.

8.2. Generating functions of Toeplitz matrices

(a) We consider a class of (tr)-complete Toeplitz matrices $M_n(f)$, $f \in C$, where C is a subset of all bounded, real-valued, and $(\mathfrak{X})$-measurable functions defined on X,

$$M_n(f) = \left\{ \int_X \phi_\nu(x)\,\overline{\phi_\mu(x)}\,f(x)\,dx;\; \nu,\mu = 0, 1, \ldots, n-1 \right\}.$$

Let $\Gamma \subset C$ and have the following properties. Γ forms a linear algebra over the field of real numbers [see 8.1 (b)]. Further, Γ is complete in C, so that for any $f \in C$ and $\epsilon > 0$ there is a function $g \in \Gamma$ so that $\|f - g\| < \epsilon$. Clearly, if we can deal with the matrices $M_n(g)$, $g \in \Gamma$, we can study the general case, $f \in C$, by approximating $f(x)$ by functions from Γ. We do not even have to suppose as much as this. In fact we have the following theorem:

THEOREM. *Suppose that the* (tr)-*complete class of matrices* $M_n(g)$, $g \in \Gamma$, *satisfies the relation*

$$\lim_{n \to \infty} n^{-1}\,\mathrm{tr}\, M_n(g) = L(g), \tag{1}$$

where L is a given linear operator in Γ; then the class of Toeplitz matrices $M_n(f)$, $f \in C$, has the asymptotic eigenvalue distribution determined by the moments

$$\mu_s = L(f^s), \quad s = 1, 2, \ldots.$$

Proof. First let us show that the $M_n(g)$ have an asymptotic eigenvalue distribution. It follows from the (tr)-completeness that for any positive integer s

$$\lim_{n \to \infty} n^{-1}\,\mathrm{tr}\,\{[M^s(g)]_n - M_n^s(g)\} = 0.$$

Noting that $[M^s(g)]_n = M_n(g^s)$ we find, if $\lambda_\nu^{(n)}$ denote the eigenvalues of $M_n(g)$,

$$\lim_{n \to \infty} n^{-1} \sum_{\nu=1}^n (\lambda_\nu^{(n)})^s = \lim_{n \to \infty} n^{-1}\,\mathrm{tr}\, M_n^s(g) = \lim_{n \to \infty} n^{-1}\,\mathrm{tr}\, M_n(g^s).$$

But the definition of Γ implies that $g^s \in \Gamma$ so that (1) is applicable and

$$\lim_{n \to \infty} n^{-1} \sum_{\nu=1}^\infty (\lambda_\nu^{(n)})^s = L(g^s) = \mu_s;$$

hence the $\lambda_\nu^{(n)}$ have the asymptotic distribution determined by the moments μ_s.

To complete the proof we start from an arbitrary $f \in C$ and approximate it by an element $f^* \in \Gamma$, so that $\|f - f^*\| < \epsilon$. From 7.3 it follows that

$$| M_n(f) - M_n(f^*) | < \epsilon,$$

and the theorem of 7.4 (a) completes the proof by noting that L is a bounded functional which can be extended to C in the usual manner.

(b) We note that if a subset of functions γ exists such that its linear hull is Γ, it is sufficient to prove (1) for each $g \in \gamma$.

There are various ways to prove (1), but the following method (or some modification of it) seems to be of a rather general character. Consider the function

$$K(x; z) = \sum_{\nu=0}^{\infty} | \phi_\nu(x) |^2 z^\nu$$

in the region of the complex z-plane where the series converges. This function can be explicitly evaluated for various classical orthogonal functions. Now we introduce the *generating function* of the Toeplitz matrix under consideration:

$$G(g; z) = \sum_{\nu=0}^{\infty} \int_X | \phi_\nu(x) |^2 g(x)\, dx\, z^\nu = \sum_{\nu=0}^{\infty} a_\nu(g)\, z^\nu.$$

It is clearly regular in the unit circle $|z| < 1$, and the radius of convergence is 1 provided $\inf_X g(x) > 0$. Since the Taylor coefficients $a_\nu(g)$ are positive, we know (see Appendix) that $G(g; z)$ has a singularity at $z = 1$.

(c) We now assume that this singularity is a *pole*. This condition is often found to be satisfied. We have then in the neighborhood of $z = 1$

$$(1-z)^{-1} \inf_X g(x) \leqq G(g; z) \leqq (1-z)^{-1} \sup_X g(x), \qquad (2)$$

so that the pole is of the first order, and we will write

$$G(g; z) \cong (1-z)^{-1} A(g), \quad z \to 1. \qquad (3)$$

Now we can prove the following theorem:

THEOREM. *Consider a class $M_n(g)$, $g \in \Gamma$, of (tr)-complete Toeplitz matrices. If the generating function has a pole at $z = 1$ with residue $A(g)$, then the distribution of eigenvalues of $M_n(g)$ tends to the distribution with the moments*

$$\mu_s = A(g^s), \quad s = 1, 2, \dots.$$

9

Proof. The functional $A(g)$ is a bounded linear operator. First, it is clearly linear since

$$\operatorname{tr} M_n(c_1 g_1 + c_2 g_2) = c_1 \operatorname{tr} M_n(g_1) + c_2 \operatorname{tr} M_n(g_2),$$

so that $A(c_1 g_1 + c_2 g_2) = c_1 A(g_1) + c_2 A(g_2)$. It is bounded because (2) implies $|A(g)| \le \|g\|$.

Now, we have by definition

$$\lim_{n \to \infty} n^{-1} \operatorname{tr} M_n(g) = \lim_{n \to \infty} n^{-1} \sum_{\nu=1}^{n} \int_X |\phi_\nu(x)|^2 g(x)\, dx = \lim_{n \to \infty} n^{-1} \sum_{\nu=1}^{n} a_\nu(g),$$

provided this limit exists. But (3) holds, from which we conclude by applying a famous theorem of Hardy–Littlewood (see Appendix) that

$$\lim_{n \to \infty} n^{-1} \operatorname{tr} M_n(g) = A(g).$$

The rest of the proof follows from the theorem in (a).

8.3. Existence of a canonical distribution

(a) We consider the case when X is a finite interval $[a, b]$ on the real axis and C consists of the real-valued continuous functions defined on $[a, b]$. In this case we can prove more than theorem 8.2 (c).

THEOREM. *We assume that the class of Toeplitz matrices $M_n(g)$, $g \in \Gamma$, is* (tr)*-complete; here X and C are defined as above and Γ is a linear algebra belonging to and everywhere dense in C. If $G(g; z)$ has a pole at $z = 1$, the class of matrices $M_n(f)$, $f \in C$, has a canonical distribution.*

Proof. As we have seen in the proof of theorem 8.2 (c) the residue $A(g)$ of $G(g; z)$ at $z = 1$ is a bounded linear operator when $g \in \Gamma$. Thus it can be extended to C preserving the property of being linear and bounded. But such an operator can be written as

$$A(f) = \int_a^b f(x)\, dW(x),$$

where $W(x)$ is a function of bounded variation in $[a, b]$ (see Appendix). Using the definition of $A(f)$ we see immediately that

(i) $A(f) \ge 0$ if $f(x) \ge 0$, i.e. $A(f)$ is a positive operator.

(ii) $A(1) = 1$.

This implies, however, that $W(x)$ is nondecreasing and of variation 1 over the interval $[a, b]$, i.e. $W(x)$ is a distribution function over this interval. Now we conclude from theorem 8.2. (c) that the asymptotic eigenvalue distribution of $M_n(f)$ exists and has the moments

$$\int_{-M}^{M} f^s dD(f) = A(f^s) = \int_a^b [f(x)]^s dW(x).$$

In view of $M = \|f(x)\| < \infty$ we have in this case a finite distribution, so that the moments determine the distribution uniquely. Consequently the matrices have the canonical distribution $W(x)$.

Of course the theorem still holds if the interval $[a, b]$ is replaced by an interval in a finite-dimensional Euclidean space.

(b) Before proceeding to the study of certain Toeplitz matrices of new types it may be instructive to consider some of the results of chapter 7 in the light of what has been discussed here. Let C be the set of continuous functions with period 2π; we can take for Γ the set of trigonometric polynomials (see 1.9) and

$$\gamma = \{a e^{i\nu x} + \bar{a} e^{-i\nu x}; \ \nu = 0, 1, 2, \ldots\}.$$

For the classical Toeplitz matrices it is clear that $M_n(g)$, $g \in \Gamma$, is (tr)-complete, since

$$\{M_n(g)\}_{\nu\mu} = 0 \quad \text{if} \quad |\nu - \mu| > \text{order of } g(x);$$

see the theorem of 8.1 (b). In this case $A(g)$ is immediately obtained as

$$G(g, z) = \sum_{\nu=0}^{\infty} \frac{1}{2\pi} \int_{-\pi}^{\pi} g(x) \, dx \, z^\nu = \frac{1}{2\pi} \int_{-\pi}^{\pi} g(x) \, dx \, \frac{1}{1-z},$$

so that

$$A(g) = \frac{1}{2\pi} \int_{-\pi}^{\pi} g(x) \, dx;$$

hence the canonical distribution $dW(x) = (2\pi)^{-1} dx$ is uniform as we have seen in chapter 5 and in 7.6. Note that in this case we have $a_\nu(g) = A(g)$ for all ν, and the appeal to the Tauberian theorem is not necessary.

(c) For the classical orthogonal polynomials on a finite interval we observe that choosing Γ as the set of all polynomials, and

$$\gamma = \{x^\nu; \nu = 0, 1, \ldots\},$$

the matrices $M_n(g)$, $g \in \Gamma$, will be (tr)-complete. This can be shown in the same way as above (see Appendix).

(d) In order to study the Toeplitz matrices associated with Haar's orthonormal system (7.9) we may choose for γ all functions in this system and Γ as the linear hull of γ. Then $M_n(g)$, $g \in \Gamma$, is (tr)-complete for the same reason as above. It is clear that for $g \in \Gamma$ and for sufficiently large values of ν

$$a_\nu(g) = \int_0^1 [\phi_\nu(x)]^2 g(x) \, dx = g(P_\nu),$$

where P_ν is any point with $\phi_\nu(P_\nu) \neq 0$, say the midpoint of an interval of such values of x. When ν runs through all the 2^m values of ν corresponding to the index m (see 7.9), P_ν moves from 2^{-m-1} to $1 - 2^{-m-1}$ on a set of equally spaced points. Unless $g(x)$ is identically constant, $g(P_\nu) = a_\nu(g)$ will fluctuate without converging as ν increases. However, the points P_ν will tend to become more and more uniformly distributed over $[0, 1]$ and this will ensure the existence of a canonical distribution,

$$n^{-1} \operatorname{tr} M_n(g) = n^{-1} \sum_{\nu=0}^{n-1} g(P_\nu) \to \int_0^1 g(x) \, dx,$$

so that $dW(x) = dx$.

Applying this method to the study of Toeplitz matrices the general procedure will consist of two steps. First one has to show that the class of matrices is (tr)-complete. Then the generating function, or at least its residue at $z = 1$, has to be evaluated for functions belonging to γ. We obtain then the moments of the limiting eigenvalue distribution.

8.4. Toeplitz matrices associated with Hermite polynomials

(a) In this and the next section we deal briefly with two problems which we were not able to settle completely. First, let X be the real axis and $d\mu(x) = e^{-x^2} dx$, where dx is the ordinary Lebesgue measure. We consider the *Hermite polynomials*

$$H_n(x) = (-1)^n e^{x^2} \frac{d^n}{dx^n} e^{-x^2},$$

or after normalization,

$$p_n(x) = \pi^{-\frac{1}{4}} 2^{-\frac{1}{2}n} (n!)^{-\frac{1}{2}} H_n(x).$$

We associate with these orthornormal functions the Toeplitz matrices

$$M_n(f) = \left\{ \int_{-\infty}^{\infty} p_\nu(x) \, p_\mu(x) f(x) \, e^{-x^2} dx; \quad \nu, \mu = 0, 1, \ldots, n-1 \right\}.$$

The question arises how to choose the class C of functions $f(x)$ in the most convenient way. It is not advisable to take C as $L(-\infty, \infty)$ or

$L_2(-\infty, \infty)$ or any set of functions for which $\lim_{x \to \infty} f(x)$ exists. In fact, one can show that in these cases the limiting eigenvalue distributions are concentrated in one point. A more adequate choice is to take for C the set of all real-valued almost periodic functions (in Bohr's sense) on the real axis.

We can choose for Γ the set of all real-valued finite trigonometric sums and

$$\gamma = a e^{i\lambda x} + \bar{a} e^{-i\lambda x}, \quad -\infty < \lambda < \infty.$$

It would be desirable now to prove the (tr)-completeness of the class of matrices defined above. However, we were not able to do this. Nevertheless, it is of some interest to investigate the asymptotic eigenvalue distribution under the hypothesis that (tr)-completeness holds.

(b) We have for $|z| < 1$

$$K(x; z) = \sum_{\nu=0}^{\infty} [p_\nu(x)]^2 z^\nu = \pi^{-\frac{1}{2}} (1 - z^2)^{-\frac{1}{2}} \exp \left\{ \frac{2x^2 z}{1+z} \right\}.$$

This formula is due to Mehler (see Appendix); it holds uniformly in each bounded interval on the x-axis and for $|z| \le \rho < 1$. We then obtain, using Lebesgue's theorem on dominated convergence, the following expression for the generating function of the matrix $M_n(e^{i\lambda x})$:

$$G(e^{i\lambda x}; z) = \int_{-\infty}^{\infty} K(x; z) e^{-x^2 + i\lambda x} dx$$

$$= \pi^{-\frac{1}{2}} (1 - z^2)^{-\frac{1}{2}} \int_{-\infty}^{\infty} \exp \left\{ -x^2 \frac{1-z}{1+z} + i\lambda x \right\} dx$$

$$= (1-z)^{-1} \exp \left\{ -\frac{\lambda^2}{4} \frac{1+z}{1-z} \right\}.$$

If $\lambda = 0$ this has the residue 1 at $z = 1$; otherwise

$$\lim_{z \to 1-0} (1-z) G(e^{i\lambda x}; z) = 0.$$

Hence for $g \in \Gamma$ we have $A(g) = g_0$, where g_0 is the mean value of the expression

$$g(x) = \sum_{\nu=0}^{p} g_\nu e^{i\lambda_\nu x}; \quad \lambda_0 = 0; \; \lambda_1, \dots, \lambda_p \ne 0.$$

Hence

$$A(g) = g_0 = \lim_{A \to \infty} \frac{1}{2A} \int_{-A}^{A} g(x) \, dx = \mathfrak{M}g, \quad g \in \Gamma. \qquad (1)$$

Since the mean-value operation $\mathfrak{M}$ defined for the class of almost periodic functions is bounded and linear, it follows by a simple extension that $Af = \mathfrak{M}f$ for all $f \in C$. Now the theorem 8.2. (c) is applicable and we see that the eigenvalues of $M_n(f)$ have a limiting distribution whose moments μ_s are given by

$$\mu_s = \lim_{A \to \infty} \frac{1}{2A} \int_{-A}^{A} [f(x)]^s \, dx,$$

i.e. by the moments of the distribution of the values of the function $f(x)$.

Thus under the hypothesis that the Toeplitz matrices $M_n(f)$ form a (tr)-complete class, their asymptotic eigenvalue distribution coincides with the distribution of the values of $f(x)$ over the real axis.

8.5. Other orthogonal systems

We shall make some observations concerning the Toeplitz matrices associated with the Charlier polynomials (see Appendix) without going into a complete treatment of this problem.

(a) The *Charlier polynomials* $\phi_\nu(x)$ are defined on $X = (0, 1, 2, \ldots)$, $dx =$ counting measure and $d\mu(x) = j(x)\,dx$, where the $j(x)$ are the Poisson weights

$$j(x) = e^{-a}\frac{a^x}{x!}, \quad x = 0, 1, \ldots; \quad a > 0.$$

Then $\phi_\nu(x)$ is a polynomial of the exact degree ν satisfying the relations

$$\int_X \phi_\nu(x)\,\phi_\mu(x)\,d\mu(x) = \sum_{x=0}^{\infty} \phi_\nu(x)\,\phi_\mu(x)j(x) = \delta_{\nu\mu}.$$

It is easy to show that this is a complete system on $L_2(X)$. Indeed, let $b = (b_0, b_1, \ldots)$ be an element in $L_2(X)$ so that

$$(\phi_\nu; b) = \sum_{x=0}^{\infty} \phi_\nu(x)\,\bar{b}_x j(x) = 0 \quad \text{for} \quad \nu = 0, 1, \ldots;$$

we can employ the relation

$$\sum_{\nu=0}^{\infty} \phi_\nu(x)\,\frac{(a^{\frac{1}{2}}t)^\nu}{(\nu!)^{\frac{1}{2}}} = (1+t)^x e^{-at}$$

for small values of t and we find

$$0 = \sum_{x=0}^{\infty} b_x(1+t)^x j(x) = e^{-a}\sum_{x=0}^{\infty} b_x\frac{(a+at)^x}{x!};$$

the right member being an entire function of t we obtain immediately $b_x = 0$.

The generating function $K(x; z)$ has been evaluated by J. Meixner in terms of Charlier polynomials; expressing these in terms of Laguerre polynomials,

$$\phi_\nu(x) = (-1)^\nu a^{-\frac{1}{2}n} (\nu!)^{\frac{1}{2}} L_\nu^{(x-\nu)}(a),$$

we find

$$K(x; z) = \sum_{\nu=0}^{\infty} [\phi_\nu(x)]^2 z^\nu = e^{az} (a^{-1}z)^x x! L_x\{-az^{-1}(1-z)^2\}.$$

Now if we choose C, Γ and γ as in the last section, we have to evaluate the generating function for $g(x) = e^{i\lambda x}$. We find

$$G(g; z) = \int_0^\infty K(x; z) g(x) d\mu(x) = \sum_{x=0}^{\infty} K(x; z) e^{i\lambda x} j(x)$$

$$= e^{-a+az} \sum_{x=0}^{\infty} (z e^{i\lambda})^x L_x\{-az^{-1}(1-z)^2\}$$

$$= (1 - z e^{i\lambda})^{-1} \exp\left\{a(z-1) \frac{1-e^{i\lambda}}{1-ze^{i\lambda}}\right\}.$$

Hence

$$A(e^{i\lambda x}) = \begin{cases} 1 & \text{if} \quad \lambda = 0, \\ 0 & \text{if} \quad \lambda \not\equiv 0 \; (\text{mod } 2\pi). \end{cases}$$

We can extend this operator to the whole class C so that

$$A(f) = \lim_{N \to \infty} \frac{1}{2N} \sum_{x=-N}^{N} f(x).$$

If we knew that the class of matrices under consideration is (tr)-complete we would obtain a result very similar to the (hypothetical) result of the previous paragraph. Unfortunately, the (tr)-completeness is still an open question.

(b) Let us consider another case: X is the unit circle $|x| \leq 1$, $dx =$ Lebesgue area, and the orthonormal system is given by

$$\begin{cases} \phi_0(x) = \pi^{-\frac{1}{2}}, \\ \phi_{2\nu}(x) = \pi^{-\frac{1}{2}}(2\nu+2)^{\frac{1}{2}} r^\nu \cos \nu\theta, & \nu = 1, 2, \ldots, \\ \phi_{2\nu-1}(x) = \pi^{-\frac{1}{2}}(2\nu+2)^{\frac{1}{2}} r^\nu \sin \nu\theta, & \nu = 1, 2, \ldots, \end{cases}$$

where $x = re^{i\theta}$. Let us take for γ the set of functions

$$\gamma = \{r^\nu \cos \nu\theta, r^\nu \sin \nu\theta; \nu = 0, 1, \ldots\},$$

so that C consists of all real-valued functions $f(x)$ harmonic in the closed unit circle. For $g(x) = r^p \cos p\theta$ [or $g(x) = r^p \sin p\theta$] it is clear that $\{M(g)\}_{\nu\mu} = 0$ for sufficiently large values of $|\nu - \mu|$. Hence the theorem in 8.1 is applicable so that the matrices considered are (tr)-complete.

It is also clear that for the same choice of g we have

$$\{M(g)\}_{2\nu, 2\nu} = \frac{2\nu+2}{\pi} \int_{r=0}^{1} \int_{\theta=-\pi}^{\pi} r^{2\nu+p+1} \cos^2 \nu\theta \cos p\theta \, dr \, d\theta$$

$$= \frac{2\nu+2}{(2\nu+2+p)\pi} \int_{-\pi}^{\pi} \cos^2 \nu\theta \cos p\theta \, d\theta \to \frac{1}{2\pi} \int_{-\pi}^{\pi} \cos p\theta \, d\theta$$

$$= \frac{1}{2\pi} \int_{-\pi}^{\pi} g(e^{i\theta}) \, d\theta,$$

as ν tends to infinity. Since the same holds for $g(x) = r^p \sin p\theta$, we obtain

$$\lim_{n\to\infty} n^{-1} \operatorname{tr} M_n(f) = \frac{1}{2\pi} \int_{-\pi}^{\pi} f(e^{i\theta}) \, d\theta.$$

In other words, we have proved the existence of a canonical distribution, uniformly distributed along the boundary $|x| = 1$ of the unit circle.

The functions $f(x)$ considered are harmonic in the closed unit circle so that we have, as is well known,

$$\frac{1}{2\pi} \int_{-\pi}^{\pi} f(e^{i\theta}) \, d\theta = f(0),$$

Hence we can use as a canonical distribution the distribution with all its variation concentrated at the point $x = 0$.

8.6. Toeplitz integral kernels of the Fourier type

(a) In this section we deal with the Toeplitz operator for which $X = S = (-\infty, \infty)$, $dx = ds = $ Lebesgue measure, and

$$\phi(x, s) = (2\pi)^{-\frac{1}{2}} e^{ixs}.$$

We follow here the notation of 7.2. The transformation denoted by T in 7.2 is now the *Plancherel transform* (see Appendix). Let $f(x)$ be a real-valued, bounded and integrable function,

$$|f(x)| \leqq M < \infty, \quad \int_{-\infty}^{\infty} |f(x)| \, dx < \infty;$$

we introduce the Fourier kernel

$$K(s,t)=K(s-t)=\frac{1}{2\pi}\int_{-\infty}^{\infty}e^{i(s-t)x}f(x)\,dx.$$

For S_{α} (7.2) we choose the intervals $[0,T]$ [which yields, of course, the same result as taking the symmetric intervals $(-\frac{1}{2}T,\frac{1}{2}T)$]. Given the integral equation

$$\int_{0}^{T}K(x-y)\,\phi(y)\,dy=\lambda\phi(x),$$

we shall study the distribution of the eigenvalues for large values of T. This is clearly a problem connected with the general theory of Toeplitz forms, since the linear operator defined by $K(x,y)$ as an integral kernel is a general Toeplitz operator.

In 7.6 we have investigated the eigenvalues of the classical Toeplitz matrices approximating them by circulant matrices. In the same way we will now approximate the kernel $K(x,y)$ by a periodic one whose eigenvalues can be found directly.

(b) We introduce the function

$$f_A(x)=\frac{1}{2\pi A}\int_{-\infty}^{\infty}\left(\frac{\sin\frac{1}{2}A(x-u)}{x-u}\right)^2 f(u)\,du,\quad A>0,$$

which is integrable and satisfies the condition $|f_A(x)|\leq M$. Introducing the function

$$K_A(s)=\frac{1}{2\pi}\int_{-\infty}^{\infty}e^{isx}f_A(x)\,dx$$

we have of course

$$K_A(s)=\begin{cases}(1-|s|/A)\,K(s), & |s|\leq A,\\ 0, & |s|>A.\end{cases}$$

Then

$$|K-K_A|^2=\frac{1}{T}\int_0^T\int_0^T|K(s-t)-K_A(s-t)|^2\,ds\,dt$$

$$=\frac{2}{T}\int_0^T|K(s)-K_A(s)|^2(T-s)\,ds\leq\frac{2A^2}{T^2}\int_0^A|K(s)|^2\,ds$$

$$+2\int_A^{\infty}|K(s)|^2\,ds.$$

Defining the kernel $L_{A,T}$ by

$$L_{A,T}(s)=K_A(s)\quad\text{if}\quad-\tfrac{1}{2}T<s<\tfrac{1}{2}T,$$

and by requiring that it is periodic with period T, we have (for $A < \frac{1}{2}T$)

$$|K_A - L_{A,T}|^2 = \frac{2}{T}\int_{\frac{1}{2}T}^{T} |L_{A,T}(s)|^2 (T-s)\, ds = \frac{2}{T}\int_{0}^{\frac{1}{2}T} |L_{A,T}(s)|^2 s\, ds$$

$$= \frac{2}{T}\int_{0}^{A} |L_{A,T}(s)|^2 s\, ds \leqq \frac{2A}{T}\int_{0}^{\infty} |K(s)|^2 ds.$$

We first choose A so large that $\int_{A}^{\infty} |K(s)|^2 ds$ is very small, say $< \epsilon$. This is possible since $K(s)$ is the Fourier transform of a quadratically integrable function and hence it is itself quadratically integrable. Then, letting T tend to infinity, we see that

$$|K - L_{A,T}| \leqq |K - K_A| + |K_A - L_{A,T}| \leqq [O(T^{-2}) + 2\epsilon]^{\frac{1}{2}} + O(T^{-\frac{1}{2}}).$$

It is now easy to show that $L_{A,T}$ satisfies the conditions in theorem 7.4. Since $|K| \leqq M$, it follows from the inequality just proved that $|L_{A,T}|$ is uniformly bounded (see 7.3). Moreover, we shall prove that $\|L_{A,T}\|$ is also uniformly bounded. We can find the eigenvalues of $L_{A,T}$ easily. Indeed, putting $\phi_\nu(s) = \exp(2\pi i\nu s/T)$; $\nu = 0, \pm 1, \ldots$, we obtain

$$\int_{0}^{T} L_{A,T}(s-t)\, \phi_\nu(t)\, dt = \exp(2\pi i\nu s/T) \int_{0}^{T} L_{A,T}(t) \exp(-2\pi i\nu t/T)\, dt,$$

so that $\phi_\nu(s)$ is an eigenfunction corresponding to the eigenvalue

$$\lambda_{\nu,T} = \int_{0}^{T} L_{A,T}(t) \exp(-2\pi i\nu t/T)\, dt.$$

As $\{\phi_\nu(t); \nu = 0, \pm 1, \ldots\}$ is complete in $L_2(0, T)$, there cannot be any other eigenfunctions. We see, using Fourier's inversion formula, that

$$\lambda_{\nu,T} = f_A(2\pi\nu/T), \quad \nu = 0, \pm 1, \ldots,$$

so that $\|L_{A,T}\| = \max_{\nu} |\lambda_{\nu,T}| \leqq M$.

(c) Finally, we have to show that the distribution of the $\lambda_{\nu,T}$ converges. Let p be an integer, $p \geqq 1$. Then $f_A^p(x)$ is the Fourier transform of $K_A^{p*}(t)$, where the superscript $p*$ denotes p convolutions of $K_A(t)$ with itself. Clearly the function $[f_A(x)]^p$ is (i) integrable, (ii) differentiable, and (iii) its derivative is integrable. Thus we can apply the *Poisson summation formula* (see Appendix) and obtain

$$T^{-1} \sum_{\nu=-\infty}^{\infty} (\lambda_{\nu,T})^p = T^{-1} \sum_{\nu=-\infty}^{\infty} [f_A(2\pi\nu/T)]^p = \sum_{\nu=-\infty}^{\infty} K_A^{p^*}(\nu T).$$

For $T > pA$ the latter sum reduces to $K_A^{p^*}(0)$, which for large values of A tends to $K^{p^*}(0) = \dfrac{1}{2\pi} \displaystyle\int_{-\infty}^{\infty} [f(x)]^p \, dx.$

The assumptions of the approximation theorem are satisfied and we have the following theorem:

THEOREM. *If $f(x)$ is a real-valued, bounded and integrable function, the eigenvalues of the integral equation*

$$\int_0^T K(s-t)\,\phi(t)\,dt = \lambda\phi(s), \quad 0 < s < T,$$

have asymptotically the distribution of the values of $f(x)$ where x is distributed with density $(2\pi)^{-1}$ along the real axis.

In other words, a canonical distribution exists which is absolutely continuous with the derivative $(2\pi)^{-1}$.

Stated in other terms, this means that if the interval $[a,b]$ does not contain the origin and if $m\{f(x)=a\} = m\{f(x)=b\} = 0$ we have

$$\lim_{T \to \infty} T^{-1}\{\text{number of } \lambda\text{'s in } [a,b]\} = (2\pi)^{-1} m\{a < f(x) < b\}.$$

8.7. Toeplitz integral kernels of the Bessel type

Let us take $X = S = [0, \infty]$, $dx = ds = $ Lebesgue measure, and define the orthogonal kernel by the *Bessel functions*

$$\phi(x,s) = (xs)^{\frac{1}{2}} J_\nu(xs), \quad \Re(\nu) \geqq -\tfrac{1}{2}.$$

The transformation denoted by T in 7.2 is now the *Hankel transform* (see Appendix). To study the eigenvalues of the associated integral equation

$$\int_0^T K(s,t)\,\phi(t)\,dt = \lambda\phi(s), \quad 0 < s < T,$$

with

$$K(s,t) = (st)^{\frac{1}{2}} \int_0^\infty J_\nu(xs)\,\overline{J_\nu(xt)}\,xf(x)\,dx,$$

for a bounded, real-valued and integrable function $f(x)$, we shall use the asymptotic formula

$$x^{\frac{1}{2}} J_\nu(x) = (2/\pi)^{\frac{1}{2}} \cos (x - \alpha) + R(x),$$

where

$$\alpha = \tfrac{1}{4}\pi + \tfrac{1}{2}\nu\pi, \quad |R(x)| \leqq A(1+x)^{-1}, \quad x > 0.$$

Consider the function

$$\Delta(s, t) = \int_0^\infty \cos x(s - \alpha)\, R(tx) f(x)\, dx.$$

We have

$$\int_0^T |\Delta(s, t)|^2\, ds \leqq C \int_0^\infty |R(tx)|^2 [f(x)]^2\, dx.$$

In view of

$$\frac{1}{T} \int_0^T |R(tx)|^2\, dt \leqq \frac{A^2}{1 + Tx},$$

we see that

$$\frac{1}{T} \int_0^T \int_0^T |\Delta(s, t)|^2\, ds\, dt \leqq CA^2 \int_0^\infty \frac{[f(x)]^2}{1 + Tx}\, dx \to 0$$

as $T \to \infty$.

We introduce the Toeplitz kernel of Fourier type

$$L(s, t) = \frac{2}{\pi} \int_0^\infty \cos (sx - \alpha) \cos (tx - \alpha) f(x)\, dx.$$

Then we write

$$K(s, t) = L(s, t) + \Delta(s, t) + \Delta_1(s, t) + \delta(s, t)$$

where $\Delta_1(s, t)$ is of the same form as $\Delta(s, t)$. We have just shown that $|\Delta| \to 0$ (and the same holds for Δ_1). In order to apply the approximation theorem of 7.4 we just have to consider the last term

$$\delta(s, t) = \int_0^\infty R(sx)\, \overline{R(tx)} f(x)\, dx.$$

If $s > B$,

$$|\delta(s, t)| < A^2 \int_0^\infty \frac{|f(x)|}{1 + Bx}\, dx \to 0 \quad \text{as} \quad B \to \infty,$$

and similarly for $t > B$. Hence

$$\lim_{T \to \infty} |\delta| = 0,$$

and since the behavior of the eigenvalues of $L(s, t)$ is known we obtain the desired result.

THEOREM. *The integral kernel*

$$K(s,t) = (st)^{\frac{1}{2}} \int_0^\infty J_\nu(xs) \, \overline{J_\nu(xt)} \, xf(x) \, dx, \quad \Re(\nu) \geqq -\tfrac{1}{2},$$

where $f(x)$ *is a real-valued, bounded and integrable function, has the canonical distribution with density* π^{-1} *over the real interval* $[0, \infty]$.

It would be interesting to consider the corresponding problem for Watson transforms. It is likely that the method of 8.1–8.5 can be translated to the case of a continuous parameter. Appropriate Tauberian theorems for Laplace transforms have to be used.

PART II

APPLICATIONS OF TOEPLITZ FORMS

CHAPTER 9

APPLICATIONS TO ANALYTIC FUNCTIONS

Let
$$f(z) = \alpha_0 + \alpha_1 z + \alpha_2 z^2 + \ldots + \alpha_n z^n + \ldots$$
be an analytic function regular in the unit circle $|z| < 1$. We denote the minimum (greatest lower bound) of $\Re f(z)$ for $|z| < 1$ by $R(f)$, and the maximum (least upper bound) of $|f(z)|$ for $|z| < 1$ by $M(f)$. [In extreme cases we may have $R(f) = -\infty$ and $M(f) = +\infty$.] Certain suitably defined Toeplitz forms yield an effective instrument in order to deal with the following three problems concerning the *functionals* $R(f)$ and $M(f)$:

A. To obtain the quantities $R(f)$ and $M(f)$ as the limits of certain monotonic sequences of constants (eigenvalues) which can be computed algebraically.

B. To characterize the classes of functions $f(z)$ which are regular in the unit circle $|z| < 1$ and satisfy there the condition $\Re f(z) > 0$ and $|f(z)| < 1$, respectively, in terms of the coefficients $\alpha_0, \alpha_1, \alpha_2, \ldots, \alpha_n, \ldots$.

C. To deal with the following question. We prescribe the $n+1$ first coefficients $\alpha_0, \alpha_1, \alpha_2, \ldots, \alpha_n$ and consider the set of all functions $f(z)$ which are regular in the unit circle $|z| < 1$ and have a power series beginning with these coefficients. To each function of this kind a certain $R(f)$ and a certain $M(f)$ belongs. What is the maximum of $R(f)$ and the minimum of $M(f)$?

9.1. Matrices and forms

Dealing with the quantity $R(f)$ we shall assume that α_0 is real; also we introduce in this case the following alternate notation:
$$\alpha_0 = c_0, \quad \alpha_n = 2c_n, \quad c_{-n} = \bar{c}_n, \quad n = 1, 2, 3, \ldots. \tag{1}$$
This is in agreement with the notation used in 1.10 (a) for the harmonic function $\Re f(z)$.

(a) In the discussion of the problems A, B, C formulated in the introduction, we shall make use of the matrix

$$M = \begin{pmatrix} \alpha_0 & \alpha_1 & \alpha_2 & \ldots \\ 0 & \alpha_0 & \alpha_1 & \ldots \\ 0 & 0 & \alpha_0 & \ldots \\ \ldots & \ldots & \ldots & \ldots \end{pmatrix}. \tag{2}$$

If we employ the customary symbols of the matrix algebra we can write

$$M^* = \overline{M}' = \begin{pmatrix} \overline{\alpha}_0 & 0 & 0 & \dots \\ \overline{\alpha}_1 & \overline{\alpha}_0 & 0 & \dots \\ \overline{\alpha}_2 & \overline{\alpha}_1 & \overline{\alpha}_0 & \dots \\ \dots & \dots & \dots & \dots \end{pmatrix}. \tag{3}$$

In dealing with the functional $R(f)$ we shall consider the matrix

$$\tfrac{1}{2}(M + \overline{M}') = \tfrac{1}{2}\begin{pmatrix} 2\Re\alpha_0 & \alpha_1 & \alpha_2 & \dots \\ \overline{\alpha}_1 & 2\Re\alpha_0 & \alpha_1 & \dots \\ \overline{\alpha}_2 & \overline{\alpha}_1 & 2\Re\alpha_0 & \dots \\ \dots & \dots & \dots & \dots \end{pmatrix} = \begin{pmatrix} c_0 & c_1 & c_2 & \dots \\ c_{-1} & c_0 & c_1 & \dots \\ c_{-2} & c_{-1} & c_0 & \dots \\ \dots & \dots & \dots & \dots \end{pmatrix}.$$
$$\tag{4}$$

The second form makes use of the alternate notation (1) introduced above; these matrices are of the Toeplitz type.

Studying the functional $M(f)$ another matrix (h_{pq}) will be of importance defined by the condition

$$h_{pq} = \alpha_p \overline{\alpha}_q + \alpha_{p-1}\overline{\alpha}_{q-1} + \dots + \alpha_0 \overline{\alpha}_{q-p}, \quad p \leqq q, \tag{5}$$

and $h_{qp} = \overline{h}_{pq}; p, q = 0, 1, 2, \dots$. We can write

$$(h_{pq}) = \overline{M}'M. \tag{6}$$

(b) The Hermitian form associated with the matrix (4) is

$$\tfrac{1}{2}(M + \overline{M}') = \sum_{p,\, q=0,1,2,\dots} c_{q-p} u_p \overline{u}_q = \Re \sum_{n=0}^{\infty} \alpha_n (u_0 \overline{u}_n + u_1 \overline{u}_{n+1} + \dots), \tag{7}$$

which is of course a Toeplitz form. Assuming that $f(z)$ is regular on the unit circle $|z| = 1$, $z = e^{ix}$, this form can be written as follows:

$$\frac{1}{2\pi} \int_{-\pi}^{\pi} \Re f(e^{ix}) \left| \sum_{n=0}^{\infty} u_n e^{inx} \right|^2 dx. \tag{8}$$

The Hermitian form associated with the matrix (6) is

$$\overline{M}'M = \sum_{p,\, q=0,1,2,\dots} h_{pq} u_p \overline{u}_q = \sum_{n=0}^{\infty} |\alpha_0 u_\nu + \alpha_1 u_{\nu+1} + \alpha_2 u_{\nu+2} + \dots|^2. \tag{9}$$

9.2. Problem A concerning $R(f)$

Problem A has been formulated in the introduction. We shall use the notation 9.1 (1).

(a) THEOREM. *Let* $f(z) = c_0 + 2 \sum\limits_{n=1}^{\infty} c_n z^n$, c_0 *real*, $c_{-n} = \bar{c}_n$, *be regular in the unit circle* $|z| < 1$. *We denote by* $\lambda^{(n)}$ *the lowest eigenvalue of the Toeplitz matrix*

$$
\begin{pmatrix}
c_0 & c_1 & c_2 & \cdots & c_n \\
c_{-1} & c_0 & c_1 & \cdots & c_{n-1} \\
\cdots & \cdots & \cdots & \cdots & \cdots \\
c_{-n} & c_{-n+1} & c_{-n+2} & \cdots & c_0
\end{pmatrix}. \tag{1}
$$

The quantities $\lambda^{(n)}$ *form a nonincreasing sequence and*

$$
\lim_{n \to \infty} \lambda^{(n)} = R(f). \tag{2}
$$

The matrix (1) is the nth section of the infinite Hermitian matrix $\tfrac{1}{2}(M + M')$ defined by 9.1 (4). The quantity $\lambda^{(n)}$ is the minimum of the Toeplitz form

$$
\begin{aligned}
T_n &= \sum_{p,\,q=0,1,\,\ldots\,n} c_{q-p} u_p \bar{u}_q \\
&= \lim_{r \to 1-0} \sum_{p,\,q=0,1,\,\ldots,\,n} c_{q-p} r^{|p-q|} u_p \bar{u}_q \\
&= \lim_{r \to 1-0} \frac{1}{2\pi} \int_{-\pi}^{\pi} \Re f(r e^{ix}) \left| \sum_{\nu=0}^{n} u_\nu e^{i\nu x} \right|^2 dx, \tag{3}
\end{aligned}
$$

under the side condition $\sum\limits_{\nu=0}^{\infty} |u_\nu|^2 = 1$. Hence the sequence $\lambda^{(n)}$ is nonincreasing. From the integral representation (3) of T_n we conclude that

$$
\lambda^{(n)} \geqq R(f). \tag{4}
$$

(b) Let $0 < \rho < 1$; the form (3) associated with the function $f(\rho z)$ will be

$$
\sum_{p,\,q=0,1,\,\ldots,\,n} c_{q-p} \rho^{|p-q|} u_p \bar{u}_q.
$$

We denote by $\lambda^{(n)}(\rho)$ the minimum of this form under the side condition $\sum\limits_{\nu=0}^{n} |u_\nu|^2 = 1$. If $\{v_\nu\}$ is a unit vector for which $\lambda^{(n)}(\rho)$ is attained, we have

$$
\begin{aligned}
\lambda^{(n)}(\rho) &= \sum_{p,\,q=0,1,\,\ldots,\,n} c_{q-p} \rho^{|p-q|} v_p \bar{v}_q \\
&\geqq \min_{x} \sum_{p,\,q=0,1,\,\ldots,\,n} c_{q-p} \rho^{|p-q|} e^{i(p-q)x} v_p \bar{v}_q,
\end{aligned}
$$

where the minimum refers to x, $-\pi \leqq x \leqq \pi$. The latter sum is a harmonic function of ρ, x so that the minimum diminishes when ρ increases. Thus for $\rho < \rho_1 < 1$

$$\lambda^{(n)}(\rho) \geqq \min_x \sum_{p, q=0, 1, \ldots, n} c_{q-p} \rho_1^{|p-q|} e^{i(p-q)x} v_p \bar{v}_q,$$

and the latter sum is $\geqq \lambda^{(n)}(\rho_1)$; hence $\lambda^{(n)}(\rho)$ is a decreasing function of ρ and $\lambda^{(n)}(\rho) \geqq \lambda^{(n)}$.

(c) Let $0 < \rho < 1$. We have

$$\lambda^{(n)}(\rho) = \min \frac{1}{2\pi} \int_{-\pi}^{\pi} \Re f(\rho e^{ix}) \left| \sum_{\nu=0}^{n} u_\nu e^{i\nu x} \right|^2 dx, \quad \sum_{\nu=0}^{n} |u_\nu|^2 = 1, \qquad (5)$$

so that according to 5.2 (10)

$$\lim_{n \to \infty} \lambda^{(n)}(\rho) = \min_x \Re f(\rho e^{ix}),$$

consequently

$$\lim_{n \to \infty} \lambda^{(n)} \leqq \min_x \Re f(\rho e^{ix}).$$

If ρ increases to 1 the minimum on the right tends to $R(f)$, and this, together with (4), establishes the assertion.

9.3. Problem B concerning $R(f)$

We shall use again the notation 9.1 (1).

(a) THEOREM. *The power series* $f(z) = c_0 + 2 \sum_{n=1}^{\infty} c_n z^n$, c_0 *real,* $c_{-n} = \bar{c}_n$, *converges in the unit circle* $|z| < 1$ *and has there a positive real part if and only if the Toeplitz forms* T_n [9.2 (3)] *are all nonnegative. More precisely, there are two cases possible:*

(i) *all forms* T_n *are positive definite;*

(ii) *there exists an integer* $m, m \geqq 1$, *so that* T_n *is positive definite for* $n \leqq m-1$ *and nonnegative semidefinite for* $n \geqq m$.

Case (ii) *occurs if and only if*

$$f(z) = \sum_{\nu=1}^{m} \rho_\nu \frac{1 + \epsilon_\nu z}{1 - \epsilon_\nu z}, \quad m \geqq 1, \qquad (1)$$

where $\rho_\nu > 0$, $|\epsilon_\nu| = 1$ *and* $\epsilon_k \neq \epsilon_l$ *if* $k \neq l$; $k, l = 1, 2, \ldots, m$. *In this case* $R(f) = 0$.

The theorem yields a complete characterization of the class $\Re f(z) > 0$ for $|z| < 1$, or, what is the same, $R(f) \geqq 0, f(z) \not\equiv 0$. Another obviously equivalent characterization is the following:

(i') $\lambda^{(n)} > 0$ for all n,

(ii') $\lambda^{(n)}>0$ for $n\leq m-1$ and $\lambda^{(n)}=0$ for $n\geq m$, where $\lambda^{(n)}$ is used in the same sense as in theorem 9.2.

If $\lambda^{(n)}=0$ for all n, we must have $f(z)\equiv 0$; we write then $m=0$ [cf. (f)]. Obviously (i) can be interpreted as the case $m=\infty$. The case $f(z)=c_0$, $c_0>0$, is trivial.

(b) First we note that, assuming $\lambda^{(n)}\geq 0$, we must have

$$\begin{vmatrix} c_0 & c_n \\ c_{-n} & c_0 \end{vmatrix}\geq 0,$$

so that $|c_n|\leq c_0$; thus $f(z)$ must be then regular in the unit circle $|z|<1$. In view of theorem 9.2 the condition $R(f)\geq 0$ is equivalent with $\lambda^{(n)}\geq 0$.

The sequence $\{\lambda^{(n)}\}$ is nonincreasing and has a nonnegative limit. Thus we have either $\lambda^{(n)}>0$ for all n or $\lambda^{(m)}=0$ for a certain m, in which case $\lambda^{(n)}=0$, $n\geq m$. Let m be the least integer of this kind. The first case corresponds to (i), the second to (ii).

(c) Let us discuss the equivalent conditions (ii) and (ii'). Assuming that $m\geq 1$ and $f(z)$ has the form (1) we see that condition (ii) [or (ii')] is fulfilled. Indeed, we have in this case

$$T_n=\sum_{\nu=1}^{m}\rho_\nu\,|\,u_0+u_1\bar\epsilon_\nu+u_2\bar\epsilon_\nu^2+\ldots+u_n\bar\epsilon_\nu^n\,|^2;\tag{2}$$

this form is positive definite as long as $n\leq m-1$ and nonnegative semidefinite for $n\geq m$.

The proof of the converse is more complicated. We offer two different lines of argument.

(d) *First method.* We use the results of 4.1. We have to show that from condition (ii) the special case (1) follows. We choose n so large that the coefficients $c_1, c_2, \ldots, c_n$ are not all zero and $\lambda^{(n)}=0$. There exists an integer $m=m(n)$, $1\leq m\leq n$, so that the Toeplitz form

$$T_h=\sum_{p,\,q=0,1,\ldots,h}c_{q-p}u_p\bar u_q\tag{3}$$

is positive definite for $h\leq m-1$ and nonnegative semidefinite for $m\leq h\leq n$. This means that $\lambda^{(h)}>0$ for $h\leq m-1$ and $\lambda^{(h)}=0$ for $h\geq m$. We notice that m is independent of n.

We consider the form T_m; there exists a nonzero vector $(v_0, v_1, \ldots, v_m)$ for which this form is zero. This vector is, except for a factor, *uniquely determined* (cf. 4.1). According to theorem 4.1 we have

$$c_k=\sum_{\nu=1}^{m}\rho_\nu\epsilon_\nu^k,\quad \rho_\nu>0,\quad |\epsilon_\nu|=1;\quad k=0,1,\ldots,m,\tag{4}$$

where the ϵ_ν are all different. The quantities ρ_ν and ϵ_ν are uniquely determined by the vector $\{v_\nu\}$ just defined. Thus ρ_ν, ϵ_ν do not change if we pass from n to $n+1$ so that (4) holds for all k. Hence $f(z)$ must have the special form (1).

(e) *Second method.* Let $\lambda^{(h)} > 0$ for $h \leq m-1$ and $\lambda^{(h)} = 0$ for $h \geq m$. We denote by $(v_0, v_1, \ldots, v_m)$ a nonzero vector for which $T_m = 0$. Then T_n, $n \geq m$, is stationary for

$$u_0 = u_1 = \ldots = u_{\mu-1} = 0; \quad u_\mu = v_0, u_{\mu+1} = v_1, \ldots, u_{\mu+m} = v_m;$$

$$u_{\mu+m+1} = \ldots = u_n = 0, \quad (5)$$

where $0 \leq \mu \leq n - m$, i.e.

$$\sum_{q=0}^{n} c_{q-p} \bar{u}_q = \sum_{q=0}^{n} c_{p-q} u_q = 0, \quad p = 0, 1, \ldots, n, \quad (6)$$

must hold for the special vector (5). Thus

$$c_{p-\mu} v_0 + c_{p-\mu-1} v_1 + \ldots + c_{p-\mu-m} v_m = 0,$$

or

$$c_l v_0 + c_{l-1} v_1 + \ldots + c_{l-m} v_m = 0, \quad (7)$$

where $-(n-m) \leq l \leq n$. Since n is arbitrarily large, (7) holds for all integral values of l.

Choosing first $l > m$, we conclude that

$$(v_0 + v_1 z + \ldots + v_m z^m) f(z) = A_0 + A_1 z + \ldots + A_m z^m \quad (8)$$

is a polynomial of degree m. Moreover,

$$A_k = 2(c_k v_0 + c_{k-1} v_1 + \ldots + c_1 v_{k-1}) + c_0 v_k. \quad (9)$$

[For $k = 0$ the first term on the right of (9) is missing.]

Choosing l according to the condition $l < 0$ we find that

$$(\bar{v}_m + \bar{v}_{m-1} z + \ldots + \bar{v}_0 z^m) f(z) = B_0 + B_1 z + \ldots + B_m z^m \quad (10)$$

must be also a polynomial of degree m. Moreover,

$$B_{m-k} = c_0 \bar{v}_k + 2(c_1 \bar{v}_{k+1} + c_2 \bar{v}_{k+2} + \ldots + c_{m-k} \bar{v}_m). \quad (11)$$

[For $k = 0$ the second term on the right of (11) is missing.]

Finally, choosing $0 \leq l \leq m$ we obtain

$$A_l + \bar{B}_{m-l} = 0. \quad (12)$$

Now we replace z by z^{-1} in (8) and multiply by z^m:

$$(\bar{v}_m + \bar{v}_{m-1} z + \ldots + \bar{v}_0 z^m) \bar{f}(z^{-1}) = \bar{A}_m + \bar{A}_{m-1} z + \ldots + \bar{A}_0 z^m. \quad (13)$$

Comparing this with (10) and taking (12) into account,

$$\bar{f}(z^{-1}) = -f(z) \tag{14}$$

follows.

A rational function $f(z)$ satisfying (14) can be regular in $|z| < 1$ only if its poles are all *on* the unit circle. It can satisfy the inequality $\Re f(z) > 0$ in $|z| < 1$ only if these poles are all simple. (Otherwise that part of a neighborhood of a pole $z = \epsilon$, $|\epsilon| = 1$, which is in $|z| < 1$ would be mapped onto an angle $\geqq 2\pi$.) Hence $f(z)$ must have the form

$$\sum_{\nu=1}^{m'} \rho_\nu \frac{1 + \epsilon_\nu z}{1 - \epsilon_\nu z},$$

where $m' \leqq m$ and $|\epsilon_\nu| = 1$; $\epsilon_k \neq \epsilon_l$, $k \neq l$. Inserting this in (14) we find $\rho_\nu = \bar{\rho}_\nu$, so that ρ_ν is real. If z approaches the unit circle along the radius where $\epsilon_\nu z$ is real and positive, we find that sgn $\Re f(z)$ coincides with sgn ρ_ν so that $\rho_\nu > 0$. Since T_{m-1} is positive definite, m' must be $= m$.

(f) Finally, we note that the case $m = 0$ (i.e. $\lambda^{(n)} = 0$ for all n), is trivial. Indeed, in view of $R(f) \geqq 0$ we have $\Re f(z) \geqq 0$, $|z| < 1$; moreover $\lambda^{(0)} = c_0 = 0$, so that $f(z) \equiv 0$.

9.4. Problem C concerning $R(f)$

THEOREM. *Let us consider the class of all power series $f(z)$ which are regular in $|z| < 1$ and begin with the given terms $c_0 + 2 \sum\limits_{k=1}^{n} c_k z^k$, c_0 real, $c_{-k} = \bar{c}_k$. We denote by $\lambda^{(n)}$ the lowest eigenvalue of the Toeplitz form T_n [9.2 (3)]. Then for every function $f(z)$ of this class*

$$R(f) \leqq \lambda^{(n)}. \tag{1}$$

The sign $=$ holds if and only if $f(z)$ has the following special form:

$$f(z) = \lambda^{(n)} + \sum_{\nu=1}^{m} \rho_\nu \frac{1 + \epsilon_\nu z}{1 - \epsilon_\nu z}, \quad 1 \leqq m \leqq n, \quad \rho_\nu > 0, |\epsilon_\nu| = 1, \tag{2}$$

provided $c_1, c_2, \ldots, c_n$ are not all zero; here $\epsilon_k \neq \epsilon_l$ for $k \neq l$ and the quantities $m, \rho_\nu, \epsilon_\nu$ are uniquely determined. In the case $c_1 = c_2 = \ldots = c_n = 0$ the sign $=$ holds if and only if $f(z) = c_0 = \lambda^{(n)}$.

Cf. 9.2 (4). Let $R(f) = \lambda^{(n)}$; we consider $\phi(z) = f(z) - \lambda^{(n)}$ and use theorem 9.3 [cf. (ii) and (ii')]. If $c_1 = c_2 = \ldots = c_n = 0$ we have $\lambda^{(n)} = c_0$ and $R(\phi) = 0$, $\phi(0) = 0$; in view of 9.3 (b) we must have then $c_k = 0$ for all k, i.e. $\phi(z) \equiv 0$.

9.5. An equivalent form of theorem 9.3

We shall deal with another characterization of the class $\Re f(z) > 0$, $|z| < 1$, using the Toeplitz determinants associated with the given power series rather than the eigenvalues of the Toeplitz forms. We employ again the notation 9.1 (1).

(a) THEOREM. *The power series* $f(z) = c_0 + 2 \sum_{n=1}^{\infty} c_n z^n$, c_0 *real,* $c_{-n} = \bar{c}_n$, *converges in the unit circle* $|z| < 1$ *and has there a positive real part if and only if the Toeplitz determinants*

$$D_n = \begin{vmatrix} c_0 & c_1 & c_2 & \cdots & c_n \\ c_{-1} & c_0 & c_1 & \cdots & c_{n-1} \\ c_{-2} & c_{-1} & c_0 & \cdots & c_{n-2} \\ \cdots & \cdots & \cdots & \cdots & \cdots \\ c_{-n} & c_{-n+1} & c_{-n+2} & \cdots & c_0 \end{vmatrix}, \quad n = 0, 1, 2, \ldots, \quad (1)$$

are positive. The only exception is when $f(z)$ *has the form* 9.3 (1); *we have then* $D_n > 0$ *for* $n \leq m - 1$ *and* $D_n = 0$ *for* $n \geq m$.

The function $f(z)$ *is identically zero if and only if all determinants* D_n *vanish* $(m = 0)$.

The proof of this theorem is slightly more intricate than that of theorem 9.3.

(b) We have to show that the conditions (i) and (ii) of theorem 9.3, or the conditions denoted by (i') and (ii') in 9.3 (a), are equivalent to the following conditions:

(i″) $D_n > 0$ for all n;

(ii″) $D_n > 0$ for $n \leq m - 1$ and $D_n = 0$ for $n \geq m$.

The addition concerning the case $m = 0$ will be dealt with at the end of this section.

The identity of (i') and (i″) is trivial. As to (ii') and (ii″), let us assume (ii'). Then $f(z)$ must have the form 9.3 (1). The associated forms 9.3 (2) are positive definite for $n \leq m - 1$ and nonnegative semi-definite for $n \geq m$. Hence assertion (ii″) concerning the determinants D_n follows.

(c) We assume now that (ii″) holds. This implies the positive-definite character of the form T_n as long as $n \leq m - 1$, or $\lambda^{(n)} > 0$, $n \leq m - 1$. Moreover, $\lambda^{(m)}$ must be zero. Indeed, if $\lambda^{(m)}$ would be negative, some other eigenvalue of the form T_m would be zero. In view of the separation property of the eigenvalues (see Appendix) the form T_{m-1} would possess a nonpositive eigenvalue which contradicts to the positive definite character of this form. Owing to theorem 4.1 we conclude that 9.3 (4) holds for $k \leq m$. Our purpose is to prove that 9.3 (4) holds also for $k > m$, that is, for all k.

The proof is based on induction. We assume that 9.3 (4) holds for $k \leq N$ and we shall prove it for $k = N + 1$; $N \geq m$. We consider the singular form

$$T_n = T_{2N-m+1} = \sum_{\nu=1}^{m} \rho_\nu \, | \, u_0 + u_1 \bar{\epsilon}_\nu + \ldots + u_n \bar{\epsilon}_\nu^n \, |^2$$

$$+ 2\Re \sum_{h=N+1}^{m} (c_h - c_h^*) \, (u_0 \bar{u}_h + u_1 \bar{u}_{h+1} + \ldots + u_{n-h} \bar{u}_n),$$

$$n = 2N - m + 1, \quad (2)$$

where we use the notation

$$c_h^* = \sum_{\nu=1}^{m} \rho_\nu \epsilon_\nu^h, \quad h \geq N + 1. \quad (3)$$

The linear transformation

$$\left.\begin{array}{l} u_0 = U_0, \quad u_1 = U_1, \ldots, u_{N-m} = U_{N-m}, \\ u_0 + u_1 \bar{\epsilon}_\nu + u_2 \bar{\epsilon}_\nu^2 + \ldots + u_n \bar{\epsilon}_\nu^n = U_{N-m+\nu}, \quad \nu = 1, 2, \ldots, m, \\ u_{N+1} = U_{N+1}, \ldots, u_n = U_n, \quad n = 2N - m + 1, \end{array}\right\} \quad (4)$$

is nonsingular because its determinant

$$[\bar{\epsilon}_\nu^{N-m+1}, \bar{\epsilon}_\nu^{N-m+2}, \ldots, \bar{\epsilon}_\nu^N], \quad \nu = 1, 2, \ldots, m, \quad (5)$$

is different from zero. In terms of the new variables we can write

$$T_n = T_{2N-m+1} = \sum_{\nu=1}^{m} \rho_\nu \, | \, U_{N-m+\nu} \, |^2$$

$$+ 2\Re \sum_{h=N+1}^{n} \gamma_h (U_0 \bar{U}_h + U_1 \bar{U}_{h+1} + \ldots + U_{n-h} \bar{U}_n),$$

$$n = 2N - m + 1, \quad (6)$$

where γ_h stands for $c_h - c_h^*$.

The matrix of (6) is of the type

$$\begin{pmatrix} 0 & 0 & \Gamma \\ 0 & R & 0 \\ \Gamma^* & 0 & 0 \end{pmatrix}, \quad (7)$$

where R is the diagonal matrix with elements $\rho_1, \rho_2, \ldots, \rho_m$ and the matrix Γ has the form

$$\begin{pmatrix} \gamma_{N+1} & \gamma_{N+2} & \cdots & \gamma_n \\ 0 & \gamma_{N+1} & \cdots & \gamma_{n-1} \\ \cdots & \cdots & \cdots & \cdots \\ 0 & 0 & \cdots & \gamma_{N+1} \end{pmatrix}. \tag{8}$$

Hence the discriminant of T_n is, apart from nonvanishing factors, $|\gamma_{N+1}|^{2n-2N} = |\gamma_{N+1}|^{2(N-m+1)}$ so that γ_{N+1} must be zero, that is, $c_{N+1} = c_{N+1}^*$. This establishes the assertion. In fact, $D_h > 0$ for $h \leqq m-1$ and the vanishing of the determinants D_m and $D_{m+1}, D_{m+3}, D_{m+5}, \cdots$ is sufficient to conclude that $f(z)$ has the special form 9.3(1).

(d) As to the case $m = 0$ we can show that the condition

$$D_0 = D_1 = D_3 = D_5 = \ldots = 0$$

has already the consequence

$$c_0 = c_1 = c_2 = \ldots = 0.$$

Indeed, $c_0 = D_0 = 0$. Let $c_0 = c_1 = \ldots = c_N = 0$; we shall prove that $c_{N+1} = 0$. The determinant D_{2N+1} has the form

$$\begin{pmatrix} 0 & \Delta \\ \Delta^* & 0 \end{pmatrix}$$

where

$$\Delta = \begin{pmatrix} c_{N+1} & c_{N+2} & \cdots & c_{2N+1} \\ 0 & c_{N+1} & \cdots & c_{2N} \\ \cdots & \cdots & \cdots & \cdots \\ 0 & 0 & \cdots & c_{N+1} \end{pmatrix};$$

thus we have $|\det \Delta|^2 = 0$, $c_{N+1} = 0$.

9.6. Problem A concerning $M(f)$

Problem A was formulated in the introduction to this chapter. We return again to the original notation $f(z) = \sum_{n=0}^{\infty} \alpha_n z^n$.

(a) THEOREM. *Let* $f(z) = \sum_{n=0}^{\infty} \alpha_n z^n$ *be regular in the unit circle* $|z| < 1$. *We denote by* $(\mu^{(n)})^2$, $\mu^{(n)} \geqq 0$, *the highest eigenvalue of the Hermitian form* (h_{pq}), $p, q = 0, 1, \ldots, n$, *where*

$$h_{pq} = \alpha_p \bar{\alpha}_q + \alpha_{p-1} \bar{\alpha}_{q-1} + \ldots + \alpha_0 \bar{\alpha}_{q-p} \quad for \quad p \leqq q; \quad h_{qp} = \bar{h}_{pq}. \tag{1}$$

The quantities $\mu^{(n)}$ form a nondecreasing sequence and

$$\lim_{n \to \infty} \mu^{(n)} = M(f). \tag{2}$$

The matrix (1) is the nth section of the infinite matrix $M'\overline{M}$ defined by 9.1 (6). The quantity $(\mu^{(n)})^2$ is the maximum of the Hermitian form

$$S_n = \sum_{p,q=0,1,\ldots,n} h_{pq} u_p \overline{u}_q = \sum_{\nu=0}^{n} |\alpha_0 u_\nu + \alpha_1 u_{\nu+1} + \ldots + \alpha_{n-\nu} u_n|^2$$

$$= \lim_{r \to 1-0} \sum_{\nu=0}^{n} |\alpha_0 u_\nu + \alpha_1 u_{\nu+1} + \ldots + \alpha_{n-\nu} u_n|^2 r^{2n-2\nu}$$

$$\leq \lim_{r \to 1-0} \frac{1}{2\pi} \int_{-\pi}^{\pi} |f(re^{ix}) \sum_{\nu=0}^{n} u_{n-\nu} r^\nu e^{i\nu x}|^2 dx \tag{3}$$

under side condition $\sum_{\nu=0}^{n} |u_\nu|^2 = 1$. Hence the sequence $\{\mu^{(n)}\}$ is nondecreasing.

From the inequality (3) we conclude, moreover, that

$$\mu^{(n)} \leq M(f). \tag{4}$$

(b) Let $0 < \rho < 1$; the form S_n associated with the function $f(\rho z)$ is

$$\sum_{\nu=0}^{n} |\alpha_0 u_\nu + \alpha_1 \rho u_{\nu+1} + \ldots + \alpha_{n-\nu} \rho^{n-\nu} u_n|^2. \tag{5}$$

We denote by $[\mu^{(n)}(\rho)]^2$, $\mu^{(n)}(\rho) \geq 0$, the maximum of this form, $\sum_{\nu=0}^{n} |u_\nu|^2 = 1$. If $\{v_\nu\}$ is a unit vector for which this maximum is attained, we have

$$[\mu^{(n)}(\rho)]^2 = \sum_{\nu=0}^{n} |\alpha_0 v_\nu + \alpha_1 \rho v_{\nu+1} + \ldots + \alpha_{n-\nu} \rho^{n-\nu} v_n|^2$$

$$\leq \max_x \sum_{\nu=0}^{n} |\alpha_0 v_\nu + \alpha_1 \rho e^{ix} v_{\nu+1} + \ldots + \alpha_{n-\nu} \rho^{n-\nu} e^{i(n-\nu)x} v_n|^2,$$

where $-\pi \leq x \leq \pi$. In view of a well-known generalization of the maximum principle (see Appendix) the maximum on the right is increasing (nondecreasing) with ρ. Thus for $\rho < \rho_1 < 1$

$$[\mu^{(n)}(\rho)]^2 \leq \max_x \sum_{\nu=0}^{n} |\alpha_0 v_\nu + \alpha_1 \rho_1 e^{ix} v_{\nu+1} + \ldots + \alpha_{n-\nu} \rho_1^{n-\nu} e^{i(n-\nu)x} v_n|^2$$

$$= \max_x \sum_{\nu=0}^{n} |\alpha_0 e^{i\nu x} v_\nu + \alpha_1 \rho_1 e^{i(\nu+1)x} v_{\nu+1} + \ldots + \alpha_{n-\nu} \rho_1^{n-\nu} e^{inx} v_n|^2.$$

The latter sum is $\leq [\mu^{(n)}(\rho_1)]^2$; hence $\mu^{(n)}(\rho)$ is an increasing function of ρ and $\mu^{(n)}(\rho) \leq \mu^{(n)}$.

(c) Let $0 < \rho < 1$. The quantity $[\mu^{(n)}(\rho)]^2$ is the maximum of (5), $\sum_{\nu=0}^{n} |u_\nu|^2 = 1$. Choosing $u_\nu = (n+1)^{-\frac{1}{2}}$ we find that

$$[\mu^{(n)}(\rho)]^2 \geq \frac{1}{n+1} \sum_{\nu=0}^{n} |\alpha_0 + \alpha_1 \rho + \ldots + \alpha_{n-\nu} \rho^{n-\nu}|^2,$$

so that

$$\lim_{n \to \infty} \mu^{(n)} \geq \lim_{n \to \infty} \mu^{(n)}(\rho) \geq |\alpha_0 + \alpha_1 \rho + \alpha_2 \rho^2 + \ldots| = |f(\rho)|.$$

Applying this result to $f(e^{i\gamma}z)$, γ real, we obtain for the same limits the lower bound $|f(e^{i\gamma}\rho)|$, so that

$$\lim_{n \to \infty} \mu^{(n)} \geq \max_{|z|=\rho} |f(z)|.$$

Since this is true for all ρ, the limit in question is $\geq M(f)$. Comparison of this result with (4) yields (2).

9.7. Problem B concerning $M(f)$

We denote again by $(\mu^{(n)})^2$, $\mu^{(n)} \geq 0$, the maximum of the form S_n defined in 9.6, $\sum_{\nu=0}^{n} |u_\nu|^2 = 1$.

(a) THEOREM. *The function* $f(z) = \sum_{n=0}^{\infty} \alpha_n z^n$ *is regular in the unit circle* $|z| < 1$ *and satisfies the inequality* $|f(z)| < 1$ *for* $|z| < 1$ *if and only if* $\mu^{(n)} \leq 1$ *for all* n. *More precisely, there are two cases possible:*

(i) *we have* $\mu^{(n)} < 1$ *for all* n;

(ii) *there is an integer* m, $m \geq 1$, *so that* $\mu^{(n)} < 1$ *for* $n \leq m-1$ *and* $\mu^{(n)} = 1$ *for* $n \geq m$.

Case (ii) *occurs if and only if* $f(z)$ *has the form*

$$f(z) = e^{i\gamma} \prod_{k=1}^{m} \frac{z + \omega_k}{1 + \bar{\omega}_k z}$$

$$= e^{i\gamma} \frac{a_0 + a_1 z + \ldots + a_m z^m}{\bar{a}_m + \bar{a}_{m-1} z + \ldots + \bar{a}_0 z^m}, \quad \gamma \text{ real}, \quad |\omega_k| < 1, a_m = 1. \quad (1)$$

In this case $M(f) = 1$.

If $\mu^{(n)} = 1$ for all n, we must have $f(z) = \alpha_0$, $|\alpha_0| = 1$; we write then $m = 0$ [cf. (e)].

(b) For the proof we note that $\mu^{(n)} \leq 1$ involves $\sum_{\nu=0}^{n} |\alpha_\nu|^2 \leq 1$ [cf. 9.6 (3), $u_n = 1$, $u_\nu = 0$ for $\nu < n$], so that $f(z)$ must be regular in the unit circle $|z| < 1$. In view of theorem 9.6 the condition $M(f) \leq 1$ is equivalent with $\mu^{(n)} \leq 1$.

(c) Next we shall discuss condition (ii), $m \geq 1$. Let $f(z)$ have the special form (1), $M(f) = 1$; we have from 9.6 (3)

$$(\mu^{(m)})^2 \geq \sum_{\nu=0}^{m} |\alpha_0 u_\nu + \alpha_1 u_{\nu+1} + \ldots + \alpha_{m-\nu} u_m|^2 : \sum_{\nu=0}^{m} |u_\nu|^2,$$

where $\{u_\nu\}$ is an arbitrary nonzero vector. Now

$$\alpha_0 \bar{a}_{m-\nu} + \alpha_1 \bar{a}_{m-\nu+1} + \ldots + \alpha_\nu \bar{a}_m = e^{i\gamma} a_\nu, \quad 0 \leq \nu \leq m,$$

so that choosing $u_\nu = \bar{a}_\nu$

$$(\mu^{(m)})^2 \geq \sum_{\nu=0}^{m} |a_\nu|^2 : \sum_{\nu=0}^{m} |a_\nu|^2 = 1; \tag{2}$$

hence $\mu^{(m)} = 1$, consequently, since $M(f) = 1$,

$$\mu^{(n)} = 1 \quad \text{for} \quad n \geq m \tag{3}$$

follows.

On the other hand, let $\{v_0, v_1, \ldots, v_{m-1}\}$ be a unit vector for which $\mu^{(m-1)}$ is attained; writing

$$f(z) (v_{m-1} + v_{m-2} z + \ldots + v_0 z^{m-1}) = \beta_0 + \beta_1 z + \beta_2 z^2 + \ldots, \tag{4}$$

we have

$$(\mu^{(m-1)})^2 = \sum_{\nu=0}^{m-1} |\alpha_0 v_\nu + \alpha_1 v_{\nu+1} + \ldots + \alpha_{m-1-\nu} v_{m-1}|^2 = \sum_{\nu=0}^{m-1} |\beta_\nu|^2$$

$$< \sum_{\nu=0}^{\infty} |\beta_\nu|^2 = \frac{1}{2\pi} \int_{-\pi}^{\pi} |f(z)(v_{m-1} + v_{m-2} z + \ldots + v_0 z^{m-1})|^2 dx$$

$$= \frac{1}{2\pi} \int_{-\pi}^{\pi} |v_{m-1} + v_{m-2} z + \ldots + v_0 z^{m-1}|^2 dx = \sum_{\nu=0}^{m-1} |v_\nu|^2 = 1, \quad z = e^{ix},$$

i.e. $\mu^{(m-1)} < 1$ unless (4) is a polynomial of degree $m - 1$. This is, however, impossible in the case (1) since the numerator of $f(z)$ is a polynomial of the precise degree m, and $|\omega_k| < 1$.

(d) We assume now that $\mu^{(h)} < 1$ for $h \leq m - 1$ and $\mu^{(h)} = 1$ for $h \geq m$. We denote by $(v_0, v_1, \ldots, v_m)$ a unit vector for which $S_m = 1$, so that

$$|\alpha_0 v_0 + \alpha_1 v_1 + \ldots + \alpha_m v_m|^2 + |\alpha_0 v_1 + \ldots + \alpha_{m-1} v_m|^2 + \ldots + |\alpha_0 v_m|^2 = 1. \tag{5}$$

Since $S_{m-1} < 1$, the last component v_m must be different from zero.

Let $n \geqq m$, $0 \leqq \nu \leqq n - m$; we write in 9.6 (3):

$$u_0 = u_1 = \ldots = u_{\nu-1} = 0; \quad u_\nu = v_0, u_{\nu+1} = v_1, \ldots, u_{\nu+m} = v_m;$$
$$u_{\nu+m+1} = \ldots = u_n = 0,$$

yielding

$$S_n = | \alpha_\nu v_0 + \alpha_{\nu+1} v_1 + \ldots + \alpha_{\nu+m} v_m |^2 + | \alpha_{\nu-1} v_0 + \alpha_\nu v_1 + \ldots + \alpha_{\nu+m-1} v_m |^2$$
$$+ \ldots + | \alpha_1 v_0 + \alpha_2 v_1 + \ldots + \alpha_{m+1} v_m |^2 + | \alpha_0 v_0 + \alpha_1 v_1 + \ldots + \alpha_m v_m |^2$$
$$+ | \alpha_0 v_1 + \ldots + \alpha_{m-1} v_m |^2 + \ldots + | \alpha_0 v_m |^2 \leqq (\mu^{(n)})^2 = 1. \tag{6}$$

This has the consequence that

$$\alpha_k v_0 + \alpha_{k+1} v_1 + \ldots + \alpha_{k+m} v_m = 0, \quad 1 \leqq k \leqq \nu, \tag{7}$$

holds. Thus (7) holds for all $k \geqq 1$. This result implies that

$$f(z) (v_m + v_{m-1} z + \ldots + v_0 z^m) = A_0 + A_1 z + \ldots + A_m z^m \tag{8}$$

is a polynomial of degree m so that $f(z)$ is a rational function. Moreover, we have according to (5)

$$| A_0 |^2 + | A_1 |^2 + \ldots + | A_m |^2 = 1.$$

Now

$$1 = \sum_{k=0}^{m} | A_k |^2 = \frac{1}{2\pi} \int_{-\pi}^{\pi} | f(z) (v_m + v_{m-1} z + \ldots + v_0 z^m) |^2 \, dx$$

$$\leqq \frac{1}{2\pi} \int_{-\pi}^{\pi} | v_m + v_{m-1} z + \ldots + v_0 z^m |^2 \, dx = \sum_{\nu=0}^{m} | v_\nu |^2 = 1, \quad z = e^{ix},$$

so that $f(z)$ must be of constant modulus 1 on the unit circle $| z | = 1$. Since $f(z)$ is regular in $| z | < 1$, it must have the form (1). [Cf. (8), $v_m \neq 0$.]

(e) The previous argument needs only a slight modification if $m = 0$, i.e. $\mu^{(n)} = 1$, $n \geqq 0$. First, $S_0 = | \alpha_0 |^2 | u_0 |^2$, so that $| \alpha_0 | = 1$. Now for $n \geqq 1$ we set

$$u_0 = u_1 = \ldots = u_{n-1} = 0, \quad u_n = 1$$

and obtain

$$S_n = | \alpha_n |^2 + | \alpha_{n-1} |^2 + \ldots + | \alpha_0 |^2 \leqq 1,$$

so that $\alpha_1 = \alpha_2 = \ldots = \alpha_n = 0$. Thus $f(z) = \alpha_0 = e^{i\gamma}$, γ real.

9.8. Problem C concerning $M(f)$

THEOREM. *Let us consider the class of all power series $f(z)$ which are regular in $| z | < 1$ and begin with the given terms $\sum_{k=0}^{n} \alpha_k z^k$. We denote by*

$(\mu^{(n)})^2$, $\mu^{(n)} \geq 0$, *the highest eigenvalue of the form* S_n [9.6 (3)]. *Then for every function of this class*

$$M(f) \geq \mu^{(n)}. \tag{1}$$

Let $\mu^{(n)} > 0$; *the sign* = *holds in* (1) *if and only if* $f(z)$ *has the following special form*:

$$f(z) = \mu^{(n)} e^{i\gamma} \prod_{k=1}^{m} \frac{z + \omega_k}{1 + \overline{\omega}_k z}, \quad \gamma \text{ real}, \ |\omega_k| < 1, \tag{2}$$

provided $|\alpha_0| < \mu^{(n)}$; *here the quantities* m *and* ω_k *are uniquely determined. In the case* $|\alpha_0| = \mu^{(n)}$ *the sign* = *holds if and only if* $f(z) = \alpha_0 = \mu^{(n)} e^{i\gamma}$, γ *real*.

Cf. 9.6 (4). Let $M(f) = \mu^{(n)} > 0$; we can assume that $\mu^{(n)} = 1$. Let first $|\alpha_0| < 1$; we apply theorem 9.7 [cf. case (ii)]. Next let $|\alpha_0| = 1$; then $\mu^{(h)} = 1$ for all $h \geq 0$ so that [cf. 9.7 (e)] $f(z) = e^{i\gamma}$, γ real.

9.9. An equivalent form of theorem 9.7

Following the analogy to 9.5 we shall deal now with another convenient characterization of the class $|f(z)| \leq 1$, $|z| < 1$, using instead of the highest eigenvalues of the forms S_n defined in 9.6, certain determinants formed by the coefficients of the given power series.

(a) THEOREM. *The power series* $f(z) = \sum\limits_{n=0}^{\infty} \alpha_n z^n$ *converges in the unit circle* $|z| < 1$ *and satisfies there the condition* $|f(z)| < 1$ *if and only if the determinants*

$$H_n = \det(\delta_{pq} - h_{pq}), \quad p, q = 0, 1, 2, \ldots, n; \ n = 0, 1, 2, \ldots, \tag{1}$$

are all positive. Here h_{pq} *is defined by* 9.6 (1). *The only exception is when* $f(z)$ *has the form* 9.7 (1); *we have then* $H_n > 0$ *for* $n \leq m - 1$ *and* $H_n = 0$ *for* $n \geq m$.

We have $f(z) = e^{i\gamma}$, γ *real, if and only if all determinants* H_n *vanish* $(m = 0)$.

In view of the previous considerations it suffices to prove the following two facts:

(i) If there is an integer m, $m \geq 1$, such that $H_n > 0$ for $n \leq m - 1$ and $H_n = 0$ for $n \geq m$, then $f(z)$ has the form 9.7 (1).

(ii) If all determinants H_n are zero, we have $f(z) = e^{i\gamma}$, γ real.

Case (ii) can be interpreted as the case $m = 0$.

The proof of (i) is rather complicated; it requires a certain generalization of the determinants H_n. The proof of (ii) is simple; it turns out that the condition $H_0 = H_1 = H_3 = H_5 = \ldots = 0$ has already the consequence $\alpha_0 = e^{i\gamma}$, $\alpha_1 = \alpha_2 = \ldots = 0$ [cf. 9.5 (d)].

(b) It is convenient to consider a more general situation. Let

$$f(z) = \frac{A(z)}{B(z)}, \quad A(z) = \sum_{n=0}^{\infty} \alpha_n z^n, \quad B(z) = \sum_{n=0}^{\infty} \beta_n z^n, \tag{2}$$

and let us assume that $\beta_0 \neq 0$. We form the following generalization of the determinants H_n:

$$L_n = \det (k_{pq} - h_{pq}), \quad p, q = 0, 1, 2, \ldots, n, \tag{3}$$

where h_{pq} is defined as in 9.6 (1) and similarly

$$k_{pq} = \beta_p \bar{\beta}_q + \beta_{p-1} \bar{\beta}_{q-1} + \ldots + \beta_0 \bar{\beta}_{q-p}, \quad p \leq q, \quad k_{qp} = \bar{k}_{pq}. \tag{4}$$

We prove now the following theorem:

THEOREM. *With the function* $f(z) = A(z)/B(z)$ *we associate the determinants* L_n *[cf. (2)–(4) and 9.1 (5)]. Let* $m \geq 1$, *and* $L_n > 0$ *for* $n \leq m - 1$, $L_n = 0$ *for* $n \geq m$. *Then* $f(z)$ *must be a rational function of the form*

$$f(z) = e^{i\gamma} \prod_{k=1}^{m} \frac{z + \omega_k}{1 + \bar{\omega}_k z}, \quad \gamma \text{ real}, \ |\omega_k| < 1. \tag{5}$$

Let $L_n = 0$ *for all* n $(m = 0)$; *then* $f(z) = e^{i\gamma}$, γ *real.*

From here both (i) and (ii) follow by setting $B(z) = 1$.

(c) Let us deal first with the case $m = 0$, i.e. $L_n = 0$ for all n. Since $L_0 = k_{00} - h_{00} = |\beta_0|^2 - |\alpha_0|^2 = 0$, we have $\alpha_0 = \epsilon \beta_0$, $|\epsilon| = 1$. Also $L_1 = (k_{00} - h_{00})(k_{11} - h_{11}) - |k_{01} - h_{01}|^2 = 0$, hence $\alpha_0 \bar{\alpha}_1 = \beta_0 \bar{\beta}_1$, $\alpha_1 = \epsilon \beta_1$. Let us assume that $\alpha_\nu = \epsilon \beta_\nu$, $1 \leq \nu \leq N$; we shall prove that $\alpha_{N+1} = \epsilon \beta_{N+1}$. Indeed, the determinant L_{2N+1} can be written in this form

$$\begin{vmatrix} 0 & \Delta \\ \Delta^* & G \end{vmatrix},$$

where the matrix Δ is defined as follows:

$$\Delta = \begin{pmatrix} l_{0,N+1} & l_{0,N+2} & \cdots & l_{0,2N+1} \\ l_{1,N+1} & l_{1,N+2} & \cdots & l_{1,2N+1} \\ \cdots & \cdots & \cdots & \cdots \\ l_{N,N+1} & l_{N,N+2} & \cdots & l_{N,2N+1} \end{pmatrix}, \quad l_{pq} = k_{pq} - h_{pq};$$

G is a certain matrix with $N+1$ rows and columns. In view of the theorem of Laplace we have $\det \Delta = 0$. Now for $0 \leq p \leq N$, $0 \leq q \leq N$

$$l_{p,N+1+q} = \beta_p \bar{\beta}_{N+1+q} + \beta_{p-1}\bar{\beta}_{N+q} + \ldots + \beta_0 \bar{\beta}_{N+1+q-p}$$

$$- \alpha_p \bar{\alpha}_{N+1+q} - \alpha_{p-1}\bar{\alpha}_{N+q} - \ldots - \alpha_0 \bar{\alpha}_{N+1+q-p}$$

$$= \alpha_p (\bar{\epsilon}\bar{\beta}_{N+1+q} - \bar{\alpha}_{N+1+q})$$

$$+ \alpha_{p-1}(\bar{\epsilon}\bar{\beta}_{N+q} - \bar{\alpha}_{N+q}) + \ldots + \alpha_0 (\bar{\epsilon}\bar{\beta}_{N+1+q-p} - \bar{\alpha}_{N+1+q-p}),$$

so that the matrix Δ is the product of the following two matrices:

$$\begin{pmatrix} \alpha_0 & 0 & \ldots & 0 \\ \alpha_1 & \alpha_0 & \ldots & 0 \\ \ldots & \ldots & \ldots & \ldots \\ \alpha_N & \alpha_{N-1} & \ldots & \alpha_0 \end{pmatrix},$$

$$\begin{pmatrix} \bar{\epsilon}\bar{\beta}_{N+1} - \bar{\alpha}_{N+1} & \bar{\epsilon}\bar{\beta}_{N+2} - \bar{\alpha}_{N+2} & \ldots & \bar{\epsilon}\bar{\beta}_{2N+1} - \bar{\alpha}_{2N+1} \\ \bar{\epsilon}\bar{\beta}_{N} - \bar{\alpha}_{N} & \bar{\epsilon}\bar{\beta}_{N+1} - \bar{\alpha}_{N+1} & \ldots & \bar{\epsilon}\bar{\beta}_{2N} - \bar{\alpha}_{2N} \\ \ldots & \ldots & \ldots & \ldots \\ \bar{\epsilon}\bar{\beta}_{1} - \bar{\alpha}_{1} & \bar{\epsilon}\bar{\beta}_{2} - \bar{\alpha}_{2} & \ldots & \bar{\epsilon}\bar{\beta}_{N+1} - \bar{\alpha}_{N+1} \end{pmatrix}.$$

The elements under the main diagonal of the second matrix are zero. In view of $\alpha_0 \neq 0$ we conclude that $\bar{\epsilon}\bar{\beta}_{N+1} - \bar{\alpha}_{N+1} = 0$, $\alpha_{N+1} = \epsilon\beta_{N+1}$.

(d) Let $m \geq 1$. Since

$$L_0 = |\beta_0|^2 - |\alpha_0|^2 > 0$$

we have $|f(0)| = |\alpha_0/\beta_0| < 1$. We define the functions

$$A_1(z) = \sum_{n=0}^{\infty} \alpha_n^{(1)} z^n, \quad B_1(z) = \sum_{n=0}^{\infty} \beta_n^{(1)} z^n, \quad f_1(z) = \frac{A_1(z)}{B_1(z)} \tag{6}$$

in the following way:

$$\left.\begin{array}{l} A_1(z) = z^{-1}[\beta_0 A(z) - \alpha_0 B(z)], \\ B_1(z) = [\bar{\beta}_0 B(z) - \bar{\alpha}_0 A(z)], \quad B_1(0) = \beta_0^{(1)} \neq 0, \end{array}\right\} \tag{7}$$

so that

$$\left.\begin{array}{l} f_1(z) = z^{-1}\dfrac{\beta_0 A(z) - \alpha_0 B(z)}{\bar{\beta}_0 B(z) - \bar{\alpha}_0 A(z)} = \dfrac{\beta_0}{\bar{\beta}_0} z^{-1} \dfrac{f(z) - f(0)}{1 - \overline{f(0)}f(z)}, \\[2mm] f(z) = \dfrac{\alpha_0 + \bar{\beta}_0 z f_1(z)}{\beta_0 + \bar{\alpha}_0 z f_1(z)}. \end{array}\right\} \tag{8}$$

From (7) we conclude the relations

$$\alpha_n^{(1)} = \beta_0 \alpha_{n+1} - \alpha_0 \beta_{n+1}, \quad \beta_n^{(1)} = \bar{\beta}_0 \beta_n - \bar{\alpha}_0 \alpha_n, \quad n = 0, 1, 2, \ldots. \tag{9}$$

We denote by $\mathfrak{L}_n$ the Hermitian form having the elements of L_n as coefficients:

$$\mathfrak{L}_n(u_0, u_1, \ldots, u_n) = \sum_{p, q = 0, 1, \ldots, n} (k_{pq} - h_{pq})\, u_p \overline{u}_q = \sum_{p, q = 0, 1, \ldots, n} l_{pq} u_p \overline{u}_q. \tag{10}$$

Similarly we set

$$\mathfrak{L}^{(1)}_{n-1}(u_1, u_2, \ldots, u_n)$$
$$= \sum_{p, q = 1, 2, \ldots, n} (k^{(1)}_{p-1, q-1} - h^{(1)}_{p-1, q-1})\, u_p \overline{u}_q = \sum_{p, q = 1, 2, \ldots, n} l^{(1)}_{p-1, q-1} u_p \overline{u}_q, \tag{11}$$

where $h^{(1)}_{pq}$, $k^{(1)}_{pq}$, $l^{(1)}_{pq}$ belong to $A_1(z)$ and $B_1(z)$ in a similar fashion as h_{pq}, k_{pq}, l_{pq} belong to $A(z)$ and $B(z)$ respectively.

(e) We prove the identity

$$L_0 l_{pq} - \bar{l}_{0p} l_{0q} = l^{(1)}_{p-1, q-1}, \quad p, q = 1, 2, 3, \ldots. \tag{12}$$

For the proof we assume that $p \leq q$ and note that

$$L_0(\beta_p \bar{\beta}_q - \alpha_p \bar{\alpha}_q) - (\bar{\beta}_0 \beta_p - \bar{\alpha}_0 \alpha_p)\,(\beta_0 \bar{\beta}_q - \alpha_0 \bar{\alpha}_q)$$
$$+ (\bar{\beta}_0 \beta_{p-1} - \bar{\alpha}_0 \alpha_{p-1})\,(\beta_0 \bar{\beta}_{q-1} - \alpha_0 \bar{\alpha}_{q-1})$$
$$= (\bar{\beta}_0 \beta_{p-1} - \bar{\alpha}_0 \alpha_{p-1})\,(\beta_0 \bar{\beta}_{q-1} - \alpha_0 \bar{\alpha}_{q-1}) - (\beta_0 \alpha_p - \alpha_0 \beta_p)\,(\bar{\beta}_0 \bar{\alpha}_q - \bar{\alpha}_0 \bar{\beta}_q),$$

or

$$L_0(l_{pq} - l_{p-1, q-1}) - \bar{l}_{0p} l_{0q} + \bar{l}_{0, p-1} l_{0, q-1} = \beta^{(1)}_{p-1} \overline{\beta^{(1)}_{q-1}} - \alpha^{(1)}_{p-1} \overline{\alpha^{(1)}_{q-1}}.$$

In the last identity we replace p, q by $p-1, q-1$, then $p-2, q-2$, etc., finally by $1, q-p+1$. Since

$$-L_0 l_{0, q-p} + \bar{l}_{0, 0} l_{0, q-p} = 0,$$

we obtain (12) by adding these identities.

The relation (12) admits of a simple interpretation in terms of the Hermitian forms $\mathfrak{L}_n, \mathfrak{L}^{(1)}_n$. Indeed,

$$L_0 \mathfrak{L}_n(u_0, u_1, \ldots, u_n) = L_0 \sum_{p, q = 0, 1, \ldots, n} l_{pq} u_p \overline{u}_q$$
$$= L_0^2 |u_0|^2 + 2 L_0 \Re u_0(l_{01} \overline{u}_1 + l_{02} \overline{u}_2 + \ldots + l_{0n} \overline{u}_n)$$
$$+ L_0 \sum_{p, q = 1, 2, \ldots, n} l_{pq} u_p \overline{u}_q$$
$$= |L_0 u_0 + \bar{l}_{01} u_1 + \bar{l}_{02} u_2 + \ldots + \bar{l}_{0n} u_n|^2$$
$$+ \sum_{p, q = 1, 2, \ldots, n} (L_0 l_{pq} - \bar{l}_{0p} l_{0q})\, u_p \overline{u}_q$$
$$= |L_0 u_0 + \bar{l}_{01} u_1 + \bar{l}_{02} u_2 + \ldots + \bar{l}_{0n} u_n|^2$$
$$+ \mathfrak{L}^{(1)}_{n-1}(u_1, u_2, \ldots, u_n). \tag{13}$$

In the last step the identity (12) was taken into account.

(f) The relation (8) between $f(z)$ and $f_1(z)$ has, by Schwarz's lemma, the consequence that $|f(z)| \leq 1$ in $|z| < 1$ holds if and only if we have $|f_1(z)| \leq 1$ in $|z| < 1$. The relation (13) between the associated forms $\mathfrak{L}_n$ and $\mathfrak{L}_n^{(1)}$ can be interpreted as the first step of the classical Jacobi transformation of the given form $\mathfrak{L}_n$ into a sum of squares. Hence the corresponding determinants L_n and $L_{n-1}^{(1)}$ are at the same time positive or zero.

These facts serve as the basis of a mathematical induction from $m-1$ to m. Let $L_n > 0$ for $n \leq m-1$ and $L_n = 0$ for $n \geq m$. We have then $L_{n-1}^{(1)} > 0$ for $n \leq m-1$ and $L_{n-1}^{(1)} = 0$ for $n \geq m$, or $L_n^{(1)} > 0$ for $n \leq m-2$ and $L_n^{(1)} = 0$ for $n \geq m-1$. (In the case $m = 1$ we have $L_n^{(1)} = 0$ for all n.) Assuming the validity of our assertion for $m-1$ (instead of m) we conclude that

$$f_1(z) = e^{i\gamma} \frac{p(z)}{p^*(z)}, \quad \gamma \text{ real},$$

where $p(z)$ is a polynomial of degree $m-1$ with leading term z^{m-1} and $p^*(z) = z^{m-1}\overline{p}(z^{-1})$ is its reciprocal polynomial. The zeros of $p(z)$ are all in the unit circle $|z| < 1$.

From (8) we conclude that

$$f(z) = \frac{\overline{\beta}_0}{\beta_0} e^{i\gamma} \frac{kp^*(z) + zp(z)}{p^*(z) + \overline{k}zp(z)}, \quad k = \frac{\alpha_0}{\overline{\beta}_0} e^{-i\gamma},$$

where $|k| < 1$. The numerator of the last fraction is a polynomial $q(z)$ of degree m with leading term z^m and its reciprocal polynomial $q^*(z)$ is identical with the denominator. Also, for $|z| \geq 1$,

$$\left| \frac{kp^*(z)}{zp(z)} \right| \leq k < 1,$$

so that the zeros of $q(z)$ are all in the unit circle $|z| < 1$.

In view of the case $m = 0$ settled in (c) this establishes the assertion.

CHAPTER 10

APPLICATIONS TO PROBABILITY THEORY

In both the present chapter and the next we consider certain problems of the theory of stochastic processes. We intend to show that an important class of these problems can be dealt with by applying known results from the theory of Toeplitz forms.

10.1. Introduction

(a) Let us discuss first those basic concepts of the theory of probability which will be used below. On an abstract set Ω, the reference space, a σ-algebra $\mathfrak{F}$ of subsets S is defined. To each element $S \in \mathfrak{F}$ a probability $P(S)$ is assigned in such a way that P is a *probability measure*, i.e.

(i) P is completely additive, so that if $S_\nu \in \mathfrak{F}$, $\nu = 1, 2, \ldots$, and the S_ν are disjoint sets, $S_\nu \cap S_\mu = 0$ for $\nu \neq \mu$, we have

$$P\left(\bigcup_{\nu=1}^{\infty} S \right) = \sum_{\nu=1}^{\infty} P(S_\nu).$$

(ii) P is nonnegative.

(iii) The total space has probability one, $P(\Omega) = 1$.

The following interpretation is well known. The elements ω of Ω are the 'elementary events', the sets S in $\mathfrak{F}$ (the 'measurable sets') the compound events we consider, and $P(S)$ is the relative weight of S. The last statement can be made more precise but we need not go into that now.

The reference space, together with the measurable sets and the probability measure, are said to form a *probability space*, denoted by $(\Omega, \mathfrak{F}, P)$.

A real-valued function $x(\omega)$ defined on Ω is called a *stochastic variable* if it is measurable (with respect to $\mathfrak{F}$), i.e. if the set

$$\{x(\omega) < a\} \in \mathfrak{F}$$

for every real a. This definition is adopted of course with the aim to assign probabilities to events of this kind. The extension to complex-valued stochastic variables is immediate.

(b) As an example we consider the case when $\Omega = [0, 1]$, $\mathfrak{F}$ consists of the Borel sets in this interval, and P is the Lebesgue measure. Let us write the real number ω, $0 \leqq \omega \leqq 1$, as a decimal fraction

$$\omega = x_1 x_2 x_3 \dots.$$

The digits x_t, $t = 1, 2, \dots$, are uniquely determined by ω if we exclude an unbroken sequence of 9's in the decimal fraction. Instead of x_t we may write $x_t(\omega)$, $t = 1, 2, \dots$. It is clear that for a fixed positive integer t the function $x(\omega)$ is a stochastic variable so that in this way a collection of stochastic variables arises. *Such an indexed set of stochastic variables is said to form a stochastic process.* Or more formally:

Consider a given probability space $(\Omega, \mathfrak{F}, P)$ and a set of indices $T = \{t\}$. If for each $t \in T$ the function $x_t(\omega)$ is a stochastic variable (considered as a function of ω), $x_t(\omega)$ is a stochastic process when t, ω varies over $T \times \Omega$.

The set T can be finite, denumerable or nondenumerably infinite. We will deal mainly with the cases when T consists of all integers or of all real numbers.

In the above example it is clear that we have the probabilities

$$P\{x_1(\omega) = i\} = 10^{-1} \quad \text{for} \quad i = 0, 1, \dots, 9,$$

and also

$$P\{x_1(\omega) = i, x_2(\omega) = j\} = 100^{-1} \quad \text{for} \quad i, j = 0, 1, \dots, 9.$$

In the usual terminology $x_1(\omega)$ and $x_2(\omega)$ are said to be (stochastically) independent, since we have

$$P\{x_1(\omega) = i, x_2(\omega) = j\} = P\{x_1(\omega) = i\} \cdot P\{x_2(\omega) = j\}.$$

The definition is analogous if we consider $x_t(\omega)$ for more than two distinct values of t.

This is a very simple example of a stochastic process because of the independence of the stochastic variables constituting the process. The typical difficulties arise in the opposite case, namely, when dependence is involved; our first aim is to characterize one such form of dependence.

(c) For a stochastic variable $x(\omega)$ which is integrable over the reference space Ω with respect to the probability measure P, we define the mean-value operator E by

$$Ex(\omega) = \int_\Omega x(\omega) \, dP(\omega).$$

This is the mean value of the stochastic variable. For a stochastic process $x_t(\omega)$ we form the quantity (if it exists) $m_t = Ex_t(\omega)$, called the *mean-value function*. We shall assume throughout this chapter that $m_t \equiv 0$; otherwise we can consider instead the process $x_t - m_t$ which has obviously a vanishing mean-value function.

We also introduce the *covariance function* $r_{s,t} = Ex_s(\omega)\overline{x_t(\omega)}$, and assume that

$$E\,|\,x_t(\omega)\,|^2 = \int_\Omega |\,x_t(\omega)\,|^2\,dP(\omega) < \infty$$

for every $t \in T$. Under this condition both the mean-value function m_t and the covariance function $r_{s,t}$ exist, as we can see by applying Schwarz's inequality.

If $x_s(\omega)$ and $x_t(\omega)$ are independent, i.e.

$$P\{x_s(\omega) \leqq a, x_t(\omega) \leqq b\} = P\{x_s(\omega) \leqq a\} . P\{x_t(\omega) \leqq b\},$$

we have

$$r_{s,t} = \int_\Omega x_s(\omega)\,\overline{x_t(\omega)}\,dP(\omega) = \int_\Omega x_s(\omega)\,dP(\omega) \int_\Omega \overline{x_t(\omega)}\,dP(\omega) = m_s\overline{m_t} = 0.$$

Although the converse is not true in general, the covariance function yields a characterization of the dependence of the stochastic variables $x_s(\omega)$ and $x_t(\omega)$ which is adequate for many purposes.

10.2. The geometry of a stochastic process

(a) A stochastic process $x_t(\omega)$, $t \in T$, can be considered from another point of view. In the space of functions defined on Ω which are $(\mathfrak{F})$-measurable and quadratically integrable with respect to P, we introduce the scalar product in the way usual in L_2:

$$(g, h) = Eg\bar{h} = \int_\Omega g(\omega)\,\overline{h(\omega)}\,dP(\omega),$$

and the norm $\|g\| = (g, g)^{\frac{1}{2}}$. The convergence corresponding to this norm is called convergence in the mean; thus a sequence of functions $f_n(\omega) \in L_2(\Omega)$, $n = 1, 2, \ldots$, converges in the mean to $f(\omega) \in L_2(\Omega)$ if $\|f_n - f\| \to 0$ as $n \to \infty$. We write then $f(\omega) = \text{l.i.m.} f_n(\omega)$.
$$\qquad\qquad n \to \infty$$

Starting from the process $x_t(\omega)$ we consider its linear hull, i.e. the set of all finite linear combinations,

$$L(x) = \left\{ \sum_{\nu=1}^{n} c_\nu x(t_\nu);\ t_\nu \in T,\ c_\nu \text{ complex constants} \right\}.$$

Closing this linear manifold with respect to convergence in the mean *we obtain a space $L_2(x)$ which has all the properties of a complex Hilbert space (separable or not)*. Indeed, the following axioms are satisfied:

(i) The space is linear so that it is closed under addition and under multiplication with complex numbers. These two operations satisfy the usual rules of linear algebra.

(ii) A scalar product (f, g) is defined such that

$$(cf, g) = c(f, g),\qquad(1)$$

$$(f+g, h) = (f, h) + (g, h),\qquad(2)$$

$$(f, g) = \overline{(g, f)},\qquad(3)$$

$$(f, f) = \|f\|^2 > 0 \ \text{ for } \ f \neq 0 \quad \text{and} \quad \|f\| = 0 \ \text{ for } \ f = 0.\qquad(4)$$

A metric is defined in the space by the definition of distance $\|f - g\|$ between two elements f and g.

(iii) The space is complete, i.e. Cauchy sequences converge to elements in the space: if $f_n \in L_2(x)$, $\|f_n - f_m\| \to 0$ as n, $m \to \infty$, there exists an element f in the space with $\|f_n - f\| \to 0$ as $n \to \infty$.

One may note that this space $L_2(x)$ does not necessarily contain all functions quadratically integrable over Ω with respect to P.

In this way the stochastic variable $x_t(\omega)$ for a fixed value of $t \in T$ becomes a point P_t in the Hilbert space $L_2(x)$. As t varies, P_t describes a curve in $L_2(x)$. If this curve is continuous in t (to be able to make such a statement we must have a topology in T) we say that the process is *continuous in the mean*; we have then $\|x_\tau(\omega) - x_t(\omega)\| \to 0$ as $\tau \to t$.

(b) So far we have considered a very general class of stochastic processes. From now on we will restrict ourselves to an important subclass, namely, to stationary processes. They are defined in the following way.

Let T be an Abelian group. The process $x_t(\omega)$ is said to be (weakly) *stationary* if for every s, t, $h \in T$ we have $r_{s,t} = r_{s+h, t+h}$; we may say also that the geometry of the process is invariant with respect to translations of t. It is clear that under this condition there is a function $R(h)$ of a single argument so that $r_{s,t} = R(s - t)$.

For such a process we have

$$\|x_{t+h}(\omega) - x_t(\omega)\|^2 = 2R(0) - 2\Re[R(h)],\qquad(5)$$

so that it is continuous in the mean provided $R(h)$ is continuous at $h=0$. In fact $R(t)$ is then continuous for all t since

$$| R(t+\epsilon) - R(t) | = | (x_{t+\epsilon} - x_t, x_0) | \le \| x_{t+\epsilon} - x_t \| . \| x_0 \|.$$

The converse is also true [i.e. continuity in the mean implies continuity of $R(h)$], since (a)

$$\Im[R(h)] = \Im[(x_{t+h}, x_t)] = \Im[\| x_t \|^2 + (x_{t+h} - x_t, x_t)] = \Im[(x_{t+h} - x_t, x_t)]$$

tends to zero with h if the process is continuous in the mean, and (b) $\Re[R(h)] \to R(0)$. Together (a) and (b) imply that $R(h) \to R(0)$ as $h \to 0$.

10.3. The spectrum of a stationary process

(a) From here on we will consider only the case when T consists of the real line or of the real integers. These will be denoted as the continuous and the discrete case, respectively. We mention that a good deal of what follows can be obtained under the weaker assumption that T is a locally compact Abelian group (see Appendix).

(b) First, let us consider the discrete case. For any n the *covariance matrix*

$$\mathfrak{M}_n = \{r_{t+i, t+j}; \ i, j = 1, 2, ..., n\}$$
$$= \{R(i-j); \ i, j = 1, 2, ..., n\}$$

is nonnegative. Indeed, for an arbitrary vector z with components $z_1, z_2, ..., z_n$ in unitary n-space we have

$$z\mathfrak{M}_n z^* = \sum_{\nu, \mu = 1}^{n} z_\nu \bar{z}_\mu R(\nu - \mu) = \| \sum_{\nu = 1}^{n} z_\nu x_\nu(\omega) \|^2 \ge 0.$$

But then we can apply the result proved in 1.11 and 4.2 concerning the trigonometric moment problem, and we obtain immediately the following theorem:

THEOREM. *The covariance function $r_{s,t} = Ex_s(\omega)\,\overline{x_t(\omega)}$ of a stationary stochastic process with $Ex_t(\omega) \equiv 0$, $E | x_t\omega) |^2 < \infty$, can be represented as a Fourier–Stieltjes integral*

$$r_{s,t} = R(s-t) = \int_{-\pi}^{\pi} e^{i(s-t)\lambda} \, dF(\lambda) \tag{1}$$

with a bounded and nondecreasing function $F(\lambda)$. This function is uniquely determined at all points of continuity and it is called the spectral

*distribution function of the process. The set of jump points of $F(\lambda)$ is
called the spectrum of the process.*

Usually $F(\lambda)$ is normalized by the condition that it is continuous
from the right.

(c) For the continuous case we have a similar result.

Indeed, let $x_t(\omega)$, $-\infty < t < \infty$, be a stationary process with covariance function $R(t)$. If $x_t(\omega)$ is continuous in the mean we have
seen in 10.2 that $R(t)$ is continuous for all t.

For any $A > 0$ we have

$$\int_{-2A}^{2A} \left(1 - \frac{|\lambda|}{2A}\right) e^{-it\lambda}\, d\lambda = 2A \left(\frac{\sin At}{At}\right)^2,$$

and multiplying this relation by $(2\pi)^{-1}(1 - \epsilon\,|\,t\,|)\,R(t)$ and integrating
over $[-1/\epsilon, 1/\epsilon]$ we obtain

$$\int_{-2A}^{2A} \left(1 - \frac{|\lambda|}{2A}\right) f_\epsilon(\lambda)\, d\lambda = \frac{1}{\pi} \int_{-A/\epsilon}^{A/\epsilon} \left(\frac{\sin t}{t}\right)^2 \left(1 - \frac{\epsilon}{A}\,|\,t\,|\right) R\left(\frac{t}{A}\right) dt, \quad (2)$$

where

$$f_\epsilon(\lambda) = \frac{1}{2\pi} \int_{-1/\epsilon}^{1/\epsilon} (1 - \epsilon\,|\,t\,|)\, e^{-it\lambda}\, R(t)\, dt. \quad (3)$$

Since $|\,R(t)\,| \leq R(0)$ we see from (2) that

$$\left|\int_{-2A}^{2A} \left(1 - \frac{|\lambda|}{2A}\right) f_\epsilon(\lambda)\, d\lambda\right| \leq R(0) \frac{1}{\pi} \int_{-A/\epsilon}^{A/\epsilon} \left(\frac{\sin t}{t}\right)^2 dt$$

$$< R(0) \frac{1}{\pi} \int_{-\infty}^{\infty} \left(\frac{\sin t}{t}\right)^2 dt = R(0). \quad (4)$$

But

$$f_\epsilon(\lambda) = (2\pi\epsilon)^{-1} \int_{-1}^{1} (1 - |\,s\,|)\, e^{-is\lambda/\epsilon}\, R(\epsilon^{-1}s)\, ds$$

$$= (2\pi\epsilon)^{-1} \int_{0}^{1} \int_{0}^{1} e^{-iu\lambda/\epsilon + iv\lambda/\epsilon}\, R[\epsilon^{-1}(u-v)]\, du\, dv,$$

and since $R(t)$ is nonnegative definite [which can be seen by applying
the continuous analog of the argument in (b)] it is clear that $f_\epsilon(\lambda) \geq 0$.
Thus we conclude from (4), $A \to \infty$, that

$$\int_{-\infty}^{\infty} f_\epsilon(\lambda)\, d\lambda \leq R(0),$$

and the Fourier inversion formula is applicable; since $R(t)$ is continuous it yields everywhere in $[-1/\epsilon, 1/\epsilon]$

$$(1 - \epsilon |t|) R(t) = \int_{-\infty}^{\infty} e^{it\lambda} f_\epsilon(\lambda) \, d\lambda.$$

Now we let ϵ tend to zero. For any t the left member tends to $R(t)$ and the so-called continuity theorem for characteristic functions (see Appendix) implies that the functions

$$F_\epsilon(\lambda) = \int_{-\infty}^{\lambda} f_\epsilon(x) \, dx$$

converge to a bounded nondecreasing function $F(x)$ at all points of continuity of the latter function; also

$$R(t) = \int_{-\infty}^{\infty} e^{it\lambda} \, dF(\lambda).$$

We can state now the following theorem:

THEOREM. *If $x_t(\omega)$ is a stationary stochastic process which is continuous in the mean and has the covariance function*

$$R(t) = (x_{s+t}, x_s) = E x_{s+t} \bar{x}_s,$$

we have

$$R(t) = \int_{-\infty}^{\infty} e^{it\lambda} \, dF(\lambda),$$

where $F(\lambda)$ is bounded and nondecreasing so that $R(s - t)$ is a Toeplitz kernel.

It is convenient to normalize $F(\lambda)$ as being continuous from the right. As before $F(\lambda)$ can be shown to be uniquely determined.

(d) As is well known (cf. 1.3), every bounded and nondecreasing function $F(\lambda)$ can be written as the sum of three components

$$F(\lambda) = F_a(\lambda) + F_j(\lambda) + F_s(\lambda)$$

with the following properties. The component $F_a(\lambda)$ is absolutely continuous and it is the integral of the almost everywhere existing derivative of $F(\lambda)$:

$$F_a(\lambda) = \frac{1}{2\pi} \int^{\lambda} f(x) \, dx, \quad f(\lambda) = 2\pi \frac{d}{d\lambda} F(\lambda);$$

the factor 2π is introduced for convenience in the later calculations.

The nonnegative and integrable function $f(\lambda)$ is called the *spectral density* of the process.

The second component $F_j(\lambda)$ is a step function:

$$F_j(\lambda) = \sum_{\lambda_\nu \leqq \lambda} \Delta F(\lambda_\nu);$$

it is constant except at the discontinuities λ_ν of $F(\lambda)$, where $F_j(\lambda)$ has the same jump $\Delta F(\lambda_\nu)$ as $F(\lambda)$. Finally, $F_s(\lambda)$ is continuous and $F'_s(\lambda) = 0$ almost everywhere.

In practical situations we deal mostly with processes having an absolutely continuous spectrum, $F(\lambda) \equiv F_a(\lambda)$, or else an absolutely continuous spectrum with a few discontinuities superimposed. In the present chapter we will study the absolutely continuous case and in the next chapter the statistical problems arising from the presence of an added discrete component in the spectrum.

10.4. The spectral representation of a stationary process

We need one more result before we proceed to the application of Toeplitz forms to the study of stationary processes. For this purpose we consider a stationary stochastic process x_t, $-\infty < t < \infty$, which is continuous in the mean.

(a) On the linear manifold $L(x)$ consisting of all finite linear combinations of the type $\sum\limits_{\nu=1}^{n} c_\nu x_{t_\nu}$, we define a transformation T_t carrying $L(x)$ onto itself by the relation

$$T_t \left\{ \sum_{\nu=1}^{n} c_\nu x_{t_\nu} \right\} = \sum_{\nu=1}^{n} c_\nu x_{t_\nu + t}.$$

We have

$$\left\| \sum_{\nu=1}^{n} c_\nu x_{t_\nu} \right\|^2 = \sum_{\nu, \mu=1}^{n} c_\nu \bar{c}_\mu (x_{t_\nu}, x_{t_\mu}) = \sum_{\nu, \mu=1}^{n} c_\nu \bar{c}_\mu R(t_\nu - t_\mu),$$

and

$$\left\| \sum_{\nu=1}^{n} c_\nu x_{t_\nu + t} \right\|^2 = \sum_{\nu, \mu=1}^{n} c_\nu \bar{c}_\mu (x_{t_\nu + t}, x_{t_\mu + t}) = \sum_{\nu, \mu=1}^{n} c_\nu \bar{c}_\mu R(t_\nu - t_\mu),$$

so that $\| T_t z \| = \| z \|$ for $z \in L(x)$.

Now we extend this transformation to $L_2(x)$ in the following obvious way. Any $z \in L_2(x)$ can be approximated in the mean by elements from $L(x)$:

$$z = \underset{\nu \to \infty}{\text{l.i.m.}} z_\nu, \quad z_\nu \in L(x), \quad \nu = 1, 2, \ldots.$$

But

$$\| T_t z_n - T_t z_m \|^2 = \| z_n - z_m \|^2 \to 0 \quad \text{as} \quad n, m \to \infty;$$

hence the sequence $T_t z_n$ converges in the mean. Let us call the limiting element $T_t z$. This definition does not depend upon the choice of the particular sequence z_ν; indeed, if $z = \mathrm{l.i.m.}_{\nu \to \infty} z_\nu'$, $z_\nu' \in L(x)$, we find

$$\| T_t z_\nu - T_t z_\nu' \| = \| z_\nu - z_\nu' \| \to 0 \quad \text{as} \quad \nu \to \infty.$$

It is clear that T_t is a unitary transformation. Furthermore, this set of transformations forms a group; indeed $T_a T_b = T_{a+b}$. We need now a continuity property of this group.

(b) Let $u, v \in L_2(x)$. We shall prove that $(T_t u, v)$ is a continuous function of t. First we consider an element $u' = \sum_{\nu=1}^{n} c_\nu x_{t_\nu}$ in L with $\| u - u' \| < \epsilon$. Then

$$\| T_t u' - u' \| = \left\| \sum_{\nu=1}^{n} c_\nu (x_{t_\nu + t} - x_{t_\nu}) \right\| \leqq \sum_{\nu=1}^{n} | c_\nu | \, \| x_{t_\nu + t} - x_{t_\nu} \| \to 0 \quad \text{as} \quad t \to 0.$$

But

$$\| T_t u - u \| \leqq \| T_t u' - u' \| + \| T_t (u - u') \| + \| u - u' \| \leqq \| T_t u' - u' \| + 2\epsilon.$$

From this we conclude that the left member tends to zero with t. Schwarz's inequality yields

$$| (T_t u, v) - (T_s u, v) |^2 \leqq \| (T_t - T_s) u \|^2 \cdot \| v \|^2 = \| T_{t-s} u - u \|^2 \cdot \| v \|^2,$$

which completes the proof of the continuity. Thus we have the following lemma:

LEMMA. *There is a group of transformations* T_t, $-\infty < t < \infty$, *defined on $L_2(x)$ with the following properties:*

   (i) $T_t x_0 = x_t$,
   (ii) T_t *is a unitary transformation of $L_2(x)$ onto itself,*
   (iii) T_t *is an Abelian group with the composition rule* $T_a T_b = T_{a+b}$,
   (iv) $(T_t u, v)$ *is a continuous function of t.*

This makes it possible to apply Stone's theorem (see Appendix) on the representation of a group of unitary operators to the present situation. We remind the reader of this important result.

THEOREM OF STONE. *Let $\{T_t\}$, $-\infty < t < \infty$, be a group of unitary operators defined in a Hilbert space $\mathfrak{H}$ and such that $(T_t u, v)$ is a con-*

tinuous function of t for every choice of $u, v \in \mathfrak{H}$. *Then there is a representation*

$$T_t = \int_{-\infty}^{\infty} e^{it\lambda} \, dE_\lambda,$$

where E_λ *is a resolution of the identity.*

The integral must be taken as a Riemann–Stieltjes integral. The operator E_λ is normalized by the condition that it is continuous from the right.

(c) Combining the lemma proved above with Stone's theorem we obtain

$$x_t = \int_{-\infty}^{\infty} e^{it\lambda} \, dZ(\lambda),$$

where we have written $Z(\lambda) = E_\lambda x_0$ and $Z(\lambda)$ is continuous from the right. Using the properties defining a resolution of the identity we can characterize $Z(\lambda)$ as follows:

(i) l.i.m. $Z(\lambda) = 0$, l.i.m. $Z(\lambda) = x_0$,
$\quad\quad\lambda \to -\infty \quad\quad\quad\quad \lambda \to \infty$

(ii) $(Z(\lambda), Z(\mu)) = (Z(\nu), Z(\nu)) = \| Z(\nu) \|^2$, where $\nu = \min(\lambda, \mu)$,

(iii) $(x_s, x_t) = \int_{-\infty}^{\infty} e^{i(s-t)\lambda} \, d \| Z(\lambda) \|^2$.

But according to 10.3

$$(x_s, x_t) = R(s-t) = \int_{-\infty}^{\infty} e^{i(s-t)} dF(\lambda).$$

Since $F(\lambda)$ is uniquely determined and in view of the normalization of $F(\lambda)$ and $Z(\lambda)$, the function $F(\lambda)$ must coincide with $\| Z(\lambda) \|^2$ everywhere.

Let us also note that if $\lambda_1 < \lambda_2 < \lambda_3 < \lambda_4$ we have

$$(Z(\lambda_2) - Z(\lambda_1), Z(\lambda_4) - Z(\lambda_3)) = F(\lambda_2) - F(\lambda_1) - F(\lambda_2) + F(\lambda_1) = 0,$$

so that increments of the stochastic process $Z(\lambda)$ over disjoint intervals are orthogonal to each other. Such a process is said to be an *orthogonal process*. We have now proved the following theorem:

THEOREM OF CRAMÉR. *Any stationary process* x_t *which is continuous in the mean can be represented in the form*

$$x_t = \int_{-\infty}^{\infty} e^{it\lambda} \, dZ(\lambda),$$

where $Z(\lambda)$ is an orthogonal process with

$$\| Z(\lambda) \|^2 = E \mid Z(\lambda) \mid^2 = F(\lambda).$$

In the case of a discrete parameter the analogous result holds except the integration is extended over the interval $[-\pi, \pi]$,

$$x_t = \int_{-\pi}^{\pi} e^{it\lambda} \, dZ(\lambda).$$

The integrals must be interpreted as limits in the mean of Riemann–Stieltjes sums. Also in the discrete case $\| Z(\lambda) \|^2 = F(\lambda)$ [10.3 (b)].

10.5. Prediction of stationary processes

Let us consider a set of stochastic variables $\{y_\alpha\}$, where the index α ranges over some set A which can be finite, denumerably or non-denumerably infinite. Each of these variables has been observed so that their values are supposed to be known. There is another stochastic variable Y, the value of which is unknown, and we want to make a statement concerning the value Y is likely to take provided all the y_α's are known. In the extreme case when Y is independent of $\{y_\alpha\}$, clearly no help is given by the latter variables, since their values do not influence the (conditional) probability distribution of Y. On the other hand, the stronger the dependence is between Y and the y_α's, the more precise can the statement concerning Y be made.

If the y_α's are the past values of a stochastic process x_t and Y is the value of x_{t+h} at some future time point, we are dealing with a problem of *prediction*.

(i) The observed variables, say x_t for $t \leqq 0$, span a subspace $\mathfrak{H} \subset L_2(x)$, and as our predictor x_h^* of the value x_h, $h > 0$, we will choose an element in $\mathfrak{H}$. This means that we use *linear predictors* and we suppose the *entire past* of the process as known.

(ii) We shall assume that x_t is *stationary*, continuous in the mean (in case t is a continuous parameter) and having an absolutely continuous spectrum with spectral density $f(\lambda)$.

(iii) To be able to choose between different predictors we introduce an *optimality criterion*: The mean-square error $E \mid x_h^* - x_h \mid^2 = \| x_h^* - x_h \|^2$ shall be made as small as possible. It is clear that such a predictor exists and is unique and given by $x_h^* = Px_h$, where P stands for the operator projecting upon the subspace $\mathfrak{H}$.

In this and the next sections we shall deal with the discrete case. The spectrum is then situated in the interval $[-\pi, \pi]$. We consider the set of all complex-valued functions $g(\lambda)$ belonging to

$$L_2[dF(\lambda); \ -\pi, \pi].$$

As well known, this becomes a Hilbert space $L_2(F)$ if we accept the usual definition of the scalar product:

$$(g, h) = \int_{-\pi}^{\pi} g(\lambda) \, \overline{h(\lambda)} \, dF(\lambda).$$

There is a relation between $L_2(x)$ and $L_2(F)$ which is very useful in view of its simplicity. We define a transformation S by putting $S e^{it\lambda} = x_t$ and extend it linearly so that

$$S \sum_{\nu=1}^{n} c_\nu e^{it_\nu \lambda} = \sum_{\nu=1}^{n} c_\nu x(t_\nu).$$

Using the spectral representation of the covariance function we obtain

$$\left\| \sum_{\nu=1}^{n} c_\nu x(t_\nu) \right\|^2 = \sum_{\nu,\mu=1}^{n} c_\nu \bar{c}_\mu R(t_\nu - t_\mu) = \int_{-\pi}^{\pi} \left| \sum_{\nu=1}^{n} c_\nu e^{it_\nu \lambda} \right|^2 dF(\lambda) = \left\| \sum_{\nu=1}^{n} c_\nu e^{it_\nu \lambda} \right\|^2.$$

$$(1)$$

We extend now S to the whole space $L_2(F)$ by using convergence in the mean which determines Sg, $g \in L_2(F)$, uniquely, as the isometry (1) easily shows. The reader can also verify that

$$Sg = \int_{-\pi}^{\pi} g(\lambda) \, dZ(\lambda). \tag{2}$$

Thus we have proved the following theorem:

THEOREM. *The transformation S defined by (2) is a one-to-one isometric mapping of $L_2(F)$ onto $L_2(x)$. Any linear problem in $L_2(F)$ can be translated into one in the $L_2(x)$ space and vice versa.*

Hence we can rephrase the prediction problem as follows. In the subspace of $L_2(F)$ spanned by the elements $1, e^{-i\lambda}, e^{-2i\lambda}, \ldots$, we seek the element $\Phi(\lambda)$ minimizing the norm

$$\| \Phi(\lambda) - e^{i\lambda} \|^2 = \int_{-\pi}^{\pi} | \Phi(\lambda) - e^{i\lambda} |^2 dF(\lambda) = \min.$$

If this function can be found the best predictor is given by

$$x_1^* = \int_{-\pi}^{\pi} \Phi(\lambda)\, dZ(\lambda).$$

As we intend to show, this minimum problem belongs to the theory of Toeplitz forms.

10.6. Deterministic processes

Considering the best predictor x_h^* for h units of time ahead and the corresponding minimum *prediction error*

$$e_h = \| x_h^* - x_h \|^2,$$

we may ask first whether $e_h = 0$ can occur. A process x_t such that $e_h = 0$ clearly represents a singular case of extremely strong dependence between the successive stochastic variables forming the process. Such a process is said to be *deterministic*. In this section we shall characterize these processes.

(i) The condition $e_1 = 0$ means that we can approximate x_1 as closely as we wish by linear combinations of $x_0, x_{-1}, \ldots$. But the stationary character implies then that x_2 can be approximated in the same way by $x_1, x_0, x_{-1}, \ldots$; since x_1 is an element of the subspace spanned by $x_0, x_{-1}, \ldots$, we can approximate x_2 by elements of this latter subspace. Thus $e_2 = 0$, and by this reasoning we see that $e_h = 0$ for all h.

(ii) Now let $e_1 > 0$. If we employ the symbol $l(\ )$ for an arbitrary linear combination of the elements inside the parentheses we have, according to the definition,

$$e_h = \min \| x_h - l(x_0, x_{-1}, \ldots) \|^2,$$

$$e_{h+1} = \min \| x_{h+1} - l(x_0, x_{-1}, \ldots) \|^2.$$

The process being stationary, the last equation can be written as follows:

$$e_{h+1} = \min \| x_h - l(x_{-1}, x_{-2}, \ldots) \|^2 \geqq \min \| x_h - l(x_0, x_{-1}, \ldots) \|^2 = e_h,$$

so that in the present case no e_h vanishes.

Thus we have only two cases: either all e_h vanish or all of them are positive. We need only consider e_1:

$$e_1 = \lim_{n \to \infty} \| x_1 - l(x_0, x_{-1}, \ldots, x_{-n+1}) \|^2$$

and

$$\left\| x_1 - \sum_{\nu=0}^{n-1} c_\nu x_{-\nu} \right\|^2 = \int_{-\pi}^{\pi} |p_n(e^{i\lambda})|^2 dF(\lambda),$$

where

$$p_n(e^{i\lambda}) = e^{i\lambda} - \sum_{\nu=0}^{n-1} c_\nu e^{-i\nu\lambda}.$$

The integral to be minimized can be written as follows:

$$\int_{-\pi}^{\pi} |u_0 + u_1 z + u_2 z^2 + \ldots + u_n z^n|^2 dF(\lambda),$$

where $u_0 = 1$, $u_j = -\bar{c}_{j-1}$ for $1 \leq j \leq n$, and $z = e^{i\lambda}$. This is identical [apart from the factor $(2\pi)^{-1}$] with 3.1 (1) so that $e_1 = (2\pi)^{-1} \lim_{n \to \infty} \mu_n$, using the notation of chapter 3. We proved in 3.1 that the latter limit is zero if and only if

$$\int_{-\pi}^{\pi} \log f(\lambda) \, d\lambda = -\infty.$$

[For the definition of $f(\lambda)$ see 10.3 (d).]

THEOREM. *A stationary stochastic process depending upon a discrete time parameter and having an absolutely continuous spectrum is deterministic if and only if*

$$\int_{-\pi}^{\pi} \log f(\lambda) \, d\lambda = -\infty.$$

To avoid the singular case of a deterministic process we assume from now on that the logarithm of the spectral density is integrable.

10.7. Representation of nondeterministic processes

(a) The x_t are orthogonal stochastic variables only in special cases. However, it is often possible to represent the process as certain linear combinations of orthogonal stochastic variables. To describe this representation we consider a sequence ξ_t, $-\infty < t < \infty$, of such variables: $E\xi_s \bar{\xi}_t = \delta_{st}$. We assume as usual that the mean values vanish. Now we form a new process, the so-called *moving average*,

$$x_t = \sum_{\nu=0}^{\infty} a_\nu \xi_{t-\nu},$$

where the series converges in the mean if and only if $\sum\limits_{\nu=0}^{\infty} |a_\nu|^2 < \infty$. Assuming this the covariance function will be for $s > t$

$$R(s-t) = \sum_{\nu=0}^{\infty} \bar{a}_\nu a_{\nu+s-t}, \tag{1}$$

or in matrix form

$$R = A^*A, \tag{2}$$

where R is the covariance matrix $R = \{R(\nu-\mu), \; -\infty < \nu, \mu < \infty\}$ and A is the subdiagonal matrix

$$A = \{a_{\nu-\mu} \text{ if } \nu - \mu \geqq 0, \; 0 \text{ if } \nu - \mu < 0\}.$$

These matrices are classical Toeplitz matrices corresponding to the functions $f(\lambda)$ and $a(e^{-i\lambda})$, respectively, $R = T\{f(\lambda)\}$, $A = T\{a(e^{-i\lambda})\}$, where $a(z) = \sum\limits_{\nu=0}^{\infty} a_\nu z^\nu$; this power series converges in the mean on the unit circle $|z| = 1$. In the present situation the coefficients a_ν are not necessarily real; however, this is without importance. As we know relation (1) [or the equivalent relation (2)] implies that almost everywhere $f(\lambda) = |a(e^{-i\lambda})|^2$.

The function $a(z)$ belongs to the class H_2 (cf. 1.1) so that by 1.13 we have

$$\int_{-\pi}^{\pi} \log f(\lambda) \, d\lambda > -\infty. \tag{3}$$

Hence in order that a stochastic process can be represented as a moving average it is necessary that it is nondeterministic. We will show now that this condition is also sufficient.

(b) Since the logarithm of the spectral density is integrable we must have $f(\lambda) > 0$ almost everywhere. Then we can define a new process by

$$Z_\xi(\lambda) = \int_{-\pi}^{\lambda} [\phi(\lambda)]^{-1} dZ(\lambda),$$

where $\phi(\lambda)$ is a measurable 'square root' of $f(\lambda)$, $|\phi(\lambda)|^2 = f(\lambda)$. It is clear that the above integral exists and defines an orthogonal process; we have for the norm

$$\|Z_\xi(\lambda)\|^2 = \int_{-\pi}^{\lambda} |\phi(\lambda)|^{-2} dF(\lambda) = (2\pi)^{-1}(\lambda+\pi).$$

Then we will obtain a stationary process by defining

$$\xi_t = \int_{-\pi}^{\pi} e^{it\lambda} dZ_\xi(\lambda) \tag{4}$$

and the corresponding spectral distribution function will be $(2\pi)^{-1}(\lambda+\pi)$; the covariances are

$$E\xi_s\bar{\xi}_t=(\xi_s,\xi_t)=\frac{1}{2\pi}\int_{-\pi}^{\pi}e^{i(s-t)\lambda}\,d\lambda=\delta_{st};$$

the ξ_t are orthogonal and normalized.

Under the assumptions made above there exists a function $G(\lambda)\in L_2[d\lambda;-\pi,\pi]$ such that almost everywhere

$$G(\lambda)=\frac{1}{2\pi}\sum_{\nu=0}^{\infty}G_\nu e^{-i\nu\lambda},\quad f(\lambda)=|\,G(\lambda)\,|^2,$$

(cf. 1.14). The function $\phi(\lambda)$ which was not completely specified above is now chosen as $G(\lambda)$. Then we have for all t

$$x_t=\int_{-\pi}^{\pi}e^{it\lambda}\,G(\lambda)\,dZ_\xi(\lambda).$$

Since

$$G(\lambda)=\frac{1}{2\pi}\sum_{\nu=0}^{n}G_\nu e^{-i\nu\lambda}+\rho_n(\lambda)$$

with $\|\rho_n\|\to0$ as $n\to\infty$, we have, using (4),

$$x_t=\frac{1}{2\pi}\sum_{\nu=0}^{n}G_\nu\xi_{t-\nu}+Z_n.$$

Here

$$\|Z_n\|^2=\frac{1}{2\pi}\int_{-\pi}^{\pi}|\,\rho_n(\lambda)\,|^2\,d\lambda\to0\quad\text{as}\quad n\to\infty,$$

so that

$$x_t=\frac{1}{2\pi}\sum_{\nu=0}^{\infty}G_\nu\xi_{t-\nu}$$

in the sense of convergence in the mean. This proves the sufficiency of the condition and completes the proof of the following theorem:

THEOREM. *A necessary and sufficient condition for a stationary process with an absolutely continuous spectrum to be representable as a one-sided* (backwards in time) *moving average is that it is non-deterministic.*

(c) We illustrate this result by the following simple example. Let $f(\lambda)=(1-2a\cos\lambda+a^2)^{-1}$, $-1<a<1$. Since $\log f(\lambda)$ is integrable the stochastic process x_t with $f(\lambda)$ as spectral density must be representable as a moving average. We can write

$$f(\lambda) = |\, 1 - a\, e^{-i\lambda}\, |^{-2},$$

so that we may choose

$$G(\lambda) = (1 - a\, e^{-i\lambda})^{-1} = \sum_{\nu=0}^{\infty} a^\nu e^{-i\nu\lambda},$$

i.e. $G_\nu = 2\pi a^\nu$. Hence x_t is represented in the form

$$x_t = \sum_{\nu=0}^{\infty} a^\nu \xi_{t-\nu}.$$

Note that $x_t \perp \xi_\nu$ for $\nu > t$ and the ξ's can be determined simply by the relation

$$x_{t+1} - a x_t = \xi_{t+1}.$$

A stationary process satisfying such a difference equation with a stochastic disturbance is called an autoregressive process (of order one).

(d) Generalizing this case we consider a process with spectral density $f(\lambda) = [u(\lambda)]^{-1}$, where $u(\lambda)$ is a positive trigonometric polynomial of order p. We know (see 1.12) that $u(\lambda)$ can be written as

$$u(\lambda) = |\, Q(e^{i\lambda})\, |^2,$$

where

$$Q(z) = q_0 + q_1 z + q_2 z^2 + \ldots + q_p z^p$$

is a polynomial in z of degree p and with no zeros in $|z| \leq 1$. Then

$$x_t = \frac{1}{2\pi} \sum_{\nu=0}^{\infty} G_\nu \xi_{t-\nu},$$

where $(2\pi)^{-1} G_\nu$ are the Taylor coefficients of $[Q(z)]^{-1}$. Using the relation $Q(z)\,[Q(z)]^{-1} = 1$ we have

$$\left.\begin{array}{l} q_0 G_0 = 2\pi, \\[2mm] \displaystyle\sum_{\nu=0}^{\mu} q_\nu G_{\mu-\nu} = 0, \quad \mu \geq 1;\ q_\nu = 0 \text{ for } \nu > p. \end{array}\right\} \tag{5}$$

But

$$q_0 x_{t+p} + q_1 x_{t+p-1} + \ldots + q_p x_t$$

$$= \frac{q_0}{2\pi} \sum_{-p}^{\infty} G_{\nu+p} \xi_{t-\nu} + \frac{q_1}{2\pi} \sum_{-p+1}^{\infty} G_{\nu+p-1} \xi_{t-\nu} + \ldots + \frac{q_p}{2\pi} \sum_{0}^{\infty} G_\nu \xi_{t-\nu} = \xi_{t+p}.$$

Just as before the process satisfies a stochastic difference equation, now of order p, with constant coefficients and with a stochastic disturbance ξ which is orthogonal, $\xi_s \perp \xi_t$ for $s \neq t$. This is called an autoregressive process of order p.

10.8. Construction of the best predictor

(a) We proceed now to the explicit determination of the best predictor x_1^* one unit of time ahead for a nondeterministic process. If we use only $x_0, x_{-1}, x_{-2}, \ldots, x_{-n+1}$ for the prediction, we must minimize

$$\left\| x_1 - \sum_{\nu=0}^{n-1} c_\nu x_{-\nu} \right\|^2 = \frac{1}{2\pi} \int_{-\pi}^{\pi} |u_0 + u_1 z + u_2 z^2 + \ldots + u_n z^n|^2 f(\lambda)\, d\lambda,$$

where $u_0 = 1, u_j = -\bar{c}_{j-1}$ for $1 \leq j \leq n$ and $z = e^{i\lambda}$. We know (see 2.2) that this minimum μ_n is given by

$$\mu_n^{-1} = s_n(0,0) = \sum_{\nu=0}^{n} |\phi_\nu(0)|^2,$$

where the $\{\phi_\nu(z)\}$ are the polynomials orthogonal on the unit circle $|z| = 1$ with respect to the weight function $f(\lambda)$. The minimum is obtained for

$$u_n(z) = u_0 + u_1 z + u_2 z^2 + \ldots + u_n z^n = \mu_n s_n(0,z) = \mu_n \sum_{\nu=0}^{n} \overline{\phi_\nu(0)}\, \phi_\nu(z).$$

The predictor (using a finite part of the past only) is then

$$x_{1,n}^* = \sum_{\nu=0}^{n-1} c_\nu x_{-\nu} = -\sum_{\nu=0}^{n-1} \bar{u}_{\nu+1} x_{-\nu} = -\int_{-\pi}^{\pi} \sum_{\nu=0}^{n-1} \bar{u}_{\nu+1} e^{-i\nu\lambda}\, dZ(\lambda)$$

$$= -\int_{-\pi}^{\pi} e^{i\lambda}\{\overline{u_n(e^{i\lambda})} - 1\}\, dZ(\lambda).$$

Now we show that $u_n(z)$ converges in a certain sense and we shall obtain an expression for its limit. For $n < m$

$$\int_{-\pi}^{\pi} |s_n(0,z) - s_m(0,z)|^2 f(\lambda)\, d\lambda = \sum_{\nu=n+1}^{m} |\phi_\nu(0)|^2 = \mu_m^{-1} - \mu_n^{-1} \to 0,$$

as $n, m \to \infty$. We have $f(\lambda) = \lim_{r \to 1-0} |g(re^{i\lambda})|^2$ almost everywhere where $g(z)$ is of the class H_2 (cf. 1.1) with no zeros in $|z| < 1$, $g(0)$ real and positive (see 1.14). But writing $t_n(z) = g(z) s_n(0, z)$ the above relation implies that there is an element $H(z)$ in H_2 such that

$$\|t_n - H\|^2 = \int_{-\pi}^{\pi} |t_n(z) - H(z)|^2 d\lambda \to 0 \quad \text{as} \quad n \to \infty.$$

Hence for any ρ, $0 < \rho < 1$, the functions $t_n(z)$ converge uniformly in $|z| \leq \rho$ to $H(z)$ so that

$$\lim_{n \to \infty} s_n(0, z) = \frac{H(z)}{g(z)},$$

uniformly in $|z| \leq \rho$. According to 3.4 we must have then

$$H(z) = [g(0)]^{-1}.$$

Thus

$$\lim_{n \to \infty} \int_{-\pi}^{\pi} |s_n(0, z) - [g(0) g(z)]^{-1}|^2 f(\lambda) d\lambda = 0,$$

and since $\mu_n \to \mu = [g(0)]^2$ we have

$$\lim_{n \to \infty} \int_{-\pi}^{\pi} |u_n(z) - g(0)/g(z)|^2 f(\lambda) d\lambda = 0.$$

Using the isometric correspondence (defined by the representation in 10.5) between the Hilbert spaces spanned by the process and by the exponential functions, respectively, we find the best predictor

$$x_1^* = \text{l.i.m.}_{n \to \infty} x_{1,n}^* = \int_{-\pi}^{\pi} e^{i\lambda} [1 - g(0)/\overline{g(e^{i\lambda})}] dZ(\lambda).$$

We note that $g(e^{i\lambda})$ introduced in the present section corresponds to the function $\overline{G(\lambda)}$ of 10.7; we have

$$g(e^{i\lambda}) = \overline{G(\lambda)} = \frac{1}{2\pi} \sum_{\nu=0}^{\infty} \bar{G}_\nu e^{i\nu\lambda}.$$

(b) We have used before, $dZ(\lambda)/\overline{g(e^{i\lambda})} = dZ_\xi(\lambda)$, which implies

$$x_1^* = \int_{-\pi}^{\pi} e^{i\lambda} \{\overline{g(e^{i\lambda})} - g(0)\} dZ_\xi(\lambda)$$

$$= \int_{-\pi}^{\pi} \sum_{\nu=1}^{\infty} \frac{1}{2\pi} G_\nu e^{-i(\nu-1)\lambda} dZ_\xi(\lambda) = \frac{1}{2\pi} \sum_{\nu=1}^{\infty} G_\nu \xi_{1-\nu}.$$

Since

$$x_1 = \frac{1}{2\pi} \sum_{\nu=0}^{\infty} G_\nu \xi_{1-\nu},$$

we find

$$\| x_1^* - x_1 \|^2 = \frac{1}{4\pi^2} | G_0 |^2 = \frac{1}{4\pi^2} \left| \int_{-\pi}^{\pi} G(\lambda)\, d\lambda \right|^2,$$

and in view of

$$\frac{1}{2\pi} \int_{-\pi}^{\pi} \overline{G(\lambda)}\, d\lambda = \frac{1}{2\pi i} \int_{|z|=1} g(z)\, \frac{dz}{z} = g(0),$$

we obtain, as we should, $\| x_1^* - x_1 \|^2 = [g(0)]^2 = \mu$. In view of 1.14 (10) we find for the error of prediction:

$$\| x_1^* - x_1 \|^2 = \exp\left\{ \frac{1}{2\pi} \int_{-\pi}^{\pi} \log f(\lambda)\, d\lambda \right\}.$$

Thus we have proved the following theorem:

THEOREM. *Let x_t be a stationary and nondeterministic stochastic process with the spectral representation*

$$x_t = \int_{-\pi}^{\pi} e^{it\lambda}\, dZ(\lambda)$$

and with the spectral density $f(\lambda) = 2\pi \dfrac{dF(\lambda)}{d\lambda} = 2\pi \dfrac{d}{d\lambda} \| Z(\lambda) \|^2$. *Then the best linear predictor x_t^* of the value of x_t (in the sense of minimum mean-square error), when $x_{t-1}, x_{t-2}, \ldots$, have been observed, is given by*

$$x_t^* = \int_{-\pi}^{\pi} e^{it\lambda} \{ 1 - g(0)/\overline{g(e^{i\lambda})} \}\, dZ(\lambda),$$

where $g(e^{i\lambda})$ is obtained from $f(\lambda)$ as in section 1.14.
    Let

$$x_t = \frac{1}{2\pi} \sum_{\nu=0}^{\infty} G_\nu \xi_{t-\nu}$$

be the moving average representation (which exists according to the theorem proved in 10.7). Another representation of the best predictor is the following:

$$x_t^* = \frac{1}{2\pi} \sum_{\nu=1}^{\infty} G_\nu \xi_{t-\nu}.$$

The minimum prediction error is given by

$$\| x_t^* - x_t \|^2 = E\, | x_t^* - x_t |^2 = \frac{1}{4\pi^2} | G_0 |^2 = \exp\left\{ \frac{1}{2\pi} \int_{-\pi}^{\pi} \log f(\lambda)\, d\lambda \right\}.$$

In this theorem we have considered $x_{t+\nu}$ instead of $x_{1+\nu}$. Clearly the generality of the formulas is based on the stationary character of the process.

(c) As a simple example let us consider an autoregressive process of the first order [see 10.7 (c)]. Then

$$x_{t+1} - ax_t = \xi_{t+1}, \quad -1 < a < 1,$$

where the ξ's are orthogonal and normalized stochastic variables. The moving average representation is

$$x_t = \sum_{\nu=0}^{\infty} a^\nu \xi_{t-\nu},$$

so that according to the theorem just proved

$$x_t^* = \sum_{\nu=1}^{\infty} a^\nu \xi_{t-\nu} = x_t - \xi_t = ax_{t-1}.$$

In this case the best predictor is simply proportional to the last observation. The prediction error is 1.

10.9. Prediction h units of time ahead

(a) If $x_0, x_{-1}, x_{-2}, \ldots$ have been observed and we want to predict the value of $x_h, h > 0$, the above procedure has to be slightly modified. We must choose now the c's as to minimize

$$\left\| x_h - \sum_{\nu=0}^{n-h} c_\nu x_{-\nu} \right\|^2 = \frac{1}{2\pi} \int_{-\pi}^{\pi} |u_0 + u_h z^h + u_{h+1} z^{h+1} + \ldots + u_n z^n|^2 f(\lambda)\, d\lambda,$$

where $u_0 = 1, u_j = -\bar{c}_{j-h}$ for $h \leq j \leq n$. In other words, we seek a polynomial $u_n(z) = u_0 + u_1 z + u_2 z^2 + \ldots + u_n z^n$, minimizing the Toeplitz form

$$\frac{1}{2\pi} \int_{-\pi}^{\pi} |u_n(z)|^2 f(\lambda)\, d\lambda$$

under the side conditions

$$u_n(0) = 1, \quad u_n'(0) = u_n''(0) = \ldots = u_n^{(h-1)}(0) = 0.$$

This minimum problem can be treated as in the last section in a direct manner. Here we shall use a different approach. Let $L_2(x; t)$ denote the subspace spanned by the elements $x_t, x_{t-1}, x_{t-2}, \ldots$ in the Hilbert space $L_2(x)$. The projection operator corresponding to $L_2(x; t)$ will be denoted by P_t. Then the best linear predictor is $x_h^* = P_0 x_h$. We have seen that

$$x_1 = \frac{1}{2\pi} \sum_{\nu=0}^{\infty} G_\nu \xi_{1-\nu};$$

the prediction of x_1 when all the values of x_t before the time $t = 1$ have been observed, will be

$$x_1^* = \frac{1}{2\pi} \sum_{\nu=1}^{\infty} G_\nu \xi_{1-\nu}, \quad x_1 - x_1^* = \frac{1}{2\pi} G_0 \xi_1.$$

Of course $x_1^* \in L_2(x; 0)$, so that the last equation yields $\xi_1 \in L_2(x; 1)$. Because of the stationary condition we have, in general, $\xi_t \in L_2(x; t)$.

In view of

$$x_h = \frac{1}{2\pi} \sum_{\nu=0}^{\infty} G_\nu \xi_{h-\nu},$$

we obtain

$$x_h^* = \frac{1}{2\pi} \sum_{\nu=0}^{\infty} G_\nu P_0 \xi_{h-\nu},$$

where the sum should be again interpreted as a limit in the mean. But from what we have just seen it is clear that $P_0 \xi_{h-\nu} = \xi_{h-\nu}$ for $\nu \geq h$. Since

$$(\xi_\mu, x_t) = \frac{1}{2\pi} \sum_{\nu=0}^{\infty} \bar{G}_\nu (\xi_\mu, \xi_{t-\nu}) = 0$$

for $\mu > t$, we have $\xi_\mu \perp L_2(x; t)$, so that the best predictor h steps ahead is

$$x_h^* = \frac{1}{2\pi} \sum_{\nu=h}^{\infty} G_\nu \xi_{h-\nu},$$

with the minimum prediction error

$$\| x_h^* - x_h \|^2 = \frac{1}{4\pi^2} \sum_{\nu=0}^{h-1} | G_\nu |^2.$$

(b) The predictor can also be expressed in terms of the spectral representation of the process. Indeed, let

$$G_h(\lambda) = \frac{1}{2\pi} \sum_{\nu=0}^{h-1} G_\nu e^{-i\nu\lambda}, \quad G(\lambda) = G_h(\lambda) + R_h(\lambda),$$

and let us form the stochastic variable

$$y = \int_{-\pi}^{\pi} e^{ih\lambda} \{ 1 - G_h(\lambda)/G(\lambda) \} \, dZ(\lambda).$$

We have

$$y = \int_{-\pi}^{\pi} e^{ih\lambda} R_h(\lambda)\, dZ_\xi(\lambda) = \frac{1}{2\pi} \sum_{\nu=h}^{\infty} \int_{-\pi}^{\pi} e^{i(h-\nu)\lambda} G_\nu dZ_\xi(\lambda)$$

$$= \frac{1}{2\pi} \sum_{\nu=h}^{\infty} G_\nu \xi_{h-\nu} = x_h^*.$$

This yields the following theorem:

THEOREM. *The predictor x_{t+h}^* for h units of time ahead when $x_t, x_{t-1}, \ldots$ have been observed can be written as*

$$x_{t+h}^* = \int_{-\pi}^{\pi} e^{i(t+h)\lambda} \{1 - G_h(\lambda)/G(\lambda)\}\, dZ(\lambda)$$

with

$$G_h(\lambda) = \frac{1}{2\pi} \sum_{\nu=0}^{h-1} G_\nu e^{-i\nu\lambda}$$

or in the equivalent form

$$x_{t+h}^* = \frac{1}{2\pi} \sum_{\nu=h}^{\infty} G_\nu \xi_{t+h-\nu}.$$

The minimum prediction error is

$$\| x_{t+h}^* - x_{t+h} \|^2 = \frac{1}{4\pi^2} \sum_{\nu=0}^{h-1} |G_\nu|^2.$$

(c) As an example we consider an autoregressive process of order p satisfying the stochastic difference equation

$$q_0 x_{t+p} + q_1 x_{t+p-1} + \ldots + q_p x_t = \xi_{t+p}, \quad (\xi_\nu, \xi_\mu) = \delta_{\nu\mu}.$$

We have seen [10.7 (d)] that this process can be represented in the form

$$x_t = \frac{1}{2\pi} \sum_{\nu=0}^{\infty} G_\nu \xi_{t-\nu},$$

where $G_\nu, Q(z)$ (and also q_ν) have the same meaning as in 10.7(d). The best linear predictor h steps ahead is

$$x_{t+h}^* = \frac{1}{2\pi} \sum_{\nu=h}^{\infty} G_\nu \xi_{t+h-\nu}$$

$$= \frac{1}{2\pi} \sum_{\nu=h}^{\infty} G_\nu(q_0 x_{t+h-\nu} + q_1 x_{t+h-\nu-1} + \ldots + q_p x_{t+h-\nu-p}) = \sum_{\nu=0}^{\infty} A_\nu x_{t-\nu},$$

where

$$A_\nu = \frac{1}{2\pi} \sum_{s=0}^{\min(p,\nu)} G_{\nu-s+h} q_s.$$

For $\nu > p$, we obtain, in view of 10.7 (5),

$$A_\nu = \frac{1}{2\pi} \sum_{s=0}^{p} G_{\nu-s+h} q_s = 0,$$

so that the best predictor uses only the observations $x_\tau, t-p+1 \leqq \tau \leqq t$, although the entire past is available. The prediction error increases with h, from $(2\pi)^{-2} |G_0|^2$ for $h=1$ and converges to

$$\frac{1}{4\pi^2} \sum_{\nu=0}^{\infty} |G_\nu|^2 = \|x_0\|^2$$

as h tends to infinity, as might be expected.

(d) As we have seen, we can construct the best predictor either from the moving-average representation of the process or from the spectral representation. Although the latter method appears more difficult, in many cases it is in fact easier and corresponds in a more direct way to the design of the physical apparatus which computes the prediction. Let $\mathfrak{F}$ denote a linear filter acting upon the vectors $(\ldots, c_{-1}, c_0, c_1, \ldots) = c$; $\mathfrak{F}c$ should be complex-valued. Denoting the vector with components $c_\nu = \delta_{j\nu}$ by ϵ_j we set $\mathfrak{F}\epsilon_j = f_j$. Assuming that $\mathfrak{F}$ is bounded,

$$|\mathfrak{F}c| \leqq \text{const.} \, \|c\|,$$

we can write

$$\mathfrak{F}c = \sum_{j=-\infty}^{\infty} f_j c_j.$$

The numbers f_j denote the *response* of the filter to a unit input at time j. Physical filters obeying the cause-effect law must have $f_j = 0$ for $j > 0$.

The filter can also be characterized by its *frequency response* function

$$\phi(\lambda) = \sum_{j=-\infty}^{\infty} f_j e^{ij\lambda};$$

this sum converges in the mean on $[-\pi, \pi]$, since $\|\mathfrak{F}\|^2 = \Sigma |f_j|^2$ is finite. For an input function $e^{ij\lambda}$ the quantity $|\phi(\lambda)|$ measures the *gain* and $\arg \phi(\lambda)$ the *phase shift* corresponding to the frequency λ.

If this filter should operate on the process x_t we must also require that the sum defining the output of $\mathfrak{F}x_t$ converges in the mean. We obtain without difficulty that

$$\mathfrak{F}x_t = \int_{-\pi}^{\pi} \phi(\lambda) \, dZ(\lambda),$$

$$\|\mathfrak{F}x_t\|^2 = \int_{-\pi}^{\pi} |\phi(\lambda)|^2 f(\lambda) \, d\lambda,$$

and the convergence of the latter integral is necessary and sufficient for the existence of $\Im x_t$.

In this terminology the best linear predictor h steps ahead corresponds to a physical filter with the frequency response function

$$\phi(\lambda) = e^{ih\lambda}\{1 - G_h(\lambda)/G(\lambda)\}.$$

10.10. An asymptotic study of the finite linear predictor

(a) We have considered so far mainly the best linear predictor which can be obtained when the entire past has been observed. Let us assume now that $x_0, x_{-1}, x_{-2}, \ldots, x_{-n+1}$ are known and x_1 has to be predicted; we obtain then the best linear predictor

$$x^*_{1,\,n} = \int_{-\pi}^{\pi} e^{i\lambda}\{1 - \overline{u_n(e^{i\lambda})}\}\,dZ(\lambda),$$

where

$$u_n(z) = \mu_n s_n(0, z);$$

for the definition of these quantities see 10.8 (a). In general, $\mu_n > \mu = \lim_{n\to\infty} \mu_n$, and it is of importance to form an idea of the rate of decrease of $\delta_n = \mu_n - \mu$ to zero as n tends to infinity.

(b) First let us consider the very favorable situation when this decrease is exponential: $\delta_n < K_1 d^n$, $0 < d < 1$. (The constants $K_1, K_2, \ldots$ to be used in this section are independent of n.)

We have [2.2 (10)]

$$\delta_n = \left\{\sum_{\nu=0}^{n} |\phi_\nu(0)|^2\right\}^{-1} - \left\{\sum_{\nu=0}^{\infty} |\phi_\nu(0)|^2\right\}^{-1}$$

$$= \mu_n \mu \sum_{\nu=n+1}^{\infty} |\phi_\nu(0)|^2 \geq \mu^2 |\phi_{n+1}(0)|^2,$$

so that $\phi_n(0)$ decreases also exponentially: $|\phi_n(0)| < K_2 d^{\frac{1}{2}n}$. Using 3.4 (4) we find $|\phi_n(z)| \leq K_3 R^n$ uniformly for $|z| \leq R$, $R > 1$. Choosing $R < d^{-\frac{1}{2}}$, we see that

$$\sum_{\nu=0}^{\infty} \overline{\phi_\nu(0)}\,\phi_\nu(z)$$

converges uniformly in $|z| \leq R$ and the limit function (which is, of course, the analytic continuation of $[g(0)g(z)]^{-1}$) is analytic in this region. Hence $g(z)$ is analytic and free of zeros in $|z| < R$, so that the spectral density of the process can be written as the product of two functions: $f(\lambda)=f_1(\lambda)f_2(\lambda)$ almost everywhere with $f_1(\lambda)=g(e^{i\lambda})$, $f_2(\lambda)=\bar{g}(e^{-i\lambda})$, where $\bar{g}(z)$ is the function obtained from $g(z)$ by forming conjugate-complex coefficients in its Taylor series about $z=0$. Of course $\bar{g}(z)$ is also analytic and different from zero in $|z|<R$, and $\bar{g}(z^{-1})$ has this property in $|z|>R^{-1}$. Hence $f(\lambda)$ coincides almost everywhere in $[-\pi,\pi]$ with an analytic function of λ that does not vanish.

We assume conversely that the last assertion holds. We intend to show then that δ_n decreases exponentially. Indeed,

$$\delta_n=\mu_n-\mu \le \|\sigma_n(z)\|^2 - \|g(0)/g(z)\|^2,$$

where $\sigma_n(z)$ is an arbitrary polynomial of degree n whose constant term is 1. The norm is the one introduced in 10.5 for $L_2(F)$. Let us choose $\sigma_n(z)$ as the nth partial sum of the Taylor series of $g(0)/g(z)$,

$$\sigma_n(z)=\sum_{\nu=0}^{n}\gamma_\nu z^\nu.$$

Of course $\gamma_0=1$, and in view of the assumption $|\gamma_\nu|<K_4(R-\epsilon)^{-\nu}$, so that

$$\delta_n \le \{\|\sigma_n(z)\|+\|g(0)/g(z)\|\}\{\|\sigma_n(z)\|-\|g(0)/g(z)\|\}$$

$$\le K_5\|\sigma_n(z)-g(0)/g(z)\|=K_5\left\|\sum_{\nu=n+1}^{\infty}\gamma_\nu z^\nu\right\|\le K_6(R-\epsilon)^{-n},$$

which proves the assertion. We have the following theorem:

THEOREM. *A necessary and sufficient condition that $\delta_n=\mu_n-\mu$ decreases at least exponentially to zero as n tends to infinity, is that $f(\lambda)$ coincides in $[-\pi,\pi]$ almost everywhere with a function which is analytic for real λ and has no real zeros.*

(c) It is natural to ask what happens if we relax the conditions on $f(\lambda)$. A partial answer is given by the following theorem:

THEOREM. *Let $f(\lambda)$ be defined almost everywhere by the expression*

$$f(\lambda)=p(\lambda)\prod_{\nu=1}^{s}|e^{i\lambda}-e^{i\lambda_\nu}|^{2\alpha_\nu},$$

where $p(\lambda)$ is positive with k ($k\ge 4$) integrable derivatives, α_ν are positive integers, and λ_ν are distinct points in $-\pi\le\lambda<\pi$. Then two cases are possible:

(i) *Let $f(\lambda)$ have no zeros, $s=0$; then $\delta_n=o(n^{\frac{5}{2}-k})$.*

(ii) *Let $s > 0$; then we can only assert that $\delta_n = O(n^{-1})$.*

Proof. Let us consider first the case when no zeros are present, $s = 0$. Then, integrating by parts and using the Riemann–Lebesgue lemma, we see that the Fourier coefficients of $\log f(\lambda)$ are $o(n^{-k})$. Let us recall the construction of $g(z)$ [1.14 (b)]. We can write

$$g(z) = \exp\left\{\tfrac{1}{2}k_0 + \sum_{n=1}^{\infty} (k_n - il_n) z^n\right\},$$

where the k's and l's are the cosine and sine coefficients of the Fourier series of $\log f(\lambda)$, respectively. Thus $g(e^{i\lambda})$ has bounded and integrable derivatives in $[-\pi, \pi]$ up to and including the order $k - 2$ which holds also for $[g(e^{i\lambda})]^{-1}$. Hence the coefficients γ_n used in (b) are $o(n^{2-k})$, so that

$$\delta_n \leq K_5 \left\| \sum_{\nu=n+1}^{\infty} \gamma_\nu z^\nu \right\| \leq K_5 \max f(\lambda) \left\{ \sum_{\nu=n+1}^{\infty} |\gamma_\nu|^2 \right\}^{\frac{1}{2}} = o(n^{\frac{5}{2}-k}).$$

(d) When zeros occur on the boundary $|z| = 1$ the proof becomes more involved; in order to avoid cumbersome calculations we shall consider only the case $s = 1$, $\alpha_1 = 1$; we can assume that $\lambda_1 = 0$. Let us consider the expression

$$\|u_n(z) - g(0)/g(z)\|^2 = \frac{1}{2\pi} \int_{-\pi}^{\pi} |u_n(z) - g(0)/g(z)|^2 f(\lambda)\, d\lambda,$$

where $u_n(z)$ is an arbitrary polynomial with the constant term 1. This expression is equal to

$$\frac{1}{2\pi} \int_{-\pi}^{\pi} |u_n(z)(1-z) - g(0)/g_p(z)|^2 p(\lambda)\, d\lambda$$

$$\leq (2\pi)^{-1} \max p(\lambda) \int_{-\pi}^{\pi} |u_n(z)(1-z) - g(0)/g_p(z)|^2\, d\lambda,$$

where $g_p(z)$ is the function related to $p(\lambda)$ in the same way as $g(z)$ is to $f(\lambda)$; we have $g(z) = g_p(z)(1-z)$. Now the function

$$g(0)/g_p(z) = \sum_{\nu=0}^{\infty} d_\nu z^\nu, \quad d_0 = 1,$$

is analytic in $|z| < 1$. Let us choose $u_n(z) = u_0 + u_1 z + \ldots + u_n z^n$ as follows:
$$u_\nu = d_0 + d_1 + \ldots + d_\nu - \nu D/n, \quad 0 \leq \nu \leq n,$$

where $D = D_n$ is defined by $d_0 + d_1 + \ldots + d_n = D$, so that

$$u_\nu - u_{\nu-1} = d_\nu - D/n \quad \text{for} \quad 1 \leq \nu \leq n \quad \text{and} \quad u_0 = 1, \quad u_n = 0.$$

Hence

$$\frac{1}{2\pi}\int_{-\pi}^{\pi} |u_n(z)(1-z) - g(0)/g_p(z)|^2 d\lambda = D_n^2/n + \sum_{\nu=n+1}^{\infty} |d_\nu|^2.$$

Now $g_p(e^{i\lambda})$ has at least two bounded derivatives; hence D_n must converge as n tends to infinity. The second term in the right-hand member is $o(n^{-1})$ and the theorem is proved in this case.

(e) As an example let us consider the finite moving average

$$x_t = \xi_t - \rho\xi_{t-1}, \quad (\xi_s, \xi_t) = \delta_{st}, \quad 0 \leq \rho \leq 1.$$

The spectral density is $f(\lambda) = |1 - \rho e^{i\lambda}|^2$. The covariance matrix is

$$\{r_{s,t}; 0 \leq s, t \leq n\} = \begin{pmatrix} 1+\rho^2 & -\rho & 0 & \cdots & 0 \\ -\rho & 1+\rho^2 & -\rho & \cdots & 0 \\ \cdots & \cdots & \cdots & \cdots & \cdots \\ 0 & 0 & 0 & \cdots & 1+\rho^2 \end{pmatrix};$$

the determinant of this Toeplitz matrix has been computed in 5.3 (a). First let $0 \leq \rho < 1$; we obtain

$$D_n = \frac{1 - \rho^{2n+4}}{1 - \rho^2},$$

so that (2.2)

$$\mu_n = \frac{D_n}{D_{n-1}} = \frac{1 - \rho^{2n+4}}{1 - \rho^{2n+2}}.$$

Then $\mu = \lim_{n\to\infty} \mu_n = 1$ and

$$\delta_n = \mu_n - \mu = \frac{\rho^{2n}(\rho^2 - \rho^4)}{1 - \rho^{2n+2}}$$

decreases indeed exponentially.

If $\rho = 1$ we obtain instead the Toeplitz determinant $D_n = n+2$ and

$$\mu_n = \frac{n+2}{n+1} \to \mu = 1$$

as n tends to infinity. In this case the decrease is slower:

$$\delta_n = \mu_n - \mu = (n+1)^{-1},$$

due to the presence of a zero of $f(\lambda)$ at $\lambda = 0$.

10.11. Linear stationary problems and Toeplitz forms

The reader may have observed by now that the theory of Toeplitz forms is a convenient tool in the study of stationary stochastic processes, not only in solving problems of prediction but also in other respects. Some of these applications belong to the next chapter since they are of a statistical nature, but we can already now indicate the general nature of these applications.

(a) Let x_t be a stationary process with discrete time and the spectral density $f(\lambda)$. We study the values of x_t, $t \in S$, where S is a set of integers, and expecially the stochastic variables obtained as linear combinations

$$L(x) = \sum_{t \in S} c_t x_t.$$

Since the covariance matrix of our process is of the Toeplitz type it is clear that the square of the norm (i.e. the variance) of $L(x)$ is a Toeplitz form

$$\| L(x) \|^2 = \sum_{s,\, t \in S} c_s \bar{c}_t r_{s-t} = \frac{1}{2\pi} \int_{-\pi}^{\pi} | u(e^{i\lambda}) |^2 f(\lambda)\, d\lambda,$$

where $u(z)$ is the 'Laurent polynomial'

$$u(z) = \sum_{t \in S} c_t z^t.$$

The norm is not changed if we multiply $u(z)$ by a power of z since $|z| = |e^{i\lambda}| = 1$. Hence we can always assume that $u(z)$ is an ordinary polynomial of z.

The general problem will be to minimize this norm under certain side conditions on $u(z)$. We have studied in considerable detail the situation when $S = 0, -1, -2, \ldots, -n$ and the side condition is $c_0 = 1$. The problem is identical with that of the best linear finite predictor; after the modification of $u(z)$ mentioned above the side condition can be written as $u(0) = 1$. Similarly, dealing with the prediction h steps ahead we obtain conditions of the form $c_0 = 1$, $c_\nu = 0$, $1 \leq \nu \leq h-1$, or in equivalent form $u(0) = 1$, $u^{(\nu)}(0) = 0$, $1 \leq \nu \leq h-1$. *Hence prediction corresponds to imposing conditions on $u(z)$ at the point $z = 0$.*

(b) In some important practical cases it is known that the mean value of the process is not zero but given by

$$m_t = E x_t = \mu\, e^{i\lambda t},$$

where $-\pi \leq \lambda < \pi$ and μ is an unknown constant. It is natural to require then that the predictor x_0^* should have *correct expected value*, i.e.

$$E x_0^* \equiv m_0 \equiv \mu,$$

irrespective of the value of μ. The left-hand side can be written as

$$-E\left\{\sum_{t=-1}^{-n} c_t x_t\right\} = -\mu \sum_{t=-1}^{-n} c_t e^{i\lambda t},$$

so that we must have

$$1 = -\sum_{t=-1}^{-n} c_t e^{i\lambda t} = -u(e^{i\lambda}) + c_0,$$

and since c_0 should be 1, the extra condition can be written simply $u(e^{i\lambda}) = 0$. Hence, *in addition to the conditions at $z=0$, we obtain another condition on $u(z)$ at the point $z = e^{i\lambda}$.*

A further case of less practical interest is when the mean-value sequence m_t is a damped harmonic:

$$m_t = \mu \zeta^t, \quad |\zeta| < 1.$$

If we still want predictors with correct expected value we are led to *the condition $u(\zeta) = 0$ at the point ζ in the interior of the unit circle.*

Recapitulating, we have found that *the linear problems associated with stationary stochastic processes with a discrete time parameter can be treated by means of the theory of the classical Toeplitz forms. The stationary processes and the Toeplitz forms are linked by the theorems in 10.3 and 10.4.*

10.12. Representation of continuous stationary processes

It is natural to investigate the possibility of extending the results discussed in 10.5–10.11 to stationary processes depending upon a continuous time parameter. While it is rather easy to guess the necessary formal modifications, some care is needed in carrying out the details in a rigorous manner. As a start we prove in this section the analog of the representation of 1.14 and its probability interpretation as given in 10.7.

(a) Let x_t be a stationary process which is continuous in the mean. Assuming as before that the spectrum is absolutely continuous we denote the spectral density by $f(\lambda)$ so that

$$R(t) = (x_{s+t}, x_s) = \frac{1}{2\pi} \int_{-\infty}^{\infty} e^{it\lambda} f(\lambda)\, d\lambda.$$

Instead of 10.7 (3) we assume now that

$$\int_{-\infty}^{\infty} \log f(\lambda) \frac{d\lambda}{1+\lambda^2} > -\infty; \tag{1}$$

the integral is then finite since $\log x < x, x > 0$, and $f(\lambda)$ is integrable. Making the substitution

$$\lambda = \operatorname{tg}(\tfrac{1}{2}\mu), \quad \frac{1+i\lambda}{1-i\lambda} = e^{i\mu}, \tag{2}$$

and writing $f(\lambda) = f_d(\mu)$ we have

$$\int_{-\pi}^{\pi} \log f_d(\mu)\, d\mu = 2 \int_{-\infty}^{\infty} \log f(\lambda)\, \frac{d\lambda}{1+\lambda^2} > -\infty.$$

Hence, according to 10.7, $f_d(\mu)$ can be considered as the spectral density corresponding to a non-deterministic discrete process and

$$f_d(\mu) = |G_d(\mu)|^2$$

almost everywhere with

$$G_d(\mu) = \frac{1}{2\pi} \sum_{\nu=0}^{\infty} G_\nu e^{-i\nu\mu}, \quad \sum_{\nu=0}^{\infty} |G_\nu|^2 < \infty;$$

the first sum should be interpreted as a limit in the mean. We have, using the orthonormal property of the exponential functions,

$$\delta_{kl} = \frac{1}{\pi} \int_{-\infty}^{\infty} \frac{(1-i\lambda)^l}{(1+i\lambda)^{l+1}} \frac{(1+i\lambda)^k}{(1-i\lambda)^{k+1}}\, d\lambda = \frac{1}{2\pi} \int_{-\pi}^{\pi} e^{i(k-l)\mu}\, d\mu,$$

so that the functions

$$\pi^{-\frac{1}{2}} \frac{(1-i\lambda)^k}{(1+i\lambda)^{k+1}}, \quad k = 0, 1, \ldots,$$

form an orthonormal set in $L_2[d\lambda; -\infty, \infty]$. We introduce the function

$$G(\lambda) = G_d(\mu) = \frac{1}{2\pi} \sum_{\nu=0}^{\infty} G_\nu \frac{(1-i\lambda)^\nu}{(1+i\lambda)^{\nu+1}}, \tag{3}$$

which belongs also to $L_2[d\lambda; -\infty, \infty]$; hence it has a Plancherel transform $\gamma(t)$:

$$G(\lambda) = \operatorname*{l.i.m.}_{A \to \infty} \frac{1}{2\pi} \int_{-A}^{A} e^{-i\lambda t} \gamma(t)\, dt.$$

Since

$$\operatorname*{l.i.m.}_{A \to \infty} \frac{1}{2\pi} \int_{-A}^{A} e^{i\lambda t} \frac{(1-i\lambda)^\nu}{(1+i\lambda)^{\nu+1}}\, d\lambda = 0$$

for $t < 0$, it is clear that $\gamma(t)$ also vanishes for negative values of t. We have $f(\lambda) = |G(\lambda)|^2$.

This representation of $f(\lambda)$ in terms of a function $G(\lambda)$ which is a one-sided Plancherel transform, can be compared with the result proved in 1.14.

(b) Since $G(x)$ vanishes almost nowhere on the real line we can introduce a stochastic process

$$\zeta(\lambda) = \int_0^\lambda [G(x)]^{-1} dZ(x),$$

where $Z(\lambda)$ is the spectral process corresponding to x_t.

Then $\| \zeta(\lambda) \|^2 = (2\pi)^{-1} | \lambda |$. Also let

$$\xi(\lambda) = (2\pi)^{-\frac{1}{2}} \int_{-\infty}^\infty \frac{e^{ix\lambda} - 1}{ix} d\zeta(x).$$

We consider two intervals $[\lambda_1, \lambda_2]$ and $[\lambda_3, \lambda_4]$; we have then

$$(\xi(\lambda_2) - \xi(\lambda_1), \xi(\lambda_4) - \xi(\lambda_3)) = \frac{1}{4\pi^2} \int_{-\infty}^\infty \frac{e^{ix\lambda_2} - e^{ix\lambda_1}}{ix} \cdot \frac{e^{-ix\lambda_4} - e^{-ix\lambda_3}}{-ix} dx = 0$$

if the two intervals are disjoint, and $= (2\pi)^{-1} (\lambda_2 - \lambda_1)$ if they coincide. This is just Parseval's relation. Hence $\xi(\lambda)$ is also an orthogonal process (see 10.4).

We have

$$x_t = \int_{-\infty}^\infty e^{it\lambda} dZ(\lambda) = \int_{-\infty}^\infty e^{it\lambda} G(\lambda) d\zeta(\lambda)$$

$$= \int_{-\infty}^\infty e^{it\lambda} \left\{ \underset{A\to\infty}{\text{l.i.m.}} \frac{1}{2\pi} \int_{-A}^A e^{-i\lambda s} \gamma(s) ds \right\} d\zeta(\lambda) = (2\pi)^{-\frac{1}{2}} \int_{s=0}^\infty \gamma(s) d\xi(t-s),$$

where the interchanging of the order of integration is easily justified. Hence we have obtained the following theorem:

THEOREM. *If the stationary process x_t is continuous in the mean and has a spectral density $f(\lambda)$ satisfying*

$$\int_{-\infty}^\infty \log f(\lambda) \frac{d\lambda}{1+\lambda^2} > -\infty,$$

the process can be represented as a moving average:

$$x_t = (2\pi)^{-\frac{1}{2}} \int_{s=0}^\infty \gamma(s) d\xi(t-s), \tag{4}$$

where $\gamma(s)$ is quadratically integrable and $\xi(s)$ is an orthogonal process with $\| d\xi(s) \|^2 = (2\pi)^{-1} ds$.

10.13. Prediction of a continuous parameter process

(a) Let us consider the stationary process x_t which is continuous in the mean and has a spectral density $f(\lambda)$ satisfying the condition 10.12 (1). This process has been observed for $t < 0$ and we want to predict its value at the time $t = h > 0$. Denoting the predictor by x_h^* we require in analogy to the discrete case (see 10.8) that

$$x_h^* \in L_2(x;\ 0), \| x_h^* - x_h \| = \min,$$

which yields of course $x_h^* = P_0 x_h$, where P_0 is the projection operator associated with the manifold $L_2(x;\ 0)$. So far this is scarcely more than the definition of the best predictor. To establish the relation between the present problem and the Toeplitz forms we write tentatively

$$x_h^* = \int_{-\infty}^{0} x_t\, dw(t),$$

where $w(t)$ is a function of bounded variation. We define $w(t) = w(0)$ for $0 < t < h$ and $w(t) = w(0) - 1$ for $h < t < \infty$. Then

$$x_h^* - x_h = \int_{-\infty}^{\infty} x_t\, dw(t),$$

and the norm to be minimized can be written as follows:

$$\| x_h^* - x_h \|^2 = \int_{-\infty}^{\infty} \int_{-\infty}^{\infty} R(s-t)\, dw(s)\, \overline{dw(t)};$$

this is a Toeplitz form corresponding to the Toeplitz kernel

$$R(s-t) = \frac{1}{2\pi} \int_{-\infty}^{\infty} e^{i(s-t)\lambda} f(\lambda)\, d\lambda;$$

this type of kernel was studied in 8.6. The minimum problem formulated above represents a generalization of the problem dealt with in 3.1.

The following difficulty should be mentioned. Seeking the best *finite* predictor in the discrete case we dealt with a finite dimensional vector space. All elements of this space could be represented as sums of the form $\sum_0^n c_\nu x_{-\nu}$. In the present case, however, the space spanned by $x_t,\ -T < t < 0$, has a denumerably infinite dimension. While the set of all elements of the form $\int_{-T}^{0} x_t\, dw(t)$ is everywhere dense in this space, it is not true in general that every element of the space can be written in such a form. This fact is the source of some complications.

(b) Using the theorem in the last section we obtain

$$x_h^* = (2\pi)^{-\frac{1}{2}} \int_{s=0}^{\infty} \gamma(s) \, d\xi^*(h-s),$$

where $\xi^*(\tau) = P_0 \xi(\tau)$. Since $\xi(\tau)$ is an orthogonal process and x_t can be written as in 10.12 (4), we have $x_t \perp \xi_\tau$ if $\tau > t$. Hence $\xi^*(h-s) = 0$ for $s > h$.

In order to calculate $\xi^*(h-s)$ for $0 < s < h$ we are going to show that $L_2(x; \tau) = L_2(\xi; \tau)$. We know already, in view of 10.12 (4), that $L_2(x; \tau) \subseteq L_2(\xi; \tau)$. Assuming that in the last relation no strict equality holds, there is a nonzero element $z \in L_2(\xi; \tau)$ such that $(x_t, z) = 0$ for all $t \leq \tau$. In view of the stationary character of the process we need only consider one time point, say $\tau = 0$. Since $\xi(t)$ is an orthogonal process, z can be written in the form

$$z = \int_{-\infty}^{0} a(s) \, d\xi(s)$$

and

$$\|z\|^2 = \frac{1}{2\pi} \int_{-\infty}^{0} |a(s)|^2 \, ds < \infty.$$

Hence

$$(x_t, z) = \frac{1}{2\pi} \int_{-\infty}^{0} \gamma(t-s) \, \overline{a(s)} \, ds, \quad t < 0. \tag{1}$$

Forming the Fourier transforms and taking into account that $a(s) = 0$ for $s > 0$, we find

$$\int_{-\infty}^{\infty} e^{it\lambda} G(\lambda) \, \overline{A(\lambda)} \, d\lambda = 0, \quad t < 0, \tag{2}$$

where $A(\lambda)$ is the Fourier transform of $a(s)$.

Now there are functions $h_\nu(s)$ (see Appendix) such that

$$\frac{(1-i\lambda)^{\nu-1}}{(1+i\lambda)^{\nu+1}} = \int_{-\infty}^{0} e^{it\lambda} h_\nu(t) \, dt, \quad \nu = 1, 2, 3, \ldots, \tag{3}$$

where $h_\nu(s)$ is exponentially decreasing for large negative values of t. Hence we obtain from (2), multiplying by $h_\nu(t)$ and integrating,

$$\int_{-\infty}^{\infty} \left(\frac{1-i\lambda}{1+i\lambda} \right)^{\nu} G(\lambda) \, \overline{A(\lambda)} \, \frac{d\lambda}{1+\lambda^2} = 0, \quad \nu = 1, 2, 3, \ldots.$$

Using the transformation 10.12 (2) we find that

$$\int_{-\pi}^{\pi} e^{-i\nu\mu} G_d(\mu) \, \overline{A_d(\mu)} \, d\mu = 0, \quad \nu = 1, 2, 3, \ldots, \tag{4}$$

where $G_d(\mu)$ has been defined by 10.12 (3) and $A_d(\mu) = A(\lambda)$.

Let us return for a moment to the discrete case. The analogous question for this case was resolved in 10.9 with the result

$$L_2(x; \tau) = L_2(\xi; \tau).$$

We could have treated the discrete problem according to the procedure of the present section, obtaining an equation of the form (4); thus we have reduced our present problem to the discrete case in which the solution is already known. Hence we can state now that $A_d(\mu) = A(\lambda) = 0$ almost everywhere, implying that $a(s) = 0$ and $L_2(x; \tau) = L_2(\xi; \tau)$.

The best predictor is then

$$x_h^* = (2\pi)^{-\frac{1}{2}} \int_{s=h}^{\infty} \gamma(s) \, d\xi(h-s),$$

with the prediction error to be computed from

$$x_h^* - x_h = -(2\pi)^{-\frac{1}{2}} \int_{s=0}^{h} \gamma(s) \, d\xi(h-s).$$

THEOREM. *For a stationary stochastic process which is continuous in the mean and has a spectral density* $f(\lambda)$ *satisfying*

$$\int_{-\infty}^{\infty} \log f(\lambda) \frac{d\lambda}{1+\lambda^2} > -\infty,$$

the best predictor can be obtained in the following explicit form:

$$x_{t+h}^* = (2\pi)^{-\frac{1}{2}} \int_{s=t}^{\infty} \gamma(t+h-s) \, d\xi(s),$$

$$\| x_{t+h}^* - x_{t+h} \|^2 = (2\pi)^{-2} \int_0^h | \gamma(s) |^2 \, ds.$$

This holds when the process x_s *has been observed for* $-\infty < s < t$. *The orthogonal process* $\xi(s)$ *was defined in 10.12.*

10.14. Deterministic processes

A process x_t is said to be deterministic if $L_2(x; t) = L_2(x)$ for every real t. This is of course isometrically equivalent to the fact that the subspace spanned by

$$\{e^{it\lambda}, e^{i(t-1)\lambda}, e^{i(t-2)\lambda}, \ldots\}$$

coincides with $L_2[dF; -\infty, \infty]$, i.e. with the Hilbert space of all functions quadratically integrable with respect to $F(\lambda)$. (See 10.5.) This is a completeness problem analogous to that discussed in 3.3.

We have seen already that under the condition 10.12 (1) the process is nondeterministic. Now we assume

$$\int_{-\infty}^{\infty} \log f(\lambda) \frac{d\lambda}{1+\lambda^2} = -\infty.$$

We use the transformation 10.12 (2). It is known (see 3.3 and 10.6) that $\{1, e^{-i\mu}, e^{-2\mu}, \ldots\}$ spans the entire Hilbert space of functions defined on $[-\pi, \pi]$ with the weight function $f_d(\mu) = f(\lambda)$. This implies that the set $\left\{\left(\frac{1+i\lambda}{1-i\lambda}\right)^\nu, \nu \leq 0\right\}$ is complete in $L_2(dF)$; it remains to show that each function $\left(\frac{1+i\lambda}{1-i\lambda}\right)^\nu$, $\nu \leq 0$, can be approximated by a linear combination of the functions $e^{it\lambda}$, $t \leq 0$. This follows easily from the fact that for $k \geq 1$

$$\left(\frac{1-i\lambda}{1+i\lambda}\right)^k = (-1)^k + \frac{p_{k-1}(\lambda)}{(1+i\lambda)^k},$$

where $p_{k-1}(\lambda)$ is a polynomial of degree $k-1$. The first term is $(-1)^k e^{it\lambda}$ for $t=0$; the second term can be written as a Fourier transform and approximated in the same way as it was done at the end of the last section. The result then follows:

THEOREM. *A stationary stochastic process x_t continuous in the mean and with an absolutely continuous spectrum of spectral density $f(\lambda)$, is deterministic if and only if*

$$\int_{-\infty}^{\infty} \log f(\lambda) \frac{d\lambda}{1+\lambda^2} = -\infty.$$

10.15. A simple example

We consider a stationary stochastic process with the covariance function $R(t) = e^{-|t|}$. A simple calculation shows that the spectrum is absolutely continuous with the spectral density $f(\lambda) = 2(1 + \lambda^2)^{-1}$. Since

$$\int_{-\infty}^{\infty} \log \frac{2}{1+\lambda^2} \frac{d\lambda}{1+\lambda^2} > -\infty,$$

the process is nondeterministic and should be representable as a one-sided moving average. Carrying out the calculations as described in the last section we obtain $\gamma(s) = 2^{\frac{3}{2}} \pi e^{-s}$, $s > 0$, and

$$x_t = 2\pi^{\frac{1}{2}} \int_0^{\infty} e^{-s} d\xi(t-s);$$

the best linear predictor is

$$x_{t+h}^* = 2\pi^{\frac{1}{2}} \int_h^{\infty} e^{-s} d\xi(t+h-s) = e^{-h} x_t.$$

The error of prediction becomes

$$\| x_{t+h} - x_{t+h}^* \|^2 = \| x_{t+h} - e^{-h} x_t \|^2 = 1 - e^{-2h}.$$

One may note that in the present case the best predictor is actually of the Stieltjes integral form discussed in 10.13 with the weight function $w(s) = 0$ for $s < t$ and $w(t+0) = e^{-h}$. If the covariance function is of the form $p(t) e^{-|t|}$, where $p(t)$ is a polynomial of the kth degree, x_{t+h}^* will be a linear combination of $x_t, x_t', x_t'', ..., x_t^{(k)}$.

10.16. Other applications to the theory of probability

In the previous part of the present chapter we have studied some questions related to stochastic processes from the point of view of Toeplitz forms. Various important linear problems have been reduced to a type familiar to us from the theory of Toeplitz forms. Although the theory of stationary stochastic processes is that part of the calculus of probability where Toeplitz forms have been applied in the most systematic manner, there are other topics of great interest which might be discussed by similar methods.

In order to give the reader an idea of how and why Toeplitz forms are useful for certain other probability problems we shall sketch an approach to the problem of *random walk*.

(a) Let $X_1, X_2, \ldots$ be independent stochastic variables with the symmetric frequency function $K(x)$. We consider a particle in Brownian motion on the real line starting out from the point $x=0$ at time $t=0$. The parameter t runs through the nonnegative integers, and the total displacement of the particle after t units of time is supposed to be represented by $S_t = X_1 + X_2 + \ldots + X_t$. If S_t takes values outside of an interval $[-p, p]$ the particle is absorbed by the 'barriers' $x = \pm p$. We seek expressions for *the probability P_T that the particle is not to be absorbed in T steps*.

We have

$$P_T = \int_E K(x_1) K(x_2) \ldots K(x_T)\, dx_1 dx_2 \ldots dx_T,$$

where the domain of integration is

$$E = \{-p < x_1 < p,\ -p < x_1 + x_2 < p,\ \ldots,\ -p < x_1 + x_2 + \ldots + x_T < p\}.$$

Changing variables:

$$y_i = p + x_1 + x_2 + \ldots + x_i, \quad i = 1, 2, \ldots, T,$$

we find

$$P_T = \int_0^{2p} \int_0^{2p} \ldots \int_0^{2p} K(y_1 - p)\, K(y_2 - y_1) \ldots K(y_T - y_{T-1})\, dy_1 dy_2 \ldots dy_T,$$

since the Jacobian of the transformation is one. This convolution integral can be computed with the aid of the Toeplitz integral equation

$$\int_0^{2p} K(u - v) f(v)\, dv = \lambda f(u).$$

Denoting the eigenvalues of this equation by λ_ν and the associated eigenfunctions by $\phi_\nu(u)$ we find easily, since P_T can be considered as the integral of an iterated kernel,

$$P_T = \sum_{\nu=1}^{\infty} \lambda_\nu^T \phi_\nu(p) \int_0^{2p} \phi_\nu(u)\, du.$$

While this is an explicit expression for the probability in question, it is not suitable for practical use, since the eigenvalues and eigenfunctions of the kernel $K(u - v)$ are difficult to calculate in general. We observe, however, that if the characteristic function

$$c(\lambda) = E\, e^{i\lambda X} = \int_{-\infty}^{\infty} e^{i\lambda x} K(x)\, dx$$

of the stochastic variables is absolutely integrable, then

$$K(u-v) = \frac{1}{2\pi} \int_{-\infty}^{\infty} e^{-i(u-v)\lambda} c(\lambda)\, d\lambda,$$

and since $K(x)$ was assumed to be symmetric, $K(-x)=K(x)$, the characteristic function $c(\lambda)$ will be real-valued. Hence $K(u-v)$ is a Toeplitz kernel of the type discussed in chapter 8. Unfortunately, the results in that chapter are not immediately applicable to the present problem, but the close connection is apparent, and it seems reasonable that useful approximations for P_T can be obtained in this manner.

(b) A different although related problem is the following. Let $X_1, X_2, \ldots$ be independent symmetric stochastic variables with

$$P\{X_j = \nu\} = c_\nu, \quad c_\nu = c_{-\nu}, \quad \sum_{-\infty}^{\infty} c_\nu = 1.$$

We assume that the series $\sum_{-\infty}^{\infty} \nu c_\nu$, representing the mean, is absolutely convergent; this series is equal to zero, of course. We introduce the characteristic function

$$f(\lambda) = E\,e^{i\lambda X} = \sum_{-\infty}^{\infty} c_\nu e^{i\nu\lambda}.$$

Then $f'(\lambda)$ exists and we assume that this function satisfies a Lipschitz condition
$$|f'(\lambda_1) - f'(\lambda_2)| < K\,|\lambda_1 - \lambda_2|^\alpha, \quad 0 < \alpha < 1.$$

Let us consider the partial sums $S_\nu = \sum_{j=1}^{\nu} X_j$. We seek the expected value of the stochastic variable

$$M_m = \max\,(0, S_1, S_2, \ldots, S_{m-1}),$$

conditioned by the event $S_m = 0$. For this purpose we introduce the eigenvalues $\lambda_j^{(n)}$ of the Toeplitz matrix $\{c_{\nu-\mu}; \nu,\mu = 0, 1, \ldots, n\}$ and consider the relation to be discussed below in 11.7:

$$\lim_{n\to\infty}\left\{\sum_{j=1}^{n+1} (\lambda_j^{(m)})^s - \frac{n+1}{2\pi}\int_{-\pi}^{\pi} [f(\lambda)]^s\, d\lambda\right\}$$

$$= -2 \sum_{-\infty < l_1, \ldots, l_{s-1} < \infty} \max\,(0, l_1, l_1+l_2, \ldots, l_1+l_2+\ldots+l_{s-1})$$

$$\times c_{l_1} c_{l_2} \cdots c_{l_{s-1}} c_{l_1+l_2+\ldots+l_{s-1}}. \quad (1)$$

The right-hand member will be denoted by $-E_s$. Then it is easily seen that

$$| E_s | \leqq 2(s-1) \left(\sum_{-\infty}^{\infty} c_\nu \right)^{s-2} \sum_{-\infty}^{\infty} | \nu | c_\nu.$$

The same bound can be shown to hold for the quantity inside the curly brackets in (1), for every n. Now in the neighborhood of $z=0$.

$$\lim_{n \to \infty} \sum_{s=1}^{\infty} \frac{z^s}{s} \left\{ \sum_{j=1}^{n+1} (\lambda_j^{(n)})^s - \frac{n+1}{2\pi} \int_{-\pi}^{\pi} [f(\lambda)]^s \, d\lambda \right\} = - \sum_{s=1}^{\infty} \frac{z^s}{s} E_s.$$

If $D_n(g)$ denotes the Toeplitz determinant associated with the positive function $g(\lambda)$ and $G(g)$ the geometric mean of $g(\lambda)$ we obtain

$$\lim_{n \to \infty} \{\log D_n(1-zf) - (n+1) \log G(1-zf)\} = \sum_{s=1}^{\infty} \frac{z^s}{s} E_s.$$

By applying the theorem in 5.5, an alternate form of this limit arises, namely,

$$\sum_{l=1}^{\infty} l \, | \, h_l(z) \, |^2, \quad h_l(z) = \frac{1}{2\pi} \int_{-\pi}^{\pi} \log[1 - zf(\lambda)] e^{-il\lambda} d\lambda.$$

Expanding $h_l(z)$ and comparing the coefficients of z^s we obtain (writing m in place of s)

$$\sum \max (0, l_1, l_1 + l_2, \ldots, l_1 + l_2 + \ldots + l_{m-1}) \, c_{l_1} c_{l_2} \cdots c_{l_{m-1}} c_{l_1 + l_2 + \ldots + l_{m-1}}$$

$$= \frac{m}{2} \sum_{l=1}^{\infty} l \sum_{k=1}^{m-1} \frac{1}{k(m-k)} \frac{1}{2\pi} \int_{-\pi}^{\pi} [f(\lambda)]^k e^{-il\lambda} d\lambda \frac{1}{2\pi} \int_{-\pi}^{\pi} [f(\lambda)]^{m-k} e^{il\lambda} d\lambda.$$

Noting that $[f(\lambda)]^k$ is the characteristic function of S_k and using the Fourier inversion formula we see that

$$\frac{1}{2\pi} \int_{-\pi}^{\pi} [f(\lambda)]^k e^{-il\lambda} d\lambda = P\{S_k = l\}.$$

We observe also that

$$P\{S_m = 0\} E\{M_m \mid S_m = 0\} = \sum \max (0, l_1, l_1 + l_2, \ldots, l_1 + l_2 + \ldots + l_{m-1})$$

$$c_{l_1} c_{l_2} \cdots c_{l_{m-1}} c_{l_1 + l_2 + \ldots + l_{m-1}};$$

taking into account that $c_{-\nu} = c_\nu$, we obtain the desired result:

$$P\{S_m = 0\} E\{M_m \mid S_m = 0\} = \frac{m}{2} \sum_{l=1}^{\infty} l \sum_{k=1}^{m-1} \frac{P\{S_k = l\} P\{S_{m-k} = -l\}}{k(m-k)}.$$

CHAPTER 11

APPLICATIONS TO STATISTICS

11.1. Linear estimation

In this chapter we shall deal with statistical problems related to the theory of Toeplitz forms. In certain cases the results previously obtained for these forms will be immediately applicable to the problems in question, in other cases modifications and extensions will be needed. Certain problems in linear estimation can be considered as special cases of the problem studied in 3.2. However, our attention will be concentrated on the boundary case $|\zeta| = 1$, and we will need an asymptotic expression for the quantity $\mu_n(\zeta)$ defined in 3.2, as n tends to infinity.

(a) As in the previous chapter we shall study certain important special cases illustrating the general idea of employing Toeplitz forms.

Let x_t be a stationary stochastic process with a discrete time parameter. We introduce the mean value $m_t = Ex_t$, the covariance function $R(s-t) = E(x_s - m_s)\overline{(x_t - m_t)}$, and the spectral density $f(\lambda)$; the spectrum is assumed to be absolutely continuous. Under the hypothesis that the mean-value function can be written as $m_t = \mu\,e^{it\lambda_0}$, where λ_0 is a known real constant, we want to *estimate* μ by using the observations $x_{-n}, x_{-n+1}, \ldots, x_n$. This estimate μ^* of μ should of course be a function of the observations, $\mu^* = \mu^*(x_{-n}, x_{-n+1}, \ldots, x_n)$ chosen in such a way that the error of estimation $\mu^* - \mu$ becomes as small as possible. The last statement needs a more precise formulation since μ^* varies over the $(2n+1)$-dimensional sample space spanned by the vectors $(x_{-n}, x_{-n+1}, \ldots, x_n)$. How this should be done is a question belonging to the theory of *statistical inference*.

(b) In the present context we will restrict ourselves to *linear* functions as estimates,

$$\mu^*(x_{-n}, x_{-n+1}, \ldots, x_n) = \sum_{\nu=-n}^{n} c_\nu x_\nu,$$

where the c's are complex constants. We will choose that linear function which minimizes the norm of the estimation error,

$$\|\mu^* - \mu\|^2 = E\,|\,\mu^* - \mu\,|^2 = \min$$

under the side condition

$$\sum_{\nu=-n}^{n} c_\nu e^{i\nu\lambda_0} = 1.$$

This condition means that we allow only estimates with correct expectation, $E\mu^* = \mu$, identically in μ. Such estimates are called *unbiased* and were briefly mentioned in 10.11.

The problem for the parameters $c_{-n}, c_{-n+1}, \dots, c_n$ can be written as follows:

$$\frac{1}{2\pi} \int_{-\pi}^{\pi} \left| \sum_{\nu=-n}^{n} c_\nu e^{i\nu\lambda} \right|^2 f(\lambda)\, d\lambda = \min,$$

$$\sum_{\nu=-n}^{n} c_\nu e^{i\nu\lambda_0} = 1,$$

which is the problem on Toeplitz forms studied in 3.2 with $\zeta = e^{i\lambda_0}$. Another way of writing this is

$$cRc^* = \min, \quad c\epsilon = 1,$$

where c is the vector $(c_{-n}, c_{-n+1}, \dots, c_n)$, ϵ is the column vector with components

$$e^{-in\lambda_0}, e^{-i(n-1)\lambda_0}, \dots, e^{in\lambda_0} \quad \text{and} \quad R = \{R(\nu - \mu);$$

$$\nu, \mu = -n, -n+1, \dots, n\}.$$

We use the symbol $c^* = \bar{c}'$. An arbitrary vector c satisfying $c\epsilon = 1$ can be written in the form $c = K\epsilon^*R^{-1} + d$, where $d\epsilon = 0$ and K is the scalar $(\epsilon^*R^{-1}\epsilon)^{-1}$. Now $R^* = R$, so that $cRc^* = K^2\epsilon^*R^{-1}\epsilon + dRd^*$. Since R is a positive-definite matrix [see 10.3 (1)] we find that the minimum is attained for $c = (\epsilon^*R^{-1}\epsilon)^{-1}\epsilon^*R^{-1}$, and the minimum is $M_n = (\epsilon^*R^{-1}\epsilon)^{-1}$. The solution is unique. Although these are explicit expressions for c and M_n their practical value is moderate, since they involve the cumbersome calculation of the inverse of a matrix R of high order. Therefore adequate approximations are needed.

11.2. Existence of consistent estimates

(a) We consider the problem of the last section for large values of n. A reasonable requirement for a good estimate is that its mean-square error becomes small as n increases. More formally we shall say that μ_n^* forms a sequence of *consistent estimates* if

$$\lim_{n \to \infty} \| \mu_n^* - \mu \| = 0.$$

Our first aim is to find out whether there exist consistent estimates in the present situation. Let us consider the estimates constructed in the last section. They represent the solution of the problem considered in 3.2 for $\zeta = e^{i\lambda_0}$. We observe that ζ is a point on the boundary of the unit circle. Since the sequence $\|\mu_n^* - \mu\|^2$ is nonincreasing, it tends to a limit M_∞ as n tends to infinity. We want to show that $M_\infty = 0$.

Suppose that the spectral density is bounded, $f(\lambda) \leqq c < \infty$. Then $R \leqq cI$, where I is the identity matrix and hence $R^{-1} \geqq c^{-1}I$, so that $\epsilon^* R^{-1} \epsilon \geqq c^{-1} \|\epsilon\|^2 = c^{-1}(2n+1)$. Thus $M_n \leqq (2n+1)^{-1}c$ and tends to zero; hence *if the spectral density is bounded there exist consistent estimates of μ and $M_n = O(n^{-1})$.*

(b) It is not difficult to see that this result holds more generally. Indeed, let us consider the estimates

$$\mu_L^* = (2n+1)^{-1} \sum_{\nu=-n}^{n} x_\nu e^{-i\nu\lambda_0},$$

i.e. $c_\nu = (2n+1)^{-1} e^{-i\nu\lambda_0}$. Clearly this is an unbiased estimate. Further

$$\|\mu_L^* - \mu\|^2 = \frac{1}{2\pi} \int_{-\pi}^{\pi} \left| \sum_{\nu=-n}^{n} c_\nu e^{i\nu\lambda} \right|^2 f(\lambda)\, d\lambda$$

$$= \frac{1}{2\pi} \frac{1}{(2n+1)^2} \int_{-\pi}^{\pi} \left(\frac{\sin (n+\tfrac{1}{2})(\lambda-\lambda_0)}{\sin \tfrac{1}{2}(\lambda-\lambda_0)} \right)^2 f(\lambda)\, d\lambda.$$

The last expression is closely related to the Fejér means; expressing these means by the Fourier coefficients of $f(\lambda)$ and using the Riemann–Lebesgue lemma (see Appendix), we obtain the desired result

$$\lim_{n\to\infty} \|\mu_L^* - \mu\|^2 = 0.$$

Thus: *If the spectrum is absolutely continuous there exist consistent estimates.* Simple examples indicate that this cannot hold for arbitrary spectra.

(c) Let us consider now the more general situation when

$$m_t = \mu \int_{-\pi}^{\pi} e^{it\lambda}\, d\mu(\lambda),$$

where $\mu(\lambda)$ is a complex-valued function of bounded variation. The spectral distribution function $F(\lambda)$ is in this case not necessarily absolutely continuous. When is it possible to estimate μ consistently?

As before we must have

$$\left. \begin{aligned} \int_{-\pi}^{\pi} |\, u_n(e^{i\lambda})\,|^2\, dF(\lambda) &= \min, \\ 1 = \sum_{\nu=-n}^{n} c_\nu \int_{-\pi}^{\pi} e^{i\nu\lambda}\, d\mu(\lambda) &= \int_{-\pi}^{\pi} u_n(e^{i\lambda})\, d\mu\,(\lambda), \end{aligned} \right\} \tag{1}$$

where

$$u_n(z) = \sum_{\nu=-n}^{n} c_\nu z^\nu.$$

Schwarz's inequality yields

$$1 \leq \left\{ \int_{-\pi}^{\pi} |\, u_n(e^{i\lambda})\,|\,|\, d\mu(\lambda)\,| \right\}^2 \leq \left\{ \sum_\nu |\, u_n(e^{i\lambda_\nu^{(m)}})\,|\,|\, \Delta\mu(\lambda_\nu^{(m)})\,| \right\}^2 + \epsilon$$

$$\leq \sum_\nu |\, u_n(e^{i\lambda_\nu^{(m)}})\,|^2\, \Delta F(\lambda_\nu^{(m)}) \sum_\nu \frac{|\, \Delta\mu(\lambda_\nu^{(m)})\,|^2}{\Delta F(\lambda_\nu^{(m)})} + \epsilon,$$

where $[-\pi, \pi]$ has been divided by a net $-\pi < \lambda_1^{(m)} < \lambda_2^{(m)} < \ldots < \lambda_m^{(m)} < \pi$. If this net is sufficiently fine, ϵ can be made as small as required.

It is well known that the quantity

$$H_m = \sum_\nu \frac{|\, \Delta\mu(\lambda_\nu^{(m)})\,|^2}{\Delta F(\lambda_\nu^{(m)})}$$

is nondecreasing when the net becomes more refined. The limit (finite or not) is denoted by

$$H = \int_{-\pi}^{\pi} \frac{|\, d\mu(\lambda)\,|^2}{dF(\lambda)},$$

which is a so-called *Hellinger integral*. We have proved that

$$\liminf_{n \to \infty} \| \mu_n^* - \mu \|^2 \geq 1/H.$$

Actually we have equality in the above relation. Indeed, let

$$\phi^{(m)}(\lambda) = H_m^{-1} \frac{\overline{\Delta\mu(\lambda_\nu^{(m)})}}{\Delta F(\lambda_\nu^{(m)})} \quad \text{for} \quad \lambda_\nu^{(m)} < \lambda \leq \lambda_{\nu+1}^{(m)}.$$

Except for small neighborhoods of $\lambda_\nu^{(m)}$ this function can be uniformly approximated by trigonometric polynomials, and choosing the net so that the points of discontinuity of $\mu(\lambda)$ and $F(\lambda)$ do not coincide with $\lambda_\nu^{(m)}$, we obtain

$$\left. \begin{aligned} \int_{-\pi}^{\pi} |\, \phi^{(m)}(\lambda)\,|^2\, dF(\lambda) &= H_m^{-1}, \\ \int_{-\pi}^{\pi} \phi^{(m)}(\lambda)\, d\mu(\lambda) &= 1. \end{aligned} \right\}$$

If $H_m = \infty$ for a finite m, there must be a ν for which

$$\frac{\Delta\mu(\lambda_\nu^{(m)})}{\Delta F(\lambda_\nu^{(m)})} = \infty.$$

Then we would choose $\phi^{(m)}(\lambda) = [\Delta\mu(\lambda_\nu^{(m)})]^{-1}$ in $\lambda_\nu^{(m)} < \lambda \leq \lambda_{\nu+1}^{(m)}$ and zero otherwise and carry out the same approximation procedure leading to the previous relations.

Now choosing again the nets infinitely refined we find for this particular choice of estimates

$$\lim_{n \to \infty} \| \mu_n^* - \mu \|^2 = 1/H.$$

We have thus proved that *the limit of the minimum mean square error is $1/H$. Particularly, there are consistent estimates of μ if and only if the Hellinger integral H diverges.*

(d) In the situation studied in (a) and (b) the function $\mu(\lambda)$ is constant except at the point $\lambda = \lambda_0$, where it has the jump 1. Hence $H = +\infty$ or $< +\infty$, respectively, according as the spectral distribution function is continuous or not at $\lambda = \lambda_0$. Thus we have *the necessary and sufficient condition for the existence of consistent estimates of μ; the spectrum of the process must be continuous at $\lambda = \lambda_0$.*

As a byproduct we obtain a result belonging actually to chapter 10, since it is of probabilistic nature. Let x_t be a stationary process with mean zero. Having observed the values of the process at the time points $\ldots, -2, -1, +1, +2, \ldots$, is it possible to *interpolate* the value of x_0 exactly by linear estimates?

Consider the expression

$$M_n = \min \left\| x_0 - \sum_{\nu=-n}^{n} d_\nu x_\nu \right\|^2 = \min \left\| \sum_{\nu=-n}^{n} c_\nu x_\nu \right\|^2,$$

where $d_0 = 0$ and hence $c_0 = 1$. This minimum problem is exactly of the same form as (1) with the side condition $c_0 = 1$ which corresponds to $d\mu(\lambda) = (2\pi)^{-1} d\lambda$. We are then in the position to write down the interpolation error immediately:

$$\lim_{n \to \infty} M_n = 4\pi^2 \left\{ \int_{-\pi}^{\pi} \frac{(d\lambda)^2}{dF(\lambda)} \right\}^{-1}.$$

Exact interpolation is possible if and only if the Hellinger integral in the denominator diverges.

11.3. Best linear estimate

(a) Let us return now to the case when $m_t = \mu e^{it\lambda_0}$ and when the process has an absolutely continuous spectrum. We have seen that consistent estimates of μ exist. It is then natural to search for the best one among them. We will now denote the observations by $x_0, x_1, ..., x_n$. If by 'best' we mean the estimate μ_0^* (which has minimum variance among all unbiased estimates formed by linear combinations of $x_0, x_1, ..., x_n$), according to 11.1 we have

$$\mu_0^* = (\epsilon^* R^{-1}\epsilon)^{-1}\,\epsilon^* R^{-1}x,$$

where x stands for the column vector $(x_0, x_1, ..., x_n)$. The mean-square error is $\|\mu_0^* - \mu\|^2 = (\epsilon^* R^{-1}\epsilon)^{-1}$, and this can also be written as $\|\mu_0^* - \mu\|^2 = \sigma_n^{-1}$, where

$$\sigma_n = \sum_{\nu=0}^{n} |\phi_\nu(e^{i\lambda_0})|^2.$$

Here $\{\phi_\nu(z)\}$ denote the polynomials orthonormal with respect to $(2\pi)^{-1}f(\lambda_0)$ on the unit circle $|z|=1$ (see 2.1). Now if the conditions of 3.5 are satisfied, we know that

$$\phi_n(e^{i\lambda_0}) = \overline{\{G(\lambda_0)\}}^{-1}e^{in\lambda_0} + \epsilon_n, \quad \epsilon_n \to 0 \text{ as } n \to \infty,$$

where $G(\lambda)$ has been defined in 10.7 (b). But then

$$\sigma_n/n \to [f(\lambda_0)]^{-1},$$

so that

$$\|\mu_0^* - \mu\|^2 \cong f(\lambda_0)/n \quad \text{as} \quad n \to \infty. \tag{1}$$

While this yields an asymptotic expression for the mean-square error of the best linear estimate of μ, it does not enable us to compute μ_0^* in practice except in a few special cases. For the general case approximations are needed.

(b) We consider the unbiased estimate

$$\mu_L^* = \frac{1}{n+1}\sum_{\nu=0}^{n} x_\nu e^{-i\nu\lambda}$$

introduced in the last section. We saw that it has the mean-square error

$$\|\mu_L^* - \mu\|^2 = \frac{1}{2\pi}\frac{1}{(n+1)^2}\int_{-\pi}^{\pi}\left(\frac{\sin\frac{n+1}{2}(\lambda-\lambda_0)}{\sin\frac{1}{2}(\lambda-\lambda_0)}\right)^2 f(\lambda)\,d\lambda.$$

If the spectral density is continuous at $\lambda = \lambda_0$ we know from the properties of the Fejér kernel that

$$\| \mu_L^* - \mu \|^2 \cong f(\lambda_0)/n \quad \text{as} \quad n \to \infty. \tag{2}$$

Combining (1) and (2) we obtain the following theorem:

THEOREM. *Let x_t be a stationary process with mean value $m_t = \mu e^{it\lambda_0}$ and spectral density $f(\lambda)$. Let $f(\lambda)$ be positive and have a modulus of continuity $\omega(\delta)$ satisfying $\omega(\delta) = O(\delta^\alpha)$, $0 < \alpha \leq 1$. Then the estimate μ_L^* is asymptotically as good as any other unbiased linear estimate of μ. The mean-square error is given asymptotically by*

$$\| \mu_L^* - \mu \|^2 \cong \| \mu_0^* - \mu \|^2 \cong f(\lambda_0)/n.$$

If the mean value m_t is a more general linear expression in terms of known sequences but with unknown coefficients, guessing the form of an asymptotically efficient approximation of the best estimates is not so easy. It has been shown recently (see Appendix) that in many important cases the so-called least-square estimates satisfy this requirement. Without entering into a complete discussion of this topic we shall indicate in (c) the type of argument which is a modification of the proof used in (a) and (b). At the same time the conditions of the theorem above will be somewhat relaxed.

(c) Let us deal with the same situation as before but for an auto-regressive process with the spectral density (see 10.7)

$$f(\lambda) = \left| \sum_{\nu=0}^p b_\nu z^\nu \right|^{-2}, \quad z = e^{i\lambda},$$

where the polynomial $\sum_{\nu=0}^p b_\nu z^\nu$ has all its zeros in $|z| < 1$, $b_p > 0$. We have seen that in this case for $m \geq 0$ [see 2.4 (8)]

$$\phi_{m+p}(z) = \sum_{\nu=0}^p b_\nu z^{m+\nu},$$

so that

$$n^{-1} \sum_{\nu=0}^n | \phi_\nu(e^{i\lambda_0}) |^2 = [f(\lambda_0)]^{-1} + o(1).$$

Now let $f(\lambda)$ be an arbitrary *positive and continuous* spectral density; if ϵ is a positive number, polynomials $p_1(z)$ and $p_2(z)$ can be found such that

$$\begin{aligned} f_1(\lambda) &= | p_1(z) |^{-2} \leq f(\lambda) \leq | p_2(z) |^{-2} = f_2(\lambda), \\ f_2(\lambda) &- f_1(\lambda) < \epsilon, \quad z = e^{i\lambda}. \end{aligned}$$

But the norm of a linear estimate

$$\left\| \sum_{\nu=0}^{n} c_\nu (x_\nu - m_\nu) \right\|^2 = \frac{1}{2\pi} \int_{-\pi}^{\pi} \left| \sum_{\nu=0}^{n} c_\nu e^{i\nu\lambda} \right|^2 f(\lambda)\, d\lambda$$

is clearly a monotonic functional of f. Hence the norm $\| \mu_0^* - \mu \|^2$ is situated in an interval (α_n, β_n) with

$$\alpha_n \cong f_1(\lambda_0)/n, \quad \beta_n \cong f_2(\lambda_0)/n,$$

and since $f_1(\lambda_0) - f(\lambda_0)$ and $f_2(\lambda_0) - f(\lambda_0)$ can be made as small as required by choosing ϵ sufficiently small, we find

$$\| \mu_0^* - \mu \|^2 \cong f(\lambda_0)/n.$$

THEOREM. *If the spectral density $f(\lambda)$ is positive and continuous the estimate μ_L^* is asymptotically as good as the best estimate μ_0^*.*

(d) As an example let us consider the simple case when $\lambda_0 = 0$ and x_t is a moving average $x_t = \xi_t - r\xi_{t-1}$, so that $f(\lambda) = 1 + r^2 - 2r \cos \lambda$. If $-1 < r < 1$ the conditions of the theorem in (c) are fulfilled and μ_L^* must be an asymptotically efficient estimate. However, if $r = 1$ the spectral density is zero at $\lambda = 0$, and it will be interesting to determine the consequences of this fact. First, it is clear that

$$\mu_L^* = \frac{1}{n+1} \sum_{t=0}^{n} x_t = \frac{1}{n+1} (\xi_n - \xi_{-1})$$

and $\| \mu_L^* \|^2 = 2(n+1)^{-2}$.

In order to find the norm of μ_0^* we use the explicit form of $\phi_\nu(z)$ (see Appendix):

$$\phi_\nu(z) = [(\nu+1)(\nu+2)]^{-\frac{1}{2}} \{ (\nu+1) z^\nu + \nu z^{\nu-1} + \ldots + 1 \}. \tag{3}$$

Then $| \phi_\nu(1) |^2 = (\nu+1)(\nu+2)/4$ and

$$\sigma_n = \sum_{\nu=0}^{n} | \phi_\nu(1) |^2 \cong n^3/12.$$

Thus

$$\| \mu_0^* \|^2 = \sigma_n^{-1} \cong 12n^{-3} \quad \text{and} \quad \lim_{n \to \infty} (\| \mu_0^* \| : \| \mu_L^* \|) = 0.$$

We see that in this case μ_L^* is far from being asymptotically efficient.

11.4. Best linear estimates; continuous case

(a) The analogous problem for stochastic processes with a continuous time parameter is slightly more difficult. We assume that the unknown mean value (corresponding to $\lambda_0 = 0$) is m and that the process x_t has been observed in the interval $[0, T]$. Among all unbiased linear estimates of m we choose the one of minimum norm. The *existence of such an estimate is* easily proved.

Indeed, we consider the set of estimates of the form

$$m^* = \sum_{\nu=1}^{n} c_\nu x_{t_\nu}, \quad t_\nu \in [0, T], \tag{1}$$

where n is an arbitrary positive integer and the c_ν are complex constants such that $\sum_{\nu=1}^{n} c_\nu = 1$. Closing this set under convergence in the mean we obtain a set M of elements belonging to the Hilbert space $L_2(0, T)$ spanned by x_t, $t \in [0, T]$.

If $y, z \in M$, we have clearly $\alpha y + (1 - \alpha) z \in M$ for all α. In particular, M is *convex*. Now we want to show that there is a unique element $m^* \in M$ such that

$$\| m^* \|^2 = \inf_{y \in M} \| y \|^2 = c.$$

We can apply a well-known argument. Let $m_\nu^* \subset M$ and $\| m_\nu^* \| \to c$ as $\nu \to \infty$. Then the parallellogram law yields

$$\| m_\nu^* - m_\mu^* \|^2 + \| m_\nu^* + m_\mu^* \|^2 = 2 \| m_\nu^* \|^2 + 2 \| m_\mu^* \|^2.$$

But $\frac{1}{2}(m_\nu^* + m_\mu^*) \in M$ so that according to the definition of c we obtain

$$\| m_\nu^* - m_\mu^* \|^2 \leq 2 \| m_\nu^* \|^2 + 2 \| m_\mu^* \|^2 - 4c \to 0.$$

Hence $\{m_\nu^*\}$ is a Cauchy sequence and converges to an element $m^* \in M$ and of the norm $\| m^* \| = c^{\frac{1}{2}}$. This element must be unique; indeed, if μ^* had the same properties, the parallelogram law used again implies $\mu^* = m^*$.

If $s, t \in [0; T]$, for any δ the estimate $m^* + \delta x_s - \delta x_t$ will be unbiased and we must have

$$\| m^* + \delta x_s - \delta x_t \|^2 \geq \| m^* \|^2,$$

so that

$$|\delta|^2 \| x_s - x_t \|^2 + 2\Re \delta (m^*, x_s - x_t) \geq 0.$$

This is possible for every δ only if $(m^*, x_s - x_t) = 0$, that is,

$$(m^*, x_t) = V, \quad t \in [0, T],$$

where V is a constant. Since m^* belongs to the space spanned by x_t, $t \in [0, T]$, it is clear that the above equation determines m^* uniquely.

The constant V has a simple interpretation. Indeed, m^* is the limit in the mean of sums of the form (1) so that

$$\| m^* \|^2 = \lim (m^*, \Sigma c_\nu x_{t_\nu}) = \lim \Sigma \bar{c}_\nu (m^*, x_{t_\nu}) = V \lim \Sigma \bar{c}_\nu = V.$$

Thus we have obtained the following theorem:

THEOREM. *Let x_t be a stochastic process with the unknown but constant mean value m. The process is observed for $t \in [0, T]$. Then there exists a unique unbiased estimate m^* of minimum variance. The estimate is the unique solution among all unbiased estimates satisfying the integral equation*

$$(m^*, x_t) \equiv V, \quad t \in [0, T].$$

The constant V is the minimum variance.

(b) Our next step will be to express m^* in a more convenient form in the case when x_t is a stationary process. Let $\hat{x}_t = P_0 x_t$, where P_0 is the projection operator associated with the Hilbert space $L_2(0, T)$. We have

$$\| \hat{x}_s - \hat{x}_t \| \leq \| x_s - x_t \|,$$

so that $\hat{x}_t$ is continuous in the mean and hence integrals of $\hat{x}_t$ over finite intervals have a meaning. We are going to show that the integral

$$K = \int_{-\infty}^{\infty} \hat{x}_t \, dt \tag{2}$$

exists and that K is proportional to m^*. More precisely we have the following theorem:

THEOREM. *Let x_t be a stationary process satisfying the following conditions:*

(i) *It has an absolutely continuous spectrum and is nondeterministic; hence (see 10.12) it can be written as follows:*

$$x_t = \int_{-\infty}^{t} g(t - \tau) \, d\xi(\tau). \tag{3}$$

(ii) *The spectral density at $\lambda = 0$ is positive, $f(0) > 0$.*
(iii) $g(u) = (1 + u^2)^{-1} . O(1).$
Then there exists a constant γ so that

$$m^* = \gamma \int_{-\infty}^{\infty} \hat{x}_t \, dt. \tag{4}$$

[For the sake of simplicity the factor $(2\pi)^{-\frac{1}{2}}$ has been omitted in (3).]

Proof. Consider $\hat{x}_t$ for a value of $t > T$. Introducing the prediction x_t^* for the value of x_t when x_s has been observed for $-\infty < s < T$, we have $x_t^* = P_{-\infty} x_t = \hat{x}_t + z_t$, $z_t \perp \hat{x}_t$, where $P_{-\infty}$ is the projection operator for $L_2(-\infty, T)$. Hence

$$\|\hat{x}_t\|^2 \leq \|x_t^*\|^2 = \int_{-\infty}^{T} |g(t-u)|^2 \, du = (t-T)^{-3}.O(1)$$

and

$$\int_{T}^{\infty} \|\hat{x}_t\| \, dt < \infty.$$

Similarly

$$\int_{-\infty}^{0} \|\hat{x}_t\| \, dt < \infty$$

so that the integral (2) has a meaning and defines an element in $L_2(0, T)$.

Now K is the limit in the mean of a sequence K_n of Riemann sums

$$K_n = \sum_{\nu=1}^{n} \hat{x}_{t_\nu}, \quad t_\nu = t_\nu^{(n)}.$$

But then for $s \in [0, T]$ we have

$$(K, x_s) = \lim_{n \to \infty} \sum_{\nu=1}^{n} (\hat{x}_{t_\nu}, x_s) = \lim_{n \to \infty} \sum_{\nu=1}^{n} (x_{t_\nu}, x_s) = \int_{-\infty}^{\infty} R(t) \, dt,$$

in view of $(\hat{x}_t, x_s) = (x_t, x_s) = R(t-s)$; $R(t)$ is absolutely integrable since $(t > T)$

$$|R(t)| = |(x_t, x_0)| = |(\hat{x}_t, x_0)| \leq \|\hat{x}_t\| . \|x_0\|$$
$$= (t-T)^{-\frac{3}{2}}.O(1),$$

and similarly for $t < 0$.

We have by Fourier's inversion formula

$$f(0) = \int_{-\infty}^{\infty} R(t) \, dt.$$

Since $f(0) \neq 0$, according to condition (ii) we can find a constant γ_T such that
$$(\gamma_T K, x_s) = V_T, \quad s \in [0, T],$$

where V_T is the minimum variance introduced in theorem (a). We have to choose $\gamma_T = V_T/f(0)$. But then the best unbiased estimate is $m^* = \gamma_T K$, see theorem (a), and the assertion is proved.

(c) The following example may be illuminating. We consider the real stationary process dealt with in 10.15 with the covariance function $R(t) = e^{-|t|}$. Tentatively we use for the best estimate the form

$$m^* = \int_0^T x_t \, dW(t);$$

here $W(t)$ is of bounded variation so that the integral has a meaning. We must have

$$(m^*, x_s) = \int_0^T e^{-|t-s|} \, dW(t) \equiv V, \quad s \in [0, T]. \tag{5}$$

Let us try the choice

$$W(t) = \begin{cases} 0, & t = 0, \\ a + bt, & 0 < t < T, \\ a + bT + c, & t = T. \end{cases}$$

Then

$$\int_0^T e^{-|t-s|} \, dW(t) = a e^{-s} + b \int_0^T e^{-|t-s|} \, dt + c e^{-(T-s)}$$

$$= 2b + (a - b) e^{-s} + (c - b) e^{-(T-s)}.$$

Choosing $a = b = c$ we find

$$1 = \int_0^T dW(t) = a + bT + c = b(2 + T)$$

so that $b^{-1} = 2 + T$ and the best estimate becomes

$$m^* = (2 + T)^{-1} \left\{ x_0 + \int_0^T x_t \, dt + x_T \right\}.$$

The corresponding variance (i.e. the constant V) is $V = 2b = 2(2 + T)^{-1}$.

This estimate was found by solving the equation (5) by trial and error. A more systematic and constructive procedure is possible by using theorem (b). It is easily shown that

$$\hat{x}_t = \begin{cases} e^t x_0, & t < 0, \\ x_t, & 0 < t < T, \\ e^{-(t-T)} x_T, & T < t. \end{cases}$$

Then

$$K = \int_{-\infty}^\infty \hat{x}_t \, dt = x_0 + \int_0^T x_t \, dt + x_T$$

and γ_T is found to be $(2 + T)^{-1}$, yielding the same expression for m^* as above.

We observe that for $T \to \infty$ the quantity m^* is asymptotically equivalent to

$$m_L^* = T^{-1} \int_0^T x_t dt$$

in the sense that $\lim_{T \to \infty} (\|m_L^*\|/\|m^*\|) = 1$. This holds more generally as is shown by the following theorem which extends theorems 11.3 (b) and (c).

THEOREM. *Under the conditions of theorem* (b) *the estimate*

$$m_L^* = T^{-1} \int_0^T x_t dt$$

is asymptotically efficient, i.e.

$$\|m_L^*\| \cong \|m^*\| \quad as \quad T \to \infty.$$

Moreover, $\|m^*\|^2 \cong f(0)/T$.

Proof. We know that [see theorem (b)]

$$m^* = \gamma_T \int_{-\infty}^{\infty} \hat{x}_t dt = \gamma_T \left\{ \int_0^T x_t dt + K_1 + K_2 \right\},$$

where

$$K_1 = \int_{-\infty}^0 \hat{x}_t dt, \quad K_2 = \int_T^{\infty} \hat{x}_t dt.$$

First, we have to find an asymptotic expression for γ_T. From the proof of theorem (b) we infer that

$$\|K_1\| \leq \int_{-\infty}^0 \|\hat{x}_t\| dt < A,$$

where A does not depend upon T. A similar inequality holds for $\|K_2\|$. Then it is clear that

$$\|m^*\|^2 = |\gamma_T|^2 f(0) \, T\{1 + o(1)\}.$$

Using an argument similar to that in 11.2 (b) we obtain

$$\left\| \int_0^T x_t dt \right\|^2 = \frac{2}{\pi} \int_{-\infty}^{\infty} \left(\frac{\sin \frac{1}{2} T\lambda}{\lambda} \right)^2 f(\lambda) \, d\lambda \cong f(0) \, T.$$

On the other hand, $\|m^*\|^2 = \gamma_T f(0)$, so that $\gamma_T \cong T^{-1}$ and then $\|m^*\|^2 \cong f(0)/T \cong \|m_L^*\|^2$, which completes the proof.

11.5. Distribution of quadratic forms

We turn now to problems of another type. The most important groups of statistical problems studied so far in connection with stationary processes are:

(i) Estimation of the *mean value components*.

(ii) Estimation of the *spectrum*.

The first group has been treated in some special cases in 11.2–11.4. Other types of statistical inference than estimation may of course be considered.

Let x_t be a real and normally distributed stationary process with a discrete time parameter and with an absolutely continuous spectrum. Assuming that the process has been observed for $t=1,2,...,n$, it is required to find an estimate $f^*(\lambda)$ for the spectral density $f(\lambda)$. It is clear that $f^*(\lambda)$ must be a function of $x_1, x_2, ..., x_n$ and there are reasons to require that this function should be a *quadratic form*. Further, it is reasonable to choose a nonnegative form.

Thus we are led to consider an estimate of the form

$$f^* = n^{-1}x^*Wx = x^*Fx, \quad F = W/n,$$

where $x=(x_1, x_2, ..., x_n)$ and the matrix W is nonnegative. To be able to use this estimate practically we need an expression (exact or approximate) for its distribution. It is easy to obtain an explicit form for the characteristic function which is, however, difficult to handle in computations.

We know that the covariance matrix of the observations

$$R = \left\{ r_{\nu-\mu} = \frac{1}{2\pi} \int_{-\pi}^{\pi} e^{i(\nu-\mu)\lambda} f(\lambda)\, d\lambda; \; \nu,\mu=1,2,...,n \right\} \tag{1}$$

is positive definite. Hence the normal distribution of x can be characterized by a frequency function

$$p(x) = (2\pi)^{-\frac{1}{2}n} (\det R)^{-\frac{1}{2}} \exp\{-\tfrac{1}{2}x^*R^{-1}x\}.$$

The characteristic function of f^* is

$$\phi_n(\alpha) = E\exp(i\alpha f^*) = (2\pi)^{-\frac{1}{2}n}(\det R)^{-\frac{1}{2}} \int \exp\{x^*[i\alpha F - \tfrac{1}{2}R^{-1}]x\}\, dx,$$

where the integration is extended over the entire n-space. This integral can be evaluated (see Appendix) with the result

$$\phi_n(\alpha) = \{\det(I - 2i\alpha RF)\}^{-\frac{1}{2}}.$$

Denoting the eigenvalues of RF by $\lambda_1, \lambda_2, \ldots, \lambda_n$ this reduces to

$$\log \phi_n(\alpha) = -\frac{1}{2} \sum_{\nu=1}^{n} \log (1 - 2i\alpha\lambda_\nu), \tag{2}$$

which is not too convenient an expression, partly because the λ_ν are, in general, difficult to compute and partly because it is difficult to carry out the Fourier inversion leading to the frequency function for f^*.

The two first moments of f^* will be needed and can be obtained by expanding (2) in a power series in α:

$$\left.\begin{aligned} m &= Ef^* = \sum_{\nu=1}^{n} \lambda_\nu, \\ \sigma^2 &= E(f^* - m)^2 = 2 \sum_{\nu=1}^{n} \lambda_\nu^2. \end{aligned}\right\} \tag{3}$$

In almost all important cases W is a Toeplitz matrix,

$$W = \left\{ \frac{1}{2\pi} \int_{-\pi}^{\pi} e^{i(\nu-\mu)\lambda} w(\lambda)\, d\lambda;\ \nu, \mu = 1, 2, \ldots, n \right\},$$

and R is of the form (1). This makes it possible to obtain useful approximations by applying certain earlier results.

11.6. The normal approximation

We consider the normalized stochastic variable $z = \sigma^{-1}(f^* - m)$. It has a characteristic function $\psi_n(\alpha)$ for which

$$\log \psi_n(\alpha) = -\frac{1}{2} \sum_{\nu=1}^{n} \log (1 - 2i\alpha\lambda_\nu/\sigma) - i\alpha m/\sigma = \tfrac{1}{2}\alpha^2 + d_n$$

and

$$|d_n| \leqq A\, |\alpha|^3 \sigma^{-3} \sum_{\nu=1}^{n} |\lambda_\nu|^3. \tag{1}$$

In order to find a suitable bound for λ_ν we consider the matrices R and W. Assuming that

$$0 < c_1 \leqq f(\lambda) \leqq c_2, \quad 0 \leqq w(\lambda) \leqq c_3, \tag{2}$$

we obtain from 7.3: $\|R\| \leqq c_2, \|W\| \leqq c_3$. If λ is an eigenvalue of $M = RF$, there is a normalized vector x, $\|x\| = 1$, such that $Mx = \lambda x$ and hence $x^*Mx = \lambda x^*x = \lambda$. Now since R is Hermitian,

$$|\lambda| = |x^*Mx| = |x^*RFx| = |(Rx, Fx)| \leqq \|Rx\| \cdot \|Fx\| \leqq \|R\| \cdot \|F\|$$
$$\leqq c_2 c_3/n.$$

Consequently,

$$|\lambda_\nu| \leq c_2 c_3 / n \qquad (3)$$

and

$$d_n \leq A(\sigma^{-1} c_2 c_3 |\alpha|)^3 n^{-2}. \qquad (4)$$

Recalling that

$$f^* = (2\pi n)^{-1} \sum_{\nu,\,\mu=1}^{n} w_{\nu-\mu} x_\nu x_\mu, \qquad w_k = \frac{1}{2\pi} \int_{-\pi}^{\pi} e^{ik\lambda} w(\lambda) \, d\lambda,$$

and using the relation valid for normal stochastic variables:

$$E[x_\nu x_\mu - r_{\nu-\mu}][x_{\nu'} x_{\mu'} - r_{\nu'-\mu'}] = r_{\nu-\nu'} r_{\mu-\mu'} + r_{\nu-\mu'} r_{\mu-\nu'},$$

it is easily verified that $\sigma^2 = E(f^* - m)^2$ is a monotonic functional in $f(\lambda)$ and hence σ^2 is at least as large as the value σ_0^2 computed for $f(\lambda) = c_1$ [see (1)]. In this case we have $r_\nu = c_1 \delta_{\nu 0}$ so that

$$\sigma_0^2 = 2c_1^2 n^{-2} \sum_{\nu,\,\mu=1}^{n} w_{\nu-\mu}^2 = 2c_1^2 n^{-1} \sum_{k=-n+1}^{n-1} (1 - |k|/n) w_k^2 \geq \text{const.}\, n^{-1}.$$

Hence $\sigma^{-3} = O(n^{\frac{3}{2}})$ so that in view of (2) and (3) we conclude from (1) that $d_n = O(n^{-\frac{1}{2}})$, consequently

$$\lim_{n \to \infty} \psi_n(\alpha) = e^{-\frac{1}{2}\alpha^2}.$$

This yields the following theorem:

THEOREM. *Let x_t be a real stationary process with mean zero and a spectral density bounded away from zero and infinity. If W is a Toeplitz matrix associated with a bounded weight function $w(\lambda) = w(-\lambda)$, the estimate $f^* = n^{-1} x^* W x$ is asymptotically normally distributed with the parameters given in 11.5 (3).*

11.7. Closer approximations

(a) In order to evaluate, in the approximate sense, m and σ^2 of the last section, we may use properties of the Toeplitz forms discussed in earlier chapters. Recalling 11.5 (3) we ask in a slightly more general way for an asymptotic expression of

$$\mu_{s,n} = n^{-1} \sum_{\nu=1}^{n} \lambda_\nu^s \qquad (1)$$

as n tends to infinity. Since the λ_ν are eigenvalues of the product RF of Toeplitz matrices, we can apply the results of chapter 7 (cf. especially

7.4 dealing with a general version of the present problem) and we find that

$$\mu_{s,n} \cong (2\pi)^{-1} n^{-s} \int_{-\pi}^{\pi} [f(x)]^s [w(x)]^s dx. \tag{2}$$

Expanding $\log \phi_n(\alpha)$ in power series we have for small values of α [note that $\lambda_\nu \neq 0$ since $\det(RF) = \det R \det F \neq 0$]

$$\log \phi_n(\alpha) = \sum_{s=1}^{\infty} k_s(i\alpha)^s/s!,$$

where the k_s are the so-called *cumulants* of the stochastic variable f^*. We find

$$k_s = 2^{s-1}(s-1)! \sum_{\nu=1}^{n} \lambda_\nu^s, \quad s = 1, 2, \ldots, \tag{3}$$

so that (2) yields the following approximation for the cumulants:

$$k_s' = \frac{2^{s-1}(s-1)!}{n^{s-1}} \frac{1}{2\pi} \int_{-\pi}^{\pi} [f(x)]^s [w(x)]^s dx. \tag{4}$$

Especially for $s = 1, 2$ we have

$$\left. \begin{aligned} k_1' &= m' = \frac{1}{2\pi} \int_{-\pi}^{\pi} f(x) w(x) dx, \\ k_2' &= (\sigma')^2 = \frac{2}{n} \frac{1}{2\pi} \int_{-\pi}^{\pi} [f(x)]^2 [w(x)]^2 dx. \end{aligned} \right\} \tag{5}$$

The normalized variable $z' = (\sigma')^{-1}(f^* - m')$ has cumulants l_s which are approximately given by

$$\left. \begin{aligned} l_1 &= 0, \quad l_2 = 1, \\ l_s &\cong c_s n^{1-\frac{1}{2}s}, \quad s > 2, \quad n \to \infty, \end{aligned} \right\} \tag{6}$$

where the constants c_s can be computed from (4).

(b) The asymptotic expression (6) for l_s has been computed without estimating the remainder term. To be able to use these approximations in practice in an adequate way it is necessary to obtain an idea of the *error of the approximation*. A bound for these errors can easily be found.

Indeed, suppose that the functions $f(\lambda)$ and $w(\lambda)$ have bounded derivatives of the second order. Then the condition of theorem 8.1 is satisfied so that the matrices in question are trace complete. Of course we choose $X=[-\pi,\pi]$ and $\phi_\nu(x)=(2\pi)^{-\frac{1}{2}}e^{i\nu x}$ corresponding to the classical Toeplitz forms. Let p in this theorem be equal to $2s$ and put

$$f_1(x)=f_3(x)=\ldots=f_{2s-1}(x)=f(x),$$
$$f_2(x)=f_4(x)=\ldots=f_{2s}(x)=w(x).$$

Then the definition of a trace complete set of Toeplitz matrices tells us that (see 8.1)

$$\lim_{n\to\infty} n^{-1}\operatorname{tr}\{[M_n(f)\,M_n(w)]^s-M_n(f^sw^s)\}=0,$$

or, if the eigenvalues of the matrix $M_n(f)\,M_n(w)$ are denoted by μ_ν,

$$\lim_{n\to\infty}\left\{n^{-1}\sum_{\nu=1}^{n}\mu_\nu^s-\frac{1}{2\pi}\int_{-\pi}^{\pi}[f(x)]^s\,[w(x)]^s\,dx\right\}=0,$$

which is in accordance with the expression for $\mu_{s,n}$ found earlier in this section. But in the proof of the theorem in 8.1 we showed actually slightly more, namely, that the expression in the curly brackets above tends to zero as n^{-1}. Hence

$$\mu_{s,n}=n^{-1}\sum_{\nu=1}^{n}\lambda_\nu^s=(2\pi)^{-1}n^{-s}\int_{-\pi}^{\pi}[f(x)]^s\,[w(x)]^s\,dx+O(n^{-s-1}). \qquad (7)$$

In the usual cases it is often possible to obtain exact expressions for k_1 and in certain simple cases also for k_2. Then the normalized variable $z^*=k_2^{-\frac{1}{2}}(f^*-k_1)$ has the cumulants [see above (6)]

$$\left.\begin{aligned}l_1&=0, \quad l_2=1,\\ l_s&=c_s n^{1-\frac{1}{2}s}+O(n^{-\frac{1}{2}s}), \quad s>2, \quad n\to\infty.\end{aligned}\right\} \qquad (8)$$

The bounds for the error in l_3 and l_4 are of the order $n^{-\frac{3}{2}}$ and n^{-2}, respectively. Since l_5 is of the order $n^{-\frac{3}{2}}$, it is clear that we will, in general, not gain very much in precision by employing for the approximation more than the four first cumulants.

(c) However, this is true only if our bounds are of the same order as the true error. The question whether this holds has been answered so far only for the case when RW is itself a Toeplitz matrix, which does not hold generally (except of course when R or W is the identity matrix). We have the following theorem:

THEOREM. *Let us consider the Toeplitz matrix*

$$R_n=\{r_{\nu-\mu};\ \nu,\mu=0,1,\ldots,n\}, \quad r_k=\frac{1}{2\pi}\int_{-\pi}^{\pi}e^{ikx}f(x)\,dx,$$

where f(x) is a real and even function such that

$$\sum_{k=1}^{\infty} k \, | \, r_k \, | < \infty.$$

If $\lambda_0^{(n)}, \lambda_1^{(n)}, \ldots, \lambda_n^{(n)}$, are the eigenvalues of R_n, the following relation holds:

$$\lim_{n \to \infty} d_n = \lim_{n \to \infty} \left\{ \sum_{\nu=0}^{n} (\lambda_\nu^{(n)})^s - \frac{n+1}{2\pi} \int_{-\pi}^{\pi} [f(x)]^s dx \right\}$$

$$= -2\sum \{ \max (0, l_1, l_1 + l_2, \ldots, l_1 + l_2 + \ldots + l_{s-1}) \}$$

$$r_{l_1} r_{l_2} \cdots r_{l_{s-1}} r_{l_1 + l_2 + \ldots + l_{s-1}}; \quad (9)$$

moreover, we have the bound

$$| \, d_n \, | \leqq 2\sum \max (0, l_1, l_1 + l_2, \ldots, l_1 + l_2 + \ldots + l_{s-1})$$

$$| \, r_{l_1} \, | \, | \, r_{l_2} \, | \ldots | \, r_{l_{s-1}} \, | \, | \, r_{l_1 + l_2 + \ldots + l_{s-1}} \, |. \quad (10)$$

The summations are extended over $-\infty < l_1, l_2, \ldots, l_{s-1} < \infty$.

Proof. Considering the special case $s = 3$, which is representative for the general situation, we have

$$\sum_{\nu=0}^{n} (\lambda_\nu^{(n)})^3 = \operatorname{tr} R^3 = \sum r_{i_1 - i_2} r_{i_2 - i_3} r_{i_3 - i_1},$$

with i_1, i_2, i_3 taking the values from 0 to n. Introducing the characteristic function $\psi(i)$ for this set of integers:

$$\psi(i) = \begin{cases} 1 \text{ for } i = 0, 1, \ldots, n, \\ 0 \text{ otherwise,} \end{cases}$$

we have

$$\sum_{\nu=0}^{n} (\lambda_\nu^{(n)})^3 = \sum \psi(i_1) \, \psi(i_2) \, \psi(i_3) \, r_{i_1 - i_2} r_{i_2 - i_3} r_{i_3 - i_1}.$$

Changing to the new variables $j_1 = i_1$, $j_2 = i_2 - i_1$ and $j_3 = i_3 - i_2$ we obtain instead

$$\sum_{\nu=0}^{n} (\lambda_\nu^{(n)})^3 = \sum \psi(j_1) \, \psi(j_1 + j_2) \, \psi(j_1 + j_2 + j_3) \, r_{j_2} r_{j_3} r_{j_2 + j_3}.$$

It is now useful to observe that the sum

$$\sum_{j_1} \psi(j_1) \, \psi(j_1 + j_2) \, \psi(j_1 + j_2 + j_3)$$

$$= n + 1 - \{ \max (0, j_2, j_2 + j_3) - \min (0, j_2, j_2 + j_3) \},$$

provided the right-hand member is positive; otherwise the sum is zero.

Using the condition of the theorem it follows that

$$\sum \max \left(|j_2|, |j_2+j_3|\right)|r_{j_2}||r_{j_3}||r_{j_2+j_3}| < \infty,$$

and hence the sum

$$\sum \{\max (0, j_2, j_2+j_3) - \min (0, j_2, j_2+j_3)\} r_{j_2} r_{j_3} r_{j_2+j_3}$$

converges absolutely. But $M^3(f) = M(f^3)$, so that

$$\sum r_{j_2} r_{j_3} r_{j_2+j_3} = \frac{1}{2\pi} \int_{-\pi}^{\pi} [f(x)]^3 \, dx.$$

Since $r_j = r_{-j}$ we find

$$\sum \max (0, j_2, j_2+j_3) \, r_{j_2} r_{j_3} r_{j_2+j_3} = \sum \max (0, -j_2, -j_2-j_3) \, r_{j_2} r_{j_3} r_{j_2+j_3}$$

$$= -\sum \min (0, j_2, j_2+j_3) \, r_{j_2} r_{j_3} r_{j_2+j_3},$$

which implies the desired relation (9).

The bound (10) is derived in a similar way. We have

$$\sum_{\nu=0}^{n} (\lambda_\nu^{(n)})^3 - \frac{n+1}{2\pi} \int_{-\pi}^{\pi} [f(x)]^3 \, dx$$

$$= -\sum_{S} \{\max (0, j_2, j_2+j_3) - \min (0, j_2, j_2+j_3)\} r_{j_2} r_{j_3} r_{j_2+j_3}$$

$$- (n+1) \sum_{S^*} r_{j_2} r_{j_3} r_{j_2+j_3},$$

where S is the set of integers j_2, j_3 such that the expression in the curly brackets is at most equal to $n+1$; S^* is the complementary set. Hence

$$\left| \sum_{\nu=0}^{n} (\lambda_\nu^{(n)})^3 - \frac{n+1}{2\pi} \int_{-\pi}^{\pi} [f(x)]^3 \, dx \right|$$

$$\leq \sum_{S} \{\max (0, j_2, j_2+j_3) - \min (0, j_2, j_2+j_3)\} |r_{j_2}||r_{j_3}||r_{j_2+j_3}|$$

$$+ (n+1) \sum_{S^*} |r_{j_2}||r_{j_3}||r_{j_2+j_3}|$$

$$\leq \sum \{\max (0, j_2, j_2+j_3) - \min (0, j_2, j_2+j_3)\} |r_{j_2}||r_{j_3}||r_{j_2+j_3}|$$

$$= 2 \sum \max (0, j_2, j_2+j_3) |r_{j_2}||r_{j_3}||r_{j_2+j_3}|,$$

which completes the proof.

(d) This theorem shows that under the stated condition the error

$$\mu_{s,\,n} - \frac{1}{2\pi} \int_{-\pi}^{\pi} [f(x)]^s \, dx$$

is exactly of the order n^{-1}. To validate generally the remarks on the error of approximation of the cumulants of the stochastic variable one would have to extend this theorem to products of Toeplitz matrices.

An example which, although very simple, has a certain statistical interest is $f(x) = \cos x$. Then the $n+1$ rowed Toeplitz matrix is given by

$$
R = \begin{pmatrix} 0 & \tfrac{1}{2} & 0 & \cdots & \cdots \\ \tfrac{1}{2} & 0 & \tfrac{1}{2} & \cdots & \cdots \\ \cdots & \cdots & \cdots & \cdots & \cdots \\ \cdots & \cdots & \cdots & \tfrac{1}{2} & 0 \end{pmatrix}
$$

with the eigenvalues [see 5.3 (8)]

$$
\lambda_\nu = \cos \frac{(\nu+1)\pi}{n+2}, \quad \nu = 0, 1, \ldots, n.
$$

Using the Euler–MacLaurin summation formula we find

$$
\mu_{s,n} = \frac{1}{n+1} \sum_{\nu=0}^{n} \left(\cos \frac{(\nu+1)\pi}{n+2} \right)^s
$$

$$
= \frac{1}{n+1} \int_0^{n+2} \left(\cos \frac{\pi x}{n+2} \right)^s dx - \frac{1+(-1)^s}{2(n+1)}
$$

$$
+ \frac{\pi}{(n+1)(n+2)} \int_0^{n+2} P_1(x)\, s \left(\cos \frac{\pi x}{n+2} \right)^{s-1} \sin \frac{\pi x}{n+2}\, dx,
$$

where $P_1(x) = [x] - x + \tfrac{1}{2}$. Hence

$$
\mu_{s,n} - \frac{1}{2\pi} \int_{-\pi}^{\pi} \cos^s x\, dx = \frac{1}{2\pi(n+1)} \int_{-\pi}^{\pi} \cos^s x\, dx - \frac{1+(-1)^s}{2(n+1)}
$$

$$
+ \frac{s}{n+1} \int_0^{\pi} P_1 \left(\frac{n+2}{\pi} x \right) \cos^{s-1} x \sin x\, dx.
$$

The dominating term of the error will be for an even $s = 2l$

$$
\frac{1}{n+1} \left\{ 2^{-2l} \binom{2l}{l} - 1 \right\};
$$

for odd s the order is $o(n^{-1})$.

11.8. The continuous case

Some of the results of the last two sections have been extended to stochastic processes with a continuous time parameter. We will consider a slightly different situation of considerable interest.

(a) Let x_t be a real and normal stationary process continuous in the mean with mean zero and with spectral density $f(\lambda)$. The process is put through a square law device, the output of which is fed into a linear filter with the continuous response function $K(t)$. We shall assume that $K(t)$ is bounded and integrable over $[0, \infty]$. The output y_t of this filter is given then by

$$y_t = \int_{-\infty}^{0} K(t+s)\, x_s^2 \, ds.$$

We want to find the probability distribution of y_t. Since y_t is also stationary, there is no restriction to fix the time, $t=0$.

We consider the Hermitian integral kernel

$$H(s,t) = [K(s)]^{\frac{1}{2}} R(s-t) [K(t)]^{\frac{1}{2}} \tag{1}$$

[where $R(t)$ is the covariance function of x_t] which is of the Hilbert–Schmidt type (see 7.1), since

$$\int_{-\infty}^{\infty} \int_{-\infty}^{\infty} [H(s,t)]^2 \, ds\, dt < \infty.$$

Let λ_j and $\phi_j(t)$ be the eigenvalues and eigenfunctions of the integral equation

$$\int_{-\infty}^{\infty} H(s,t)\, \phi(t)\, dt = \lambda \phi(s).$$

If $z_j, j=1,2,\ldots$, are normally distributed stochastic variables with mean zero, variance one, and independent of each other, the sum

$$z_t = \sum_{j=1}^{\infty} \lambda_j^{\frac{1}{2}} z_j \phi_j(t) \tag{2}$$

will converge in the mean for each value of t. Indeed, since $R(s-t)$ and hence also $H(s,t)$ is a nonnegative kernel, Mercer's theorem tells us that

$$H(s,t) = \sum_{j=1}^{\infty} \lambda_j \phi_j(s)\, \phi_j(t) \tag{3}$$

converges absolutely. Thus

$$H(t,t) = \sum_{j=1}^{\infty} \lambda_j [\phi_j(t)]^2 < \infty,$$

so that the mean convergence of (2) is established.

(b) The linear way in which z_t was derived from the sequence z_j implies that z_t is a normal process with mean value zero and with the covariance function (1), as can be seen by combining (2) and (3). Thus we conclude that the probability distribution of z_t and $[K(t)]^{\frac{1}{2}} x_t$ are identical provided the values of these processes are considered simultaneously for a finite or denumerable number of time points. Hence we find easily that y_0 has the same probability distribution as

$$\int_{-\infty}^{0} z_s^2 \, ds = \sum_{j=1}^{\infty} \lambda_j z_j^2.$$

The characteristic function of this stochastic variable is obtained by applying a simple limit procedure to 11.5 (2), and we find for its logarithm

$$\log \phi(\alpha) = -\frac{1}{2} \sum_{j=1}^{\infty} \log (1 - 2i\alpha\lambda_j).$$

The cumulants of y_0 are given by

$$k_\mu = 2^{\mu-1}(\mu-1)! \sum_{j=1}^{\infty} \lambda_j^\mu.$$

Assuming that $K(s) = L(\beta s)$, $\beta > 0$, where $L(t) \in L_2[0, \infty]$ and $L(t)$ is bounded and continuous, we seek asymptotic expressions for k_μ provided β is small. The following result on the eigenvalues of a type of Toeplitz integral equation (see also 8.6) is useful.

THEOREM. *We assume that*

(i) $\qquad R(t) \in L[-\infty, \infty], \quad R(t) = \frac{1}{2\pi} \int_{-\infty}^{\infty} e^{it\lambda} f(\lambda) \, d\lambda,$

where $f(\lambda) \geq 0$ *and* $f(\lambda)$ *is even, bounded and integrable.*

(ii) $L(t) \in L_2(0, \infty)$ *and* $L(t)$ *is bounded and continuous. We consider the integral equation*

$$\int_{-\infty}^{\infty} L(\beta s) \, R(s-t) \, L(\beta t) \, \phi(t) \, dt = \lambda \phi(s), \quad \beta > 0.$$

Then

$$\lim_{\beta \to 0} \beta \sum_{j=1}^{\infty} (\lambda_j(\beta))^{\mu} = \frac{1}{2\pi} \int_0^{\infty} [L(s)]^{2\mu} \, ds \int_{-\infty}^{\infty} [f(\lambda)]^{\mu} \, d\lambda. \qquad (4)$$

Proof. As is well known, we have

$$\sum_{j=1}^{\infty} (\lambda_j(\beta))^{\mu} = \underbrace{\int \cdots \int}_{\mu} [L(\beta t_1) \ldots L(\beta t_{\mu})]^2 \, R(t_1 - t_2) \, R(t_2 - t_3)$$
$$\ldots R(t_{\mu} - t_1) \, dt_1 \, dt_2 \ldots dt_{\mu}.$$

Changing variables to

$$\begin{cases} \beta t_{\mu} = s_{\mu}, \\ \beta t_{\mu-1} = s_{\mu} + \beta s_{\mu-1}, \\ \cdots\cdots\cdots\cdots\cdots\cdots\cdots\cdots \\ \beta t_1 = s_{\mu} + \beta s_{\mu-1} + \ldots + \beta s_1, \end{cases}$$

we find

$$\beta \sum_{j=1}^{\infty} [\lambda_j(\beta)]^{\mu} = \underbrace{\int \cdots \int}_{\mu} [L(s_{\mu} + \beta s_{\mu-1} + \ldots + \beta s_1)]^2 \ldots [L(s_{\mu})]^2 R(s_1) \, R(s_2)$$
$$\ldots R(s_{\mu-1}) R(s_1 + \ldots + s_{\mu-1}) \, ds_1 \, ds_2 \ldots ds_{\mu}.$$

The integrand is dominated by

$$\text{const.} \, [L(s_{\mu})]^2 \, | \, R(s_1) \, R(s_2) \ldots R(s_{\mu-1}) \, |,$$

which is integrable over the μ-space. When β tends to zero the integrand converges to

$$[L(s_{\mu})]^{2\mu} \, R(s_1) \, R(s_2) \ldots R(s_{\mu-1}) \, R(s_1 + \ldots + s_{\mu-1}),$$

so that indeed (4) follows.

Substituting $K(t) = L(\beta t)$ we see that the normalized stochastic variable $\sigma^{-1}(y_0 - m)$ has for small values of β the cumulants

$$k_1' = 0, \quad k_2' = 1,$$

$$k_{\mu}' \cong \text{const.} \, \beta^{\mu/2-1}, \quad \mu > 2; \quad \beta \to 0.$$

Hence as the *time constant* $1/\beta$ of the filter increases the cumulants of order higher than two tend to zero. This implies that y_0 is asymptotically normally distributed with given first and second moments.

One may note the following interesting consequence of the theorem closely related to the discussion in 8.6:

COROLLARY. *Under the conditions of the previous theorem the following is true. Let* $N(u, v)$ *denote the number of eigenvalues* $\lambda_j(\beta)$ *situated in the interval* $[u, v]$, $0 < u < v$. *Assuming that the plane measure of the set in the* $s \times \lambda$-*plane*

$$m\{[K(s)]^2 f(\lambda) = a \text{ or } b\} = 0,$$

we have

$$\lim_{\beta \to 0} \beta N(u, v) = \frac{1}{2\pi} m\{a < [K(s)]^2 f(\lambda) < b\}.$$

We do not enter into the proof, which runs along lines similar to those of the proof of theorem 8.6.

APPENDIX

(NOTES AND REFERENCES)

CHAPTER 1

1.2.–1.6. Concerning the definitions and results of these paragraphs see, for instance, St. Saks, *Theory of the Integral*, 2d ed. (New York, 1937); or F. Riesz–B. Sz. Nagy[1], chapters I, II, III; or H. Cramér[3], chapters 1–9.

1.3. As to (a) see F. Riesz–B. Sz. Nagy, p. 53. The theorems in (b) and (c) are due to E. Helly, 'Über lineare Funktionaloperationen', *Sitzungsberichte der math.-naturwiss. Klasse der Akademie in Wien*, Abt. IIa, vol. 121 (1912), pp. 268–71.

1.4. The theorem in (a) has been communicated to us by Professor Kakutani. It will play an essential role in the proof of the theorem in 3.1 [see 3.1(f)].

1.5. Cf. F. Riesz–B. Sz. Nagy[1], p. 110. The important representation (3) is due to F. Riesz, 'Sur certains systèmes singuliers d'équations intégrales', *Annales scientifiques de l'École Normale Supérieure*, ser. 3, vol. 28 (1911), pp. 33–62.

1.6. These important theorems are due to P. Fatou, 'Séries trigonométriques et séries de Taylor', *Acta Mathematica*, vol. 30 (1906), pp. 335–400. Concerning (a) see p. 375, concerning (b) see p. 378. Another slightly more general formulation of (a) is as follows. Let $f_n(x) \geqq 0, f_n \in L$. Then

$$\int_{-\pi}^{\pi} \liminf_{n \to \infty} f_n(x)\, dx \leqq \liminf_{n \to \infty} \int_{-\pi}^{\pi} f_n(x)\, dx.$$

1.7. Cf. M. H. Stone[1], chapter I.

1.8. As to the theorem of F. Riesz–E. Fischer, see F. Riesz–B. Sz. Nagy[1], pp. 58 and 70. The orthogonalization is called sometimes the Gram–E. Schmidt process. The polynomials $\phi_n(x)$ introduced in (d) (i) are commonly called the orthogonal polynomials associated with the distribution $d\alpha(x)$. Cf. 6.4. The polynomials $\phi_n(x)$ defined in (d) (ii) have been introduced by G. Szegő[5, II]; they will be studied in chapters 2 and 3.

1.9. We may choose for $t(x)$, for instance, the Fejér means of the partial sums of the ordinary Fourier series of the function $f(x)$ (cf. A. Zygmund, *Trigonometrical Series*, 2d ed. (New York, 1952), pp. 45–7). In this case we have the additional advantage that $t(x)$ remains between the maximum and minimum of the function $f(x)$. As to the theorem in (b), cf. D. Jackson, *The Theory of Approximation*, American Mathematical Society, Colloquium Publications no. 11 (1930), p. 7.

1.10. In the proof of the theorem in (b) the Poisson kernel might be replaced by the Fejér kernel. The study of the Toeplitz forms, in particular of their eigenvalues, is the central topic of the present book. Cf. chapters 4, 5 and 7.

1.11. (a) Concerning various moment problems, cf. J. A. Shohat–J. D. Tamarkin[1]. (b) The essential content of this section is the following theorem: Any harmonic function $f(r, x)$ which is regular and positive in the unit circle $r < 1$, can be represented in the form

$$f(r, x) = \frac{1}{2\pi} \int_{-\pi}^{\pi} \frac{1 - r^2}{1 - 2r \cos(x - \theta) + r^2}\, d\alpha(\theta),$$

where $\alpha(\theta)$ is a distribution function. This important result is due to F. Riesz (see the paper quoted in 1.5, p. 60). The proof of the text is due to G. Herglotz. A continuous convex function $F(x)$ satisfies a Lipschitz condition

$$|F(x_1) - F(x_2)| \leqq A |x_1 - x_2|$$

(a consequence of the definition), which implies absolute continuity; the derivative $F'(x)$ exists except for a denumerable set of values. Cf. J. L. W. V. Jensen, 'Sur les fonctions convexes et les inégalités entre les valeurs moyennes', *Acta Mathematica*, vol. 30 (1906), pp. 175–93. Let $\alpha(x)$ and $\beta(x)$ be two solutions; we conclude (as in the text) that $\alpha(x) - \beta(x) = 0$ except for the points of discontinuity of $\alpha(x)$ and $\beta(x)$. The number of these points is denumerable and at each point of discontinuity x_0 we must have

$$\alpha(x_0 - 0) - \beta(x_0 - 0) = 0, \quad \alpha(x_0 + 0) - \beta(x_0 + 0) = 0.$$

Thus $\alpha(x)$ and $\beta(x)$ can differ only at such points x_0 where $\alpha(x_0 - 0) < \alpha(x_0 + 0)$.

1.12. (a) Concerning this elegant representation, cf. L. Fejér, 'Über trigonometrische Polynome', *Journal für die reine und angewandte Mathematik*, vol. 146 (1916), pp. 53–82, §§ 1, 2. The theorem is due to L. Fejér and F. Riesz. Cf. also T. J. Stieltjes, *Oeuvres complètes*, vol. 1, pp. 99–104. Another representation of nonnegative trigonometric polynomials $f(x)$ is the following:

$$f(x) = \left| \sum_{\nu=0}^{n} u_\nu (\cos \tfrac{1}{2}x)^{n-\nu}(\sin \tfrac{1}{2}x)^\nu \right|^2,$$

where u_ν are complex numbers. Cf. E. Fischer, p. 242. (b) The polynomial $g(z)$ defined in (b) $[g(z) \neq 0$ in $|z| < 1]$ enjoys the following extremum property. Let us consider all representations $f(x) = |\gamma(z)|^2$, $z = e^{ix}$, where $\gamma(z)$ is a polynomial of degree n; let z be fixed, $|z| < 1$. The quantity $|\gamma(z)|$ is a maximum if $\gamma(z) = \epsilon g(z)$, $|\epsilon| = 1$. An analogous property holds in the case dealt with in 1.14.

1.13. The L-integrability of $\log |\rho(e^{ix})|$ was found by G. Szegö in 1920 [7]. The elegant argument used in the text is due to F. Riesz; published first in a joint paper (1920, in Hungarian) with G. Szegö; cf. also F. Riesz, 'Über die Randwerte einer analytischen Funktion', *Mathematische Zeitschrift*, vol. 18 (1923), pp. 87–95, also, 'Sur les suites des fonctions analytiques', *Acta Szeged*, vol. 1 (1923), pp. 1–10.

1.14. This theorem is due to G. Szegö [7], published first in a joint paper with F. Riesz (see 1.13). The original proof for (c) was based on the use of Toeplitz forms and on a theorem to be proved in 3.1 (a). Concerning Jensen's inequality, cf. *loc. cit.* 1.11, p. 187.

1.15. Cf. G. Szegö[8], 10.3 (pp. 270–3). (b) The convergence of the integral (1) can be replaced by the more general condition that

$$\int_{-\pi}^{\pi} |\log f(\theta) - \log f(x)| \left| \cot \frac{x-\theta}{2} \right| d\theta$$

is convergent.

1.16. These theorems have a considerable literature. Concerning a simple proof of the theorem in (a) cf. G. Pólya–G. Szegö, vol. 2, p. 90, problem 82. The special case in (b) was pointed out by M. Riesz, 'Eine trigonometrische Interpolationsformel und einige Ungleichungen für Polynome', *Jahresbericht der Deutschen Mathematiker-Vereinigung*, vol. 23 (1915), pp. 345–68. The proof of the text is due to O. Szász.

1.17. These polynomials represent a generalization of the polynomials introduced by G. Faber, 'Über polynomische Entwicklungen', *Mathematische Annalen*, vol. 57 (1903), pp. 389–408.

1.18. Concerning the application of the theorem in (c) to the eigenvalues of a membrane cf. R. Courant–D. Hilbert, *Methoden der mathematischen Physik*, I, 2d ed. (Berlin, 1931), pp. 16–18. Concerning the history and background of this important characterization of the eigenvalues see G. Pólya, 'Estimates for the eigenvalues', *Studies in Mathematics and Mechanics, Presented to Richard von Mises* (New York, 1954), pp. 200–7.

1.19, 1.20. For a complete treatment of the topics dealt with in these sections, the reader is referred to F. Riesz–B. Sz. Nagy.

1.20. (b) Concerning the projection operator, cf. F. Riesz–B. Sz. Nagy, p. 264. (c) For a proof of the theorem of Hilbert and the meaning of the integral (2) we refer to F. Riesz–B. Sz. Nagy, pp. 272–3.

CHAPTER 2

Concerning the topics dealt with in chapter 2, cf. G. Szegö[8], chapter XI, pp. 280–8. As the orthogonal polynomials of a real interval [cf. 1.8 (d) (i)] are connected with the Hankel matrices $(c_{\mu+\nu})$, so are the polynomials $\phi_n(z)$ of the present chapter with the Toeplitz matrices $(c_{\nu-\mu})$. Concerning a relation of the orthogonal polynomials of a real and finite interval to the polynomials $\phi_n(z)$, cf. G. Szegö, *Ibid.* pp. 287–8; see 6.4.

CHAPTER 3

3.1. In the absolutely continuous case $d\alpha(x) = w(x)\,dx$ this theorem was proved by G. Szegö[5, I], p. 194, Satz XVII. The minimum μ_n is of course $= D_n/D_{n-1}$, where the D_n are the Toeplitz determinants defined in 2.1 (b). The general case of an arbitrary distribution $d\alpha(x)$ was treated first by A. N. Kolmogorov and M. G. Krein; cf. N. I. Achieser, p. 261. Our method is different from that used by these authors.

3.2. In the absolutely continuous case $d\alpha(x) = w(x)\,dx$ this theorem was found by G. Szegö[5, I], p. 185, Satz XII.

3.3. This completeness theorem was first formulated by A. N. Kolmogorov and M. G. Krein; cf. N. I. Achieser, pp. 261–3.

3.4. Concerning these results see G. Szegö[8], chapter XII. Cf. also J. Geronimus[1], where further references to the Russian literature can be found.

3.5. Cf. G. Szegö[8], chapter XII.

CHAPTER 4

4.1. This basic theorem has been mentioned in the Preface. The present proof follows the line of G. Szegö[10].

CHAPTER 5

As will be seen in chapters 9, 10 and 11, Toeplitz forms have many applications to the theory of functions, to probability theory and to statistics. Other possibilities of applications have not yet been developed systematically. Here is a simple example illustrating how Toeplitz matrices appear in the theory of crystal structures.

Let us consider a *one-dimensional crystal* idealized in the following way. It consists of material points of equal mass m and situated at (x_ν, y_ν), where $x_\nu = \nu$. The potential energy is given by the quadratic form $U = \Sigma u_{\nu\mu} y_\nu y_\mu$ with a symmetric matrix $(u_{\nu\mu})$. The crystal is supposed to be *homogeneous* which implies that the coefficients $u_{\nu\mu}$ depend only on the coordinate difference $\nu - \mu$, $u_{\nu\mu} = u_{\nu-\mu}$. The boundaries are kept fixed, say $y = 0$ for $\nu < 0$ and $\nu > n$. The equations of motion are

$$m\ddot{y}_\nu = -\frac{\partial U}{\partial y_\nu} = -\sum_{\mu=0}^{n} u_{\nu\mu} y_\mu, \quad \nu = 0, 1, \ldots, n.$$

As usual we put $y_\nu = c_\nu e^{i\lambda t}$ and obtain

$$m\lambda^2 c_\nu - \sum_{\nu=0}^{n} u_{\nu\mu} c_\mu = 0.$$

In order that nontrivial solutions exist λ^2 must be an eigenvalue of the *Toeplitz matrix* $\{m^{-1} u_{\nu-\mu}; \nu, \mu = 0, 1, \ldots, n\}$. For the further study of the motion it is necessary to evaluate these eigenvalues or find adequate approximations for them.

Explicit solutions can be found only in special cases, but as we have seen in chapter 5 one can find asymptotic expressions (valid for large values of n) for the *distribution* of the eigenvalues. This model can be considered, of course, as the discrete analog of a vibrating string.

5.1. Concerning H. Weyl's theory of 'equal distributions', cf., for instance, G. Pólya–G. Szegö, vol. 1, p. 70.

5.2. (b) The theorem formulated in (b) is due to G. Szegö, cf. [5, I], p. 194, Satz XVIII. Concerning a direct proof of (11), see J. Ullman[1]. (d) The first proof of (12) [and (13)] can be found in G. Szegö[1] under somewhat more restrictive conditions than in the later papers.

5.3. These examples have been discussed at various places. Cf. for instance, M. Kac–W. L. Murdock–G. Szegö, pp. 783–5, 788–9.

5.4. For this paragraph see *ibid.* 5.3, pp. 785–90. (d) Observe the different notations of 1.18 (c) and 5.4 (d) for the eigenvalues.

5.5. For this paragraph see G. Szegö[9]. (a) The bound $h_n = O(n^{-1-\alpha})$ follows from general theorems on approximations. Cf. C. de la Vallée Poussin, *Leçons sur l'approximation des fonctions d'une variable réelle* (Paris, 1919), p. 16. (f) As to Privalov's theorem cf. A. Zygmund, *op. cit.* 1.9., p. 156. Concerning the theorem on approximations used in (f) see de la Vallée Poussin, *op. cit.* p. 27, théorème V.

CHAPTER 6

6.1. (b) The polynomials $p_n(x)$ which are orthogonal on a given analytic Jordan curve have been introduced by G. Szegö[6]. (c) As to the Hermitian forms (11) cf. M. Kac–W. L. Murdock–G. Szegö, chapter II.

6.2. (b) A similar argument is used in G. Szegö[8], pp. 363–4.

6.3. The eigenvalues of the Hankel forms of a finite interval were first studied by G. Szegö[3].

6.4. Cf. the remarks on chapter 2. As to the theorem in (d) cf. G. Szegö[8], p. 290, theorem 12.1.2.

6.5. Cf. 6.1 (c).

CHAPTERS 7 AND 8

The topics discussed in chapters 7 and 8 have been studied only recently (there are only a few publications dealing with these questions) and the results are far from complete. The properties of a Toeplitz operator in the general sense were considered by U. Grenander[4]. The section on integral equations in M. Kac–W. L. Murdock–G. Szegö deals with an analog of Toeplitz matrices depending on a continuous parameter. See also M. Kac[2].

7.1. (a) Concerning completely continuous operators, cf. F. Riesz–B. Sz. Nagy, pp. 231 and 362.

7.2. (a) For the concept of an orthogonal kernel see S. Bochner, 'Inversion formulae and unitary transformations', *Annals of Mathematics*, vol. 35 (1934), pp. 111–5. Cf. also F. Riesz–B. Sz. Nagy, p. 296. (c) For the Fourier–Plancherel transform see 8.6.

7.4. (c) The theorem on the asymptotic behavior of the eigenvectors of a Toeplitz matrix is not very satisfactory. In certain applications of the theory of Toeplitz forms, e.g. in estimation theory, one needs an asymptotic statement on the eigenvectors, but to be useful, this statement must be considerably stronger than that of the present theorem. To obtain such a result, one may be forced to consider special types of Toeplitz matrices.

7.5. (a) The approximation of $f(x)$ is carried out as in E. Hopf, *Ergodentheorie* (Berlin, 1937), p. 6. (c) The Radon–Nikodym derivative is discussed in P. R. Halmos, *Measure Theory* (New York, 1950), §§ 31, 32, pp. 128–36, and in F. Riesz–B. Sz. Nagy, pp. 136–7.

7.7. (a) The Gauss–Jacobi formula used in this section is discussed in G. Szegö[8], p. 46. (c) The theorem used here is due to G. Szegö[8], p. 46. (c) The theorem used here is due to G. Szegö[8], p. 303. Concerning the example cf. also 6.3.

7.8. The reader will find more details about the topic discussed in the beginning of this section in R. Courant–D. Hilbert, *op. cit.* 1.18, p. 250. For the asymptotic formula of $u_n(t)$, cf. E. W. Hobson, 'On a general convergence theorem and the theory of the representation of a function by series of normal functions', *Proceedings of the London Mathematical Society*, ser. 2, vol. 6 (1908), pp. 349–95; see in particular p. 379.

7.9. (a) Concerning the Haar System, see A. Haar, 'Zur Theorie der orthogonalen Funktionensysteme', I, *Mathematische Annalen*, vol. 69 (1910), pp. 331–71, in particular pp. 361–71. Cf. also S. Kaczmarz–H. Steinhaus, *Theorie der Orthogonalreihen* (New York, 1951), 120–2.

8.1. The concept of linear algebra is discussed, for instance, in G. Birkhoff–S. MacLane, *A Survey of Modern Algebra* (New York, 1953), p. 239. The concept of (tr)-complete classes of Toeplitz matrices is helpful; for such classes the problem of finding the asymptotic eigenvalue distribution is reduced to an analytic problem which is often easy to solve. Little is known about the relation between (tr)-completeness and the properties of the orthonormal system that generates the Toeplitz matrices. Cf. J. Ullman. (d) Concerning the Radon–Nikodym derivative, cf. 7.5(c).

8.2. (b) (c) Cf. E. C. Titchmarsh, *The Theory of Functions* (Oxford, 1939), pp. 214 and 226.

8.3. (a) See 1.5. (c) We have to use in this case the explicit expression for the generating functions; cf. four 'Notes' of G. N. Watson in the *Journal of the London Mathematical Society*, vol. 8 (1933) and vol. 9 (1934). In the case of Legendre polynomials, for example, the generating function will be an elliptic integral. As an alternative procedure we might compute then $a_\nu(g)$, $g \in \Gamma$, directly by an elementary though somewhat tedious method. Without giving the derivation here we mention that in this case $a_\nu(g)$ converges to a finite value as ν tends to infinity.

8.4. (b) Mehler's formula is discussed in G. Szegö[8], p. 371; 23.

8.5. In this section we use various properties of the Charlier polynomials which can be found in G. Szegö[8], p. 34 and in J. Meixner, 'Erzeugende Funktionen der Charlierschen Polynome', *Mathematische Zeitschrift*, vol. 44 (1938), pp. 531–5; p. 533. See also A. Erdélyi, *Higher Transcendental Functions*, vol. 2 (New York, 1953), 10.12.17.

The following remarks are of some interest.

(a) According to chapters 5 and 7 a matrix of the form

$$\left\{ M_n(dF) = \frac{1}{2\pi} \int_{-\pi}^{\pi} e^{i(\nu-\mu)x} dF(x); \; \nu, \mu = 0, 1, \ldots, n \right\}, \tag{1}$$

where $F(x)$ is bounded and non-decreasing in $[-\pi, \pi]$, has an eigenvalue distribution which converges to the distribution of $dF_a(x)/dx = f(x)$, the derivative of the absolutely continuous component of $F(x)$. This result concerns the average behavior of the eigenvalues and does not imply anything about an individual eigenvalue.

We will show now, that it is possible to find the asymptotic behavior of the 'highest' eigenvalues of (1), provided n is large. Let the points of discontinuities of $F(x)$ be $x_1, x_2, \ldots$ with the corresponding jumps $F_1, F_2, \ldots$, where the numbering has been made so that $F_1 \geqq F_2 \geqq \ldots$. For a positive integer p we write

$$F(x) = F_p(x) + G_p(x) + F_a(x) + F_s(x) = F_p(x) + H_p(x),$$

where $F_a(x)$ denotes the absolutely continuous, and $F_s(x)$ the singular component; $F_p(x)$ is the jump-function

$$F_p(x) = \sum_{x_m \leqq x, \, m \leqq p} F_m,$$

and $G_p(x)$ the remainder of the jump part of $F(x)$,

$$G_p(x) = \sum_{x_m \leqq x, \, m > p} F_m.$$

We form the matrix $M_n(dH_p)$. In order to obtain a bound for its norm we consider the corresponding quadratic form

$$|z^* M_n(dH_p) z| = \left| \sum_{\nu, \mu=0}^{n} h_{\nu-\mu} z_\nu \bar{z}_\mu \right| \leqq \sum_{k=-n}^{n} |h_k| \sum_{\substack{0 \leqq \nu, \mu \leqq n: \\ \nu - \mu = k}} |z_\nu \bar{z}_\mu|$$

$$\leqq \left\{ (2n+1) \sum_{k=-n}^{n} |h_k|^2 \right\}^{\frac{1}{2}}.$$

Consequently (see 7.3) the norm of $n^{-1} M_n(dH_p)$ is not greater than

$$\left\{ \frac{2n+1}{n^2} \sum_{k=-n}^{n} |h_k|^2 \right\}^{\frac{1}{2}} \to 2 \left\{ \sum_{m=p+1}^{\infty} F_m^2 \right\}^{\frac{1}{2}} \quad \text{as} \quad n \to \infty,$$

which can be made arbitrarily small by choosing p sufficiently large.

Let us now consider the eigenvalues of the matrix $n^{-1} M_n(dF_p)$. We have

$$n^{-1} z^* M_n(dF_p) z = \sum_{k=1}^{p} F_k |(z, \xi_k)|^2,$$

where the vectors ξ_k are defined as follows:

$$\{\xi_k\}_\nu = (n+1)^{-\frac{1}{2}} e^{-i\nu x_k}, \quad \nu = 0, 1, \ldots, n.$$

In view of

$$(\xi_k, \xi_l) = \begin{cases} 1 & \text{if } k = l, \\ \dfrac{1}{n+1} \dfrac{1 - e^{i(x_l - x_k)(n+1)}}{1 - e^{i(x_l - x_k)}} = O(1) & \text{if } k \neq l, \end{cases}$$

the system $\xi_1, \xi_2, \ldots, \xi_p$ is normalized and asymptotically orthogonal. It is then easy to see that when n tends to infinity and j is an integer $1 \leq j \leq p$, the jth largest eigenvalue of the matrix $n^{-1} M_n(dF_p)$ tends to F_j.

In view of the fact that $\|n^{-1} M_n(dH_p)\|$ is small and using 1.18(c) we have proved the following. While we have seen previously that the majority of the eigenvalues of a Toeplitz–Stieltjes matrix $M_n(dF)$ behave on the average like the values of the derivative $dF_a(x)/dx$, we can now also make a statement concerning the individual behaviour of the 'highest' eigenvalues. If we denote the ordered jumps of $F(x)$ by $F_1 \geq F_2 \geq \ldots$ and their number by $N \leq \infty$, then the jth largest eigenvalue $(1 \leq j \leq N)$ of $n^{-1} M_n(dF)$ tends to F_j as n tends to infinity.

(b) Let α_ν, $\nu = 0, 1, 2, \ldots$, be an increasing sequence of nonnegative integers with $\alpha_0 = 0$; we write $\alpha_{-\nu} = \alpha_\nu$. We consider the matrix

$$A_n(f) = \left\{ \frac{1}{2\pi} \int_{-\pi}^{\pi} e^{i\alpha_{\nu - \mu} x} f(x)\, dx; \quad \nu, \mu = 1, 2, \ldots, n \right\}$$

for $f \in L_2(-\pi, \pi)$. In order to find the eigenvalue distribution of $A_n(f)$ we note that it can be written as a classical Toeplitz matrix $A_n(f) = M_n(\hat{f})$, where

$$\hat{f}(x) = \text{l.i.m.} \sum_{p \to \infty}^{p} (f; e^{i\alpha_\nu x})\, e^{i\nu x} = Lf;$$

$$(f; e^{i\alpha_\nu x}) = \frac{1}{2\pi} \int_{-\pi}^{\pi} f(t)\, e^{-i\alpha_\nu t} dt,$$

so that the eigenvalues of $A_n(f)$ are asymptotically distributed as the values of $\hat{f} = Lf$. If, for example, $\alpha_\nu = m\nu$, where m is a positive integer, we have

$$Lf = \frac{1}{m} \left\{ f\left(\frac{x}{m}\right) + f\left(\frac{x + 2\pi}{m}\right) + \ldots + f\left(\frac{x + 2(m-1)\pi}{m}\right) \right\}.$$

(c) Take $X = [0, \pi]$, $dx = $ Lebesgue measure and the complete system in $L_2(0, \pi)$

$$\phi_\nu(x) = (2/\pi)^{\frac{1}{2}} \cos \nu x, \quad \nu = 0, 1, \ldots;$$

the transformation denoted by T in 7.2 is in this case the cosine transform. Consider the Toeplitz matrix

$$M_n(f) = \left\{ \frac{2}{\pi} \int_0^{\pi} \cos \nu x \cos \mu x f(x)\, dx; \quad \nu, \mu = 0, 1, \ldots, n-1 \right\},$$

where $f(x)$ is real, bounded and measurable. Now $M_n(f) = A_n(f) + B_n(f)$, where

$$A_n(f) = \left\{ \frac{1}{\pi} \int_0^{\pi} \cos (\nu - \mu) x f(x)\, dx; \quad \nu, \mu = 0, 1, \ldots, n-1 \right\},$$

$$B_n(f) = \left\{ \frac{1}{\pi} \int_0^{\pi} \cos (\nu + \mu) x f(x)\, dx; \quad \nu, \mu = 0, 1, \ldots, n-1 \right\}.$$

The element in $B_n(f)$ tends to zero as $\nu + \mu \to \infty$ (in view of the Riemann–Lebesgue lemma); hence it is clear that $|B_n| \to 0$ as $n \to \infty$. But as we know the asymptotic eigenvalue distribution of

$$A_n(f) = \left\{ \frac{1}{2\pi} \int_{-\pi}^{\pi} e^{i(\nu-\mu)x} f(x)\, dx;\ \nu,\ \mu = 0, 1, \ldots, n-1 \right\}$$

[where we have defined $f(x) = f(-x)$ for negative arguments], we see that $M_n(f)$ has the canonical distribution with density π^{-1} in $X = [0, \pi]$.

8.6. (a) For the Plancherel transform cf. F. Riesz–B. Sz. Nagy, p. 291. (b) The case of a periodic kernel was treated by J. Egerváry. (c) The theorem is due to M. Kac–W. L. Murdock–G. Szegö. Their argument is slightly different from that of the text. As to the Poisson summation formula, cf. S. Bochner[2], p. 37.

8.7. S. Bochner[2], p. 180, discusses the Hankel transform.

CHAPTER 9

The problems dealt with in this chapter have an extensive literature. We mention here only the papers of C. Carathéodory–L. Fejér and of I. Schur[2]. The methods used in the text when we deal with the problems A, B, C, will be slightly different from those employed in the papers quoted above.

9.3. (a) This theorem is a more precise formulation of theorem 1.10 (b). (d) (e) The first proof is based on 4.1, the second on certain arguments closely related to those used in the proof of theorem 4.1.

9.5. This argument is different from those existing in the literature. It follows a line analogous to that of I. Schur for the class $|f(z)| \leq M$. Cf. 9.9. However, the problem of 9.5 is much simpler than that of 9.9. (c) Let K be any Hermitian form of the $n+1$ variables $u_0, u_1, \ldots, u_n$ and K_1 the form of n variables $u_0, u_1, \ldots, u_{n-1}$ arising from K for $u_n = 0$. The lowest eigenvalue of K_1 is not greater than the second lowest eigenvalue of K. This follows from the theorem in 1.18 (c) since $u_n = 0$ is a special linear condition imposed on the variables $u_0, u_1, \ldots, u_n$.

9.6.–9.9. The subject matter is so arranged that the corresponding problems concerning $\Re f(z)$ and $|f(z)|$ are dealt with in a parallel manner.

9.6. (b) Concerning the generalization of the maximum principle used here, cf. Pólya–Szegö, vol. 1, p. 142, problem 299.

9.9. This is a somewhat simplified presentation of the discussion of the case 9.7 (1) due to I. Schur[1], pp. 218–20.

CHAPTER 10

The reader who is not familiar with the linear theory of stochastic processes will find a clear exposition of the basic ideas of this theory in K. Karhunen[1].

10.1. We did not go into details concerning the choice of the probability space in situations encountered in practice. Indeed, the study of this complicated problem would carry us too far in a direction outside the scope of the present book. For a thorough account of this question we refer to J. L. Doob[1].

10.2. For the axioms of a Hilbert space, cf. for instance, F. Riesz–B. Sz. Nagy, p. 195. We have not assumed that the space $L_2(x)$ is separable since this is not essential in the present context. However for most stochastic processes dealt with in practice the separability condition is satisfied. The reader can easily verify this for the processes which are continuous in the mean. As to the 'continuity theorem' for characteristic functions used here, cf. Cramér[3], p. 96.

10.3. (a) For the case that T is a compact Abelian group, cf. Kampé de Fériet[1]. (c) The theorem is due to S. Bochner[2]. The simple proof given here is due to H. Cramér[1].

10.4. (b) For a proof of Stone's theorem and a further discussion the reader is referred to F. Riesz–B. Sz. Nagy, pp. 377–90. (c) The theorem in (c) is due to H. Cramér[2] who proved it in the case of a continuous parameter.

10.5. The reader familiar with statistics will notice that the construction of the best linear predictor is the same problem as to find the linear regression lines for a simultaneous probability distribution; the only difference is that in the present situation we have to deal with a Hilbert space instead of the usual finite-dimensional sample space.

10.6–10.7. To avoid complications that would obscure the general approach we have assumed throughout these sections that all spectra are absolutely continuous.

10.7. The representation of a stationary process as an infinite moving average (plus a deterministic component) is due to H. Wold[1], as are also the concepts of deterministic and nondeterministic processes. The theorem in (b) is due to A. Kolmogorov[1].

10.8.–10.9. The explicit construction of the best predictor is due to A. Kolmogorov and N. Wiener; the latter dealt also with the case of a continuous time parameter.

10.9. A direct treatment of the problem of this paragraph can be found in U. Grenander–M. Rosenblatt[1].

10.10. For a complete discussion see U. Grenander–M. Rosenblatt[1].

10.11. It is true in general that adding a side condition tends to increase the resulting minimum norm of $L(x)$. However, it can be shown that the *same* prediction error is obtained whether we impose the condition $u(\zeta) = 0$, $|\zeta| = 1$, or not. See U. Grenander–M. Rosenblatt[1]. For $|\zeta| < 1$ this does not hold. The relation between problems of prediction and the theory of Toeplitz forms was pointed out by U. Grenander[3].

10.12. Originally the representation of a continuous stationary process was derived in other ways; see K. Karhunen[2] for an argument which is analogous to that given in 10.7.

10.13. We denote by $l_n(x) = L_n^{(-1)}(x)$ the Laguerre polynomials corresponding to the parameter $\alpha = -1$ [Szegö 8, p. 97, (5.1.6)]. Then for real λ and for $n = 1, 2, 3, \ldots$,

$$\frac{(1 - i\lambda)^{n-1}}{(1 + i\lambda)^{n+1}} = \frac{(-1)^n}{2} \int_{-\infty}^{0} e^{it\lambda + t} l_n(-2t) \, dt.$$

This follows by forming the generating functions of both sides.

10.14. The method used in 10.12–10.14 is due to N. I. Achieser[2] and J. L. Doob[1].

10.15. Many important special cases of the problem of this chapter can be found in N. Wiener[1].

10.16. The reader interested in further details of the topics discussed in this section may consult M. Kac[1], [2] and M. Kac–W. L. Murdock–G. Szegö[1].

CHAPTER 11

It was pointed out by U. Grenander[3] that the theory of Toeplitz forms is applicable to the linear estimation problems arising in the statistical theory of stationary processes.

11.1–11.4. The results of these sections are due to Grenander[1], [2], [3]; these papers contain a more complete discussion.

11.2. Let $\lim_{m \to \infty} a_m = 0$; then

$$\lim_{m \to \infty} \frac{(m+1)\, a_0 + m a_1 + (m-1)\, a_2 + \ldots + a_m}{(m+1)^2} = 0.$$

11.3. (b) The general problem of linear estimation for stationary processes has been treated in U. Grenander, 'On the estimation of regression coefficients in the case of an autocorrelated disturbance', *Annals of Mathematical Statistics*, vol. 25 (1954), pp. 252–72. (d) As to (3) see G. Szegö[5], II, p. 188.

11.4. (b) Here we use a criterion due to K. Karhunen[1], p. 33, in order to prove the existence of the integral K. (c) The estimation problem studied in (c) belongs clearly to the theory of Toeplitz forms associated with integral kernels $R(s-t)$. Since the method of 8.6 is not immediately applicable to the present situation, a different approach has been used. One would expect interesting results if the technique of chapters 7 and 8 could be extended to cover problems of the type just dealt with. The method of 11.3 has been successfully applied to certain more complicated cases but so far never to the question studied in (c) in spite of its importance for certain technical problems.

11.5–11.7. Various ways of approximating the probability distribution of quadratic forms in normally distributed stochastic variables were suggested by T. Koopmans[1], W. J. Dixon[1], and P. Whittle[1]. These methods implicitly use a result on the eigenvalue distribution of Toeplitz matrices; this was pointed out and discussed by U. Grenander[3]. The approximations seem to work very well in practice but some care is needed in the application in order to obtain meaningful results.

11.5. The derivation of the characteristic function of f^* can be found in H. Cramér[3], p. 120.

11.7. (c) The theorem of this section is due to M. Kac[2] whose proof we have followed. (d) There are various ways of using asymptotic expressions for the cumulants. One can choose a suitable family of frequency functions and select therein a function with cumulants coinciding with the approximate values. Various such families have been used for this purpose: The Pearson curves, Charlier's A-series, and the Laguerre series. The last alternative seems to yield particularly good approximations in the present case. The selection of such functions does not belong to the theory of Toeplitz forms so that we do not enter into a detailed discussion of this question.

11.8. A problem arising in electronics (see G. R. Arthur[1]) was the starting point for the considerations of this section. The theorem and the corollary are due to M. Kac–W. L. Murdock–G. Szegö[1].

BIBLIOGRAPHY†

ACHIESER, N. I. *Vorlesungen über Approximationstheorie* (Berlin, 1953).

ACHIESER, N. I. and KREIN, M. G.

[1] 'Über Fouriersche Reihen beschränkter summierbarer Funktionen und ein neues Extremumproblem, I', *Communications de la Société Mathématique de Kharkoff*, ser. 4, vol. 9 (1934), pp. 3–28; II, *ibid.* ser. 4, vol. 10 (1934), pp. 3–32.

[2] 'Über eine Transformation der reellen Toeplitzschen Formen und das Momentenproblem in einem endlichen Intervalle', *Communications de la Société Mathématique de Kharkoff*, ser. 4, vol. 11 (1935), pp. 21–6.

[3] 'Das Momentenproblem bei der zusätzlichen Bedingung von A. Markoff', *Communications de la Société Mathématique de Kharkoff*, ser. 4, vol. 12 (1935), pp. 13–35.

ARTHUR, G. R. 'A note on the approach of narrow band noise after a non-linear device to a normal probability density', *Journal of Applied Physics*, vol. 23 (1952), pp. 1143–4.

BERGMAN, S. 'Über die Entwicklung der harmonischen Funktionen der Ebene und des Raumes nach Orthogonalfunktionen', *Mathematische Annalen*, vol. 86 (1922), pp. 238–71.

BOCHNER, S.

[1] 'Über orthogonale Systeme analytischer Funktionen', *Mathematische Zeitschrift*, vol. 14 (1922), pp. 180–207.

[2] *Vorlesungen über Fouriersche Integrale* (Leipzig, 1932; New York, 1948).

[3] 'Inversion formulas and unitary transformations', *Annals of Mathematics*, vol. 35 (1934), pp. 111–5.

CARATHÉODORY, C. 'Über den Variabilitätsbereich der Fourierschen Konstanten von positiven harmonischen Funktionen', *Rendiconti del Circolo Matematico di Palermo*, vol. 32 (1911), pp. 193–217.

CARATHÉODORY, C. and FEJÉR, L. 'Über den Zusammenhang der Extremen von harmonischen Funktionen mit ihren Koeffizienten und über den Picard-Landauschen Satz', *Rendiconti del Circolo Matematico di Palermo*, vol. 32 (1911), pp. 218–39.

CRAMÉR, H.

[1] 'On the representation of a function by certain Fourier integrals', *Transactions of the American Mathematical Society*, vol. 46 (1939), pp. 191–201.

[2] 'On harmonic analysis in certain functional spaces', *Arkiv för Mat., Astron., Fysik*, 1942, no. 12, 7 pp.

[3] *Mathematical Methods of Statistics* (Princeton, 1946).

DIXON, W. J. 'Further contributions to the problem of serial correlation', *Annals of Mathematical Statistics*, vol. 15 (1944), pp. 119–44.

DOOB, J. L. *Stochastic Processes* (New York, 1953).

EKLIND, J. R. and JUNG, J. *Estimation of the Spectral Density.* (Unpublished manuscript.)

EGERVÁRY, J. *Az integrálegyenletek egy osztályáról* (Thesis; Budapest, 1914).

FEJÉR, L. 'Über trigonometrische Polynome', *Journal für die reine und angewandte Mathematik*, vol. 146 (1915), pp. 53–82.

† This Bibliography contains only items which have some, though frequently rather distant, relation to Toeplitz forms. Other sources are quoted in the Appendix.

FISCHER, E. 'Über das Carathéodorysche Problem, Potenzreihen mit positivem reellen Teil betreffend', *Rendiconti del Circolo Matematico di Palermo*, vol. 32 (1911), pp. 240–56.

FROBENIUS, G. 'Ableitung eines Satzes von Carathéodory aus einer Formel von Kronecker', *Sitzungsberichte der Kgl. Preussischen Akademie der Wissenschaften*, 1912, pp. 16–31.

GERONIMUS, J.
  [1] 'On the trigonometric moment problem', *Annals of Mathematics*, vol. 47 (1946), pp. 742–61.
  [2] 'On the orthogonal polynomials of V. A. Steklov', *Doklady Akademii Nauk SSSR*, vol. 83 (1952), pp. 5–8. [Russian.]
  [3] 'On some extremal problems in the space $L_\sigma^{(p)}$', *Mat. Sbornik*, N.S., vol. 31 (73) (1952), pp. 3–26. [Russian.]

GRENANDER, U.
  [1] 'Stochastic processes and statistical inference', *Arkiv för Matematik*, vol. 1 (1950), pp. 195–277.
  [2] 'On empirical spectral analysis of stochastic processes', *Arkiv för Matematik*, vol. 1 (1952), pp. 503–31.
  [3] 'On Toeplitz forms and stationary processes', *Arkiv för Matematik*, vol. 1 (1952), pp. 555–71.
  [4] 'A contribution to the theory of Toeplitz matrices', *Transactions of the American Mathematical Society*, vol. 79 (1955), pp. 124–40.

GRENANDER, U. and ROSENBLATT, M. 'An extension of a theorem of G. Szegö and its application to the study of stochastic processes', *Transactions of the American Mathematical Society*, vol. 76 (1954), pp. 112–26.

HERGLOTZ, G. 'Über Potenzreihen mit positivem, reellem Teil im Einheitskreise', *Berichte über Verhandlungen der Kgl.-sächs. Gesellschaft der Wissenschaften zu Leipzig, Mathematisch-Physikalische Klasse*, vol. 63 (1911), pp. 501–11.

KAC, M.
  [1] 'Random walk in the presence of absorbing barriers', *Annals of Mathematical Statistics*, vol. 16 (1945), pp. 62–7.
  [2] 'Toeplitz matrices, translation kernels and a related problem in probability theory', *Duke Mathematical Journal*, vol. 21 (1954), pp. 501–9.

KAC, M., MURDOCK, W. L. and SZEGÖ, G. 'On the eigenvalues of certain hermitian forms', *Journal of Rational Mechanics and Analysis*, vol. 2 (1953), pp. 767–800.

KAMPÉ DE FÉRIET, J. 'Analyse harmonique des fonctions aléatoires stationnaires d'ordre 2 définies sur un groupe abélien localement compact', *Comptes Rendus Académie des Sciences, Paris*, vol. 226 (1948), pp. 868–70.

KARHUNEN, K.
  [1] Über linear Methoden in der Wahrscheinlichkeitsrechnung, *Annales Academiae Scientiarum Fennicae*, ser. A, 1947, no. 37, 79 pp. [Thesis.]
  [2] 'Über die Struktur stationärer zufälliger Funktionen', *Arkiv för Matematik*, vol. 1 (1952), pp. 141–60.

KOLMOGOROV, A. N. 'Stationary sequences in Hilbert space', *Bulletin of the University of Moscow*, vol. 2 (1941), 40 pp. [Russian.]

KOOPMANS, T. 'Serial correlation and quadratic forms in normal variables', *Annals of Mathematical Statistics*, vol. 13 (1942), pp. 14–33.

KREIN, M. G.
  [1] 'Über eine neue Klasse von Hermiteschen Formen und über eine Verallgemeinerung des trigonometrischen Momentenproblems, I', *Bulletin de l'Académie des Sciences de l'URSS*, ser. 7, vol. 6 (1933), pp. 1259–75.

[2] 'On a generalization of some investigations of G. Szegö, W. M. Smirnov, and A. N. Kolmogorov', *Doklady Academii Nauk SSSR*, vol. 46 (1945), pp. 91–4.

[3] 'On a problem of extrapolation of A. N. Kolmogorov', *Doklady Academii Nauk SSSR*, vol. 46 (1945), pp. 306–9.

MATHIAS, M. 'Über positive Fourier-Integrale', *Mathematische Zeitschrift*, vol. 16 (1923), pp. 103–25.

PÓLYA, G. and SZEGÖ, G. *Aufgaben und Lehrsätze aus der Analysis*, 2 vols. (Berlin, 1925, 1954; New York, 1945).

RIESZ, F. 'Über ein Problem des Herrn Carathéodory', *Journal für die reine und angewandte Mathematik*, vol. 146 (1915), pp. 83–7.

RIESZ, F. and NAGY, B. Sz. *Leçons d'analyse fonctionnelle* (Budapest, 1952).

SCHUR, I.

[1] 'Über einen Satz von C. Carathéodory', *Sitzungsberichte der Kgl. Preussischen Akademie der Wissenschaften*, 1912, pp. 4–15.

[2] 'Über Potenzreihen, die im Innern des Einheitskreises beschränkt sind, I, II', *Journal für die reine und angewandte Mathematik*, vol. 147 (1916), pp. 205–32; vol. 148 (1917), pp. 122–45.

SHOHAT, A. J. and TAMARKIN, J. D. *The Problem of Moments*, Mathematical Surveys, no. 1 (New York, 1943).

STONE, M. H. *Linear Transformations in Hilbert Space and their Applications to Analysis*, American Mathematical Society, Colloquium Publications, no. 15 (New York, 1932).

SZÁSZ, O. 'Über harmonische Funktionen und L-Formen', *Mathematische Zeitschrift*, vol. 1 (1918), pp. 140–62.

SZEGÖ, G.

[1] 'Ein Grenzwertsatz über die Toeplitzschen Determinanten einer reellen positiven Funktion', *Mathematische Annalen*, vol. 76 (1915), pp. 490–503.

[2] 'A Toeplitz-féle formákról', *Mathematikai és természettudományi értesitő*, vol. 35 (1917), pp. 185–222.

[3] 'A Hankel-féle formákról', *Mathematikai és természettudományi értesitő*, vol. 36 (1918), pp. 497–538.

[4] 'Über einen Satz des Herrn Carathéodory', *Jahresbericht der Deutschen Mathematiker-Vereinigung*, vol. 28 (1920), pp. 131–7.

[5] 'Beiträge zur Theorie der Toeplitzschen Formen, I, II', *Mathematische Zeitschrift*, vol. 6 (1920), pp. 167–202; vol. 9 (1921), pp. 167–90.

[6] 'Über orthogonale Polynome, die zu einer gegebenen Kurve der komplexen Ebene gehören,' *Mathematische Zeitschrift*, vol. 9 (1921), pp. 218–70.

[7] 'Über die Randwerte analytischer Funktionen', *Mathematische Annalen*, vol. 84 (1921), pp. 232–44.

[8] *Orthogonal Polynomials*, American Mathematical Society, Colloquium Publications, no. 23 (New York, 1939).

[9] 'On certain hermitian forms associated with the Fourier series of a positive function', *Festskrift Marcel Riesz* (Lund, 1952), pp. 228–38.

[10] 'On a theorem of C. Carathéodory', *Studies in Mathematics and Mechanics, Presented to Richard von Mises* (New York, 1954), pp. 62–6.

TOEPLITZ, O.

[1] 'Zur Transformation der Scharen bilinearer Formen von unendlichvielen Veränderlichen', *Nachrichten der Kgl. Gesellschaft der Wissenschaften zu Göttingen, Mathematisch-physikalische Klasse*, 1907, pp. 110–15.

[2] 'Zur Theorie der quadratischen Formen von unendlichvielen Variablen', *Nachrichten der Kgl. Gesellschaft der Wissenschaften zu Göttingen, Mathematisch-physikalische Klasse*, 1910, pp. 489–506.

[3] 'Zur Theorie der quadratischen und bilinearen Formen von unendlich-vielen Veränderlichen. I. Teil: Theorie der *L*-Formen', *Mathematische Annalen*, vol. 70 (1911), pp. 351–76.

[4] 'Über die Fouriersche Entwicklung positiver Funktionen', *Rendiconti del Circolo Matematico di Palermo*, vol. 32 (1911), pp. 191–2.

ULLMAN, J. *On the Eigenvalues of Certain Hermitian Forms*, Technical Report no. 28 for the Office of Naval Research (Stanford University, 1952).

VERBLUNSKY, S. 'On positive harmonic functions: a contribution to the algebra of Fourier series', *Proceedings of the London Mathematical Society*, ser. 2, vol. 38 (1934), pp. 125–57.

WHITTLE, P. *Hypothesis Testing in Time Series Analysis* (Uppsala, 1951).

WIENER, N. *Extrapolation, Interpolation, and Smoothing of Stationary Time Series* (New York, 1949).

WOLD, H. *A Study in the Analysis of Stationary Time Series*, 2d ed. (Stockholm, 1953).

INDEX

CPSIA information can be obtained
at www.ICGtesting.com
Printed in the USA
LVHW081057300320
651625LV00019B/1348